MILLE MIGLIA

THE WORLD'S GREATEST ROAD RACE

Anthony Pritchard

First published in March 2007

A catalogue record for this book is available
from the British Library

ISBN 978 1 84425 139 1

Library of Congress catalog card no 2006935943

Published by Haynes Publishing, Sparkford,
Yeovil, Somerset BA22 7JJ, UK
Tel: 01963 442030 Fax: 01963 440001
Int. tel: +44 1963 442030 Int. fax: +44 1963 440001
E-mail: sales@haynes.co.uk
Website: www.haynes.co.uk

Haynes North America Inc.,
861 Lawrence Drive, Newbury Park,
California 91320, USA

Page layout by G&M Designs Limited,
Raunds, Northamptonshire

Printed and bound in Britain
by J. H. Haynes & Co. Ltd, Sparkford

Note: this book uses the commonly anglicised forms of Italian
names in the case of Roma = Rome, Firenze = Florence,
Venezia = Venice, Mantova = Mantua, Padova = Padua,
Torino = Turin, Milano = Milan, Livorno = Leghorn

Contents

Introduction

It would be possible to write a million words about the Mille Miglia. That would still not tell the full, intimately detailed story and would be excruciatingly boring. What I have sought to do is to write a balanced account of the 25 races (excluding the 1939 Tobruk-Tripoli event which, in reality, has nothing to do with the Mille Miglia). I have put the emphasis on personal recollections in an attempt to catch the spirit of this great event that was so vitally and flamboyantly different from any other, together with accounts of the great cars and the great drivers.

The concept was that of four great motor racing enthusiasts, who had witnessed the popularity of the Le Mans 24 Hours race, first held in 1923. The founders of the Mille Miglia were Count Aymo Maggi, Franco Mazzotti, Giovanni Canestrini (who was to write one of the most detailed books about the race) and Renzo Castagneto. At this time Maggi was only 23 years old and his close friend Mazzotti (the son of an industrialist) was 21, while the other two founders were rather more mature – Canestrini 30 and Castagneto 34.

Together they formed the concept of a race on the roads of Italy that would challenge cars and drivers to the limit. After they had considered various routes, they selected one with a length of some 1,600km. To call the race the 'Mille Miglia' (Thousand Miles) to distinguish it from other events was almost inevitable. First held in 1927, the race was banned after a serious accident in

The start of the last race in the series, in 1957. All the early classes have departed and dawn is beginning to break. Now the fastest cars are pushed out to take their places before mounting the ramp for the start. Heading this line-up is the Wolfgang von Trips Ferrari, followed by Hans Herrmann's Maserati, Peter Collins's Ferrari and Piero Taruffi's Ferrari. (Author's Collection)

1938. It was held on a closed circuit in 1940 and then revived as a road race in 1947. The Mille Miglia was one of the greatest of all motor sport events. It attracted a vast number of entries, reaching a peak of 521 starters in 1955.

This was a race in which in not just the great marques such as Alfa Romeo, Ferrari, Maserati and Mercedes-Benz competed, but also a vast number of amateur drivers with small sports cars and family saloons – even bubble cars such as the Isetta. Some merely had aspirations to take part and no serious intention of completing the course. A typical example of those drivers of less than serious intent was Ferruccio Lamborghini, who started the race in his modified Fiat Topolino, and ended it when he collided with an osteria (inn).

When the first 1,000-mile race was held, the Italian motor industry was in dire financial straits and – because the majority of makers could not afford the cost of building special cars – an added appeal was that, so far as larger-capacity cars were concerned, it would be open only to Le Mans-type cars; that meant four-seater touring models that were listed as production cars; it should be clarified, however, that the smallest-capacity classes, just as at Le Mans, accepted cars with two-seater bodywork.

Even before the first race was held, excitement gripped the Italian nation. Mussolini's Fascist government went to considerable lengths to ensure that it was a success. In many areas podestàs (administrative heads of commune, roughly what in the UK would be called a mayor) brought forward road-repair and improvement schemes. Even so, for much of the race distance, driving conditions were desperately bad.

The Fascist Militia did its best to ensure that the roads were as safe as possible by providing a system of marshalling by controlling other road users and

This photograph was taken before the first Mille Miglia, held in 1927. It shows a very happy Ing. Nicola Romeo, with Count Gaston Brilli Peri and that persistent riding mechanic, Bruno Presenti. Ing. Romeo was far less happy after an OM won the race. (Centro Documentazione Alfa Romeo)

spectators rather than competitors. Pessimists who expected a repeat of the horrors of road-racing of the early years of the Twentieth Century were to be sadly disappointed and the 'butcher's bill' was quite small over the years.

With the benefit of hindsight, one cannot but speculate how the organisers viewed the large entries of the 1950s. They were undoubtedly pleased with the success of the event, but were they aware of the potential catastrophe of so many cars of mixed performance racing together on ordinary roads? There was also the fact that, although spectators were carefully controlled in the towns, they stood on dangerous corners and wandered at will in the countryside.

Did they ever think of the death toll in the 1903 Paris-Madrid race (six confirmed dead and many unconfirmed) and tremble in their beds? The answer is, of course, that this was Italy and no such disaster was ever countenanced. Fatal accidents, of course, were

expected, because they were a part of motor racing, but not an accident of catastrophic proportions.

In its later years the race was especially popular with British entrants. It attracted such diverse cars as Healey saloons, HWM-Jaguar sports-racing cars, Triumph TR2 sports cars, Cooper-Jaguar and C-type Jaguars. It was a round in the World Sports Car Championship between 1953 and 1957. During the years that the Mille Miglia was run, a total of approximately 5300 competitors took part and it has been estimated that 100 million spectators watched the race.

A word needs to be said about the role of the 'co-driver'. Even after co-drivers ceased to be compulsory, many drivers still took someone with them. They filled a multitude of roles. Some provided company for the driver (Marco Crosara with Giannino Marzotto, for example); some were genuine mechanics (Bignami with Varzi in 1935, Norman Dewis with Moss in 1951 and Hermann Eger with Hans Herrmann in 1955); some were navigators – the classic examples of these are Denis Jenkinson with Stirling Moss in 1955–57 and Hans Klenk with Karl Kling in 1952–53. Sometimes they really were co-drivers and did their stint behind the wheel, but these were a minority.

And talking of minorities, Count Aymo Maggi enjoyed a lifestyle that was singularly exclusive. In post-war days he invited leading British teams to stay at the

Two great Italian drivers, seen in 1931 – and an interesting comparison in sizes. On the left is Tazio Nuvolari (winner in 1930 and 1933) and Giuseppe Campari (winner in 1928 and 1929). On the right is Senator Vicini of Modena. This photograph was taken at the Coppa Acerbo at Pescara. Campari was killed in an accident at Modena in 1931. (Spitzley-Zagari Collection)

Maggi ancestral home, Casa Maggi. The tales of Maggi hospitality are numerous; British guests have described how a green-liveried waiter stood behind the chair of each guest and served only him.

When persons of extreme wealth entertained with such splendour in a poverty-stricken country that only very recently had suffered the horrors and vicissitudes of war, then the success of Communism in Italy is not at all surprising. Maggi would, of course, have argued that he was providing employment and other benefits to people who would otherwise be unemployed. At the end of the day, it all depends on one's political leanings.

Whether one writes or reads about Alfa Romeo (I became hooked on the marque some 50 years ago), one is (perhaps I should say 'I am') emotionally overwhelmed by the decline of a marque that was so great and so important in the 1920s and 1930s. After the Second World War Alfa Romeo initially made a recovery that was quite outstanding in Grand Prix racing, in sports car events and with the '1900' of 1950 onwards and its smaller-capacity production car successors. It is a story that is even sadder and more heart-sickening than that of the decline and fall of such great British makes as Austin, Morris and Triumph.

There are two aspects of the Mille Miglia that should be highlighted at this point. From 1949 onwards the race

numbers represented the starting times of each car, which depended on the size of the entry. Starters left at intervals of one minute. In 1953, for example, there were 481 starters. The first car away was a Fiat that left at 2100 hours. The last starters were the Ferrari of Castellotti/Regosa, that departed at 6.37 the following morning, and the C-type Jaguar of Tony Rolt/Len Hayden which followed a minute later.

In effect it was a race purely on a time basis, but rivals in a class would catch up with each other and fight out a wheel-to-wheel duel. Throughout the race the faster cars would constantly be catching and passing slower cars, but the first car to finish on the road would usually be a car from the 'middle runners'. Within each class there was, supposedly, a lottery for the order in which drivers started, but it seems that, in the unlimited capacity sports car class at least, the starting order was often 'fiddled' to favour the leading Italian drivers. Ideally, the best place to start was last, because at each stage the driver would know the precise times of all his rivals who had started in front.

A late starting number also had its drawbacks, however (see the accounts of Robin Richards in relation to 1950 and Denis Jenkinson in 1954). If the car was not one of the fastest, or had mechanical problems that delayed it, then the spectators would assume that the last competitor had passed them. People would start wandering along the roads, bus services would begin operating, lorries would start their day's journeys, and farmers would be on the roads with their horses and carts. Driving at racing speed in these conditions surpassed 'dangerous' and there was little alternative but to throw in the towel.

Another important aspect is the question of 'road books'. All drivers, at least the sensible ones who had covered the course in training, had course notes. The making of these go back to the very early days of the race. Up to 1953 there was always a riding mechanic to give the driver some form of instructions, but from 1954 drivers could compete solo. Film maker Bill Mason recalled that in the 1953 race his driver, Dr Alberico Cacciari, had a 200-page book of tear-off route notes. Alberto Ascari's route notes for the 1954 race are published in Count Giani Marzotto's *Red Devils* (see Bibliography).

It is not entirely clear who originated these very detailed route notes that listed every corner, hill brow and hazard, but Hans Klenk claims to be the pioneer (see page 185). Klenk, who partnered Kling in a Mercedes-Benz 300 SL coupé in 1952, had all these details in coil-spring notebook form and shouted directions to the driver through a small megaphone. This clearly would not work in an open car. So, according to Klenk, the Mercedes factory devised the roll system used by Moss and Jenkinson.

This is not the story according to SM and Jenks. Jenks claimed that he first discussed the idea with American driver John Fitch, with whom he was proposing to ride in the 1954 race. Fitch did not run that year, but when it was agreed that Jenks would ride with Moss in 1955 in a Mercedes-Benz, the idea was revived. The 1955 map roller is clearly marked 'M Papier, Footscray, England.' Moss arranged to have it made with the Perspex window sealed by clear tape.

That the Mille Miglia could not last for ever was inevitable. Attitudes changed and, after the horrors and death toll of the 1903 Paris-Madrid race, it was amazing that any other road races even took place. If the question is raised, whether the Mille Miglia was held as open or closed races, the answer has to be 'both'. The roads were theoretically closed to non-racing traffic for a number of hours. In the early days this did not deter many Italian motorists from taking to the road regardless of whether or not they were officially closed. It was only the last few races that were properly marshalled with closed roads and, even then, late runners were forced to retire if delayed.

Whatever the potential horrors of the Mille Miglia, road-racing was commonplace in Italy. Apart from the Mille Miglia, there was the 671-mile Tour of Sicily that survived until 1957, the 41-mile (66.2km) Mugello circuit that lasted until 1970 and the Targa Florio which survived on the 44.7-mile (72km) Little Madonie circuit in Sicily until 1974. Interestingly, the Mugello circuit incorporated part of the course of the Mille Miglia, including the Futa and Raticosa passes.

The Targa Florio was of course also on a much shorter circuit that was lapped ten or so times, but there was very little crowd control and the spectators behaved in very much the same way as they had at the Mille Miglia. There were the same crowds that opened up to allow cars to pass down the middle between them, just as in the Mille Miglia, and there were spectators watching from the outside of corners and sitting on the parapets of bridges. Every year there were casualties, but these were not widely publicised. Whether the Mille Miglia had to end in 1957 is discussed later.

Acknowledgements

Julian Hunt deserves a very special appreciation and acknowledgment. In the 1980s he was writing his own book on the Mille Miglia and received considerable support and assistance from Denis Jenkinson. For various reasons he did not complete the book and he very kindly passed to me his notes of interviews with drivers now dead and others, and has given me the benefit of the research that he and Jenks carried out on specific cars. I greatly appreciate the support, friendship and additional input that he has given me while I was writing this book. He has also very kindly contributed the section of the book discussing the four founders of the race.

I am also very grateful to the many people who have contributed to the book in ways great and small: John Aldington (of the Frazer Nash Archives); David Baker (former Secretary of the Lancia Motor Club); Bob Berry; Gregor Fiskin; Paul Frère; Brigit Gale; Lawrence Hardwicke (of the Frazer Nash Archives); Tony Haynes; Hans Herrmann; Ingenieur Hans Klenk; Manfredini Lancia; Count Giannino Marzotto; Dr Harry Niemann (Leiter, Unternehmensgeschichte/Konzern Archiv, DaimlerChrysler); Hygen Nyncke (Konzernarchiv. Mobile Tradition, BMW); James Sitz; John Thompson.

The Founders of the Mille Miglia

In Italy, if you need anything important, you turn first to your family and friends. It is this close bond which is the key to life – and the despair of many from outside the country. Modern Italy has only existed for 100 years or so, and the tradition of inter-city or inter-region rivalry continues to this day. The Mille Miglia would not have existed but for citizens of the city of Brescia and its rivalry with Milan. Brescia lies in the valley of the River Po, to the north of the Lombardy plain, and has always been a centre for precision engineering, so in the late nineteenth century it naturally became a centre for the fledgling cycle and automobile industries.

Competitive cycle events were soon being organised, centred on the town, and the Giro d'Italia, the round-Italy cycle race, was held in Brescia from 1901. This flair for the organisation of competitive events quickly spread to motorcycles and cars and, in September 1905, the first of the Brescia Speed Weeks was held. The climax was the Coppa Florio, a race over 300 miles which attracted all the important teams.

The Fascia d'Oro road circuit outside Brescia continued in regular use until the first Italian Grand Prix in 1921, when huge crowds arrived on special trains to watch Jules Goux, driving a Ballot, average a remarkable 89mph (143kph) for 322 miles (518km). However, the construction by a well-connected syndicate of a new autodrome in the Royal Park at Monza, to the north of Milan, led to the 1922 GP being staged on the new course, and Brescia's position at the heart of motor racing declined. In 1926 the four friends got together to do something about the situation.

Count Aymo Maggi

Late in 1926 Aymo Maggi returned to Brescia after a successful season racing his private Bugatti. Born on 3 July 1903, the son of Count Berado Maggi di Gradella, he was from a wealthy landowning family with large estates at Calino, just outside Brescia, and Gradella, near Milan. Brought up to live the life of a country gentleman, he was captivated by speed from an early age, becoming a keen cyclist and motorcycle racer. He took up racing cars in 1922 and by 1926 was a successful driver of Bugattis, who would go on to drive Alfa Romeos and Maseratis all over Europe. Maggi was intelligent and perceptive, a keen amateur engineer who would finance the building of light aero engines designed by Rino Berardi.

Maggi was keenly aware that the Italian domestic motor industry was in the doldrums. All the best racing cars were being made abroad and he felt there was a need for a tough race for sports cars to encourage the Italian manufacturers to improve their products. It also smarted that Brescia had been sidelined. Over dinner one night he met two friends, Count Franco Mazzotti, his boyhood companion and fellow sportsman, and Renzo Castagneto, Editor of the Brescia sporting newspaper, *Lo Sporto Bresciano*. Castagneto was an experienced cycle and motorcycle competition organiser.

The founders of the Mille Miglia (from left): Aymo Maggi, Franco Mazzotti, Giovanni Canestrini and Renzo Castagneto.

The three talked over the need for an international sports car race and the importance of a high-profile event to Brescia in the way that the 24-Hour Race was to Le Mans. They soon decided they needed the view of someone with a wider viewpoint, so they jumped in a car and drove over to Milan where they banged on the door of their mutual friend, Giovanni Canestrini, motoring correspondent of the *Gazzetta dello Sport*, Italy's national sports newspaper. Canestrini tells how they sat in his apartment discussing the possibilities. Someone suggested that the race should run from Brescia to Rome, as it seemed like a good idea to include the capital, but if it was one-way this would give all the publicity to Rome.

How about Brescia-Rome-Brescia was the next suggestion? How far would that be? "Around 1600 kilometres", said Castagneto, "about the right distance." Mazzotti who, as a keen pilot, was used to reckoning in miles, added, "That would be a thousand miles. The Romans reckoned in miles, so we could call it the Mille Miglia." Soon they had it settled: the wealthy Mazzotti would finance the enterprise, Castagneto would organise it, Maggi would ensure the necessary approvals were obtained, and Canestrini's newspaper would provide publicity.

A road race of the type they were planning would require the co-operation of the councils and authorities in numerous towns and cities who would need to agree to the passage, closure and policing of roads. Another prerequisite would of course be the approval of the Government. The Fascist Party of Benito Mussolini had, by various means, brought about a general acceptance of national identity and imposed the will of a strong government on the rival city and regional assemblies. It was therefore essential for the Brescianos to have the Fascist politicians on their side.

Fortunately Arturo Turati, Secretary of the Party and Mussolini's deputy, had been born in Brescia and was an old friend of Aymo Maggi. After a cordial lunch, Maggi emerged with official approval and clearance for liaison between the police, army and civic authorities to run the race. In December 1926 the *Gazzetta dello Sport* announced the race to the public and they were off and running.

Aymo Maggi continued to compete in motor racing events. He was the only one of the original four to drive in the first Mille Miglia, sharing an Isotta Fraschini with Bindo Maserati, finishing sixth overall, and he continued to compete in his brainchild through the 1930s and for a final time (with Marchese Antonio Brivio, driving a Fiat Berlinetta) in 1947. He became Count Maggi in 1929 on his father's death and, in 1931, he married Camilla Calieppo, whose father had been a pioneer motorist.

Count Maggi devoted much of his time to the Mille Miglia, promoting the race at home and abroad – his friendliness and charm made him welcome all over Europe. It was almost certainly his personality and powers of persuasion behind the revitalisation of the race after the devastation of the war. Post-war, Calino became the base for almost all foreign entrants and the lavish, almost feudal, lifestyle impressed visitors almost as much as the welcome they received from the Count and Countess (who was fluent in many languages). After the last race Count Maggi's health, which had been poor for some years, declined and he died at Calino on 23 October 1961, aged only 58.

Count Franco Mazzotti

Born on 31 December 1904, the son of a wealthy banker and industrialist, Mazzotti grew up with Aymo Maggi and shared many of his interests. He became an enthusiastic and experienced pilot and took part in long-distance air races and flew the Atlantic in 1934. He was an experienced hydroplane racer and won a number of events in his boat *Mille Miglia*. He sponsored a team of Bugattis, 'Scuderia per dilettanti' and was the financial backer of the Mille Miglia until the war.

In 1930 Maggi and Mazzotti shared a 1750cc Alfa Romeo in the Mille Miglia and finished eighth overall. Count Mazzotti, Commandant of a special Air Force Combat Group, disappeared on a flight from Tunisia to Sicily in January 1942. From 1947 the title of the race was changed to the Coppa Franco Mazzotti Mille Miglia as a tribute to this gentle sportsman.

Renzo Castagneto

Born in Padua in 1892, Castagneto and his family moved to Milan when he was a child. As a young man he became an accomplished cyclist and later scored many victories in local events on motorcycles. In the early 1920s he became a successful journalist and in 1923 was director of the weekly sporting paper *Lo Sporto Bresciano*. By this time he had become more involved in the organisation of events, particularly the Giro d'Italia and the Motorcycle Grands Prix of Bari, Messina, Syracuse and Tripoli. He was also Secretary of the Brescia Football Association for many years.

Following the meeting in December 1926, the Automobile Club of Brescia was formed to organise the race and Castagneto became its first Secretary and later the permanent Director-General. He worked full time at the post and was responsible for the planning and administration of all twenty-one Mille Miglias. He was also to be seen at many other events in Italy, often officiating and giving his time to the sport he loved and his beaming smile appears in many contemporary photographs.

Giovanni Canestrini

The leading Italian motoring journalist of his generation, Canestrini was born at Rovertro, south of Trento, in 1894 and moved with his family to Milan when he was a small boy. His studies in engineering at the Turin Polytechnic were interrupted by the outbreak of World War I. After serving with the artillery he transferred to the air training school at Venaria Reale where his instructor was Arturo Ferranin, later to achieve fame as part of the Schneider Trophy Team.

Canestrini went on to become an experienced and much-decorated airman and after leaving the air force in the spring of 1924 he became the motoring correspondent of the *Gazzetta dello Sport*. Over the next 50 years he covered all the major events in Italy, and many abroad, and he came to know all the leading personalities involved in Italian motoring and motor racing. He contributed to international publications and his own book on the Mille Miglia was first published in 1967.

Overleaf: A very happy Italian trio: (from left) Baconin Borzacchini, Varzi and Danese. Borzacchini was killed when he crashed his Maserati at Monza in September 1933. (Author's Collection)

The Great Mille Miglia Drivers

ALBERTO ASCARI

(Born Milan, 13 July 1918, died Monza circuit, 26 May 1955)

Sublimely smooth, rarely ruffled during his Championship years and undoubtedly the most dominant Champion of the 1950s, Ascari was beefy, contented and a devoted family man. He was the son of Antonio Ascari who had been killed at the wheel of an Alfa Romeo P2 in the 1925 French Grand Prix at Montlhéry. In the late 1930s Ascari raced Bianchi motorcycles; he then drove one of the Tipo 815 AutoAvia cars in the 1940 Mille Miglia and an elderly Tipo 6CM Maserati in the 1940 Tripoli Grand Prix. Mussolini then brought Italy into the Second World War on the Axis side on 10 June 1940.

Ascari did not race again until 1947 when he joined Piero Dusio's 'circus' of Cisitalia single-seaters. Dusio's idea of touring with a fleet of these lithe little cars with 1,089cc Fiat engines did not prove financially successful,

Alberto Ascari was a great Italian driver who won the Formula 1 Drivers' World Championship in both 1952 and 1953. Although his record at the wheel of single-seaters was quite exceptional, he rarely drove in the Mille Miglia. After campaigning it for Ferrari in 1950 and 1951 he did not contest the race again until 1954 when he scored a brilliant victory for Lancia. Here he is seen at the wheel of a Maserati 4CLT/48 'San Remo' in the 1948 British Grand Prix at Silverstone – he finished second to team-mate Luigi Villoresi. (Guy Griffiths)

even though drivers included some famous names. Ascari competed in the first of these events, the so-called Cairo International Grand Prix held on the island of El Gézirah on 9 March. He finished second in his heat to Piero Taruffi and second in the final to Franco Cortese. The race was a financial fiasco and the series was cancelled. Later in the year he once again drove a Cisitalia in a race on the Caracalla circuit at Rome, but retired.

In 1947 Count 'Johnny' Lurani's Scuderia Ambrosiana started to enter Maserati four-cylinder supercharged 4CL cars in Grands Prix and became to all intents and purposes the works team. Luigi Villoresi was asked to lead the team and he suggested that Ascari should be his number two. The older driver had recognised something very special, very talented in Ascari's driving and Villoresi became his closest friend and mentor.

Ascari failed to make much of a mark in Formula 1 that year, but he did drive superbly in the Italian Grand Prix at Monza; he held third place ahead of one of the Alfa Romeo 158s driven by Consalvo Sanesi, but dropped back to finish fifth after a long pit stop to sort out a loose fuel tank. During 1948 Maserati introduced the much-improved 4CLT/48 car with twin-stage supercharging, generally lower construction and with a tubular chassis. These cars were usually known as the 'San Remo' model because the new Maserati made its debut in the San Remo Grand Prix.

Ascari won the San Remo race and then drove for Alfa Romeo in the French Grand Prix on the very fast Reims circuit. He finished third in the French race and, then back at the wheel of a San Remo, he was fourth in the Italian Grand Prix, won by Jean-Pierre Wimille with an Alfa Romeo. In October Villoresi and Ascari drove Maseratis in the first RAC Grand Prix at Silverstone and in the absence of the Alfa Romeos they took the first two places. In the Mille Miglia, Ascari drove a new A6.GCS 'Monofaro' Maserati and partnered by Bertocchi he ran well until he had mechanical problems.

Overall, Ascari had a season that proved a good learning curve and in itself very successful, bearing in mind that the 4CLT/48s were no match for the Alfa Romeos. Ferrari had fielded his new Tipo 125 single-stage supercharged V12 1,497cc cars in the 1948 Italian Grand Prix. Their debut was hardly spectacular, but that they had promise was undoubted and Villoresi and Ascari both agreed to drive for Ferrari in 1949. It was a year of only limited success despite the fact that Alfa Romeo had temporarily withdrawn from racing. A difference was that Ascari was now team-leader.

Ascari won the Swiss Grand Prix, the International Trophy at Silverstone and, with the latest longer-wheelbase, two-stage supercharged Ferrari was victorious in the European Grand Prix at Monza. Neither Ascari nor Villoresi drove in the Mille Miglia that year, but in

1950 they appeared with the latest 3,322cc V12 cars, but retired. Altogether, it was a poor year for both Ferrari and Ascari. At Maranello, engineer Aurelio Lampredi was feverishly working on a new line of unsupercharged Grand Prix Ferraris.

The regulations permitted unsupercharged cars up to 4,500cc as well as the more familiar 1,500cc supercharged cars and Ferrari had decided to follow the unsupercharged road, albeit that a full 4,498cc car was not ready to race until the Italian Grand Prix at Monza. Alfa Romeo had returned to racing and dominated the events in which they ran, so there were poor pickings for Ferrari. With a supercharged car, Ascari was second to Fangio (Alfa Romeo) at Monaco, he took over Serafini's 4.5 Ferrari to finish second to Farina (Alfa Romeo) in the Italian race and in the absence of the works Alfa Romeo team won the Penya Rhin Grand Prix at Barcelona.

Ascari and Villoresi reappeared in the 1951 Mille Miglia with Tipo 340 America 4,101cc Ferrari V12 sports-racing cars. While Ascari drove an open car with Touring barchetta body, Villoresi was at the wheel of a Vignale berlinetta. Ascari started the race in full darkness at 4.16am. Within a few miles he had crashed and was out of the race. It was, apparently, not an error of judgement, but a moronic spectator had pointed a powerful flashlight at Ascari's car; temporarily blinded by the light, he lost control and in the ensuing crash a spectator was killed. From then on Ascari insisted that the Mille Miglia be excluded from his contract.

The 1951 Formula 1 season witnessed a fierce battle between the ageing, overdeveloped supercharged Alfa Romeos driven by Fangio and Farina and the latest unsupercharged Ferraris with twin-plug ignition. By modern standards both Alfa Romeo and Ferrari were bulky and unwieldy and their poor roadholding was frightening. Alfa Romeo maintained their unbeaten post-war record by winning the Swiss, Belgian and European Grands Prix (the last of these held at Reims). Ferraris were, however, second in all three of these races and it was only a matter of time before the Alfa Romeos were beaten.

The breakthrough came in the British Grand Prix at Silverstone where Ascari retired because of gearbox trouble and the winner was a newcomer to the Ferrari team, beefy, balding, but dynamic Argentinean driver Froilan Gonzalez. Ascari went on to win the German and Italian races for Ferrari, but after the Maranello cars ran into tyre trouble in the Spanish Grand Prix on the Pedralbes circuit at Barcelona, Fangio won the race for Alfa Romeo and clinched his first World Championship. Ascari took second place on 25 points to the 31 of Fangio.

It was disappointment for Ascari, but in three seasons with Ferrari he had risen from an up-and-coming driver to a World Champion in waiting. Alfa Romeo

By 1949, Ascari and Villoresi were both works Ferrari drivers. Ascari, seen with his Tipo 125 V12 supercharged 1.5-litre Ferrari, is on his way to win the International Trophy race at Silverstone. Second was Giuseppe Farina with a Maserati, and Villoresi finished third. Note that at this stage in his racing career, Ascari is still wearing a linen helmet and has not yet adopted the famous blue crash helmet. (Guy Griffiths)

withdrew from Grand Prix racing at the end of 1951. The much-vaunted BRM V16 remained unreliable and there were no other contenders that were remotely competitive. So, one by one, the organisers of the World Championship Grands Prix decided to hold their races to 2,000cc unsupercharged Formula 2 rules. Ferrari had his new Tipo 500 four-cylinder Formula 2 car and, in the absence of serious opposition once Fangio had crashed his Maserati and put himself out of racing for the rest of the season, Ascari dominated Grand Prix racing.

Ascari won every Championship Grand Prix, except the Swiss race at Bremgarten which he missed because he was competing at Indianapolis. He enjoyed six victories and with wins in the first three Championship races of 1953, he had set a record of nine successive wins which still remains unbroken. Thereafter he finished fourth in the French Grand Prix, but won the British and Swiss races. For two years in succession Ascari was World Champion and at the peak of his career.

Lancia had been spending vast sums on a racing programme and were planning to race their new D50 V8 Grand Prix car designed by a team of engineers working under Vittorio Jano. Gianni Lancia offered both Ascari and Villoresi very substantial sums to drive for his team in 1954. It was the sort of money that is very difficult to refuse and so, after five seasons, they both left Ferrari. The new car was not to be ready to race until the Spanish Grand Prix in October 1954 and apart from testing Ascari might well have been described as gainfully unemployed.

Villoresi was to drive one of the team's D24 sports-racing cars in the Mille Miglia, but he was injured in a practice accident and, with remarkably good cheer, Ascari agreed to drive in his place. Other Lancias were driven by Piero Taruffi, who led prior to his retirement, Eugenio Castellotti and Piero Valenzano. The D24 was a beautifully-balanced, superb-handling car with ideal engine characteristics for road-racing. The race started in atrociously wet and dangerous conditions and initially Taruffi led. Ferrari, the marque that usually dominated the race, was running its monstrous 4.9-litre Tipo 375 Plus cars and they were most definitely not suitable for racing on ordinary roads.

At Rome, Taruffi led Ascari by a margin of 4½ minutes, Castellotti and Valenzano were already out of the race and Taruffi crashed near Florence. Ascari with the sole remaining D24 became increasingly worried about his car, which had developed an engine misfire. He won by a margin of over half-an-hour from Vittorio Marzotto with a 2-litre Ferrari Mondial, but the World Champion had suffered an enervating, draining race and at the finish, he was not merely tired, but completely exhausted, haggard and drawn.

This was the last real success that Ascari achieved. While waiting for the D50 to be ready, he drove a

Maserati 250F in the 1954 British and French Grands Prix and a Ferrari in the Italian race at Monza. There seemed to be something seriously wrong with Ascari's personality as he blatantly over-drove these cars. He also drove a Lancia sports car in the Tourist Trophy at Dundrod. The D50 finally appeared in the Spanish Grand Prix in October, but Ascari retired yet again.

By the start of the 1955 season Lancia was in severe financial trouble, but it carried on with its single-seater racing programme. In the Argentine Grand Prix, run in excruciatingly hot conditions, Ascari spun off on wet tar. The D50s appeared in minor races and Ascari won the Valentino Grand Prix held at Turin. The first round of the World Championship was the Monaco race and Ascari, leading the race after the Mercedes-Benz W196 cars retired, had a brake lock on the downhill section to the chicane and the car plunged through the straw bales into the harbour.

The car sank in the harbour in a hiss of steam, but Ascari's blue helmet bobbed to the surface and he was rescued unhurt apart from a broken nose and shock. Ten days later Ascari borrowed the Ferrari that he was to co-drive with Castellotti in the Supercortemaggiore Grand Prix at Monza and went out for a few laps. He also borrowed a crash helmet, whereas normally he would not drive without his 'lucky' blue helmet.

The exhaust note of the Ferrari could be heard rising and falling, but suddenly there was silence. Ascari had crashed at the Curva Vialone, probably because the car was running on wheel rims too narrow for its Englebert tyres. When rescuers arrived on the scene, Ascari was dying.

Although Ascari is now largely forgotten outside Italy, news-vendors' boards in Britain carried the legend 'Ascari killed.' Lancia ran a single D50 for Castellotti in the Belgian Grand Prix and then withdrew from racing. The cars were eventually handed over to Ferrari. When Ascari won his two World Championships, there was not much in the way of opposition and it would not be too unkind to describe them as 'soft' wins. His greatest success was his solo winning drive in the 1954 Mille Miglia, the race that he disliked intensely.

CLEMENTE BIONDETTI

(Born Buddusó, Sardinia, 18 August 1898, died Florence, 24 February 1955)

Biondetti, who reached the real peak of his racing career in late pre-war days, possessed a remarkable aptitude for the Mille Miglia and his greatest claim to fame was that his four wins made him more successful in the race than any other driver. He began his racing career with motorcycles in 1923 but this came to an end in 1926 when he crashed heavily at Ostia – an accident in which he allegedly broke 24 bones.

On recovering he started racing on four wheels in 1927 and initially drove a number of different makes, including Salmsons, Talbots and Bugattis. For several seasons he drove works and private Maseratis without conspicuous success. It perhaps reflects Biondetti's persistency rather than his talent that he achieved no real prominence until the 1936 Mille Miglia. In this race he drove the Alfa Romeo Monoposto with which Pintacuda had won the previous year and was partnered by Cesara.

He faced a very strong team of three new works Alfa Romeo 8C 2900A cars. By Bologna he led by 2min 40sec, a lead that he still maintained at Rome. Biondetti was delayed at Rome by time lost changing all four tyres and thereafter he gradually fell back, partly because of heavy tyre wear, partly because of a bungled refuelling stop at Perugia and maybe because of tiredness. At the finish he took fourth place behind the three works cars and was over 41 minutes behind the winner.

As a result of this performance he gained a place with Scuderia Ferrari in 1937. He retired in that year's 1,000-mile race, but in 1938, partnered by Stefani, he drove one of the latest 8C 2900B cars to victory. His record speed of 84.15mph (135.39kph) was not bettered until 1939. During 1938–40 he performed well with Alfa Romeo 158 Voiturettes and his successes included second place in the 1938 Coppa Ciano, a win in the 1939 Coppa Acerbo and second place in the Voiturette division of the Swiss Grand Prix (the Prix de Berne) and, finally, second place in the 1940 Tripoli Grand Prix.

Although Clemente Biondetti was an exceptionally able driver and knew the course of the Mille Miglia intimately, there was – inevitably – an element of luck in his four wins. Here, after his 1948 victory, he talks to Mille Miglia organiser Giovanni Canestrini. (Author's Collection)

Biondetti built this special, which combined a Biondetti-made chassis, a Ferrari body and a Jaguar XK 120 engine, together with Jaguar gearbox. He raced it in the Mille Miglia in 1951 and 1952 without success. The second year it had full-width bodywork vaguely resembling that of a C-type Jaguar. Here Biondetti is seen breaking the course record in the Firenze-Fiesole hill climb in April 1951. (Author's Collection)

A hat-trick of wins in the first three post-war Mille Miglia races in 1947–49, together with wins in the 1948–49 Tour of Sicily road races, which were as arduous as the Mille Miglia, if somewhat shorter, crowned his career. By now Biondetti was over 50, old for a racing driver even by the standards of the time. In 1950 he built a Grand Prix 'special' that combined a Ferrari Tipo 166 chassis with a Jaguar XK 120 engine. He abandoned racing this in Grands Prix after setting the slowest practice time bar two in the Italian Grand Prix but ran it in the Mille Miglia in 1951–52.

Biondetti was a member of the works Jaguar team at Le Mans in 1951. The following year he shared Stagnoli's third-place Ferrari in the Monaco Grand Prix, run that year as a sports car race, and co-driving with Cornacchia he finished second in the Pescara 12 Hours sports car race. For 1953 he joined Lancia and after a troubled race he finished eighth with one of the new D20 coupés in the Mille Miglia.

His final Mille Miglia drive was in 1954 when he finished fourth with a borrowed 2.7-litre Tipo 225 Ferrari. It was a remarkable performance, as he was a sick man aged nearly 56 and had been diagnosed as suffering from cancer a couple of years previously. His last months were bereft of pleasure, as he lived for motor racing in which he could no longer compete, and he became increasingly ill before dying at Florence on the 24 February 1955. He was one of the great men of the Mille Miglia.

RUDOLF CARACCIOLA

(Born Remagen am Rhein, 30 January 1901, died Kassel, Germany, 28 September 1959)

That Caracciola was one of the greatest drivers of the 1930s is undoubted. Many would say that he was the greatest of all because his driving was much more controlled, much less desperate than Nuvolari's and although he crashed, he did so infrequently. Despite his wonderful career with Mercedes-Benz, he had some dreadful experiences; he had crashed heavily in practice for the 1933 Monaco Grand Prix and it seemed unlikely that he would ever race again. His first wife Charly died in an avalanche, and, ultimately, two other bad crashes, both apparently caused by mechanical failures of his cars, brought his racing career to an end.

After he had completed his education and a year's military service, he went to work for the Fafnir car manufacturing company based at Aachen. Later he worked for the same company in Dresden. Determined to motor race, in 1922 he persuaded Fafnir to let him drive one of their 1.5-litre cars in a race at Avus where he finished fourth and at Rüsselheim where he won his race.

The following year he won a race in Berlin with an Ego, a light car built in the capital city.

He then went to work for Mercedes as a salesman and was soon competing in motor racing very successfully with cars provided by his employers. He won 13 events (including speed trials and hill climbs) in 1923, 25 events in 1924 and in 1926 went on to win the first German Grand Prix held in dreadfully wet weather at Avus. It was a very difficult race because of the conditions, but the opposition was not strong. That year Mercedes and Benz formally merged and Caracciola won event after event with the big Mercedes-Benz Type S cars. These were steadily developed until, in their final SSKL form, the power output was around 300bhp.

These 7-litre Mercedes-Benz SSKs ran mainly in racing car events, but even in their fastest form they were sports cars with a two-seater body and wings. Mercedes-Benz raced as a means of promoting sales of their cars and it was especially important that they performed in sports car events. In the 1930 Mille Miglia, Rudolf Caracciola at the wheel of an SSK and partnered by Christian Werner took sixth place. It was purely an exploratory entry and once the factory had concluded that it could win the race, it determined on a much more serious effort the following year.

Caracciola was also partnered by Werner in an SSK at Le Mans that year and there was a tremendous tussle between the German entry and the Bentleys. The Mercedes-Benz dominated the early hours of the race, but there were fierce battles for the lead between Birkin (blown 4½-litre Bentley) and Caracciola, and Barnato (Speed Six 6.5-litre Bentley) and Caracciola.

Two strong Bentley teams pushed Caracciola and the SSK to the car's mechanical limit. By the early hours of Sunday morning the SSK had dropped back to second place five minutes behind the Bentley of Barnato/Kidston and at 2.23am it retired because of a blown cylinder head gasket, probably the result of continuous use of the blower that could be switched in or out. In a long-distance race it was unwise to use it for sustained periods.

That the SSK and the later SSKL had an outstanding straight-line performance was undoubted, but they were also incredibly difficult cars to handle and only the most able drivers could exploit their full potential. After Le Mans, Caracciola won the European Sports Car Mountain Championship with his SSK and the Irish Grand Prix. The Irish race held in Phoenix Park, Dublin was a handicap event, but there was a battle for the outright lead between the Mercedes-Benz of Caracciola and the supercharged 4½-litre Bentley of Tim Birkin. Other SSKs were driven by Malcolm Campbell and Earl Howe and there were two other 'blower' Bentleys, but they took no part in the battle for the lead.

Caracciola and Birkin battled furiously, despite heavy rain starting to fall. It was so fierce in these

The great German Champion Rudolf Caracciola explains to his wife, Charly, the finer points of his 1931 race win with a Mercedes-Benz SSKL. Behind Caracciola is mechanic Wilhelm Sebastion (Author's Collection)

Suave, assured and vastly able: Caracciola sat for this portrait in the late 1930s, when he was at the peak of his Grand Prix racing career with Mercedes-Benz. Although he drove for the team again in 1952, his skill had diminished because of accidents and age. Another crash at Bern that year brought his racing career to an end. (Author's Collection)

dreadful conditions that it was frightening to watch. Birkin was forced to make three pit stops and although still lapping at high speed, he was dropping further and further behind. Despite the heavy rain Caracciola set a new lap record of 91.3mph (146.9kph) beating the record of 90.8mph (146.1kph) that he had set earlier in the dry. Caracciola won on scratch from Campari (Alfa Romeo) and Earl Howe with Birkin in fourth place. Caracciola also won on handicap from Victor Gillow (Riley) and Campari.

Sadly, there were to be no more battles between Mercedes-Benz and Bentley because the British company withdrew from racing at the end of 1930 due to its financial difficulties. The situation at Stuttgart-Untertürkheim was better – but not that much. In late 1930 Daimler-Benz withdrew from racing because of the economic difficulties caused by the Depression. Although the situation looked hopeless, Alfred

Neubauer managed to arrange a satisfactory deal with the Stuttgart company, which cost it almost as much as if it had continued racing.

The new arrangement was that Neubauer would act as team manager for Caracciola instead of the company. Caracciola acquired what was to be the prototype SSKL Mercedes-Benz on very favourable terms. Also made available and funded by the factory were the mechanics and a transporter. During the year Caracciola won 11 races and perhaps the most important was the Mille Miglia. He was partnered by Wilhelm Sebastian, who combined the roles of navigator and mechanic. On the face of matters the SSKL was totally unsuitable for the Mille Miglia, especially on the mountain passes, but Caracciola drove magnificently and mastered both car and course.

The SSKL lacked full support and there were at least a couple of occasions when Caracciola pulled into roadside garages and refuelled there rather than the controls where there was no back-up team. Nor was the race completely trouble free. Charles Goodacre tells on page 98 how he came across the stricken SSKL and Sebastian cadged a strong elastic rubber band off him. The incident is not too difficult to envisage; much more difficult is speculating just how the elastic band was used. Caracciola's job was, of course, made easier by the fact that the two new 8C 2300 Alfa Romeos driven by Arcangeli and Nuvolari were plagued by tyre problems and far from fully developed.

At the end of 1931 Daimler-Benz decided that they could no longer afford to support Caracciola. So he entered into an agreement to drive works Alfa Romeos. A very peculiar situation had arisen. Caracciola's car was painted white and he was not, officially, a member of the works team. Whether all the existing Alfa Romeo drivers did not want him in the team or whether it was just Campari is far from clear. For some years in the past – and it was to hold good in the future – Alfa Romeo used only Italian drivers, but Caracciola was a very exceptional driver and it seems that this apartheid was because of both his nationality and his towering ability.

One of Rudi's first drives with an Alfa Romeo in 1932 was in the Mille Miglia. Partnered by Bonini in his white 8C 2300 Monza, Caracciola battled for the lead with Nuvolari and Varzi (Bugatti) right from the start of the race and he was leading at Rome, but soon after the stop there the Monza's engine dropped a valve and he was out of the race. He finished second to Nuvolari at Monaco and took several other good places.

By the Italian Grand Prix at Monza in June, part of the prejudice against Caracciola was lifted as he now drove a red car. He achieved two major race victories during the year, both with the new Monoposto Tipo B cars: he won the German Grand Prix in accordance with team orders (it was his fourth victory in this race) and he also won the Monza Grand Prix on merit. Wins in five Mountain Hill Climbs led to him becoming European Mountain Champion for the first time (previously he had only been Sports Car Champion).

At the end of 1932 Alfa Romeo was beset with financial difficulties and withdrew from racing. Initially, Scuderia Ferrari was not allowed to have the Tipo B Monopostos and they languished at Portello. For 1933 Monégasque driver Louis Chiron and Caracciola went into partnership to race Alfa Romeo Monzas and Bugattis. It was a short-lived partnership that ended on the second day of practice at the Monaco Grand Prix. Caracciola crashed his Monza heavily into a stone wall.

The German driver claimed that a front brake had locked as he approached the chicane and he had been forced to make a snap decision between hitting the wall

and plunging into the harbour. A number of observers of the accidents, however, were of the view that Caracciola had made a rare error of judgement and left his braking too late.

As Caracciola explained in his autobiography, *A Racing Driver's World,* he believed that he was unhurt: "Only the body of the car was smashed, especially around my seat. Carefully I drew my leg out of the steel trap. Bracing myself against the frame of the body I slowly extricated myself from the seat … I tried to hurry out of the car. I wanted to show that nothing had happened to me, I was absolutely unhurt. I stepped to the ground. At that instant the pain flashed through my leg. It was a ferocious pain, as if my leg [was] being slashed with hot, glowing knives. I collapsed …"

It was a terrible injury. Caracciola's right hip was shattered at the hip joint. It was believed that he would never race again. Rudi recovered against the odds and for 1934 he signed to drive for the new Mercedes-Benz team racing in the new 750Kg Grand Prix category. At the time he signed the contract, it was far from certain whether, in fact, Caracciola would be able to race. Not long afterwards Rudi's wife Charly died – apparently from a heart attack – after her skiing party had been buried in an avalanche.

During the next few years Caracciola reigned supreme as the greatest driver in the Mercedes-Benz team, despite challenges from Fagioli, von Brauchitsch and Lang. Between the 1934 French Grand Prix held on 1 July, the debut race for the Mercedes team, and the Yugoslav Grand Prix on 3 September 1939 Caracciola won 15 major Grands Prix (this total includes a shared drive with Fagioli in the 1934 Italian Grand Prix). He was also European Champion three times.

In 1937 Caracciola married his second wife, Baby Hoffmann in Lugano, Switzerland where he had lived since 1929 (the complexities of Baby Hoffmann's relationship with Louis Chiron are outside the scope of this book) and during the war years they lived in Switzerland. Caracciola was to drive in the Indianapolis 500 Miles race in 1946. He was hoping that one of the 1939 W165 supercharged V8 voiturettes would be refurbished and released by the factory.

But it was not to be and so he drove an American Thorne Special. During qualifying the car went out of control at high speed, he crashed and suffered very serious head injuries. It seems that driver error was not in any way responsible for the accident. He eventually recovered, but by the time that he raced again in 1952 he was 51 years of age.

It was Caracciola's own wish that resulted in his inclusion in the Mercedes-Benz 300 SL Gullwing team in 1952 and it seems that Neubauer was reluctant to include him. His first race was the Mille Miglia, the event that he had won 21 years previously. Caracciola drove a car slightly less powerful than that of his team-mates and this may have been a calculated decision by Neubauer. Rudi's drive was not exactly distinguished, but he 'kept the car on the island', kept going at a reasonable turn of speed and took fourth place.

This was not quite the end of Caracciola's racing career. He next appeared with a Gullwing in the Preis von Bern, a minor race on the Bremgarten circuit. Local driver Daetwyler's 4.1-litre Ferrari expired on the first lap and the 300 SLs were unchallenged. On lap 13 of this short race Rudi's car locked a rear brake, a failing not unknown on these cars, he was unable to control the Gullwing and went off the road, colliding with a tree. His left thigh was very badly fractured and his long and brilliant driving career was at an end. It was another accident that occurred through no fault of the driver.

Caracciola is probably best remembered for his Grand Prix drives, especially in the wet, and he was universally known by the name 'Regenmeister'. In the context of this book, his greatest drive was in the 1931 Mille Miglia, a brilliant win with a difficult car and one of only two wins in the whole series by other than an Italian driver. Caracciola's health never fully recovered from the crash at Bern and when he died in 1959 in a sanatorium he was only 58 years of age.

STIRLING MOSS

(Now Sir Stirling Moss, born West Kensington, London, 17 September 1929)

AN APPRECIATION OF HIS MILLE MIGLIA DRIVES
So many books have been written about Stirling Moss that it would be otiose and tedious to summarise his career here. Tom Wisdom undoubtedly drove in more Mille Miglia races than any other British driver. Donald Healey ranks next in these particular stakes, but Moss follows with a total of six drives, three for Jaguar, his winning drive for Mercedes-Benz and two for Maserati.

Stirling's first drive in the 1,000-mile race came in 1951 when he drove a works-prepared XK 120 Roadster accompanied by Frank Rainbow of Jaguar's Experimental Department. The Jaguar drivers had carried out no practice over the circuit, which would have been a terrible mistake, if the Jaguar's race had lasted rather longer. The race started in torrential rain and Rainbow recounted to Andrew White *(Jaguar Sports Racing & Works Competition Cars to 1953):*

"I had every confidence [in Stirling]. We got on well (and we remained firm friends). We had passed a Ferrari and I remember noticing that Italy had still a lot of post-war repairs to do. We crossed a Bailey-type bridge at about 100mph [160kph] and the sound was as if all the planks

Stirling Moss was to become the greatest British racing driver of all time. This photograph, taken in about 1950, shows him at the wheel of a Cooper 500. (Guy Griffiths)

had upended themselves. The road was glistening and there was still hardly any daylight.

"Our disaster happened quickly, on the approach to a left-hander. Stirling did wonders with the wheel to no avail. The crowd parted and we hit a 'Topolino' parked where there would have otherwise been an escape road. As we got out to inspect the damage, John Lea ran over from Leslie Johnson's [XK 120] which had gone off too, and we all got out of the way and watched the antics of the last few competitors.

"We rejoined the race, but Stirling soon found that there was virtually no lock to the right. The road was drying, but we still overshot the first open garage, where Moss had decided to stop. Reversing rapidly proved our final undoing. Excessive rotation caused the reverse gear bush to seize on the idler shaft. There was a modification later as a result of our experience, but that was no help at the time! It took Stirling and me ages to get the floorboards up and the gearbox lid off.

"We did disengage the seized gear, but, by the time that we had removed the mangled bumpers and cleared the body from the wheels, we realised the first control would be closed. We made for Brescia reluctantly, realising that at the crash scene the other Jaguar must have gone back too. In Brescia we must have taken a wrong turning because we found ourselves at the top of a flight of stone steps. Not daring to engage reverse, Stirling quietly drove down the steps into the square."

In 1952 Moss drove a C-type fitted with disc brakes and he was partnered by Jaguar's works test driver Norman Dewis. It was the famous race in which Mercedes-Benz fielded a very well prepared team of 300 SL Gullwings and had tested assiduously, whereas Moss had been unable to do more than token practice. It was the first year in which a starting ramp was used at Brescia and in the heavy rain many drivers suffered wheelspin on the ramp. There were also problems with cars grounding. Quite a number of drivers elected to start from the road alongside the ramp, among them Moss.

Moss talks with World Champion Juan-Manuel Fangio in 1951, when Moss was driving Kieft-Norton 500cc Formula 3 cars. (Guy Griffiths)

Dewis told Andrew Whyte: "We yelled like mad to attract the attention of a starting official who stamped his feet and waved his arms furiously, obviously objecting to our car starting from this position. I pointed at my watch and made other signs. There were shrugs all round. At 0619 the flag fell and we were away in a series of professionally-corrected back-end slides ... it was like motoring on ice for the first hour ... small towns came and went in a flash, their streets becoming narrow lanes bordered by forests of faces swaying to and fro, like cornfields in a breeze. After two hours the car sounded perfect and our system of signalling to each other was working very well indeed."

Kling started four minutes after Moss and caught and passed the British car. Not far after Ravenna the flexible pipes from the Jaguar's exhaust manifold cracked and Dewis felt that he was being overcome by fumes. He revived himself by leaning out into the air stream. The Jaguar was unable to keep pace with Kling's 300 SL. Dewis reported to Whyte on the most frightening moment in the race:

"We caught up with the Mercedes number 613 of Caracciola who speeded-up when he saw us. Stirling managed to pass, however, only to find he was travelling much too fast to negotiate a right-hand bend. The car slid broadside and I felt as if I was hanging over my side of the car with Stirling lying on top of me. After careering along the edge, knocking over several posts, we lurched back on to the road. We both felt a bit shaken and I used a whole box of matches trying to light a cigarette."

By Rome the Jaguar had dropped to seventh place. They carried on, somewhat overcome by fumes from the exhaust and with a bad fuel leak. At Siena they drove through the flames from Biondetti's Jaguar 'Special' which had caught fire during refuelling. Because of the fuel leak they made an additional refuelling stop at the Shell depot in Florence. As they raced into the control, they hit the open passenger door of a competing Fiat and sliced it off completely. There is little doubt that by that time they were too overcome by fumes to think clearly.

The Jaguar crossed the Raticosa Pass and on the north side the front of the car slid outwards and into a boulder. The handling became unstable and when they stopped to check, they found that the steering rack bracket had detached itself from the chassis frame. They were out of the race, but after Dewis had wired up the rack tube, they were able to motor slowly to Bologna. If they had been able to keep going, they would have finished fourth. It was the only time that a British car with British crew was able to challenge for the lead in the Mille Miglia and, despite the problems and retirement, it was a magnificent performance.

Stirling Moss drove a C-type once again in the 1953 race, partnered by Mortimer Morris Goodall, who had been appointed Jaguar team manager for that season only. He was an outsider and his position in the team whereby he was senior to 'Lofty' England was deeply resented at Browns Lane.

Some lessons had been learned and Moss carried out some 6,000 miles (9,650km) of practice over a two-week period. There were three C-types entered, all very carefully prepared. Despite this none of the Jaguars made it to the finish and Moss was out of the race before Ravenna because a rear axle tube had twisted into the differential housing. The works took no more interest in the Mille Miglia and Moss did not drive in the 1954 race.

At the time of writing Stirling Moss is one of only two surviving Mille Miglia winners, the other being Giannino Marzotto who won the race twice. Who scored the greatest Mille Miglia victory is just about impossible to argue objectively. It could very well be Moss, but what can be said with absolute accuracy is that his win in 1955 is the best remembered for a number of reasons; it was highly publicised at the time by Daimler-Benz; it was reported widely throughout the world and it is still reported and commented on because of the close and brilliantly successful partnership between Moss and his navigator Denis Jenkinson.

The whole concept of detailed notes written on a roll of paper 18 feet in length in an alloy case and with the notes read through a Perspex window sealed with Sellotape caught the public imagination. So did the fact that the two men trusted each other completely. It was not simply a case of them having prepared the notes together based on what Jenkinson was able to write during practice, but Moss had the confidence that Jenkinson always knew precisely which point on the course they had reached. When Jenkinson indicated a corner and a speed, Moss accepted it implicitly.

In 1955 Mercedes-Benz entered four 300 SLRs and they were, with the works Ferraris, the fastest cars in the race and, as the 1,000 miles proved, the epitome of reliability. Two drivers, Fangio and Kling, drove solo, while Herrmann and Moss each took a passenger. Herrmann, backed up by Eger, turned in a very fine drive in this race (see page 240), but was not in the same league as Moss and Jenkinson. Denis Jenkinson was probably the greatest of all motor racing journalists and his so very detailed account of the race published in *Motor Sport* for June 1955 was the finest piece that he ever wrote.

The formidable combination of Moss and Jenkinson were entered with Maseratis in 1956 and 1957. In both years the cars failed miserably. Moss's 1956 mount was an underdeveloped, ill-handling Tipo 350S with 3,483cc engine. It was fast enough to win, but not even Moss could overcome the deplorable handling and his race ended in a crash from which he and Jenkinson were very fortunate to

escape unscathed. The following year Moss drove a monstrous V8 4.5-litre 450S, but while it seems doubtful that such a brute of a car could win the 1,000-mile race, this was never put to the test. The Maserati had to be retired within minutes of the start because of a broken brake pedal.

TAZIO NUVOLARI

(Born Casteldario, near Mantua, 18 November 1892, died 11 August 1953, Mantua)

Fifty-five or so years ago when Tazio Nuvolari was still alive, when Farina had won the first Drivers' World Championship in 1950 and the following year when Juan Fangio won the first of his five Championships, it was

Tazio Nuvolari, seen at his first motorcycle race in 1920. The machine is an Indian that belonged to his father. (Author's Collection)

axiomatic that the 'Flying Mantuan' was the greatest racing driver ever. By today's standards when men grow much taller, at 5ft 3in he was a diminutive, skinny little figure characterised by light blue linen trousers, yellow shirt (with a large 'TN' on the right-hand side of the chest) and leather wind-helmet. If it was cold, he would wear a leather waistcoat. It did not help his general appearance that he had a rather monkey-like face.

But he drove like 'a bat out of hell', highly competitive, able to screw much more out of a second-rate Alfa Romeo than anyone would have thought possible; he was always fighting to win, always battling wheel-to-wheel with his rivals and very often winning against the odds. The classic example of this was his victory with a Monoposto Alfa Romeo in the 1935 German Grand Prix, where he defeated the might of the Mercedes-Benz and Auto Union teams and left a certain Adolf greatly miffed.

Once he started to race cars, he found that he lacked the physical strength to control the heavy steering. So he started to drive on the throttle through corners, inducing

Nuvolari, probably the greatest Italian racing driver of all time, and winner of the Mille Miglia in 1933. (Author's Collection)

beautifully balanced and controlled four-wheel-drifts, a way of cornering that he is credited with inventing. There are always misconceptions about four-wheel-drifts and four-wheel-slides. The drift is when the car is beautifully balanced and has all four wheels in line. It is something that only really great drivers could achieve, while sliding through corners with the front wheels at a different angle from the rear wheels was the forte of lesser drivers

And then there were Nuvolari's crashes. It seemed that he was always crashing (in fact his record was not that bad) and then racing in a cast or a plaster corset and in great pain in his determination to achieve another victory. Any other driver who crashed as frequently as Nuvolari would be regarded critically. Not Nuvolari, his crashes were all part of his mystique and his greatness. Whether he stands up as a really great driver comparable with the later Fangio, Moss, Clark or Senna is very difficult to assess fairly. Standards and perspectives were so very different when Nuvolari was racing.

His full names were Tazio Giorgio Nuvolari and he was the eldest of three children born to Arturo and Elisa Nuvolari. He worked as a car salesman. Shortly before the outbreak of the First World War, Nuvolari met Carolina Perrina, a very attractive local girl and it seems that they fell in love. During the war Nuvolari was in the army and served as a driver. Once the war was over, Tazio returned to the motor trade and he and Carolina married. Like many drivers of the period, his grounding was in motorcycle-racing and he raced Harley-Davidsons, Indians and Bianchis.

In 1925 he drove in some minor car races. He was given a trial drive by Alfa Romeo in a P2 at Monza that year, but went off the road and crashed because the gearbox seized. This is the first recorded of Nuvolari's notorious crashes. He was badly injured and the doctors told him that he was to be confined to bed for a week. Naturally, he ignored the doctors' advice and insisted that they strapped him up in the riding position so that he could race his Bianchi ten days after the accident with the Alfa Romeo. He seemed totally indifferent to danger.

During 1927–28 he teamed up with Achille Varzi to race Bugatti Type 35s and proved by far the more successful of the two drivers. By 1930 both Nuvolari and Varzi were in the Alfa Romeo team and Tazio scored his first win in the Mille Miglia. It does seem that Jano favoured Nuvolari and deliberately misled Varzi into believing that he had a substantial lead, and inducing him to ease off.

During much of the rest of 1930 he had mixed fortunes, but he enjoyed a much more successful season in 1931. The Mille Miglia was a débâcle because the new 8C 2300 Alfa Romeos were undeveloped, but Nuvolari won four races with Alfa Romeo Monzas, among them the Targa Florio and the ten-hour Italian Grand Prix in which he co-drove with Campari.

Alfa Romeo revealed the Tipo B Monoposto Grand Prix cars in the Italian Grand Prix in June 1932. It was another successful year during which Nuvolari won the Targa Florio and the Italian and French Grands Prix, together with the Coppa Acerbo and the Coppa Ciano road races. At the end of the 1932 season, Alfa Romeo was forced to withdraw from racing for financial reasons.

The company did not make the Monopostos available to Scuderia Ferrari and that team had to struggle on with the far less competitive Alfa Romeo Monzas. Even so Nuvolari won ten races in 1933, six of them with Alfa Romeos, including Le Mans. He won the Mille Miglia for a second time that year. Because the Monzas were so uncompetitive, Nuvolari switched to Maserati in mid-season and won three races with the Bologna cars. The season ended at the San Sebastian Grand Prix in which he crashed and suffered minor head injuries.

Nuvolari drove for Maserati and Bugatti in 1934, although he appeared with an Alfa Romeo in the Mille Miglia. The press and public were expecting a fierce battle in the Mille Miglia between Nuvolari and Varzi. It was a very wet race, Varzi was racing on Pirelli Pneugrippa tyres, the poor grip in the wet of Nuvolari's Dunlops prevented him from putting up a serious challenge and he was forced to settle for second place.

Shortly afterwards Nuvolari had a bad accident in heavy rain in the Bordino Grand Prix at Alessandria. He broke his right leg, which was put in a plaster cast, but he was determined to race his Maserati in the Avusrennen on the banked circuit in Berlin three weeks later. He had the car modified so that he could operate the pedals with his left foot. He finished fifth.

For 1935 Nuvolari was persuaded to rejoin Scuderia Ferrari which was about to receive the latest Alfa Romeos. He had hoped to join Auto Union, but apparently Stuck and Varzi did not want him in the team and had enough clout to stop them signing him up. So far as Alfa Romeo and Ferrari were concerned, it was really

Nuvolari at the wheel of his Alfa Romeo at the 1937 Circuit of Masaryk, at Brno in Czechoslovakia. It was the last race that the maestro drove for Alfa Romeo. (Author's Collection)

Nuvolari's son Alberto died from nephritis in 1946 at the age of 18. Tazio, puffing away at his fag, stands on the right of the picture, with Count Trossi behind him. (Author's Collection)

a case of 'your country needs you.' By this time German domination of Grand Prix racing was almost complete. Alfa Romeos picked up wins by Nuvolari and others in minor races, but by that year's German Grand Prix at the end of July Mercedes-Benz had won six major races and Auto Union two.

At the Nürburgring the German cars dominated their home race in the early laps, but Nuvolari was gradually making his way up the field. By lap ten he was leading, but most drivers stopped to refuel at the end of lap 12. Nuvolari was stationary for 2min 14sec because the pressure-pump refuelling system had failed and the car was refuelled from churns. He resumed at his sensationally fastest and by the start of lap 22, the last lap, he was back in second place, 35sec behind von Brauchitsch (Mercedes-Benz).

Not even Nuvolari could make up that difference in 14.17 miles (22.80km). For once the gods smiled favourably on Nuvolari, for von Brauchitsch's rear tyres were badly worn and with Nuvolari pressing so hard, Mercedes racing manager Alfred Neubauer dare not call him in for a wheel-change. Half-way round that lap, the left rear tyre of the Mercedes-Benz burst and Nuvolari sailed on to one of the greatest wins in his career.

Nuvolari stayed with Alfa Romeo for another two seasons, but he did not take part in another pre-war Mille Miglia. He crashed yet again in practice for the 1936 Tripoli Grand Prix. A tyre had burst and Nuvolari was flung out of the cockpit. He was again put in a plaster cast because of broken ribs (these days the ribs would have been left to heal themselves, but the pain from broken ribs is intense). Obviously he was advised not to race and, equally obviously, he ignored that advice. He finished seventh in this race.

Later that year he pushed the Mercedes-Benz entries so hard in the Hungarian Grand Prix at Budapest that they all retired and Nuvolari led an Alfa Romeo 1–2–3 across the line. Another good win followed in the Circuit of Milan where he beat Varzi (Auto Union) back into second place. Otherwise the year 1936 proved a bonanza for Auto Union and their lead driver Bernd Rosemeyer. Even so, Nuvolari had a number of other successes, usually against heavy odds. He won the Coppa Ciano at Leghorn, leading an Alfa Romeo 1–2–3, and later in the year he won the Vanderbilt Cup Race at Roosevelt Raceway, (together with $20,000 prize money, equivalent today to around £100,000).

Tazio stayed with Alfa Romeo again in 1937, but the Milan cars were even less competitive. In April he crashed heavily in practice for the Circuit of Turin and soon afterwards his father died. Once again he competed in the Vanderbilt Cup and travelled to New York on the wonderful new French liner *Normandie* with its most impressive and delightful art deco furnishings and decorations. Not long before the giant French liner

docked in New York, Nuvolari received a cable informing him of the death of his son Giorgio, plagued by heart problems since birth.

In the 1938 Pau Grand Prix his new Tipo 308 Alfa Romeo caught fire because chassis flexing had caused the fuel tank to split. Although Nuvolari abandoned it quickly, he suffered burnt legs. He was deeply troubled that Alfa Romeo should let him drive such a bad car. He made it clear that he would never again drive an Alfa Romeo and shortly afterwards announced that he was retiring. Following the death of Bernd Rosemeyer during a record-breaking attempt in January 1938, Auto Union lacked a lead driver and with some hesitation Nuvolari joined them at the German Grand Prix in July.

For 1938 onwards the Grand Prix regulations were, in simple terms, for unsupercharged cars up to 4,500cc and supercharged cars up to 3,000cc. Auto Union were racing new supercharged 3-litre V12s. Nuvolari took a little while to adjust to these immensely powerful rear-engined cars, which were plagued initially by mechanical problems, but towards the end of the season he won the Italian and Donington Grands Prix. At Donington he raced with fractured ribs after hitting a deer in practice.

By the start of the 1939 season he was 46 years of age, but he had lost none of his forcefulness or enthusiasm. It was very much a Mercedes-Benz year and Hermann Lang won five of the year's races for Untertürkheim. Throughout the season Nuvolari was fighting it out at the front, but his only win was in the shortened Yugoslavian Grand Prix held at Belgrade on the day that the Second World War broke out.

Despite his advancing years and ill-health Nuvolari raced again after the end of the Second World War. In 1946 his younger son Alberto died from nephritis (inflammation of the kidneys) at the age of 18. During that year Tazio became very sick, and was said to be suffering from a respiratory disease caused by inhaling alcohol fuels while driving racing cars. It has never been specified what the disease was, but it may have been a form of emphysema.

Nuvolari drove in a number of single-seater races and his very last win was with a Maserati in the 1946 Albi Grand Prix. He was now 54 years of age and in the Milan Grand Prix in September he finished his heat, steering with his left hand and with his right holding a blood-stained handkerchief to his mouth.

It seemed that he would never race again, but he did compete in a number of races, including the 1947 and 1948 Mille Miglia events. These two races in themselves form part of the Nuvolari legend and resulted in some very fanciful journalism. In simple, objective terms Nuvolari drove in ten Mille Miglia races, he won twice and was second twice. Not the best record, but not far off it. Nuvolari was certainly a very great Mille Miglia driver, but was he the world's greatest driver.' Probably not, but it does no harm to believe that he was.

As an aside, in the East Midlands anyone rushing about in a car is said, in local dialect, to be 'Tazzing around.' It is an expression that reflects the tremendous and lasting impression that Nuvolari made at Donington Park in 1938.

PIERO TARUFFI

(Born, Albone Laziale, Rome, 12 October 1906, died Rome, 12 January, 1988)

Taruffi, a qualified engineer, was one of the great stalwarts of the Mille Miglia. He competed regularly from 1930 onwards and, perhaps more famously, was manager of the Gilera motorcycle racing team. Like so many Italian drivers, he had considerable experience of racing motorcycles before taking to four wheels. This was a career course that was rarely followed in England. Taruffi's first motorcycle racing experience was with a private Norton, but in 1934 he joined the company that built the Rondine (predecessor to the Gilera) and was both a works rider and development engineer.

By this time Taruffi had already set out on his career in racing on four wheels. One of his first drives was in the 1930 Mille Miglia sharing the driving of a Lancia Lambda. It was old and uncompetitive, it overheated and misfired and he and Masera did well to finish 40th. The following year Taruffi was partnered by Matrullo and drove a supercharged Tipo 61 Itala in the 1,000-mile race, but retired.

Enzo Ferrari recognised Taruffi as a 'coming man' and although he was still racing motorcycles, Scuderia Ferrari offered him a few drives. He refused to race motorcycles for the Scuderia and preferred to ride his own machines. Early successes on four wheels were a second place behind Fagioli ('Sedici Cilindri' Maserati) in the 1932 Rome Grand Prix and third place in the 1933 Eifelrennen. By 1934 Taruffi was driving works Maseratis. He worked his way up to fourth place with a four-cylinder 2.5-litre car at Monaco, only to retire on the last lap, but this was more than compensated for by a fine class win in the Mille Miglia.

Taruffi next drove the 5-litre V5 'Sedici Cilindri' car in the Tripoli Grand Prix. He used the brute power of the 16-cylinder car to build up an early lead, but on the fourth lap the brakes locked as he entered a curve. The effect of the braking was such that the tyre treads melted and the Maserati went off the track, demolishing a hoarding. Taruffi was thrown out of the car and was lucky to escape with only a broken arm. That was the end of his racing until 1935.

Piero continued his motorcycle racing career, but he also joined the Bugatti team. Molsheim was in decline and still racing the obsolescent Type 59 cars and Taruffi tried hard, but achieved nothing. He finally retired from motorcycle racing in 1937, but he joined Gilera, whom he had persuaded to take over the Rondine racing project and worked for them as development engineer and team manager. His preoccupation with Gilera was such that he was then rarely seen at the wheel of racing cars before the Second World War.

Taruffi became closely involved with Cisitalia in early post-war days. He was test driver and raced cars in a number of events from 1946 through to 1949. Endurance races included the 1948 Tour of Sicily and the 1948 Mille Miglia. He also drove a works Alfa Romeo Tipo 158 into fourth place behind team-mates Wimille, Trossi and Sanesi in the 1948 Monza Grand Prix. By 1949 Taruffi was driving for Ferrari from time to time. He was at the wheel of a Tipo 166S in that year's Mille Miglia and led until the transmission broke at Ravenna. In the Formula 2 Rome Grand Prix on the Caracalla circuit he brought his car across the line in second place behind Villoresi with a similar Ferrari.

In the pits at Silverstone during the British Grand Prix meeting in July 1952 are (left) Tony Vandervell, entrant of Ferrari Thin Wall Specials and, later, Vanwall Formula 1 cars, and (right) Italian driver Piero Taruffi. At this meeting Taruffi drove the Thin Wall Special in the Formule Libre race. He set fastest lap and won, despite being penalised a minute for jumping the start. With good reason the 'Silver Fox' was regarded as one of Italy's fastest drivers. (Guy Griffiths)

Gilera had built a new four-cylinder 500cc racing motorcycle, the work of Ing. Piero Remor. There was nothing wrong with the concept, but a great deal wrong with the execution and the new machine was, initially, a failure. Remor left Gilera to work for MV Agusta and Taruffi, who had left Gilera following the outbreak of the Second World, returned in 1950 as team manager and also acted as a development engineer. He stayed with Gilera until the end of 1955. He loved the world of motorcycle racing, but his talents on four wheels were more and more in demand. Taruffi's life became something of a juggling act, especially as he was also record-breaking with his Tarf twin-boom cars.

Piero Taruffi was one of that generation of Italian racing drivers who were quick, dependable and remained so with the passing of the years. By 1950 he was 43 years old; he still had not sorted out his priorities between Gilera and racing cars. That year he drove for Alfa Romeo in the Italian Grand Prix at Monza, but had to hand over his car to Juan Fangio. In two major non-Championship races he did particularly well. He was third with an Alfa Romeo in the Grand Prix des Nations at Geneva and third with a Ferrari in the Penya Rhin Grand Prix at Barcelona.

In 1951 he joined Ferrari on a regular basis and enjoyed a good measure of success, finishing second with his unblown 4.5-litre Ferrari in the Swiss Grand Prix and taking fifth places at both the Nürburgring and Monza. The following year World Championship racing was held to Formula 2 rules and Taruffi backed up his Ferrari team-leader Alberto Ascari superbly. There was not much in the way of opposition to the Ferraris, but Taruffi won the Swiss Grand Prix in the absence of Ascari at Indianapolis; he took third place in the French race at Rouen and second place in the British Grand Prix. It was a good enough performance for him to finish third in the Drivers' Championship.

Taruffi turned in a superb drive with a 4.1-litre Ferrari in the 1952 Mille Miglia and battled hard for the lead against the Mercedes-Benz 300 SL opposition until his car broke its transmission. He drove Tony Vandervell's Ferrari Thin Wall Special to victory in the Ulster Trophy on the Dundrod circuit near Belfast and with this car he also won the Formule Libre race at Silverstone on the day of the British Grand Prix – despite being penalised one minute for jumping the start.

He withdrew from Grand Prix racing in 1953, and joined the Lancia team to drive the new D20 3-litre coupés. In this early form the Lancias were not competitive, so Taruffi was not too upset to retire in the Mille Miglia because of brake trouble. As the years passed, so Taruffi wanted more and more to win the Mille Miglia in which he had been competing for so many years. He stayed with Lancia for 1954 and the latest D24 3.3-litre spiders were seriously competitive and just about the ideal road-racing car.

Many think that Taruffi was the fastest (and most dependable) of all Mille Miglia drivers, faster than Castellotti, faster than Moss and faster than Collins. He was certainly much more of a consistent driver than either Castellotti or Collins and he had the advantage of knowing the course intimately. Piero seemed unbeatable in the 1954 Mille Miglia and had a four-minute lead over Ascari with another Lancia at Rome. All was fine until an almost pedestrian driver running in a small capacity class crossed his line and forced him off the road near Siena. An oil pipe was torn away and the Lancia lost all its oil. Some consolation came from wins in the Tour of Sicily and the Targa Florio.

In 1955 Taruffi elected to drive a Ferrari and he appeared in the Mille Miglia at the wheel of a fast, but very fragile 3.7-litre Tipo 118 car. Like his Ferrari team-mates he was plagued by tyre problems. Even so, he put up a tremendous fight against the Mercedes-Benz 300 SLRs. He was third at Ravenna, led at Pescara, was second to Moss at Rome, but was forced to retire because of oil pump failure. Some indication of Taruffi's high standing as a driver is given by the fact that Daimler-Benz chose him to substitute for the injured Hans Herrmann in the British Grand Prix (he was fourth behind the rest of the team) and second in the Italian Grand Prix (behind Mercedes team-leader Fangio).

Taruffi drove for Maserati in the 1956 Mille Miglia. He spurned the proffered 350S that was totally lacking in development and opted instead for a normal 300S. It lacked power compared to the Ferrari opposition, but in torrential rain and on soaking, slippery roads he was second at Ravenna, but the brakes became water-logged and Taruffi smashed the car against the balustrade of a bridge on the section between Ravenna and Forli.

By the 1957 Mille Miglia, Taruffi (often referred to as the 'silver fox' because of his hair colouring) was 50 years of age. He returned to Ferrari and drove a Tipo 315S 3.8-litre V12 car. The fastest Ferraris in this were all plagued by transmission weakness and Taruffi, determined to finish the race if at all possible, drove in a much more restrained manner than in previous years. He left it to Collins to set the pace and after holding third place at Ravenna, by Pescara he was second and there he stayed until Collins retired because of transmission failure near Parma.

Taruffi won on his 13th appearance in the race and immediately announced his retirement from racing. He went on to run racing drivers' schools. His racing

Opposite: Taruffi was remarkably versatile. He raced motorcycles, managed the Gilera motorcycle racing team, and built and drove his own record-breaking cars. He had a long and distinguished motor racing career that culminated in his winning the 1957 Mille Miglia at his 13th attempt. (Guy Griffiths)

autobiography, *Works Driver,* was published in translation by Temple Press in 1964. He was also the author of *The Technique of Motor Racing* published in the UK by Motor Racing Publications. It made an interesting comparison with Denis Jenkinson's *The Racing Driver.* Jenkinson's book is a brilliant critique of racing skills, whereas Taruffi tells novices what to do.

ACHILLE VARZI

(Born Galliate, Milan, 8 August 1904, died Bremgarten, Bern, 3 July 1948)

As in all generations of motor racing there were in the 1930s certain drivers who towered above others. In this period, they were mainly Italian and German. In Italy the most dominant and much-written about personality was Tazio Nuvolari. Next came Achille Varzi and save to all who knew him well (and there were few enough of those), Varzi remains an enigma.

Facts about his career are known, well enough, but very little is understood about the man himself and to attempt to write of his thoughts and attitudes is to write sheer fiction. Unlike so many drivers, who looked scruffy and dirty when they raced, Varzi was usually the height of sartorial elegance: at race meetings he would wear a beautifully cut suit, formal shirt and silk tie. His racing overalls and linen helmet were as white and pristine as any detergent maker would have wished. His driving was very precise, very neat and very forceful.

Varzi's drug dependency came as the result of pain, stress and the only too common tendency that we all suffer from, to take the easy way out. Varzi became addicted to morphine, not so remarkable in itself, but what was remarkable was that Varzi was cured of the addiction and returned to racing. Anyone who has been involved with addicts is only too well aware that the cure from drug dependency is in reverse difficulty from the ease with which one can become addicted.

Varzi was born in Galliate near Milan on 8 August 1904 and his father was a prosperous textile manufacturer. He was one of three brothers, the others being named Anacleto and Angelo. Just like his friend and rival, Nuvolari, Achille started by racing motorcycles in the early 1920s, as did his brother Angelo. Initially, Varzi rode 500cc Sunbeam and 350cc Garelli machines. Achille rode regularly in the Isle of Man TT, apart from a full racing programme in Italy.

He was keen to switch to racing on four wheels and in 1926 bought a Type 37 Bugatti, which proved largely unsuccessful. Nuvolari set up his own team for 1928 and asked Varzi to join him. They raced much more potent Type 35 Bugattis, but overall, and not unexpectedly at this stage in Varzi's career, Nuvolari was much the more

successful of the partners. Varzi decided to go his own way and in mid-1928 he bought a P2 Alfa Romeo from Giuseppe Campari. These Grand Prix cars had been immensely successful in 1924–25 and with this car in somewhat modified form Varzi scored a string of successes in the latter part of 1928 and in 1929.

Varzi became a works Alfa Romeo driver in 1930 alongside his good friend Tazio Nuvolari. At this time Scuderia Ferrari was a small organisation that entered Alfa Romeos for private owners and it was a couple of years before they took over responsibility for the works cars. In 1930 the works entered four 6C 1750 Gran Sport cars in the Mille Miglia and among them were cars driven by Nuvolari, partnered by Guidotti (Alfa Romeo team manager in post-war years) and Achille, partnered by Canavesi.

This is the famous occasion when Nuvolari, supposedly driving without his headlights switched on, caught Varzi, surprising him completely and passing him on the road. The story is largely apocryphal in the way that it has been related. Lurani, a leading authority on the Mille Miglia says that it was in the dusk of the evening, whereas in fact it happened at 6.30 to 7 in the morning! Nuvolari had started ten minutes after Varzi so was already leading Achille on time when he caught him up on the road.

By this time in the morning dawn had broken, the weather was good and there was no reason why Varzi and Canavesi should not have been aware that Nuvolari was catching him. The truth of the matter appears to be that Commendatore Jano had misled Varzi as to the extent of his lead, a blatant and dishonest favouritism of Nuvolari (see page 89).

This helps to explain why Varzi left Alfa Romeo at the end of the year and joined the tight-fisted Ettore Bugatti and his outfit at Molsheim. There seems little doubt that at this time relations between Varzi and Alfa Romeo were at a low ebb. At Bugatti, Varzi had no luck in the Mille Miglia in 1931–33, but did win the Tunis Grand Prix in 1931–32, together with the Tripoli and Monaco Grands Prix and the Avusrennen in 1933.

It is, perhaps, a little sad to relate that the high point of Varzi's time with the Bugatti team was the 1933 Tripoli Grand Prix swindle. That year the Tripoli race was run in conjunction with an Italian state lottery (Libya was an Italian protectorate). It seems somewhat complicated, but thousands of tickets were sold and then three days before the race 30 tickets were drawn to correspond with the 30 starters. Enrico Rivio, an Italian lumber merchant, drew Varzi's name. He apparently flew to Libya and offered Varzi half his prize money should Achille win the race. The 'fix' that followed was hilarious.

This is how the late Cyril Posthumus described the outcome: "Varzi promptly contacted the other drivers, and a strange race ensued: Borzacchini and Campari retired, while Nuvolari, leading, contrived to run out of fuel with two laps to go, and stopped for a refill. As for Varzi, he had been delayed by ignition trouble, and stammered past on six of the Bugatti's eight cylinders to 'win' from Nuvolari by a foot or so." The conspiracy was obvious, but no action was taken. Instead, the short list of drivers was in future drawn immediately before the race.

In August 1933 Varzi tried out a Monoposto during practice for the Coppa Acerbo at Pescara and it was an experience that reinforced just how bad the current Grand Prix Bugatti, the Type 59, was compared to the Alfa Romeo. For 1934 Varzi left Bugatti to drive Alfa Romeos for Scuderia Ferrari. This was the first year of the 750Kg Formula and the appearance of the German teams. Varzi won six races that year, among them the Mille Miglia.

Ferrari entered Varzi with a 2.6-litre Alfa Romeo Monza in the 1,000-mile race and his main opponent was Nuvolari. Following his withdrawal from the Ferrari team, the Mantuan was at the wheel of a private Monza. Varzi had the advantage of Pirelli Pneugrippa tyres, far more effective in the wet than Nuvolari's Dunlops and won by a margin of more than eight minutes. He was partnered by Amadeo Bignami who stayed with him as his mechanic through good times and bad times. He became a true and faithful friend.

During the summer of 1934 Varzi was approached by the Auto Union team, who offered the most generous terms, he tested with them at Monza at the end of August and in November Auto Union held a reception for him at Chemnitz. It is likely that he signed the contact with Auto Union then. One source suggests that he received an annual retainer of £4,000 (the rough equivalent today of £400,000), together with a share of all winnings and he was also given a large white Horch saloon.

Despite his commitments to the German team, Varzi arranged to drive a Tipo 34 Maserati, a 3.7-litre Grand Prix car fitted with sketchy two-seater bodywork in the 1935 Mille Miglia. It was a very typical Maserati in that it was badly prepared, inadequately tested and Varzi was an early retirement. It was Varzi's third and last drive in the Mille Miglia. In 1935 Varzi's drives for Auto Union were blighted by tyre problems, but he won both the Tunis Grand Prix and the Coppa Acerbo at Pescara.

An Auto Union team-mate was Paul Pietsch, whose wife Ilse was a beautiful blonde, with a previous marriage under her belt. It seems that through the year the apparently cold and aloof Varzi started an intimate relationship with Ilse. At the end of 1934 Pietsch left Auto Union and Ilse, who joined Varzi.

In early 1936 Varzi had a minor throat operation and afterwards went testing with Auto Union at Monza. He then departed for the Winter Olympics at Garmisch-Partenkirchen where he led one of two Italian bob-sleigh teams. Varzi's team consisted of racing drivers and in the

Despite a chequered and difficult life that included a long period of drug addiction, Achille Varzi was one of the greatest drivers of his era. Early in his career Varzi was a works Bugatti driver and here he is seen with Ettore Bugatti at the 1931 French Grand Prix at Montlhéry. He and Louis Chiron won this ten-hour race driving a Bugatti Type 51. (Author's Collection)

team were Franco Cortese, Piero Taruffi and Count Felice Trossi. Not long afterwards Trossi had an operation for appendicitis.

Varzi won the 1936 Tripoli Grand Prix as the result of a decision that Italian drivers should win Italian races and German drivers should win German races. He learned that Auto Union team manager Dr Karl Feuereissen had signalled Hans Stuck to slow down, while he was shown faster signals. It was at this stage that Varzi's racing career began to fall apart. He was desperately upset by the way that the race had been fiddled and for the first time Ilse offered him morphine which he accepted.

A week later was the Tunis Grand Prix and he crashed heavily at high speed when a strong cross-wind blew his car off the road. It was a frightening crash and he was incredibly lucky to escape from it without physical injury. He was, however, very badly shaken. It was one of only two crashes in his career. The effect of it was to weaken his resolve not to take morphine, and it was rapidly becoming a habit. During the season Varzi began to play a secondary role to brilliant young newcomer, Bernd Rosemeyer.

Auto Union failed to renew Varzi's contract for 1937 and he disappeared from the racing scene. He reappeared at San Remo in July 1937 and won both his heat and the final with a 6CM Maserati. Later in the year Varzi persuaded Feuereissen that he had given up drugs and he was – initially – believed. After practice for the Czechoslovakian race, it became obvious that he was still badly affected by drugs. Again Varzi disappeared, he returned to drive (and retire) a 3-litre supercharged 8CTF Maserati at Tripoli and then disappeared yet again.

Ilse, penniless, returned to Germany and after a failed suicide attempt, she managed to give up drugs and during the war years she married a German opera singer. In 1941 Varzi married Norma, a girl he had known for many years and who must have had the most incredible patience. He was too old for military service, ran the family business and did succeed in giving up drugs altogether. An incentive was undoubtedly the difficulty in obtaining drugs in wartime Italy.

Varzi was 42 years old in 1946 but not too old to return to racing with the Alfa Romeo team. It is worth remembering that Alfa Romeo was not particularly prejudiced by age and that their 1950 team of Farina, Fangio and Fagioli had a combined age of over 130 years. A revitalised Varzi drove for Alfa Romeo for another three seasons and had regained all his old style and magic. He won at Turin in 1946, at Bari in 1947 and in addition took four second places.

Tragedy struck in practice for the 1948 Swiss Grand Prix where he lost control of his Alfa Romeo Tipo 158 in the wet at the left-hand Jordenrampe bend, hit the kerb and the car turned over; protected by only his white linen helmet, Varzi was killed instantly. For a while his name lived on; in 1949 the Argentine Automobile Club sent a team of drivers to contest European Grands Prix with Maseratis. Varzi's faithful mechanic, Amadeo Bignami, became team manager. The team called itself Squadra Achille Varzi in memory of one of Italy's greatest drivers and with the consent of his father, Menotti Varzi, it based itself in Achille's former house and workshops at Galliate.

LUIGI VILLORESI

(Born Milan, 16 May 1909, died Milan, August 1997)

If you had met Villoresi in the street, you would have known he was from Milan. His looks, his gestures and the way he talked were so typically Milanese. Luigi and his elder brother Emilio were motor racing enthusiasts from an early age. They first drove a Fiat Balilla sports car together in the 1933 Mille Miglia and finished 33rd overall in a race that for them lasted close to 19½ hours.

From then on they made regular race appearances together at the wheel of Fiat cars. In 1937 Luigi shared a Maserati with Count 'Johnny' Lurani and they were favourites to win the 1,100cc class, until their car broke its engine. The following year he co-drove a special Lancia with Forti and they won the National Sports class, finishing 14th overall. Luigi Villoresi's career had been progressing steadily.

By this time Emilio was a member of the works (Alfa Corse) Alfa Romeo team, but his racing career was to end in tragic circumstances. On Monday 20 June 1938 Alfa Romeo held a hospitality day at Monza for Alfa Romeo dealers and trade representatives. Lunch was served and afterwards Enzo Ferrari asked Emilio to do some demonstration laps with a Tipo 158 'Alfetta'. Luigi Villoresi told him that he had drunk too much wine over lunch. Ferrari overrode his objections and Emilio went out on the track with the 158. He went off the track at high speed, the car overturned and he was killed.

Obviously Luigi, who was a works Maserati driver in 1938–39, was devastated by the death of his brother, but the outcome is somewhat murky. It has been claimed that the insurers of a policy on Emilio's life had refused to pay the claim because he had been drinking. Allegedly, Ferrari refused to do anything to support the family's claim under the policy. There is so much written about Ferrari that is absolute piffle and he would have not behaved in this way.

It is also said, variously, that Luigi never forgave Ferrari or, in some versions, Alfa Romeo. He clearly had no problems in joining Ferrari for 1949 and it seems that the opportunity of driving for Alfa Romeo simply never arose. With Maserati cars Luigi was the Italian 1,500cc Champion in 1938 and 1939 and his successes included wins in the 1938 Albi Grand Prix, the 1938 Coppa Acerbo Voiturette race at Pescara and the 1939–40 Targa Florio races held in Favorita Park, Palermo for 1,500cc single-seaters.

Luigi Villoresi joined the Italian army and was captured not long after Italy entered the Second World War. Once hostilities were over, motor racing started almost immediately in France and Italy. Like other drivers, Farina, Peter Walker, Peter Whitehead, the years when Villoresi would have achieved the peak of his abilities, were the years that the world was at war and he failed to achieve the greatness that might have been expected of him.

During 1946 he drove 1,500cc supercharged Maseratis 4CLs for the Scuderia Milano and his performances included a win in the Nice Grand Prix, a collision with a lamppost in the Grand Prix des Nations at Geneva and fourth place at Milan. He also appeared with a previously unraced 1939 straight-eight 3-litre Tipo 8CL Maserati at Indianapolis, but this was not as fast as had been expected and Luigi finished a poor seventh.

For the 1947 European season Luigi Villoresi switched from Scuderia Milano to Count 'Johnny' Lurani's Scuderia Ambrosiana, which also raced 4CL Maseratis. With him went young Alberto Ascari as his number two. Generally, Ambrosiana cars were much better prepared than those from the Milan team. Although the Maserati factory did not race works single-seaters until 1952, they did race sports cars on an occasional basis and both Villoresi and Ascari drove these. The main opposition to the Ambrosiana Maseratis in 1947–48 were the all-conquering Alfa Romeo 158s, but they ran in only four races in each of these years.

Villoresi still drove o 4CLs at the beginning of 1947 when this team competed in what became known as the Temporada races, held during January and February in the Argentinean summer. In the Rosario Grand Prix he finished second to the great Achille Varzi, but he won the two races held subsequently on the Palermo Park circuit in Buenos Aires. In Europe, Villoresi's successes were limited, partly because of the sheer numbers of Maseratis racing, but he won at Nice and Lausanne. In the first post-war Mille Miglia, Villoresi drove a 2-litre Maserati and was partnered by head mechanic Guerino

Bertocchi, but they retired early in the race because of mechanical problems.

Scuderia Ambrosiana raced in the Temporada series in 1948 and Luigi won two races at Buenos Aires. Maserati introduced the improved 4CLT/48 'San Remo' model during the year, but it was still no match for the Alfa Romeos. Villoresi's successes included second place behind Ascari in the San Remo Grand Prix (scene of the debut of the new model, hence its name), third behind two Alfa 158s in the Swiss race, wins in the thinly supported Comminges Grand Prix and the Albi Grand Prix, second in the Italian Grand Prix and further wins in the RAC Grand Prix at Silverstone and the Penya Rhin Grand Prix on the Pedralbes street circuit at Barcelona. It was a very impressive record.

Ferrari had introduced his new, supercharged Tipo 125 V12 1.5-litre Grand Prix car at the 1948 Italian Grand Prix held on the Valentino Park circuit in Turin. For 1949 Villoresi and Ascari joined Ferrari. The Grand

Luigi Villoresi (right) and Alberto Ascari at Silverstone for the first Grand Prix held there in 1948. Villoresi was vastly the more experienced driver and, at the time, team-leader for Scuderia Ambrosiana. Both drivers also made occasional appearances with works Maserati sports cars. (Guy Griffiths)

Opposite: Villoresi partnered by Pasquale Cassani scored a brilliant victory in the 1951 race with this 4.1-litre Ferrari. The car was severely battered after an off-road excursion and it had developed serious gearbox trouble which meant that only first and fourth gears could be engaged. Here the car is seen at Bologna, the last time control. (Author's Collection)

Villoresi, competing his Scuderia Ambrosiana-entered Maserati 4CLT/48 San Remo at the RAC Grand Prix held at Silverstone on 2 October 1948. He won from Ascari, driving another Maserati. (Guy Griffiths)

Prix cars were largely ineffective, although in a year in which Alfa Romeo temporarily withdrew from racing, he finished second in the Belgian Grand Prix, second to Ascari in the Swiss race and won the Dutch race at Zandvoort. Villoresi did not drive in the Mille Miglia that year, but reappeared in the 1950 race at the wheel of one of the new Tipo 275 Sport 3,332cc V12 cars. He failed to finish because of mechanical problems.

Villoresi's great Mille Miglia year was 1951 when he was partnered by Cassani and drove a new Ferrari Tipo 340 America with 4,101cc V12 engine and Vignale berlinetta body. It was an extremely difficult race and even more so for Villoresi because of the sheer power of his car in the difficult conditions in which the race was run. Although it was still dry when the first starters left, all the more powerful cars set off in torrential rain which persisted for most of the race. Visibility was poor with heavy mist on the higher ground.

So many of Villoresi's opponents fell by the wayside that his victory was not so much over his rivals but more over the elements. He crashed on the flyover at Ferrara at the same spot as Sighinolfi had written of his Stanguellini. The left front wing of the Ferrari, together with headlamp, was badly smashed. At the finish he was 20 minutes ahead of Bracco with a Lancia Aurelia GT. Bracco's drive was magnificent, but he would not have finished so high up the results, but for the large number of casualties among the faster cars and the dreadful conditions.

During 1950 Ferrari had been developing new unsupercharged 4,498cc Grand Prix cars and so successes that year in Formula 1 were very few. The 1951 season witnessed a titanic battle between the Ferraris and the ageing supercharged Alfa Romeos. Ascari had consolidated his position as number one driver and Villoresi's role over the next few seasons was to support the team-leader. He never won another Grand Prix, but he was a respectable fifth in the Drivers' Championship in both 1951 and 1952. Luigi missed the Mille Miglia in 1952 and next drove a 4.1-litre Ferrari in the 1953 race, but retired very early on because of mechanical problems.

For 1954 both Ascari and Villoresi left Ferrari to drive for the Lancia team. The Grand Prix cars were not ready and he crashed with a D24 Lancia sports-racing car in practice for the Mille Miglia. By now he was only a couple of weeks short of his 45th birthday. It would be unrealistic to say other than that his talent was slipping away. He drove a 250F Maserati in few 1954 Grands

Prix and then appeared with the new D50 Lancia in the Spanish Grand Prix in October, retiring very early in the race because of brake problems.

Villoresi continued to race Lancia Grand Prix cars until the company withdrew from racing following Ascari's death. After Ferrari took over the D50 Grand Prix cars, Villoresi drove one in practice for the 1955 Italian Grand Prix, but the car was withdrawn because of tyre problems. His serious racing days were over, but he continued to race private Maserati 250Fs in Formula 1 and OSCA sports cars in 1956.

In October 1956 Villoresi crashed heavily with a 1,500cc Maserati sports car in the Rome Grand Prix at Castelfusano, suffering a broken leg. It was his last race, although he drove a Lancia to a win in the 1958 Acropolis Rally. Luigi Villoresi was not, in general terms, a great racing driver, but he was determined and highly talented and in 1951 he had proved himself to be a great Mille Miglia driver. In his last years Villoresi was desperately impoverished and a number of magazines and organisations raised funds to contribute to his upkeep. He became ill and died in a sanatorium, a broken and almost forgotten man.

Overleaf: Stirling Moss with Denis Jenkinson and their Tipo 350S Maserati on the starting ramp for the 1956 Mille Miglia. The car looked like a race-winner, but it was hopelessly underdeveloped and had major handling problems. At the start of the race probably only Moss knew just how bad it was and how slim were the prospects of success. (Author's Collection)

The Great
Marques

ALFA ROMEO

In a sense, over its thirty years the Mille Miglia reflected the stereotypes of the period. In pre-World War Two days Alfa Romeo was Italy's most successful sporting marque and probably, measured on a basis of consistency, the most successful in the world. So it is unsurprising that the cars from Portello should have scored ten wins, plus another in the first post-war race. In fact Alfa Romeo domination was so complete from 1928 onwards that interest in the Mille Miglia shifted to a considerable extent from the winning marque to the class winners and the also-rans.

There is an unbroken thread that connects Fiat, Alfa Romeo and Ferrari in terms of their competition record. Fiat was founded in 1899 and although it was destined to concentrate on mass-production and achieve sales domination in the Italian market, it had a formidable competition record. Works Fiats were regular contenders in Grand Prix racing up until 1924, by when the mantle of maintaining Italian racing prestige had passed to Alfa Romeo.

Heading the Alfa Romeo design department was one of the greatest automobile engineers of the 20th Century,

This works Alfa Romeo RLSS, seen on the Futa Pass in 1927, was driven by Count Gaston Brilli Peri/Bruno Presenti. They failed to finish because of engine problems while they were leading the race. The figure in the background to the left is Enzo Ferrari. (Centro Documentazione Alfa Romeo)

Vittorio Jano. Enzo Ferrari head-hunted Jano from Fiat and many other Alfa Romeo engineers were ex-Fiat. Prior to Jano's arrival at Alfa Romeo, the chief engineer was Giuseppe Merosi. In 1923 Merosi had produced the P1 Grand Prix car with six-cylinder twin overhead camshaft 1,990cc engine. Luigi Bazzi, later responsible for the Bi-Motore Alfa Romeo, was Enzo Ferrari's first recruit and he had left Fiat after a disagreement with their chief engineer, Fornaca.

Bazzi later became Ferrari's right-hand man, but initially he worked with Merosi on the P1. The race debut for the P1 was to have been in that year's European Grand Prix at Monza, but Alfa Romeo withdrew after leading driver Ugo Sivocci was killed in a practice accident. The P1s were never raced and it was clear beyond doubt that they would have been uncompetitive.

When Jano went to Alfa Romeo, his prime task was to build a winning Grand Prix car to comply with the 2,000cc Grand Prix formula that remained in force until the end of 1925. The result was the straight-eight, supercharged 1,987cc (61 x 85mm) P2 car that closely followed the design of the 1923 Grand Prix Fiats. The new car was ready to test early in 1924; it first ran in the Circuit of Cremona in June and won the race. Later that year the team won the European Grand Prix at Lyon and the Italian Grand Prix at Monza.

Despite the withdrawal of the team from the 1925 French Grand Prix at Montlhéry following Antonio Ascari's fatal crash, victories in the European Grand Prix

at Spa and in the Italian Grand Prix brought Alfa Romeo the newly inaugurated World Championship. In modified form the P2s were raced successfully until 1930. It was from the basic design of the P2 that Jano evolved the whole gamut of Mille Miglia winning sports cars.

In 1927 the Jano-designed twin overhead camshaft touring and sports cars were still a twinkle in their designer's eye, although they would be revealed and raceworthy by the 1928 race. The first of the Jano cars with 1,500cc single-cam engines had appeared in 1925, but these were not considered to be fast enough for the first Mille Miglia. So Alfa Romeo relied on Ing Giuseppe Merosi's six-cylinder, 2,994cc (76 x 110mm) push-rod overhead valve RLSS ('Super-Sport') cars with twin Zenith carburettors and 83bhp at 3,600rpm at the driver's command in standard form.

The earliest of these push-rod cars had first appeared in 1921 and there had followed a programme of steady development. The 1927 Mille Miglia cars had been developed by Ing Rimini, who was Alfa Romeo's racing and sales manager. They were reckoned to be good for close to 90mph (145kph). They were considered safe to 5,000rpm and had a successful competition history that went back some five years and included regular appearances in the Targa Florio. The push-rod cars in RL form scored only one win in the Sicilian road race, in 1923, but it was Alfa Romeo's first international success.

Although the Alfa Romeos were some ten mph (16kph) faster than the OMs, they proved unexpectedly unreliable for cars with such a long development history and all three works cars had mechanical problems. These 1927 Mille Miglia cars were in effect an anachronism from the past, although they were magnificent-looking cars and had a superb performance by the standards of the time.

Subsequently Alfa Romeo relied on Jano's range of six-cylinder cars. Because of the large number of variations, it is easiest to list these models in tabular form. It also has to be remembered that different designations for each model were used in Italy and the United Kingdom.

6C 1500 Turismo: 1,487cc (62 x 82mm), single overhead camshaft; power output was 44bhp at 4,200rpm; available in 10ft 2in (3,100mm) long chassis or 9ft 6in (2,895mm) short chassis; first appeared 1925, but did not enter serious production until 1927; these cars with the engine set back some further eight inches (200mm) in the frame were raced in the 1928 Mille Miglia; known as the 15/60 in the UK.

Luigi Arcangeli, partnered by Bonini, poses in this familiar but important photograph with his new 8C 2300 before the 1931 race. These cars were not yet fully developed and proved to be unreliable and plagued by tyre problems. Arcangeli led at one stage, but his car developed clutch trouble and he retired after going off the road. (Centro Documentazione Alfa Romeo)

6C 1500 Sport: 1,487cc (62 x 82mm), twin overhead camshafts; power output was 54bhp at 4,500rpm; chassis details as above; known as the 15/70 Grand Turismo in the UK; first appeared in 1928.

6C 1500 Super Sport: 1,487cc (62 x 82mm), twin overhead camshafts; Roots-type supercharger and engine set back some 15 inches (380mm) in the frame; power output was 76bhp at 4,800rpm; usually with 9ft 6in (2,895mm) wheelbase and later cars had 9ft 0in (2,745mm); first appeared in 1928; these cars were regularly raced in the Mille Miglia and had a good record of class wins.

6C 1750 Turismo: 1,752cc (65 x 88mm), single overhead camshaft; power output was 45bhp at 4,000rpm; chassis choice as for 6C 1500 Turismo; known in the UK as the 17/75; first appeared in 1929.

6C 1750 Super Sport: 1,752cc (65 x 88mm), twin overhead camshafts; power output was 55bhp at 4,200rpm; chassis choice as for 6C 1750 Turismo; known in the UK as the 17/85 Gran Turismo; first appeared in 1929.

Count Felice Trossi is seen here at the wheel of a works Alfa Romeo Tipo 158 car at the 1947 Italian Grand Prix held in Milan. Trossi was an early President of Scuderia Ferrari. He was inordinately proud of his rather prominent Roman nose. Trossi died of cancer in 1949. (Author's Collection)

6C 1750 Gran Sport: 1,752cc (65 x 88mm), twin overhead camshafts; Roots-type supercharger, fixed cylinder head on the works cars and generally as for 6C 1500 Super Sport including wheelbase length; power output was 85bhp at 4,500rpm; these cars first appeared in 1929, had a maximum speed of over 100mph (161kph); they took first and third places in the 1929 Mille Miglia and first three places in the 1930 race; these cars were known in the UK as the 17/95.

It should also be noted that in 1932 Alfa Romeo built a small run of these Jano-designed cars with 1,920cc (68 x 68mm) engines in twin-cam, but unsupercharged Gran Turismo form; power output was 68bhp at 4,500rpm and they had a four-speed synchromesh gearbox with freewheel instead of the four-speed 'crash' box of other models.

That the six-cylinder Jano Alfa Romeos were the finest sports cars of the 1920s is virtually indisputable. There were many other great sports and sporting cars during this decade, but the early 6C series combined handling, performance, quality of construction and a competition performance that, together, was unmatched by any other make. Jano had been at work on an eight-cylinder production car and this first appeared in 1931. It and its successors were to prove the greatest sporting cars of the 1930s.

Jano's new design incorporated many features of the earlier cars. The new model, designated the 8C 2300, had a straight-eight 2,336cc (65 x 88mm) engine cast in two aluminium-alloy cylinder blocks, each of four cylinders, with steel liners and an alloy crankcase. Between the two blocks of cylinders there were helical gears, one of which drove the camshafts and the other drove the supercharger, oil and water pumps and the dynamo. There were separate detachable alloy cylinder heads. The mixture was fed by a twin-choke Memini carburettor to a Roots-type supercharger. Lubrication was dry-sump.

Power output varied, but it could be as high as 155bhp at 5,200rpm. Similarities to the 6C cars were not limited to engine design, for there was, once again, a four-speed constant-mesh gearbox and a channel-section chassis with rigid axles front and rear. The version used in the Mille Miglia was the Spider Corsa with short 9ft 3in (2,820mm) wheelbase (also known in the United Kingdom as the 'Mille Miglia'), while the long-wheel variation with 10ft 2in (3,100mm) was run in fast road-race events such as Le Mans (and was known in the UK as the 'Le Mans' model).

When two cars driven by Nuvolari and Arcangeli were entered by the works in the 1931 race, it was to answer the threat from Mercedes-Benz. The new Alfa Romeos were not ready to race, they had a voracious appetite for their Pirelli tyres and this coupled with other problems resulted in a win by the SSKL. These Spider

Corsas ran again in the 1932 1,000-mile race and there were a considerable number entered. The works entered three cars with Touring bodies and Scuderia Ferrari fielded five cars with Zagato bodies. They took the first two places.

By 1933 Alfa Romeo was in severe financial difficulties and ownership of the company fell into the hands of the state-owned Instituto Recostruzione Industriale (Institute for Industrial Reconstruction) whose aims were to guide significant or vital companies back into solvency. Alfa Romeo's financial position was hardly surprising, bearing in mind that it built only 188 of the straight-eight production cars, but at the same time it was expending substantial sums re-tooling for the construction of commercial and military vehicles.

So Scuderia Ferrari now entered all cars on behalf of the works and in the 1933 race a Spider Corsa from this concern won from a privately entered Spider Corsa. There were also two Scuderia Ferrari Alfa Romeo Monza cars in the race that year. The Monza was the out-and-out racing version of the 8C 2300 and first appeared in the 1931 European Grand Prix held at Monza. These cars had two-seater bodies to comply with the then Grand Prix regulations, maximum power could be as high as 178bhp and for the Mille Miglia they were fitted with mudguards, electric starter and lighting. They could usually (but not always) be identified by a radiator cowling with slots in the sides and at the top.

By 1934 Monzas were running in the Mille Miglia with 2,632cc engines. It was a phase during which the Alfa Romeo entries were getting wilder and wilder. The

following year Scuderia Ferrari entered a Tipo B Monoposto Grand Prix car, a model that had first appeared in 1932 with 2,654cc engine. Carlos Pintacuda and the diminutive Marchese della Stufa squeezed themselves into the cockpit and won by a margin of more than 40 minutes.

At Alfa Romeo the great Jano had been working on a proper sports version of the Monoposto and the result was the 8C 2900A introduced in late 1935 and featuring the 2,905cc (68 x 100mm) engine said to develop 220bhp at 5,300rpm. There was Porsche trailing-link independent front suspension with the springs operating in engine oil, independent rear suspension by swing axles and neat open two-seater bodies. Cars of this type entered by Scuderia Ferrari in the 1936 race took the first three places. Even though only six were built, the 8C 2900A was listed as a production model.

A year later followed the 8C 2900B with general mechanical improvements and cars entered by Scuderia Ferrari took the first two places. By the 1938 race the works Alfa Corse team had absorbed Scuderia Ferrari and for a short while at least Enzo Ferrari was again an Alfa Romeo employee. The 1938 works 8C 2900Bs had especially handsome open two-seater bodies by Touring

Fangio, partnered by Sala, drove this very fast, very potent 3,560cc Tipo 6C 3000M Alfa Romeo in the 1953 race and took second place. The car had steering problems, but just how serious these were remains a matter of speculation. (Centro Documentazione Alfa Romeo)

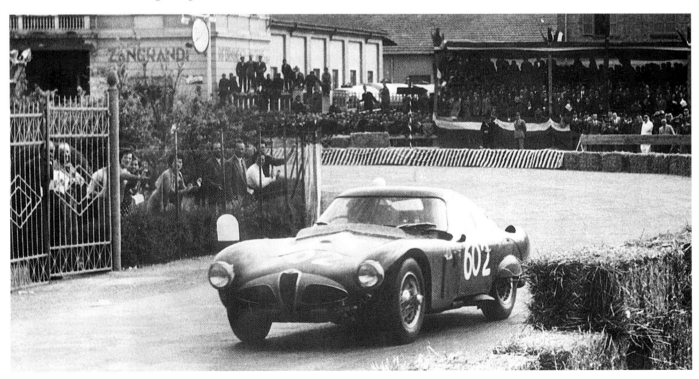

and they took the first two places in that year's Mille Miglia ahead of one of these cars privately entered.

By this time Jano had developed the new 6C 2300 and 6C 2500 models with six-cylinder engines. These cars were much cheaper to build and intended for production in relatively large numbers. Sports versions of the 2.5-litre car ran in the 1940 closed-circuit Mille Miglia, but were no match for the latest 2-litre BMWs.

Although they failed to achieve a high level of success, the Alfa Romeos entered by the works in post-war days included some fascinating 'one-offs'. In 1948 the company fielded two special versions of the production twin overhead camshaft 6C 2500 model. Reliable information about these cars is lacking, but they had a shorter than standard chassis with 9ft 2.4in (2,500mm) wheelbase, an engine that by 1950 was developing 145bhp at 5,500rpm and very aerodynamic berlinetta bodies. They had, according to Fusi, been under development since 1946. The best performances by these cars were third places in the 1949 and 1950 races.

The main thrust of Alfa Romeo's racing programme in post-World War Two days was centred on the supercharged 1,479cc straight-eight Tipo 158 Alfettas. Originally built in 1938 to run in the 'Voiturette' category, the 158s became Grand Prix cars under the

Post-war, Aston Martin achieved some remarkable performances. In 1951 David Brown riled racing manager John Wyer by lending this DB2 to journalist and very experienced competition driver Tom Wisdom. Wisdom, partnered by Tony Hume, finished 11th overall and won the category for closed cars over 2 litres. (LAT/The Autocar)

1,500cc supercharged/4,500cc unsupercharged regulations introduced for 1947.

After an initial failure in the 1946 St Cloud Grand Prix near Paris, the Alfettas won every race which the team entered until they were finally beaten by Ferrari in the 1951 British Grand Prix. By this time the Alfettas were overdeveloped and overstressed. Fangio won his first Drivers' World Championship that year and at the end of the season the team retired from Grand Prix racing.

Alfa Romeo had embarked on the development of a very advanced competition sports car, originally powered by a 1,997cc (85 x 88mm) engine and because of its very smooth, curvaceous lines became known as the Disco Volante (Flying Saucer). It would be accurate to say that it was streamlined rather than aerodynamic. Later the company built a version with a six-cylinder 2,960cc (87 x 83mm) engine said to develop 230bhp at 6,000rpm. Alfa Romeo's chief tester Consalvo Sanesi tested the 3-litre car extensively at Monza and although it had an excellent straight-line performance, the handling was difficult and it suffered from aerodynamic lift.

For 1953 this car was completely redesigned, with 3,495cc engine, much more conventional coupé bodywork by an outside coachbuilder known as Colli and new de Dion rear suspension. Three of these cars, plus a 2-litre 1952 model with conventional body, ran in the Mille Miglia that year, but only the car driven by Fangio finished and its performance is discussed on pages 190–91 and 237.

After 1953 Alfa Romeo raced only the 1900 saloons and 1,290cc Giulietta models and these enjoyed considerable success in their classes. Alfa Romeo did not make a serious return to racing until 1967 when the company's Autodelta subsidiary introduced the first of the Tipo 33 Sports Prototypes.

ASTON MARTIN

It would be realistic to say that no British car had serious prospects of winning the Mille Miglia, but the post-war sports-racing Aston Martins came close to substantial success. In pre-war days, there had been some remarkable performances at class level and the most outstanding was that of Dutchman Hertzberger with his 2-litre orange-painted Speed Model who took second place in the 2,000cc Sports category in 1937. As a racing driver, he appears to have verged on the insane, but, as recounted later, his enthusiasm was probably unbeatable.

In post-war days, the production Aston Martin DB2 with its six-cylinder, 2580cc twin overhead camshaft engine designed by W O Bentley and his team for Lagonda was a very formidable piece of machinery with a maximum speed of slightly over 115mph (185kph).

Works-entered cars were remarkably successful at Le Mans in 1950–51 and this luck, up to a point, carried over into the 1,000-mile race.

In 1951 motoring journalist and very experienced driver Tom Wisdom arranged with David Brown to borrow DB2 chassis number LML/50/8 (registration VMF 64) to drive in the Mille Miglia that year and which Brown had been using as his private road car. In 1950 this car driven by Macklin/Abecassis had finished fifth at Le Mans and won the 3,000cc class and the Index of Performance. This DB2 was prepared in the service department of the Aston Martin works at Feltham and Aston Martin racing manager John Wyer, understandably, resented this factory support for a private owner. Wisdom, partnered by Tony Hume, drove a magnificent race to finish 11th overall and win the over 2,000cc closed car class.

An inevitable result of this success was the entry of a full team of DB2s in the 1952 race. The cars entered were the two so-called 'lightweight' versions and an older car, all with 138bhp engines, that had run at Le Mans in 1951 and taken first three places in the 3,000cc class. It was pretty well mandatory to include Tom Wisdom in the team and he was now partnered by Aston Martin mechanic Fred Lown. Abecassis retired his car because of clutch failure (he was notoriously heavy on the clutch of the cars he raced), while Wisdom/Lown finished 12th overall and won what was now known as the Grand Touring class. Reg Parnell partnered by local driver Serboli finished second in the class.

At the 1951 Tourist Trophy on the Dundrod circuit in Northern Ireland the company had raced the first of the DB3 cars, the work of former Auto Union engineer, Professor Eberan-Eberhorst. He was an unimaginative engineer, dependent, apparently, on his slide-rule for even simple calculations and the DB3 was rather overweight at 1,890lb (858kg) and because of the 2.6-litre engine it was underpowered. Even after an increase in engine size to 2,922cc engine, power output was still only about 163bhp. The performance was much the same as that of a 2-litre Maserati A6GCS sports car which weighed 1,628lb (740kg) and had a power output of 160bhp.

Aston Martin entered three DB3s in the 1953 race and one of their major problems was that the team lacked the resources (and under British government fiscal policy of the time not allowed to spend sufficient money) to carry out intensive practice over the circuit. They spent ten days trying to learn the slower, more difficult parts at the expense of the faster sections. In the race Reg Parnell was partnered by photographer Louis Klemantaski and he performed exceptionally well, despite major problems.

A mounting for the Panhard rod in the rear suspension broke and at Florence team manager John Wyer was sorely tempted to withdraw the car. Parnell reportedly told him, "It's been like that for a bloody long

time – I'm going on!" Later, the throttle cable broke as he was crossing the Apennines and Parnell bodged a repair so that he could drive on full throttle with control only through the ignition switch. Remarkably, the DB3 tolerated this rough treatment and lasted the course. At the finish they were fifth overall, a second short of six minutes ahead of the Maserati A6GCS of Giletti/Bertocchi.

It is conspicuous that these two cars were so closely matched in performance; Giletti was no mean slouch and Parnell had driven exceptionally well to open up such a good lead with a very defective car. Of the other entries, Collins went off the road with the car he was sharing with young Mike Keen and finished 16th with his very battered DB3; Abecassis, partnered by Griffith, was never in contention and retired because of a loose steering rack; finally Wisdom drove again, this time accompanied by Peter Bolton, but his DB2 was eliminated by rear axle failure.

Parnell's fifth place was the best result by a British car in the history of the race. It encouraged a more determined effort by Aston Martin in 1954. By this time

In 1953 Reg Parnell, partnered by photographer Louis Klemantaski, drove this 3-litre DB3 Aston Martin. They took fifth place, the best ever Mille Miglia performance by a British car. But the DB3 was underpowered: it was only as fast as a good Italian 2-litre and it finished the race in the sort of position a good Italian 2-litre would achieve. What is significant about this photograph is how close to the road are the two women (left) and how unconcerned about the passing car. (Spitzley-Zagari Collection)

the team was racing the lighter, much improved DB3S cars, but at this stage in their development power output was still only around 182bhp at 5,500rpm. There were two cars driven by Parnell/Klemantaski and Collins/Griffith. Wyer believed – in retrospect – that 1954 represented Aston Martin's best chance to win the race and that they could well have done so but for tyre problems.

Aston Martin's problem lay in the very hardness of their Avon tyres. Wyer wanted tyres that would run through the race without change and Avon produced them for him. It was a laudable aim, but not entirely realistic. Tyres for a race like the Mille Miglia had to be exceptionally tough, but softer tyres of course gave a better grip, it was all a case of a sensible balance. The Avon tyres used by the team in this race were adequate in the dry, but they made the cars almost undriveable in the wet and 1954 was a very wet race. John Wyer threw the blame on Avon, but it is almost incredible that the Aston Martins should race on tyres that had never been tested in both wet and dry conditions.

While the handling of the DB3S was vastly superior to that of the Ferraris, especially the latest 4.9-litre Tipo 375 Plus cars, the new 3.3-litre Lancia D24 cars had both much greater power output than the Aston Martins, handling that was even better and they were in fact the ideal Mille Miglia car. Four were entered in the race and although only the car driven by Ascari finished, that was all that was required. Both the DB3S entries crashed.

Collins rose as high as fifth place at Rome, but he crashed between Rome and Siena. Not just Ascari's Lancia was in front of him, but also Paolo Marzotto/Marini with a 2-litre Ferrari Mondial. It seems inconceivable that Collins could have passed both these cars on time, even though Ascari had the benefit of facing no opposition in the late stages of the race and was able to ease off. When Parnell crashed between Popoli and L'Aquila, he was well down the field. Parnell posing by the crashed Aston Martini while Klemantaski took a photograph (and then the roles being reversed so that Klemantaski posed and Parnell clicked the shutter) is part of Mille Miglia lore.

The team entered only a single DB3S driven by Peter Collins in the 1955 race. This was of course the year of the 300 SLR Mercedes-Benz and the DB3S were still developing only 225bhp compared to the 300bhp of the German cars. Collins had a tyre blow out at high speed, he had to struggle to change the wheel on his own and, in a foul mood, set off again, driving flat-out. It was not surprising that he blew up the engine. Aston Martin also entered two DB2/4 coupés in the Special Grand Touring Group. Both retired because of defective clutches, but their prospects of success in the face of Mercedes-Benz 300 SL opposition were slim. Aston Martin failed to compete in the last two races.

Peter Collins at the wheel of his Aston Martin DB3S in the 1955 race, which was the last time Aston Martin entered the Mille Miglia. Collins was delayed by a puncture and then blew up his engine while trying to catch up on lost time. (Spitzley-Zagari Collection)

FERRARI

Italy's spiritual and actual racing successor to Alfa Romeo won eight post-war Mille Miglia races, six of them in succession. There were strong technical links between the early post-war Ferraris and the competition Alfa Romeos of 1937–39. The Tipo 158 straight-eight 1,479cc Alfa Romeo Voiturette, that as a Grand Prix car was to dominate the early post-war years of single-seater racing, was built in Ferrari's premises at Modena. This car's engine was in effect one half of the V16 Tipo 316 2,958cc Grand Prix car of 1938–39. There was also a V12 Tipo 312 3-litre Grand Prix car derived from another V12 used in the 1934–37 750kg Grand Prix formula.

The proliferation of Alfa Romeo racing engines in the late 1930s is very confusing. All these designs originated from the work of engineer Vittorio Jano, who was forced out of Alfa Romeo in 1937. Giaocchino Colombo, who had been with Alfa Romeo since 1924, was to all intents and purposes Jano's apprentice and assumed his role of engineering supremo. He was primarily responsible for both the Tipo 158 and the Tipo 316, which were based on Jano design practice. Enzo Ferrari also claimed much of the credit for these cars, but his input was very limited.

In 1936 Alfa Romeo's Managing Director, Ugo Gobbato, had brought in Wifredo Ricart, a Spaniard and strong supporter of Fascism, as technical adviser who became head of the Special Studies Department in 1940. Ricart suffered the strongest animosity from Enzo Ferrari

In 1950 the Lampredi-designed V12s made their first race appearance and Ascari and Villoresi drove Tipo 275s cars with 3,322cc engines. Here Villoresi, partnered by Cassani, is seen at the start. Although these cars were to achieve great success in a later, much-more developed form, the 1950 versions handled badly and were plagued by tyre and transmission problems. Ascari and Villoresi both retired. (LAT/The Autocar)

Clemente Biondetti is seen with his Touring Barchetta-bodied Tipo 166S in the 1949 race. He is on the cobbled section that, until shortly before, had been just a loose surface. This section between Parma and Poggia di Berceto was known as the Piantonia steps. Note the large number of spectators on the outside of the bend. Biondetti won the race for the fourth time. (Author's Collection)

The Ferrari 375 Plus

Throughout the 1950s Ferrari engine power rose in a gradual crescendo, culminating in the mighty 4.9-litre 375 Plus that appeared in 1954. Ferrari chassis design failed to keep pace with the increases in power output and the handling of the new car was totally lethal, save in the most experienced and able hands. In almost every respect the 375 Plus was, engine capacity apart, similar to its immediate predecessors.

Power unit of the 375 Plus was a development of the familiar 'long-block' Lampredi-designed engine, but with a capacity of 4,954cc. It retained the Formula 1 crankshaft of the 4.5-litre cars raced in 1953 and sold to private entrants in 1954, together with the same stroke of 74.5mm, but with new cylinder barrels of 84mm. There were now six Weber 46DCF3 twin-choke carburettors in place of the Weber four-choke type used on the 4.1-litre and 4.5-litre cars.

Initially power output was 330bhp at 6,000rpm, and the factory reckoned that the engine could be revved safely to 8,000rpm in short bursts. By the time the car was first raced, development work increased power output to 347bhp at 6,800rpm. There were no sensible comparisons with rival cars, because the 375 Plus was of much greater engine capacity than its rivals. The 3.4-litre D-type Jaguar had an output of 250bhp and the 3.3-litre Lancia D24 developed 265bhp.

The transmission was similar to that of the Lampredi-designed four-cylinder Formula 1, 2 and sports cars, by a four-speed gearbox in unit with the final drive. Lampredi followed his usual practice in chassis design, and there was a fairly simple ladder-type frame, with front suspension by a transverse leaf spring and wishbones, while at the rear there was a de Dion axle, again suspended on a transverse leaf spring. Ferrari used Houdaille shock absorbers front and rear. There were enormous drum brakes and Borrani wire-spoked wheels on Rudge-Whitworth hubs with centre-lock, triple-eared spinners.

The body was similar to that of the open two-seater built by Pinin Farina on the limited production 375MM chassis, but there was an enormous louvred bulge in the tail panel enclosing the larger fuel tank and the spare wheel and a streamlined headrest. Weight was said to be 2,110lb (957kg) and maximum speed 186mph (300kph). It is believed there were only three of these cars.

Early in 1954 Ferrari tested the new cars extensively and when Roy Pearl of *Motor Racing* magazine visited Maranello, the 'pièce de resistance', as Pearl described it, Hawthorn was testing the 375 Plus. "Mike lined up the car on the secondary road outside the factory. There was a sudden deafening roar and two very black lines of thick rubber scored the highway behind the blurred red monster. Reg Parnell [who raced a private Formula 1 Ferrari in 1954] measured them later at more than half-a-mile long.

"A roar in the distance indicated that Mike's autodrome was our 20-foot road – strewn as it was with bullock carts, Vespas, bicycles and pedestrians. Words can never describe the incredible effect of the blinding speed of Mike's first run … Once, twice more Mike did it. The roadside became quickly lined with the Ferrari mechanics, who had helped build the car. Each run was more awesome and more frightening than the last. Then Mike came in. His speed, he said, was 'about 180mph [300kph] at 5,300.' It is not hard to appreciate that this 'sports car' is even faster than the F1 Ferrari."

Ferrari first raced the 375 Plus in the 671-mile Tour of Sicily and Umberto Maglioli drove the only example entered. There was not much in the way of opposition and Maglioli led easily until he went off the road at Enna, seriously damaging the car. Then came the Mille Miglia and Ferrari's main problem was a shortage of drivers. Not only had he lost Ascari and Villoresi to Lancia, but neither Froilan Gonzalez nor Mike Hawthorn was fit to drive. Hawthorn had suffered burns when he crashed his F1 car at Siracusa and Gonzalez had suffered far less burns in rescuing him from his car, but there seemed little prospect of him being able to drive for over 11 hours without a break.

So Ferrari entered 4.9-litre cars for the veteran Farina and Maglioli. Not long after the start Farina crashed at Peschiera while avoiding spectators on the course; he suffered a broken arm and nose, while veteran mechanic

who left Alfa Corse in 1939. One of the designs created by Ricart was the Tipo 512 1,489cc Voiturette with rear-mounted flat-12 engine. The engine of this car incorporated a number of improved design features, especially as far as the valve gear was concerned.

When Enzo Ferrari set up his own car manufacturing business in the immediate post-war days, it represented "a new branch of the Alfa Romeo tradition with which he had lived for a good part of his life" (Griff Borgeson).

Colombo, acting initially as a consultant, designed the first Ferrari V12 engine in 1946; it combined Alfa Romeo design features as laid down by Jano, continued by Colombo himself and improved by Ricart. It was a V12 with the cylinders at an angle of 60° and a single overhead camshaft for each bank of cylinders.

The chosen cylinder dimensions were 55 x 52.5mm, which gave a capacity of 1,497cc. This conveniently fitted the 1.5-litre supercharged/4.5-litre unsupercharged

Luigi Parenti broke his pelvis. After a cautious start, Maglioli gave his car its "formidable and dangerous all", moved up to third place, but he, too, crashed. Except for 1954–55, Ferrari won the Mille Miglia every year between 1948 and 1957.

Apprehensions that Ferrari had overreached himself in expecting to win tortuous road races with such brutally powerful, ill-handling cars had been well founded. It was a different story on easier circuits. On the Saturday following the 1,000-mile race Gonzalez drove a 375 Plus to a win in the very wet sports car race at the International Silverstone meeting and partnered by Maurice Trintignant

Mike Hawthorn, about to test the 375 Plus on public roads near the Ferrari factory at Maranello. Dino Ferrari leans on the back of the car, while on the right are British racing driver Reg Parnell and Mike's father, Leslie Hawthorn. The very tatty appearance of the car is indicative of the extensive testing undertaken with this prototype. (Author's Collection)

he scored a narrow victory in the Le Mans 24 Hours race. In November Maglioli with a 375 Plus won the Carrera Panamericana Mexico road race. The 375 Plus was a very remarkable car in a very remarkable period of racing.

Grand Prix formula of 1947 onwards. In fact Ferrari did not race Grand Prix cars until late 1948. The first Tipo 125 sports-racing cars had this 1.5-litre engine in unsupercharged form and Franco Cortese drove a car with this engine in the 1947 Mille Miglia, but retired.

It is a truism of automobile engineering that (with the exception of cars built for specific racing formula) whatever engine capacity is chosen and considered to be the optimum, sooner or later the decision is made to

build a larger capacity version. The original Colombo-designed Ferrari V12 engine was enlarged through a number of different capacities to a final and lasting 2,953cc, the form in which it powered Bracco's 1952 winning car, the long range of 250GT cars and the Testa Rossa sports-racing car of 1958 onwards.

By 1948 Ferrari had increased the capacity of the V12 engine to 1,995cc (60 x 58.8mm) and in this form it was known as the Tipo 166. This first increase in

Piero Taruffi drove this Ferrari Tipo 340 America with very stylish Vignale body in the 1952 race. Vignale bodywork on Ferraris of this period is easily distinguishable by the 'portholes' in the wings. There were 25 America models built. It has been suggested that this car raced with a 4.5-litre engine, but it seems unlikely, even though an engine of that size is now fitted. Taruffi was leading the race until the transmission broke after the car took off over a bad bump and landed heavily. (Courtesy of Gregor Fiskin)

In the appallingly wet 1956 race, Luigi Musso drove this 3,460cc Tipo 860 Monza car. He achieved a steady race to take third place behind team-mates Eugenio Castellotti and Collins. Musso is seen driving alongside Lake Garda. (Author's Collection)

capacity was partly in response to the enlargement of the original Maserati 1.5-litre six-cylinder engine to 2 litres and partly because of the new 2-litre unsupercharged Formula 2 of 1948 onwards, The most popular version of the 2-litre car was the Tipo 166MM that featured a very elegant Touring spider body in a style known as the 'Barchetta' (little boat).

One of the remarkable features of all early Ferraris was their reliability and the Tipo 166 2-litre cars had the formidable record of winning the Mille Miglia in 1948–49, the Le Mans 24 Hours race in 1949, the Paris 12 Hours race in 1948 and 1950 and covering the highest distance in the Belgian 24 Hours race at Spa-Francorchamps in 1949 (this last race had no outright winner, only class winners). Subsequently, Ferrari won the Mille Miglia in 1950 with a 195 Sport berlinetta, with enlarged 2,341cc (65 x 58.8mm) and driven by Giannino Marzotto.

Ferrari was developing a series of larger-capacity V12s, the work of Aurelio Lampredi and these engines were known as the 'long-block' as the cylinder block was lengthened to ensure adequate spacing between bores. Ascari and Villoresi drove 'long-block' V12 cars with interim 3,322cc engines known as the Tipo 275 Sport in the 1950 Mille Miglia. Both retired because of tyre and mechanical problems. By 1951 Ferrari had ready to race

the 340 America, a V12 with a capacity of 4,101cc (80 x 68mm). Villoresi drove one of these cars with Vignale berlinetta body to a win in the 1951 Mille Miglia and the model enjoyed an exceptional competition record in both Europe and the United States.

Although Bracco drove an incredible race with a 2,953cc car to beat the Mercedes-Benz 300 SLRs in the 1952 race, there is little doubt that the fastest car in the race was Piero Taruffi's 340 America with Vignale spider body. Although this retired, one of the finest qualities of these big-capacity V12 cars was reliability, just as the smaller-capacity V12s had established. Another win by a 4.1-litre car, Giannino Marzotto's Tipo 340MM, followed in the 1953 Mille Miglia. By 1954 Ferrari was racing the even more powerful 375 Plus model (see Sidebar on page 48).

Lampredi had also produced a twin overhead camshaft four-cylinder, 1,985cc (90 x 78mm) engine that powered the Formula 2 Ferraris with which Alberto Ascari won the Drivers' World Championship in 1952–53. In late 1953 the company introduced a 2-litre sports car incorporating the mechanical components of the Formula 2 cars and this was known as the Tipo 500 Mondial. Generally these 2-litre cars were no real match for the Maserati A6GCS opposition, but Vittorio Marzotto drove one to second place overall together with a class win in the 1954 Mille Miglia and defeated the Maserati opposition.

There were also 3-litre versions of the four-cylinder sports cars derived from the engines that powered the

2.5-litre Grand Prix cars of 1954–5. The 2,999cc (103 x 90mm) Tipo 750 Monza was primarily a production model to be raced by private owners, but works tester Sergio Sighinolfi drove one into sixth place in the 1955 race. That year the main works Ferraris in the 1,000-mile race were Lampredi's latest six-cylinder cars; although these were very fast, they were also unreliable and Ferrari abandoned them before the end of the season. Maglioli did, however, drive a good race with one of these cars to finish third in the Mille Miglia behind the two leading Mercedes-Benz 300 SLRs.

It was almost an act of desperation by Ferrari to produce the Tipo 860 Monza with 3,431cc (102 x 105mm) four-cylinder engine. It made its first and very disappointing race appearance in the Tourist Trophy in September 1955, but with intensive development work it became a very formidable contender. By 1956 there had been considerable changes in the design team at Ferrari. In Formula 1 Ferrari now raced the Lancia D50 cars, which had displayed so much speed and promise in late 1954 and 1955, but without substantial success. With the cars came Vittorio Jano and a brilliant young engineer called Andrea Fraschetti, while Lampredi had departed to work for Fiat.

Ferrari dominated the results of the 1956 and 1957 Mille Miglia races. In 1956 the Scuderia ran both the Tipo 860 Monza and the new Fraschetti-designed V12 Tipo 290 of 3,490cc (73 x 69.5mm). The marque was overwhelmingly successful in this rain-soaked race and took the first five places. Fraschetti was killed in a testing accident in early 1957 by when Ferrari had ready to race another two V12 models, the 3,783cc (76 x 69.5mm) Tipo 315MM and the 4,023cc (77 x 72mm) Tipo 335 Sport.

Again, Ferrari dominated the last race in the series and veteran Piero Taruffi won with a Tipo 315MM; other Ferraris finished in second and third places. Ferrari was indeed carrying on the traditions of Alfa Romeo and apart from the Mille Miglia wins, was victor in the World Sports Car Championship in seven years of the nine in which it was run, 1953 to 1961 except 1955 (Mercedes-Benz) and 1959 (Aston Martin).

FIAT

The Mille Miglia could have existed without Fiat, but it would have been a very different race, an event for the elite only. The numbers below indicate just how large a proportion of the starters were cars of Fiat origin:

Year	Number of starters	Number of Fiats
1927	77	18
1937	124	81
1947	155	102
1957	298	50

Between 1925 and 1929 Fiat built 90,000 of these 509s, most of them with saloon or tourer bodywork. Sports versions such as this pert little car were relatively rare. They were regular competitors in early Mille Miglia races, especially after the introduction of the Utilitarian class. (Fiat Auto)

Although these statistics indicate a fall in the percentage of Fiats in later years, overall the proportion in the race was vast. Only rarely were Fiats serious contenders for places in the top ten, such as in 1948 when in a field thin in high-performance cars streamlined Fiat 1,100s finished second and third. In the main the make dominated certain of the touring classes year after year; it also made

Another very successful Mille Miglia Fiat model was the Tipo 514A. For such an inexpensive car, it had a startlingly good specification, although the 1,438cc engine was side-valve. Again, these models were very popular – and successful – in the Utilitarian class. (Fiat Auto)

a major contribution through the small constructors who used Fiat engines, gearboxes and other components; significant among these were Abarth, Bandini, Cisitalia, Ermini, Giannini, Moretti, SIATA and Stanguellini.

Until fairly recent times Fiat dominated their home market and in the 1970s some 70 to 80 per cent of cars sold in Italy were Fiats. The majority sold were small-capacity cars and the majority of Fiats running in the Mille Miglia were also of small-capacity. Most were modified to a greater or lesser extent, but it must be remembered that until the organisers became a mite selective, just anyone could enter a Fiat and many Fiat drivers, who started the race, pulled out after only covering a small part of the course. This was often done by 'young bloods'. Afterwards they had a great tale to tell.

In the early years of the race the majority of Fiats were Tipo 509 9hp two-seater cars. Introduced in 1925, these were quite advanced little cars with single overhead camshaft engines, front-wheel brakes, low-pressure tyres, single-plate clutch, thermo-syphon cooling and distinguished by a flat radiator.

Between 1952 and 1954 Fiat built only 114 of the 8V model, with a 2-litre V8 engine and a top speed of at least 110mph (177kph). Fiat failed to exploit the competition potential of these very fast – and technically sophisticated – cars, but one of them finished third in its class in the 1952 Mille Miglia. The company also failed to market the 8V properly, which resulted in abysmal sales figures. (Fiat Auto)

Between 1925 and 1929 Fiat sold 90,000 cars (there were only 172,000 private cars in total registered in Italy at this time). In the first Mille Miglia in 1927, a 509 won the 1,100cc class, but another Fiat, a Tipo 519 was the victor in the 5,000cc class. This less than inspiring model, with six-cylinder 4.8-litre engine and hydro-mechanical brakes, won the class because of a lack of opposition.

Fiat replaced the 509 in 1929 with the intensely boring and stodgy 514 with 1,438cc four-cylinder side-valve engine and these saloons, built until 1932, ran regularly in the Mille Miglia. Much more desirable however was the 514A, which was eligible for the Utilitarian class and was a remarkably pleasant little open two-seater. This car was built on the longer-wheelbase 514F van chassis; it also had a higher compression engine developing 37bhp instead of the miserable 30bhp of the saloon.

The appearance of the 514A was set off by centre-lock wire-spoke wheels and sporty wings. In standard form maximum speed was about 70mph (112kph) and the works offered a somewhat more potent 'Mille Miglia' version. Small engineering companies offered overhead valve conversions and supercharger installations. You could do a lot worse than have a 514A.

During the 1930s Fiat continued to build small-capacity cars that could do well in the Mille Miglia and other events. The first Balilla saloon appeared in 1932. It was a name that represented prevailing feelings in Italy well. Balilla was a Fascist youth organisation, the full name of which was Opera nazionale balilla per

l'assistenza e l'educazione della gioventù, founded in 1926. Balilla had been the nickname of a teenager who, according to legend, had thrown the first rock at Austrian troops in a rebellion at Genoa in 1746.

By 1934 Fiat was producing a sports version of this 995cc side-valve car, which in this form had an overhead valve engine and two or four-seater bodywork. There was a four-speed synchromesh gearbox, the fuel tank with mechanical pump was mounted in the tail, and the two-seater version had a neat little central tailfin. In standard form the maximum speed was around 72mph (116kph) and the Balilla returned about 35mpg. Around 1,200 of these cars were built.

Fiat introduced the first 500 'Topolino' (small mouse, but also used in Italian as 'Mickey Mouse') in 1936. These cars had a 569cc two-bearing, side-valve engine and in standard form they were not really up to being driven flat-out for extended distances. This gave the specialist tuning houses plenty of scope for marketing modifications. Another much-raced Fiat model was the 508C 'Millecento' introduced in 1937 and remaining available until 1948. This car had a 1,089cc four-cylinder ohv engine producing a modest 32bhp.

In standard form it was good for 70mph (thanks to low weight and good aerodynamics) and from this was developed the Tipo 508CMM, a very fast sports coupé with 42bhp engine that had lead-bronze bearings and was good for 90mph (145kph). About 400 of this high-performance model were produced between 1938 and 1940 and it provided the components for a number of small-production Fiat-based cars as well as very efficiently streamlined Fiats that were raced in small numbers.

The early post-war years were marked by continuing production of the 'Topolino' and from 1953 a unit-construction 'Millecento' with delightfully boxy lines. When production ceased in 1960 Fiat had built more than a million of these post-war 'Millecentos'. A significant car introduced by Fiat in 1952 was the rather bizarrely styled 8V with two-seater berlinetta body. These cars had a 1,996cc overhead valve V8 engine that originally developed a quite modest 105bhp, but this was later increased to 127bhp. Other features of these cars were a tubular chassis and independent suspension front and rear. There was no serious attempt to market the 8V and by the time that production ceased in 1954 only 114 had been made, 56 of which had been built up in the Siata works. These cars performed well in the GT category of the Mille Miglia, even if they were not a match for the Lancia Aurelia B20 GTs, and usually finished high up in their class.

Once the Mille Miglia had been stopped, Fiats as such were rarely raced, although developments and variations built by the small specialists proliferated. Fiat Auto is today very different from the company that

Two Stanguellinis with Fiat-based 750cc twin-cam engines, unpainted and without race numbers, line up in Bologna for scrutineering at the 1954 race. They were delightful little cars and the make – based in Modena – had, like so many small manufacturers, a big following in Italy. But outside their home country they were not competitive in the face of strong Panhard opposition. (Author's Collection)

flourished during the 1950s and poor sales of uncompetitive cars has reduced this once-flourishing and proud division of the Fiat organisation to near-insolvency.

HEALEY

There were very few British companies who tackled the Mille Miglia on a regular basis and although the Healeys were never serious contenders for outright victory, they ran consistently and successfully in post-war races. Donald Healey was a very highly regarded sporting motorist when he founded the Donald Healey Motor Company Limited at the Cape, Warwick in 1946. In pre-war days he had driven an Invicta 'S'-type car to a win in the 1931 Monte Carlo Rally and he became, first, experimental manager and, later, technical director of Triumph. During the war years he worked at Humber.

Donald Healey (holding sunglasses) faces the camera at the 1949 race, while Geoffrey Price, service manager of the Healey Motor Company, cleans the windscreen of their Westland. They finished fourth in the over 1,100cc Touring class. (LAT/The Autocar/PA-Reuter)

Initially, Healey occupied a small area in the Benford concrete mixer factory, but rapidly expanded into much larger premises at the Cape, Warwick. All early Healeys followed the same basic and very successful design. There was a box-section chassis with straight side-members and 8ft 6in (2,590mm) wheelbase. At the front there was Porsche-inspired, independent trailing link suspension, with coil springs and telescopic dampers located by a lateral link.

It was a simple and effective design, especially when combined with Riley's four-cylinder 2,443cc (80.5 x 120mm) engine. This featured twin camshafts mounted high on the cylinder block operating the pushrods and had a power output of 100bhp at 4,600rpm. Healey also used the Riley four-speed gearbox and centrifugally assisted single-plate clutch.

Initially, there was the choice of the Saloon (informally known as the Elliot after the body-builder) and the Roadster (known as the Westland for the same reason). These cars were of exceptionally light

construction and in the case of the Elliot incorporated Plexiglas side and rear windows. This model had a dry weight of only 2,240lb (1,016kg) approximately.

When a standard production Elliot running on Belgian pump fuel of notoriously low octane rating achieved over 111mph (179kph) on the Belgian motorway at Jabbeke in 1947, it became the fastest production closed car available at the time. The competition potential was enormous and it was soon exploited by Donald Healey. It should be made clear that Healeys ran in many other events in addition to the Mille Miglia.

Although quite a large number of Healeys were entered in the 1948 Mille Miglia, only three started. The Belgian Aston Martin agent L. H. 'Nick' Haines drove a works Elliot with Rudi Haller, but they retired after Rome. The other cars ran on Pirelli tyres instead of the usual Dunlops, which greatly improved the handling and they performed exceptionally well.

Donald Healey, partnered by his son Geoffrey, drove a Westland roadster and in testing with the hood up this car achieved 112mph (180kph). Donald drove the whole way, while Geoffrey read the pace notes supplied by 'Johnny' Lurani and handled the refuelling. At one stage Donald asked, "When do we reach Florence?" Geoffrey consulted the map and said, "I don't see Florence." "Where's the next control?" asked his father. "Firenze," Geoffrey replied.

Just before Rome the dynamo failed and every time they put the lights on, the engine misfired. Brake trouble developed just after Rome and the wheels locked unless very great care was taken. Shortly after Florence they collided with a large dog. In this rain-sodden race they finished ninth overall, covering the course in 17hr 26min 10sec, an average of 60.69mph (97.65kph). Although they did not win anything, it was an outstanding performance and brought the marque excellent publicity.

Better still was the performance of Lurani, partnered by Sandri, despite a broken Panhard rod which allowed the rear axle to float sideways and the tyres rub on the wheel arches. They finished 11th overall and won the International Touring category. Lurani's full account of this race is reproduced on pages 160–161.

Two works Westland cars ran in the over 1,100cc Touring class of the 1949 race and there was also an ill-fated Elliot. The handling of the Westlands had been improved by fitting an anti-roll bar at the front. Geoffrey Healey and journalist Tom Wisdom with their Westland battled throughout the race with Venturi/Sanesi (Alfa Romeo) and Lurani/Aldington (Bristol). Their starting times had been close and for much of the race these drivers were fighting it out with their rivals in sight.

Geoffrey Healey/Wisdom won their class, while Donald Healey partnered by Geoffrey Price, service manager of the Donald Healey Motor Company, took fourth place in the class. The Elliot of Cohen/Reginald Hignett crashed in an accident that killed Hignett and paralysed Cohen.

Five Healeys ran in the 1950 race and four of these were Silverstones, Riley-powered sports cars with the engine mounted further back in the chassis and stark cycle-wing bodywork. This model had appeared in 1949 and was capable of around 110mph (176kph). Wood crashed the car he was sharing with Peter Monkhouse on a flyover at Barbano di Zocco. He broke a leg, but Monkhouse was thrown out of the car and against a hoarding that carried the words 'good luck' in English; he suffered injuries that proved fatal. BBC motor sport commentator Robin Richards also crashed the Silverstone that he was sharing with Rodney Lord (Richards's full story of the race is told on pages 173–174).

The other car was a new Nash-powered prototype that was shortly to enter production in collaboration with the Nash-Kelvinator company of Kenosha, Wisconsin. The Nash-Healey gave the Warwick company the chance to break into the North American market with the backing of quite a big player. In the 1950 model year, which started in September 1949, Nash sold 191,685 cars. It was an all-time record for Nash production and placed them tenth in the car sales race.

The car raced was the prototype and was a Silverstone powered by the low output (135bhp) 3,848cc push-rod six-cylinder Nash engine and with a three-speed Nash gearbox that had Laycock de Normanville overdrive on the upper two ratios. As raced, the car had a few millimetres skimmed off the head and the exhaust opened up by a Fiat garage in Como. It would rush up to 100mph (161kph), but then run out of steam.

Healeys, Don and Geoff drove the new car, but indulged in an off-course excursion which rendered the overdrive unusable. Although they completed the course, they were too far behind to be classified. After this race, full-width bodywork was adopted (still clearly revealing

its Silverstone ancestry), the engine was modified and maximum speed rose to around 124mph (200kph). Tony Rolt and Duncan Hamilton drove it into fourth place in the Le Mans race.

In 1951 Healey returned to the Mille Miglia race with a single Nash-Healey driven by Donald and Geoffrey. The car was that raced in 1950 in the Mille Miglia and at Le Mans. It was another wet, miserable race and running with this Healey in the 'Fast' class, they finished 30th overall and fifth in their class. The works ran a second Nash-powered car in the Mille Miglia the following year, a coupé with sharply sloping roofline and built-in escape hatch. Both cars now had larger 4,138cc engines.

Donald and Geoffrey drove the coupé and they were approaching Rovigo at high speed when Donald attempted to slow the car for a bridge followed by a corner. The car responded to neither steering nor brakes. They braced themselves before colliding with a bridge abutment, but Geoffrey's head hit the windscreen which popped out of the frame; they kicked the doors open and abandoned the race.

The second was the open model and this was driven by Leslie Johnson and originally he was to be partnered by Gordon Wilkins. Wilkins was prevented from taking part by his employers and so W. A. (Bill) McKenzie, motoring correspondent of the *Daily Telegraph*, took his place. McKenzie borrowed a crash helmet and bought some bright red nylon overalls, the only ones that he could find in his size (which, to put it politely, was quite generous). The night before the race he was driven from Count Maggi's Casa Maggi to another larger villa, which would be quieter than Calino and where he could get a better night's sleep.

The line-up of Healey drivers before the 1950 race: (from left) Philip Wood, Donald Healey, Geoffrey Healey, Rodney Lord, Robin Richards and Peter Monkhouse. (LAT/The Autocar)

In the darkness just before dawn Johnson wearing a poncho over his overalls, collected McKenzie. On the drive to the start at Brescia, Johnson explored the car's handling on the streaming wet roads. At Brescia they joined the queue of sports-racing cars waiting for the off and McKenzie borrowed a dispatch rider's coat to keep himself dry. They were flagged off just before dawn and were soon running at maximum speed. After a while McKenzie settled down, at least to the extent that he began to feel frustrated by the Healey's lack of straight-line speed.

At the end of the first hour, just after Padua, they took a look at the clock and odometer and were quite pleased with their progress. Johnson shouted, "You can say you've done 108 miles [174km] on a public road in an hour." They passed two or three trucks on the road and many wrecks. They stopped once before Rome for petrol. They saw surprisingly few competing cars on the road, but had one or two dices. Once, near L'Aquila, the Healey skidded sideways for a hundred yards. On the Raticosa Pass they hit a patch of oil and went off the road into the gateway of a farm, scattering the laughing spectators.

When they reached Rome, Johnson and McKenzie got out of the car to urinate over the sandy parapet behind the petrol pumps. Just across the gulley from

them was a group of spectators who were enthusiastically cheering them on, so they thought better of the idea and modestly dashed back to the Healey. They passed the retired Jaguar of Moss/Dewis near Bologna and finished the race in the gathering dusk. As they disappeared into the trees and a steamy cloud of urine, they heard the announcement that they had finished fourth in the class and seventh overall. It was the best British result in the race up until that time.

For 1953 Healey built two new, streamlined Nash-powered cars primarily for Le Mans. American driver John Fitch, partnered by one Ray Willday, drove one of these cars in the 1,000-mile race, but retired because a brake pipe fractured early in the race. One of the new Nash-Healeys finished at Le Mans that year, but well down the field in 11th place. Nash-Healey production ceased in 1954 after only 506 cars of all types had been built. There was, however, a wind of change at the Cape, reflected in the other two cars that the team ran in the 1953 Mille Miglia.

These were new Austin-Healey 100s that were just entering production in the BMC Longbridge factory. At the 1952 Earls Court Show the Healey exhibits included the new Hundred model powered by the Austin A90 four-cylinder 2,660cc engine; it had the Austin gearbox and with stunningly smooth and stylish open two-seater body designed by Gerry Coker. The car proved the sensation of the show and after BMC took over production, Healey became solely a concern developing new models and racing high-performance versions, rather than a manufacturer.

Early Austin-Healeys had first gear blanked off, as Austin's engineers believed that the four-speed gearbox would not be strong enough to withstand the torque of the big four-cylinder engine in a chassis much lighter than that of the Atlantic touring model that it originally powered. To compensate, there was Laycock de Normanville overdrive on second and third gears operated by a switch mounted on a steering wheel spoke. The cars were raced that year by Healey in the same form.

In the Mille Miglia, their first competition outing, these handsome light green cars were very close to standard mechanically, and raced with full-width windscreen and bumpers in place. The drivers were Bert Hadley (a works Austin driver in pre-war days) who was partnered by Flight-Lieutenant Bertie Mercer and former Norton works rider Johnny Lockett, accompanied by Jock Reid (a pre-war amateur rider who with Charles Mortimer had worked for Noel Macklin during the war).

The team was based at Villa Mazzotti at Chiari, the home of Count Bindo Mazzotti. No British team ever carried out adequate training for the race, but the Healey team did at least practice the first difficult part of the race and tested the cars for maximum speed on the

On the ramp at the start of the 1954 Mille Miglia, Renzo Castagneto shakes hands with Lance Macklin, seen at the wheel of his works Austin-Healey 100. He drove a very good race with this modified production car to finish 23rd overall and fifth in his class. (LAT/The Autocar)

Passing through Lonato in the 1955 race is George Abecassis with his works 100S Austin-Healey. At one stage he was in a remarkably high fourth place and he eventually finished 11th overall. (LAT/The Autocar)

Milan-Brescia Autostrada. For pace notes, the team used those given to Geoff Healey in 1949, now in updated form.

Both cars suffered from oil frothing in the gearbox and seeping through to the clutch. Other causes, however, resulted in the retirement of the cars. Hadley/Mercer retired before reaching Ravenna when the throttle linkage came adrift. Lockett/Reid had the same problem and in each case the problem was failure of the spring-loaded ball joints. Reid cobbled together a repair using wire and they were able to continue until 16 miles (26km) from the finish where the clutch plate disintegrated.

For 1954 the works 100s featured aluminium-alloy bodies, Dunlop disc brakes, David Brown four-speed gearboxes and more highly tuned engines. One of these cars driven by Lance Macklin/George Huntoon finished third in the Sebring 12 Hours race, mainly because of the high level of retirements caused by tyre and brake problems. The Donald Healey Motor Company then entered four of these cars with new glass-fibre hard tops in the Mille Miglia. The organisers took one look at these 100s and transferred them from the Grand Touring Group to the International Sports class.

It was a fair decision that Donald Healey could not challenge, but there was to be a consequence referred to later. Healey himself withdrew and the three cars that ran were driven by veteran Monégasque driver Louis Chiron, Lance Macklin and Tom Wisdom. The last-named was the only driver of this team to have a passenger and

carried that vastly experienced old-stager Mortimer Morris Goodall, who was also Healey team manager in 1954.

The cars ran with the hard tops removed and in full sports-racing trim with aero-screens and, in the case of Chiron and Macklin, with metal tonneau covers over the passenger side. Chiron and Wisdom were forced to retire because of brake and engine problems, but an outpaced Macklin finished fifth in his class and 23rd overall; his pit stop at Rome was reported as being fastest of all runners.

Then came the bombshell. Donald Healey and the British Motor Corporation announced the team's withdrawal from European racing events. Donald Healey was piqued primarily because of the decision made less than three weeks before the 1954 Mille Miglia to allow cars in the sports car class to run with only the driver (two seats were still obligatory, although a metal cover could be fitted on the passenger side). It appears that this change in the race regulations was made at the request of the Lancia team.

Another of Healey's gripes was that teams were permitted to run two-seater racing cars as prototypes at Le Mans where the entry form had to be accompanied by a letter from the Society of Motor Manufacturers and Traders (or the National equivalent in the country concerned) stating that it accepted the entrant's assurance that the cars entered were prototypes of cars that the entrant intended to put into production. Obviously, for example, Ferrari with the 4.9-litre Tipo 375 Plus had no true intention of putting this model into production.

With the British teams, Jaguar and Aston Martin, Healey was on very thin ice because the Jaguar C-type had become a production car and its D-type was destined to be announced as a production car at the London Motor Show. Aston Martin had sold the DB3 in very small numbers and they would be announcing a production version of the DB3S at Earls Court in 1954. Although Healey's arguments had some merit, it was heavily criticised because his withdrawal from Le Mans came very late in the day. In any event the Warwick Company was planning a production version of its own rather special 1954 works cars.

The new Austin-Healey was the 100S, of which a mere 55 were built at the Cape. These cars had restyled bodies with alloy panels, a version of the A90 engine with alloy cylinder head and a power output of 132bhp, together with Dunlop disc brakes all round and a proper four-speed gearbox. Healey rebuilt the 1954 works cars to this specification, which meant little more than new body panels, and these cars retained their David Brown four-speed gearboxes.

Two of these cars ran and retired in the Carrera Pan-Americana road race in Mexico in November 1954 (they were the first British entries ever in this round of the World Sports Car Championship). At Sebring in 1955 Stirling Moss and Lance Macklin drove one of these cars into a satisfactory sixth place. Next was the Mille Miglia in which Warwick entered four 100S cars driven by Macklin, George Abecassis, Ron Flockhart and Donald Healey.

Flockhart crashed, but despite running out of fuel a long way from a control, Abecassis finished 11th overall and won the poorly supported Special Sports class. Macklin's car broke its accelerator cable and after he had fixed the throttle fully open, he drove to the finish using only the ignition switch. Donald Healey, now perhaps a little old for this game, was partnered by Cashmore in a car with full-width screen (the other drivers had single aero-screens). He retired shortly after the Rome control.

The remainder of 1955 proved disastrous for the Healey team. Warwick returned to Le Mans with a single 100S shared by Lance Macklin and Les Leston. Macklin was involved in the horrific accident that cost the lives of more than 80 spectators. It was with this car that Levegh collided and his Mercedes-Benz 300 SLR was launched into disaster and oblivion.

Macklin was again at the wheel of a works 100S in the Tourist Trophy at Dundrod in September 1955 and

deliberately ditched his car to avoid the accident that cost the lives of Jim Mayers (Cooper-Climax) and Bill Smith (Connaught). Macklin retired from racing altogether and Healey withdrew for the time being.

In the 1956 Mille Miglia the two 100S runners were private entries. Leslie Brooke/Stan Astbury missed the entrance to the bridge over the river at Siena and ploughed through the brick parapet, dropping into the meadow below. Bridge and car were badly damaged, but the occupants of the Healey escaped with a shaking. Inveterate competitor Tom Wisdom was partnered by American Walter Monaco at the wheel of a works-loaned 100S. They finished 77th overall, a disappointingly slow performance in an horrendously wet race, but good enough to take second place in the over 2,000cc limited price open class.

Tom Wisdom ran in the 1,000-mile race again in 1957, but the car was a new 100-Six production model prepared by the BMC Competitions Department at Abingdon and allegedly standard apart from a larger fuel tank. Partnered by Cecil Winby of the Bricovmo company (they manufactured Brico and Covmo pistons), Wisdom finished 37th overall and took second place in the limited price class. Healeys had run in the Mille Miglia every year since 1948, ten consecutive races, and the make's record of success was vastly superior to that of any other British marque.

LANCIA

During the years that Vincenzo Lancia controlled the company that he founded in 1906, he avoided motor racing, apart from the special Lambdas built for early Mille Miglia races. These cars had a shorter wheelbase than the production versions and tuned engines. They always appeared to be serious contenders for victory and they were handled with considerable competence by drivers who included Lancia works testers. Although these were developed in Lancia's Turin factory, none ever ran as an official works entry.

At this point it is necessary to record a conflict of evidence with regard to a V8-powered Lambda. Giacosa/Storari drove a Lambda with a DiLambda 3,960cc V8 engine in the 1931 race and they finished 21st overall, third in the over 3,000cc class. The following year this, or a similar car, was driven into eighth place by Strazza/Gismondi. A short-wheelbase Lambda with V8 engine has been found and has been authenticated by the VSCC.

This car has, however, an Astura engine of smaller-capacity than the DiLambda. If it was raced in circa 1932, it would have had a capacity of 2,604cc. There is no specific evidence of an Astura-powered car running in the race, but all Lambdas are listed in Canestrini as

'Lancia 3000' because the ordinary Lambda always had an engine of over 2,000cc and ran in the 3,000cc class.

During the 1930s a few low-cost specials appeared on Lancia chassis which were raced and there were occasional appearances by the big V8 Astura saloon that Lancia built in fairly limited numbers. The small, 1,196cc, squared-rigged Augusta saloons also ran in the touring category, but they were consistently outclassed by the Fiat opposition.

Vincenzo Lancia died in December 1936, shortly after the appearance of the Aprilia, one of the finest small sporting saloons of all time. The Aprilia continued the Lancia tradition of using a V4 single overhead camshaft engine, independent front suspension by sliding pillars and unit construction. Major advances were independent rear suspension by a transverse leaf spring, radius arms and torsion bars and superb aerodynamics. The earliest cars had a 1,352cc engine, but in 1939 capacity was increased to 1,486cc.

In absolutely standard form, maximum speed was a little over 80mph (128kph) and these cars dominated their class in the touring category of the 1,000-mile race up until about 1950. Lurani's account of his drive in the 1948 race with a 2,443cc 100mph (160kph) plus Healey Elliot saloon (see pages 160–161) makes it very clear that his main opposition came from the Aprilias of Bracco and Bornigia. That year both the Aprilia and Elliot ran in the 1,101–2,500cc touring category. The real virtues of the Aprilia were its excellent power to weight ratio, superb handling and sheer drivability.

Ing Vittorio Jano, one of the greatest automobile engineers of all time, had been sacked by Alfa Romeo in 1937 for his failure to provide more effective opposition in Grand Prix racing to Mercedes-Benz and Auto Union on the miniscule budget that the Italian government,

Although Vincenzo Lancia did not generally let his company become involved in competition work, he made an exception in respect of the Mille Miglia, for which the company built short-wheelbase versions of the Lambda, with tuned engines. The cars always ran as private entries. In the 1928 race Strazza/Varallo drove this car to a fine third place overall behind Campari/Ramponi (Alfa Romeo) and Rosa/Mazzotti (OM). (Spitzley-Zagari Collection)

Lancia entered five of their new D20 cars powered by 2.9-litre V6 engines in the 1953 Mille Miglia. This car was driven by Umberto Maglioli partnered by Carnio. They retired on the Futa Pass because of a broken oil pump. Although the highest-placed Lancia finished third in 1953, the make failed to make its mark in sports car racing until 1954 and the appearance of the far more successful 3.3-litre D24. (Louis Klemantaski)

Giani Lancia was a big man, just like his rather more eminent father. Here, at Sebring in 1954, he is sitting on the right. Behind him is Lancia managing director Panagadi and seated at the table is team manager Pasquarelli. (Author's Collection)

This is the 3.3-litre D24 Lancia that Piero Valenzano drove in the 1954 Mille Miglia. He ran well until he went off the road because of an error of judgement. He was exceedingly lucky to survive the crash without serious injury. Valenzano was killed in a later racing accident. (Author's Collection)

owners of Alfa Romeo, provided. He joined Lancia as chief engineer and controlled the engineering side of the company until 1955. At Lancia his great achievement was the development of the V6 engine. Cars of this layout powered the long-lived Aurelia and, in four overhead camshaft form, the 1953–54 sports-racing cars.

Lancia announced its successor to the Aprilia, the V6 1,754cc B10 Aurelia in early 1950. In its original form it developed a very modest 56bhp at 4,000rpm, it retained very conservatively styled four-door bodywork, but it had the very advanced feature of the four-speed gearbox in unit with the final drive. Its excellent weight distribution and independent rear suspension by trailing wishbones and coil springs gave it excellent handling and it was another immensely satisfying car to drive.

A year later Lancia introduced the B20 Aurelia GT (it was the first production car to bear the title GT or Gran Turismo) and it was a much more sporting version of the saloon. Engine capacity was now 1,991cc, power output rose to a still modest 75bhp, the wheelbase was shorter and there was new and superbly styled Pinin Farina coupé bodywork. Maximum speed in standard production form was a little over 100mph (160kph), but the works competition versions were very much faster.

Vincenzo Lancia's ultimate successor was his son, Giovanni (Gianni), born in Turin on 16 November 1924. The Lancia family held 90 per cent of the shares in Lancia and when Gianni became general manager in 1948, it was only they who could have put a ban on his excesses. The company was solvent and not under the thumb of its bankers and the managing director, Panagadi, had only limited influence.

What Lancia needed above all was capital investment to modernise production (thereby increasing the profit margin on each car sold) and new models of wider appeal than the existing staid range. Instead Gianni fell victim to the lure of motor racing. Initially Lancia raced modified versions of the Aurelia GT, in a modest enough and easily affordable competition programme. Although the Aurelia GTs scored many other successes, their best results were in the 1,000 miles race with a second place overall by Bracco behind Villoresi (4.1-litre Ferrari) in the 1951 race and third place overall by Fagioli in 1952.

Gianni Lancia's first folly came when Jano was authorised to design and develop the D20 sports racing car, followed, rapidly and at great expense, by developments of these rather unsatisfactory cars. In its original form the D20 was a very stylish coupé with a more than passing resemblance to the B20, a four overhead camshaft V6 engine developing 217bhp, a multi-tubular chassis, the gearbox in unit with the final drive and all-round independent suspension. Taruffi led the 1953 Mille Miglia with one of these cars and Bonetto drove one of them into third place.

Soon afterwards Lancia had these cars rebuilt in open form by Pinin Farina and they became known as the D23. Next came the lighter, shorter-wheelbase D24, again an open car, with new and lighter gearbox and 3,284cc engine developing 245bhp. Money seemed limitless as cars were flown to races, a team of five cars was shipped out to Mexico for the 1953 Carrera Panamericana Mexico road race and an aircraft was chartered to follow the race. Bonetto crashed one car with fatal results, but the surviving cars took the first three places after Maglioli had retired his 4.1-litre Ferrari.

So it went on, for the company had also expended a vast sum on the construction of a tower block straddling the Via Vincenzo Lancia in Turin to serve the administrative needs of the company. For the 1954 Mille Miglia, Lancia built four new cars with slightly detuned engines. With a good power to weight ratio, more than adequate performance, excellent steering, roadholding and brakes, the D24 was an ideal car for the Mille Miglia.

As narrated on page 199, D24s held the first three places in the early stages of the race and Alberto Ascari drove the sole survivor to a magnificent victory. By the handicap Tourist Trophy at Dundrod in September the team had ready two new D25 cars with 3,750cc engines developing 265bhp and still shorter wheelbase. Both retired in this 624-mile race, but D24s finished third and fourth on scratch.

All this when sales of production cars were falling and profits dropping. The final folly was the D50 Grand Prix car of extremely advanced design. Lancia lured Alberto Ascari and Luigi Villoresi to drive the new cars, but the D50s were not ready to race until the Spanish Grand Prix in October 1954. By this time Lancia was to all intents and purposes insolvent. Still Gianni failed to recognise the need for financial restraint and ran a full team in 1955 until Ascari was killed in a crash with a Ferrari sports car in practice for the Supercortemaggiore Grand Prix at Monza in June 1955.

Lancia withdrew from racing, attributing the decision to Ascari's death. Gianni was ejected from management of the company, Ferrari took over the complete team of Formula 1 cars and the racing staff, including Jano, joined the Maranello team. The Lancia family realised that they could no longer keep the company, starved of capital and unable to develop new models, afloat. Later, in 1956, they sold Lancia to the Pesenti family, who controlled the giant Italcimenti Corporation, for little more than its debts.

But what happened to the man who destroyed the company that his father founded? That he was shamed and discredited is undoubted. The writer has tried to probe the later story of Gianni Lancia, but with limited success. Gianni Lancia is, at the time of writing, very much alive and divides his time between France and Brazil. As a member of the Lancia family wrote to the author, "I am sorry not to answer the other questions to defend his privacy (very well preserved till now as you have verified)."

MASERATI

This was a marque that competed every year from the earliest days onwards, but never won the 1,000-mile race. All early Maserati sports cars were in fact two-seater racing cars based on the straight-eight 2-litre Diatto that Alfieri Maserati had built in 1925. Diatto ran into financial problems so Maserati took over the project and gave it his own name. Early Maseratis lacked the durability to survive the Mille Miglia and it was not until the early 1930s that this small company based in Bologna began to achieve a good measure of success in classes of the Mille Miglia.

In 1931 Tuffanelli, partnered by Guerino Bertocchi, won the 1,100cc class with a diminutive straight-eight Maserati and they repeated this success the following year. By 1933 Maserati had ready a four-cylinder 1,100cc engine that had greater power than its predecessors, but was fitted in a very similar chassis. This car faced a very strong works team of British MG Magnettes and retired after fighting a losing battle with the British cars. Maserati and MG clashed again in 1934, but the British team was now weaker and Piero Taruffi, partnered by Bertocchi, was formidable and won the 1,100cc class by the enormous margin of 1hr 20min.

At the 1934 Italian Grand Prix Maserati had introduced the Tipo 34 six-cylinder 3,326cc Grand Prix car and by 1935 the engine size of this model had been increased to 3,729cc. In this form power output was around 280bhp and the special car built for the 1935 Mille Miglia and driven by Achille Varzi, partnered by Bignami, should have been more than a match for the Alfa Romeo opposition. It was, sadly, too typical of Maserati incompetence that it was finished only just before the race; it had not been properly tested and was an early retirement.

But, yet again, in complete contrast, the 1,100cc Maserati of Gino Bianco, partnered – inevitably – as a sort of benign fate by Guerino Bertocchi, beat Taruffi's class record by around 27 minutes (in much more favourable weather conditions) and defeated a host of special Fiats. In 1936 Maserati prepared both 1,100 and 1,500cc four-cylinder cars and enjoyed two class wins. Bertocchi partnered racing motorcyclist Ombono Tenni in a rather wild drive to win the 2,000cc class, while Bianco, now partnered by Boccali, took the 1,100cc class. These Maseratis were fifth and sixth in overall classification, while a 2-litre car driven by

Rocco/Filippone finished tenth overall and second in the 2,000cc class.

With effect from 1 January 1937 the Orsi industrial group headed by Adolfo Orsi took over Maserati with a view to boosting its public image. Production was moved from Bologna to Modena. The new management concentrated on single-seater racing and no longer were cars built for the Mille Miglia. Lurani/Emilio Villoresi drove a private four-cylinder car in the 1937 event but they failed to finish. There were no more Maserati entries in the race until 1947 when Luigi Villoresi, partnered by Bertocchi drove the latest six-cylinder, 1,954cc A6G sports car.

Villoresi retired and there followed an interval of six years before Maserati again entered works cars in the Mille Miglia. The company rested most of its hopes in early post-World War Two days on the A6.GCS 'Monofaro', so-called because of its single headlamp mounted in the centre of the radiator grille. The rather odd positioning of the full stop was part of the official title, but rarely used. These stark sports cars with single overhead camshaft 1,979cc six-cylinder engine had a maximum speed of around 125mph (200kph). They provided very serious opposition for early 2-litre Ferraris and they were expected to do well in the new 2-litre Formula 2 that started in 1948.

Maseratis, which in reality were racing cars with wings and lights, competed regularly in pre-war Mille Miglia races. This four-cylinder Tipo 4CTR 1,100cc car was driven in the 1933 race by Tabanelli/Borgnino. They had mechanical problems, however, and were never able to challenge the team of MG Magnettes. But although they finished well down the field that year, a Maserati was to beat the MGs in the 1,100cc class in 1934. (Spitzley-Zagari Collection)

There were, however, only 16 of these cars built, for while Ferrari flourished, Maserati found itself in conflict with the Communist unions which were very powerful in Emilia Romagna. Adolfo Orsi would not give ground, production was disrupted and in 1949 the management was locked out of the Modena factory. Maserati was forced to abandon the A6.GCS, while development and preparation of the 4CLT/48 'San Remo' Grand Prix cars was carried out in a series of lock-up garages. Orsi did not regain control of the Maserati factory until 1951.

During 1951 Maserati engineer Alberto Massimino worked on a new six-cylinder 1,988cc (75 x 75mm) single-seater for Formula 2 racing. This car was designated the A6GCM, that is A-series, six-cylinder, ghisi (iron) cylinder block, competition, monoposto. The earliest cars did have a cast-iron block, but the original designation was retained after Maserati adopted aluminium-alloy cylinder blocks. Juan Fangio was to lead the team, but he was badly injured in a crash at Monza in June. The season proved one of almost complete failure.

By the end of 1952 Maserati had adopted twin-plug ignition and for 1953 there were revised cylinder dimensions of 76.2mm x 72mm, giving a capacity of 1,970cc. Power output was reckoned to be 190bhp at 9,000rpm. In the early part of 1953 Maserati put into limited production a sports version known as the A6GCS (sometimes known as 53/A6GCS, but in all cases without the full stop); this had the Formula 2 engine detuned to develop 165bhp at 6,750rpm and a very handsome body built by Maserati in-house coachbuilder Fantuzzi.

These cars were to enjoy a formidable record in the 2,000cc Sports class of the Mille Miglia. Three of them, privately owned but entered in the name of the works, ran in the 1953 race. Giletti, partnered by Bertocchi, won the class from another A6GCS. This was the eighth time

The team of Maserati A6GCS 2-litre cars, seen at the Modena factory before the 1954 race. They were exceptionally handsome cars and the body was the work of Maserati in-house coachbuilder Medardo Fantuzzi. Number 500 is the car that Luigi Musso, partnered by Zocca, drove into third place overall. Musso is standing on the extreme right of the photograph. At the back is a side view of one of the far less attractive Vignale-bodied cars that Maserati entered in the 1953 Nürburgring 1,000Km race. (Spitzley-Zagari Collection)

that Maserati chief mechanic Bertocchi had ridden in the race. He was a very brave man and his role at Maserati was very much that of a practical engineer rather than a mere mechanic. Bertocchi had joined Alfieri Maserati in 1922 at the age of 15 and it was ironic that he was to die in 1981, by when he was working for de Tomaso, as a passenger in a head-on crash with a de Tomaso customer at the wheel.

In 1954 Maserati was beaten by Vittorio Marzotto with a Ferrari, but A6GCS cars took second and third places in the 2,000cc class. The following year Maserati took the first three places in the 2,000cc class. By this time Maserati engineer Vittorio Bellentani had developed the 2,993cc 300S powered by a 245bhp enlarged version of the 250F Grand Prix car engine. The 300S lacked the sheer power of the Mercedes-Benz 300 SLR, but it had delightful steering, roadholding and braking and was liked by all who drove the model. Works driver Cesare Perdisa handled one of these cars in the 1955 race and held second place ahead of Fangio (300 SLR) until the gearbox broke.

The last two years of the Mille Miglia were disastrous for Maserati. Part of the problem in 1956 was that a large number of private owners were entering their cars and having them prepared at the works and, in addition, the factory was having to complete examples of the 150S 1,484cc sports car for which a large number of orders had been received. Moss crashed the experimental 350S because of its diabolic, unforgiving handling; Taruffi crashed his 300S, while both Perdisa (300S) and Behra (150 S) were delayed by problems arising from poor preparation. The only real consolation was the first two places in the 2,000cc Sports class by private owners with now obsolete A6GCs cars.

During 1956 Maserati had been developing the V8 4,477cc (93.8 x 81mm) Tipo 450S sports car with a new and much improved chassis. Power output was about 400hp at 7,500rpm and, according to gearing, the maximum speed was around 160–180mph (257–290kph). For the Mille Miglia these cars were fitted with a supplementary two-speed gearbox mounted between the clutch and the normal gearbox. In practice Moss found that it was possible to accelerate through the low set of five gears and then operate the push-pull control to engage high fifth.

Although these cars won the Sebring 12 Hours race and the Swedish Sports Car Grand Prix in 1957, they were so potent that only the most experienced and able drivers, such as Fangio, Moss and Behra could handle them. It is difficult to imagine that even a very skilful driver could have adequately controlled the 450S in a wet Mille Miglia, but the 1957 race was dry and, if the car had been properly prepared, Moss would have won.

It was intended that Moss and Behra should drive these cars in the Mille Miglia, but Behra non-started after a practice crash and Moss was eliminated within minutes of starting by a broken brake pedal. Maserati was destined never to win the Mille Miglia, although Scarlatti did finish fourth with a 300S in the 1957 race.

Fangio won his fifth World Championship at the wheel of the Maserati 250F in 1957, but the company was finding itself in increasing financial difficulties. Maserati withdrew its works team at the end of the year, but in 1959 returned to racing by offering private teams the famous Giulio Alfieri-designed 'Birdcage' sports-racing cars. In 1968 Citroën acquired a controlling interest in Maserati, which now built only high-speed touring cars and the engines that powered Citroën's delightful, but idiosyncratic SM saloon. Subsequently, Allesandro de Tomaso acquired control of the company and it is now a subsidiary of Fiat.

MERCEDES-BENZ

The German marque is the only foreign make to have won the Mille Miglia. The Mercedes (Daimler) side of the two companies (Mercedes and Benz merged in 1926) had already an exceptional racing record that included wins in the 1908 and 1914 French Grands Prix. It was very much the senior partner in the merger, although the struggling Benz company had been producing some exciting designs.

Notable among these were the rear-engined racing and sports cars designed by Dr Rumpler. These were a

Rudolf Caracciola, partnered by Wilhelm Sebastian in the massive blown 7-litre Mercedes-Benz SSKL, is seen on the Raticosa Pass in the 1931 Mille Miglia. It was a fine victory, but only made possible by the tyre failures and other problems suffered by the new 8C 2300 Alfa Romeos. (Author's Collection)

great pioneering effort, even if the handling was exceptionally poor because of the Benz engineers' lack of experience with this layout, but it is likely that it inspired Professor Ferdinand Porsche when he and his team designed the Auto Union Grand Prix cars of 1934 onwards. Benz also pioneered swing-axle rear suspension and diesel engines and both of these features were adopted by Mercedes-Benz.

Although the 'Grosser' Mercedes, the line of SS, SSK and SSKL large-capacity sports cars built in the late 1920s through into the early 1930s was exceptionally successful in hill climb and sports car races, it was a very brutal approach to the building of a high-performance competition car. The more powerful versions of these six-cylinder cars were built after technical director Ferdinand Porsche left the company at the end of 1928, following a stormy board meeting. He was replaced by Hans Nibel who had been mainly concerned with diesel engine and truck development at the former Benz factory at Mannheim.

During 1929–32 the company pursued a very active competition programme with the six-cylinder cars which were supercharged in all their later forms. In 1930 Caracciola drove a 7,069cc SSK (Super Sport Kurz) Mercedes-Benz in the Mille Miglia on a sort of reconnaissance. He then came back the following year with an SSKL (Super Sport Kurz Leicht) car, a model not generally sold to the public, but usually reserved for works drivers. The engine capacity remained 7,069cc, but it was fitted with high compression pistons, high-lift camshaft and usually had the 'Elephant' supercharger compressing at 12psi. Power output was over 300bhp and maximum speed around 130mph (209kph).

The sheer power and speed of the SSKL was such that Alfa Romeo had no chance of defeating it unless they entered the underdeveloped 8C 2300 cars. It was the one opportunity for Mercedes-Benz to win the Mille Miglia and Caracciola became the only German driver to do so. It was an especially important win, because without it, Alfa Romeo domination would have continued, the race would have lost much more interest than it retained in the early to mid-1930s following the Mercedes-Benz victory and it would probably have ceased being held altogether.

After Manfred von Brauchitsch ran an SSKL without success in the 1933 Mille Miglia, a period of 19 years elapsed without a Mercedes-Benz entry. During that time National Socialism had swept Germany into a maelstrom of war, atrocities and destruction. Hitler had become Chancellor in January 1933 and perished by his own hand in the Berlin bunker in April 1945. Many German cities had been destroyed by Allied bombing and bombing had completely wrecked the Mercedes-Benz factory at Stuttgart-Untertürkheim.

Germany was divided into zones, its people guilt-ridden and despised throughout Europe. The return of Mercedes-Benz to the Mille Miglia in 1952 was part of an attempt to restore international respect and respectability to the company. It was not without importance that throughout the company's history its production and marketing was closely related to its motor sport activities. Inevitably, the budget for the new racing programme was small and the company's new sports car contender, the W194 300 SL (Sport Leicht) was based on production car components.

The basis chosen for the new car was the 300 saloon with six-cylinder, single overhead camshaft 2,996cc (85 x 88mm) engine with cast-iron block that had appeared in 1951. The standard engine developed 115bhp, but in competition form as used in the 300 SL, with three Solex downdraught carburettors, the power output was about 171bhp at 5,800rpm. To reduce bonnet height, the engine was canted in the chassis at an angle of 50° to the left. The standard 300 four-speed gearbox with cast-iron casing was used.

Although Rudolf Uhlenhaut and his team of engineers used many standard components, one of the most advanced features of the new car was an elaborate multi-tubular space-frame that provided exceptional stiffness. Initially, it had been decided to fit coupé bodywork, but the side-members of the space-frame precluded the use of conventional doors, so Mercedes-Benz adopted doors that cut into the roofline where they were hinged and at the bottom terminated just above the side-members. These became known as 'gullwing doors.' It was only later in the year that the open cars appeared.

Racing manager Alfred Neubauer was unhappy with the new car because he thought that it was underpowered,

This 300 SL Gullwing, seen at the Mercedes-Benz works at Untertürkheim before the 1952 race, was driven by Hermann Lang/Grupp. Lang retired early in the race after colliding with a road marker and damaging the rear axle of the car. (DaimlerChrysler)

that it needed a five-speed gearbox and that its 15-inch (380mm) wheels with Rudge-Whitworth centre-lock hubs were too small and would result in excessive tyre wear. Uhlenhaut made it clear that if Neubauer pushed his complaints too hard, it was likely that the project would be abandoned altogether. That was not in the Racing Manager's interests and he promptly shut up.

For practice for the 1955 Mille Miglia, Stirling Moss and Denis Jenkinson used this 300 SL, seen here after a collision with an errant lorry. (LAT)

Mercedes-Benz 300 SLR

Extract from a letter dated 13 July 1995 from Denis Jenkinson to Guy Griffiths following the appearance of the Mille Miglia-winning 300 SLR at the Goodwood Festival of Speed

Dear Guy

Thank you for the set of photos from Goodwood. I'm amazed you were able to get that close, through the crowds.

The gear-gate was a masterpiece of detail engineering. They had designed it for the Grand Prix cars, but during MM practice Stirling found a tendency to change down from 5th to 2nd, instead of 5th to 4th during the heat of a moment. The basic gear pattern was arsy-tarsy to English eyes, though SM was not worried about that, but when sliding into a hairpin in 3rd and he wanted to reach sideways and snatch 2nd, he tended to get 1st by mistake.

OK if the movement was planned and he thought about it, but dicing on the open road there was no time for conscious thought, it had to be a reflex action. Out on the open road the trouble was a quick snatch from 5th to 4th to keep the revs up, and he would get 2nd. The whole gearbox had synchromesh and very close ratios. The link mechanism was perfect. Uhlenhaut rang to Stuttgart to one

The gear-change of Moss's Mille Miglia 300 SLR, photographed at the 1995 Goodwood Festival of Speed. (Guy Griffiths)

of his top henchmen, the parts arrived the next day and were fitted to the 'hack' SLR car we were using for practice.

[With the revised arrangement], you had to change progressively, 1–2–3–4–5 and 5–4–3–2–1. Reverse was opposite 1st and in your photo you can see the 'thumb'

Moss is looking at the rear of this 300 SLR during practice for the Mille Miglia, but it is in fact the car that was driven – and crashed – by Hans Herrmann. (LAT)

The Mille Miglia was the 300 SL's first race and Karl Kling came so very close to winning. Motor racing (and just about everything else) is full of ifs and buts, but if Kling had not suffered a seized hub spinner and fading brakes and if Giovanni Bracco had not been an alcoholic maniac, then Mercedes-Benz would have won the race. Later in the year the 300 SLs won minor races at Bremgarten near Bern and the Nürburgring, but, more importantly, they were victorious at Le Mans (but only after the failure of all the faster opposition) and in the Carrera Panamericana Mexico road race in November.

Mercedes-Benz originally planned to race much-modified versions of the 300 SL in 1953, but this proposal was abandoned and, instead an improved 300 SL Gullwing with fuel injection became a catalogued model, mainly for the American market. It entered production in late 1954 and by the time production ceased early in 1957 the number built totalled 1,400.

The team returned to Grand Prix racing in 1954 with the W196 car. The new car was powered by a straight-eight, 2,496cc (76.0 x 68.8mm) engine with twin overhead camshafts driven by a train of gears from the centre of the crankshaft. The engine design featured

toeing with his right foot, he went snick-snick into first, flipped the reverse catch up.

We motored forwards back on to the road, but needed a short reverse back across the road, then into first, and as he was about to change up from 1st to 2nd, I fiddled about to put the reverse catch down. As I got it down, he [engaged] second and just nipped my left thumb; but all was well, I shook it in mock anger as we tore off down the mountainside and he changed up from 2nd to 3rd. To make it all clearer this is the 'gate' pattern:

The Goodwood SLR was nearly right. The museum people made three bad boobs, which Stirling did not notice, but he never looks at original black & whites like I do. In your action photo at Goodwood you will see there is a panel behind the front wheel. This was detachable, to get at the plugs. This was removed for the race.

'Winker' lights had been added and the Perspex screen was 15mm thick, to withstand the rigours of pop-stars and retros. Our original one was the same shape, but about 5mm thick.

Cheers
Jenks

A front view of Moss's Mille Miglia 300 SLR, at Goodwood in 1995. In Jenks's letter he points out that the flashing indicators were a non-standard alteration and that the windscreen was thicker than on the original. (Guy Griffiths)

toggle to clear the gate. On the move you did not need reverse! At least not until we spun on the Radicofani! As we rolled backwards into the shallow ditch, SM with his [left] foot on the clutch and the engine still running, heeling and

mechanically opened and closed 'desmodromic' valves and Bosch high-pressure fuel injection. From this Mercedes-Benz developed a sports version for the 1955 season. This version was officially typed the W196S and the engine was typed the M196S, but the car is usually known as the 300 SLR, to emphasise its relationship with the 300 SL production model.

In the sports car the capacity of the engine was increased to 2,979cc (78 x 78mm) and it was inclined to the right in the chassis at 30 degrees from the vertical. Whereas the engine of the Grand Prix car had welded cylinder jackets made from sheet steel, the 300 SLR had aluminium-alloy cylinder blocks with integrally cast fixed cylinder head. As on the Formula 1 car, the Hirth built-up crankshaft ran in roller main and big end bearings. Power output reckoned to be around 300bhp at 7,500rpm.

Transmission was by a single-plate clutch with synchromesh on the upper four ratios. The chassis was again a multi-tubular space-frame with independent suspension: at the front by double wishbones and longitudinal torsion bars; at the rear by low-pivot swing-axles and longitudinal torsion bars with the hubs located fore and aft by a Watts linkage. Steering was left-hand.

Maximum speed according to gearing was 174–180mph (280–290kph). In 1955 there was no car that could match the performance of the 300 SLR, save for the Jaguar D-type with better aerodynamics and disc brakes – but, then only on the smooth, fast roads of the Le Mans circuit, for its roadholding was inferior.

What distinguished the Mercedes-Benz team from their rivals was their intensive pre-race training on the Mille Miglia circuit and in the race Moss/Jenkinson and Fangio took the first two places, though the other two cars of Kling and Herrmann both crashed. Mercedes-Benz success was not limited to the sports category, for production 300 SLs also took the first three places in the class for Special Gran Touring cars over 1,300cc. In addition Mercedes-Benz saloons won the over 2,000cc Modified Production Touring class and the Diesel class. Victory could not have been more complete nor Italian humiliation greater.

Mercedes-Benz withdrew from Grand Prix and sports car racing at the end of 1955, but it was not quite the end of the company's racing activities. A very strong entry of 300 SL coupés ran in the 1956 Mille Miglia; Wolfgang von Trips with a works car was a serious contender for outright victory, but he crashed while overtaking a slower car. Ferrari won the over 2,000cc GT category. Only private 300 SLs ran in the 1957 race but not one finished. Despite this dismal end to the story, Mercedes-Benz was the only foreign team to beat the Italians in a race in which most of their drivers had the major advantage of an intimate knowledge of the circuit. It was a magnificent achievement and the win of Moss/Jenkinson in 1955 remains the most famous victory in the history of the race.

OM

OM (Societa Anonima Officine Meccaniche) based in Brescia, the home of the Mille Miglia, were staunch supporters of the 1,000-mile race in its early years. What was so very different about these very high-performance cars was that they had side-valve engines. The company was founded in Milan in 1899 by the merger of Grondona Comi & C and Miani Silvestri & C. The company was a manufacturer of heavy engineering products, including railway equipment.

Although the OMs were beaten in the 1928 race, they were numerous and one did finish second. This OM, driven by Francesconi/Bassi, was rather less successful and took 12th place. It is seen on the Raticosa Pass. (Spitzley-Zagari Collection)

In 1918 OM entered the automobile business by acquiring Züst, based in Brescia. Initially, they continued to build Züst's 4,712cc four-cylinder, side-valve 25/35hp cars, which under OM ownership was typed the S305. In 1923 there appeared the first cars of their own, and the soon to be familiar design was the work of an Austrian engineer named Barratouché.

Although some interesting prototypes and an uncompetitive straight, twin-cam 1.5-litre Grand Prix car of 1926 were built, there was in reality only one home-designed production car. Initially, the company introduced a four-cylinder design, side-valve of course, with cast-iron, one-piece block, alloy crankcase, detachable cylinder head, the valves running directly in the block without guides to provide better heat dissipation and the crankshaft running in three main bearings.

The first model was the Tipo 465 introduced in 1919 and in production 1920–21 with a capacity of 1,327cc (65 x 100mm) and the very modest claimed power output of 18bhp. It was fitted with a three-speed gearbox and there was the option of short and long wheelbase lengths. It was usually sold with a four-seat torpedo (open tourer) body, it vied for the same slot in the market place as the Fiat 501 and it had no sporting pretensions. Then the 1,410cc Tipo 467 appeared in 1921 and was built until 1923. This was soon followed by the 1,496cc Tipo 469 with an engine developing 30bhp at 3,000rpm and four-speed gearbox. The initial models were the 469N and the four-wheel-brake 469S.

A rare view of an OM Superba in the 1930 Mille Miglia race. The car is a 2,221cc Compressore, driven to fifth place by Bassa and Gazzabini. Already, the great days of OM were over. (Spitzley-Zagari Collection)

Development continued with the 469S2 that had increased track and followed in 1923. It remained available until 1930 when OM introduced the final version, the 1,622cc 469S4. This car continued to be offered until private car production officially ceased in 1934. Although these last cars were regular performers in Italian racing and like all OM cars were hand-built to a substantial extent, the four-cylinder cars were very much the 'bread and butter' models of the range and it was the six-cylinder cars that achieved substantial racing successes.

In 1923 OM introduced the brilliantly successful six-cylinder version, the 1,991cc Tipo 65 Superba of almost identical design to its predecessors, but with an engine running in four main bearings. There were, initially, two versions, the 'S' with short 9ft 2in (2,800mm) wheelbase and the longer, 10ft 2in (3,100mm) wheelbase 'N'. It must be remembered that by modern standards, vintage cars had very long wheelbases. We tend to think of Lancia Lambdas as having exceptional long wheelbases, but in fact they were much the same length as contemporary OMs.

The first few cars had engines developing 40bhp at 3,600rpm. Soon power output rose significantly to 60/75bhp according to the level of tune. Four-wheel brakes were standard. 'Johnny' Lurani maintained that Ing. Ottavio Fuscaldo of Verona was responsible for the design of the Superba. In 1927 both versions had a wider track and the following year the improved 665N3 entered production. Then a year later came the 665N5 and the 665SMM with a slightly shorter 9ft 1in (2,790mm) wheelbase. All these numbers are, of course, confusing for the general reader, but they emphasise OM's policy of constant improvement.

The cars that ran in the Mille Miglia were carefully prepared and incorporated a number of modifications to increase power output. They have, however, to be distinguished from the cars marketed in the UK, which the agent, Rawlence, substantially modified. The 2-litre side-valve OM proved more than a match in 1927 for the old pushrod RLSS Alfa Romeos, but by 1928 they faced the latest twin-cam 6C 1500 Jano-designed Alfas and they were no longer fast enough to beat the best-driven of the Portello cars.

By 1929 OM had introduced the Tipo 667 Superba model of 2,221cc (67 x 105mm) and raced these cars in the Mille Miglia with supercharged engines developing around 85bhp. In this form they were known as the 665 SS MM Superba Compressore. The following year there was a further increase in engine capacity to 2.327cc (67 x 110mm), power output was 95bhp, the Mille Miglia cars were lighter and sleeker than their predecessors and roadholding had been improved. They were still no match for the latest Alfa Romeos and 1931 was to be the last year in which the OM works entered the race. The Superba had been a significant, if somewhat anachronistic contender.

By this time OM had ceased car production, but both four-cylinder and six-cylinder chassis continued to be made in commercial form. Since 1927 the company had been increasingly concentrating on the production of heavy commercial vehicles with Swiss Saurer diesel engines made under licence. OM remained an independent company, building lorries, tractors and railway rolling stock until 1968, when it was taken over by Fiat. Initially, Fiat kept the OM name alive, but the models were gradually rebadged as Fiats. As late as 2001 the name was still being used on fork-lift trucks.

At one time the OM name was still very much alive in Vintage Sports Car Club circles and Peter Binns raced a much-modified car with great success in VSCC events. In the 1960s there were still some 23 examples in the OM Register. The OM Register has now disappeared and only 15 or so OMs are listed as belonging to members of the VSCC.

OSCA

There was no competition sports car more typically Italian than the OSCA built by the surviving Maserati brothers in Bologna. These cars were beautifully constructed, but simple in concept and the majority were powered by an immensely tough twin overhead camshaft engine. They were perfect cars for private owners to enter in the smaller-capacity classes of the 1,000-mile race and they were largely unchallenged in the 1,500cc class until the Porsche 550 Spyder first ran in the event in 1954. In Italian events of a lesser nature they reigned supreme and although there are no figures available, quite a number were sold in the United States.

After they left the company they had founded, Ernesto, Ettore and Bindo Maserati set themselves up in a small works and operated under the name Officina Specializzata per la Costruzione de Automobili-Fratelli SpA. It was a dreadful mouthful and it was just as well that the brothers settled for the acronym OSCA (sometimes seen reproduced as Osca). Generally, they followed the design principles of the original Maserati

company, but most of the cars that they built were not in direct competition.

The first OSCA to enter production was the MT4 1,093cc (70 x 71mm) model with four-cylinder, single overhead camshaft engine. It had a cast-iron cylinder block, an aluminium-alloy cylinder head, Maserati-type 'finger' cam followers and a power output of 72bhp at 6,000rpm. The Maseratis installed this engine in a simple, but very effective tubular chassis with coil spring and unequal-length wishbone at the front and a rear axle suspended on quarter-elliptic springs. Transmission was by a single-plate clutch and a Fiat four-speed gearbox with synchromesh on third and top ratios.

Although cycle-wing bodies were still de rigueur, it was a handsome little car of jewel-like construction and a sheer delight to drive. The first OSCA was not ready in time to run in the 1947 race and there were no examples of the breed entered in 1948, but three OSCAs started the 1949 race. By this time OSCA had added the MT4 1350 with 1,343cc (75 x 76mm) engine to the range.

The feeling at the Bologna works was that with improvements these cars could sell very much better. In 1950 Ernesto Maserati revealed the MT2 2AD version with twin overhead camshafts driven by gear and chain. Later versions usually had rather slab-sided full-width bodies. There is no doubt that sales improved markedly around this time.

Three OSCAS ran in the 1950 Mille Miglia, all of them single-cam cars, apart from the first 1,100cc with a twin-cam engine. The works entered Luigi Fagioli, partnered by Diotavelli, and the veteran, one-time works Mercedes-Benz driver, turned in an exceptionally good performance to finish seventh overall and win the 1,100cc class. His time was just 30 seconds short of two hours faster than the Fiat that won this class in 1950.

Over the next couple of years, the OSCAs were largely unchanged, but their popularity steadily grew and there were seven 1,100cc cars in the 1951 race. Most of the race was run in heavy rain, which proved a great leveller of the performance of cars of different capacity and of course slowed all the cars. The fastest car in the class was a Stanguellini driven by Sergio Sighinolfi, who led the class initially; he went off a flyover during the night and completely wrecked his car.

World War Two fighter pilot Franco Bordoni assumed the lead in the class with his OSCA and was in the first five overall until his electric fuel pump failed and he was delayed for 40 minutes. Fagioli then assumed the lead with his OSCA and finished eighth overall, winning the 1,100cc class. His car had cycle-wing bodywork and during the race shed its right front wing. Bordoni took tenth place and a class second. Another OSCA driven by Piero Cabianca took third place in the class. At this time there was no 1,500cc sports class in which the larger-capacity cars could show their paces.

The Maserati brothers who ran OSCA: (from left) Ettore, Bindo and Ernesto. This is a posed photograph of them with a twin overhead camshaft engine, probably a 750cc unit. They were much happier running their own small company in Bologna than they had been at Maserati once it was taken over by Adolfo Orsi. (Author's Collection)

Another wet race followed in 1952. Again the 1,100cc class was an OSCA versus Stanguellini battle and again the OSCAs came out on top. Cabianca won the class with a car having a neat full-width body and Pagani and Venezian took second and third places. In 1953 OSCA ceased making the 1,352cc car, but introduced the

A view of an early OSCA, one of the first cars of the marque with 'joined-up' bodywork, seen at Brescia before the 1951 race. This 1,100cc car was driven by Pagani/Comotti who finished 20th overall and were quite well placed in their class. Although it appears that the number 221 has been painted on the right front wing, this is probably an optical illusion caused by the curvature of the bodywork and the correct number is shown. (Spitzley-Zagari Collection)

MT2 2AD model with alloy-block 1,453cc engine developing a very healthy 110bhp at 6,200rpm. The body was far more stylish than that of earlier OSCAs. There was a 1,500cc class in the 1953 Mille Miglia, but no OSCAS ran in it. That year Venezian won the 1,100cc class, but a Fiat-based 'Special' was second and Coriasco took third place in the class with his OSCA.

The greatest success in OSCA's racing history came in early 1954, but it was in a race in the United States, the Sebring 12 Hours event which was a round in the World Sports Car Championship. Stirling Moss partnered by Bill Lloyd won with a Briggs Cunningham-entered car after all the faster opposition had run into problems. It was a success that gave a great fillip to OSCA sales. There was no 1,100cc class in the 1954 Mille Miglia race and there is little doubt that these constant changes in the rules led to an element of instability. Cabianca elected to drive solo, but was beaten in the 1,500cc class by Herrmann/Linge with their Porsche 550 Spyder.

This disappointing result left sales unaffected, but it must be remembered that OSCA only built 20 or so competition cars a year and never employed more than 50 staff. In May 1954 the brothers introduced the MT2 AD 1500 with a 1,491cc (78 x 78mm) engine developing 120bhp at 6,300rpm and a maximum speed of 120mph. There was also the 2000S two-litre car, but there were only a couple of these and they never ran in the 1,000-mile race. Towards the end of 1954 OSCA moved into new and more spacious premises in San Lazzaro di Savena, about eight kilometres from central Bologna.

A further development in 1955 was the adoption of a twin-plug cylinder head on the 1,500cc car and in this form it was known as the TN-1500 ('Tipo Nuovo'). The 1,100cc cars took the first three places in their class which had been reinstated for the 1955 race. Porsche was, however, dominant in the 1,500cc class and Descollanges finished second in this class, a little over 20 minutes behind Wolfgang Seidel who won the class with his 550 Spyder.

An important OSCA development in 1956 was the Tipo 187 with 749cc (62 x 62mm) engine and it was to enjoy very considerable success. It was to prove OSCA's most successful year in the 1,000-mile race. A total of nine OSCAs were entered. Capelli won the 750cc class from a brace of Stanguellinis; Brandi and Falli were first and third in the 1,100cc class, sandwiching the Fiat-based Ermini of Menzini; and Cabianca won the 1,500cc

The heart of all OSCAs was the jewel-like twin overhead camshaft engine that combined excellent power output with above-average reliability. James Sitz photographed this partially dismantled engine when he visited the factory at San Lazzaro di Savena in 1957. (James M. Sitz)

class from Jean Behra driving a Maserati 150S. It was one of the very few occasions when there was serious, direct rivalry between the two makes.

Over the years OSCAs became much sleeker, of lower construction and with smaller frontal area. Independent rear suspension was also adopted on some cars in 1957. In the last Mille Miglia very sleek 750cc cars took first three places in their class and the marque also took first three places in the 1,500cc class. Cabianca should have run with a 1,500cc car, vying for success with the Porsche opposition, but on the eve of the race this car suffered mechanical damage that could not be repaired in time for the start. It seems that this was the first OSCA with desmodromic (mechanically operated) valves and based on a layout that Ernesto Maserati had penned as early as 1942.

OSCA continued to build sports-racing cars until 1959 and their record of success remained good. Their first Formula Junior single-seater appeared in 1958. In 1959 Fiat introduced their 1500S sporting car with a twin-cam engine designed by OSCA, but built in Turin. OSCA also built a small number of GT cars powered by this engine. The Maserati brothers were now elderly, well into their sixties, and in 1963 they sold out to MV Agusta. The marque finally disappeared in 1966.

Opposite: A view of the interior of the small OSCA works, eight kilometres outside of Bologna. Although OSCA never grasped the potential of aerodynamics in the way that companies like Lotus and EMW (in East Germany) did, the later cars were much lower and sleeker, partly because of Alessandro de Tomaso's influence. (James M. Sitz)

Overleaf: Two MG Magnette K3s arrive together at the Florence control. On the left are Tim Birkin and Bernard Rubin, who retired at Siena, and on the right Lurani and Eyston, who went on to win the race. (Author's Collection)

The Races

1927

26-27 March
Starters: 77; Finishers: 54; Distance: 1,018 miles (1,638km).
Circuit Map: See page 242.
Weather: Fine, dry throughout.

Main contenders for outright victory:

5	Count Aymo Maggi/Bindo Maserati (Isotta Fraschini Tipo 8A 7,372cc)
12	M. Danieli/Archimede Rosa (OM Tipo 665 Superba 1,991cc)
13	T. Danieli/Renato Balestrero (OM Tipo 665 Superba 1,991cc)
14	Ferdinando Minoia/Giuseppe Morandi (OM Tipo 665 Superba 1,991cc)
17	Gildo Strazza/Varallo (Lancia Lambda 2,370cc)
42	Count Gastone Brilli Peri/Bruno Presenti (Alfa Romeo RLSS 22/90 2,994cc)
43	Attilio Marinoni/Giulio Ramponi (Alfa Romeo RLSS 22/90, 2994cc)
49	'Frate Ignoto'*/Sozzi (Alfa Romeo RLSS 22/90, 2,994cc)
71	Franco Cortese/Baroncini (Itala Tipo 61 1,991cc)
99	Pugno/Bergia (Lancia Lambda, 2,370cc)

Minoia, partnered by Morandi, won the 1927 Mille Miglia with this OM, seen flat-out on the Raticosa Pass. While Minoia concentrates on his driving, Morandi has the time to wave to spectators. It was a fine victory, but the Alfa Romeo opposition was much weaker than it would be during the next few years. This OM had a lower, more tapered radiator than the other cars of the marque entered in this race. (Author's Collection)

*One can do no better than quote Hull and Slater: "Count Lurani tells us that 'Frate Ignoto' was not really a friar, but the pseudonym hid the identity of none other than the famous pioneer Arturo Mercanti, airman, automobile driver and great organiser. Mercanti was the man who 'invented' Monza Circuit and Track, which was built in the incredibly short time of 100 days in 1922. Mercanti was killed in action in the Abyssinian War in 1936 and was awarded [posthumously] a gold military medal."

The story is that Mercanti had opposed the Mille Miglia because he believed that it would draw attention away from Monza. His entry for the Mille Miglia was less than popular with certain elements of the Fascisti and hence the pseudonym. In fact the use of an obvious pseudonym was a discreet manner for him to apologise for the error of his ways! He continued to use the pseudonym in the Mille Miglia for many years. There is obviously some confusion because a 'Frate Ignoto' competed in the 1954 race.

In the first two Mille Miglia races four-seater bodywork was compulsory and so, in appearance, at least the cars looked like touring models. Outside Italy there was little awareness of the first Millie Miglia and, for example, *The Autocar* and *The Motor* devoted only a half-page to their reports of the race. Entrants (and the organisers) were very uncertain about how long the cars would take to cover the course and in reality had no idea about likely tyre consumption. There was difficulty in following the course, as at many points it was not clearly marked. This first race was very much an experiment and not just the condition of the roads, but the standards of organisation improved with the passing of the years.

Without doubt the Alfa Romeo team believed itself to be certain to win the race with its lightweight, tuned

The RLSS of Marinoni/Ramponi has just reached the summit of the Raticosa Pass; they ran well, but retired 120 miles (193km) before the finish. Road conditions were truly appalling. This photograph shows the beautiful, balanced, classic lines of this four-seater tourer. (Author's Collection)

OMs built in Brescia took the first three places in 1927, but in fourth place came this special Lancia Lambda with shortened wheelbase and tuned engine, driven by Strazza/Varallo. It crossed the finishing line 38 minutes behind the winner and, in Mille Miglia terms, the leading cars were quite closely grouped at the finish. (Spitzley-Zagari Collection)

RLSS cars, very elegant and developed by Ing Rimini; they were reckoned to be capable of close to 90mph (145kph). The side-valve OMs, however, were to provide unexpectedly stiff opposition. The six Lancia Lambdas were very short-chassis special cars capable of 80mph (129kph), powerful enough to turn in an impressive performance, even if not capable of winning the race. Other runners included a team of works-entered 3-litre Ansaldos in standard tune, but they were uncompetitive.

The 2.3-litre Bianchi works cars were also to standard specification and not likely to challenge for the lead. Among the drivers for this team was the young and inexperienced Tazio Nuvolari. Nor were the four-cylinder Diattos serious contenders for success. Suggestions that at least one of the cars was an experimental eight-cylinder (that is a touring version of the Maserati-designed 1926 Grand Prix car) seem to have been without foundation. Later in 1927 the economic conditions caught up with Diatto and production ceased.

In the 1,500cc class there were five Ceiranos and these faced little opposition, apart from a Type 40 Bugatti that was to score an unexpected success in the class. In the 1,100cc class the overhead camshaft Fiat 509s faced little opposition apart from two side-valve Amilcars, two SAMs and young Luigi Fagioli's Salmson. The SAMs were built by Societa Automobili e Motori in Legnano, Milan and were available in both side-valve and overhead-valve form. They were sports cars more in the style of contemporary French models, but did not sell well and were built only between 1924 and 1928.

The cars left the start in descending order of engine capacity, so the 7.3-litre Isotta Fraschini was first away from the start in the Piazza Vittorio at 8am. In excellent weather conditions the Alfa Romeos set the pace on the fast section between Brescia and Bologna. At Bologna the order was Brill Peri/Presenti leading Minoia/Morandi and Marinoni/Ramponi. Then it was over the Raticosa and Futa Passes and into Rome where Brilli Peri still led.

Soon it became obvious that all was not well with the leading Alfa Romeo. As the cars raced over the Somma Pass between Terni and Spoleto this RLSS developed an engine misfire and it retired at Spoleto. The actual cause of their retirement was engine seizure following the dislodgement through vibration of an oil pipe in the sump. The scales now tipped in favour of OM, with Minoia/Mirandi 11min ahead of team-mates T. Danieli/Balestrero. Then came the Alfa Romeo of Marinoni/Ramponi and in fourth place was the OM of M. Danieli/Rosa.

As night enveloped the race and the cars streamed northwards along the Adriatic coast, spectators along the route lit torches to help drivers follow the course. This was to become a Mille Miglia tradition. With more than 20 hours under their belts and very close to the finish, the Alfa Romeo of Marinoni/Ramponi retired. The exhaust pipe had sagged on to the final drive and this resulted in overheating of the final drive and transmission failure.

The OMs were now unchallenged and took first three places ahead of two Lancias. Strazza/Varallo, who finished fourth, were the first to complete the course and during the race had changed six tyres. Of the ten Lambdas entered, seven completed the course. In sixth place were Count Maggi and Bindo Maserati (the second oldest of the Maserati brothers born in 1883) with the Isotta Fraschini which they had refuelled 11 times. Maggi

Count Aymo Maggi, one of the founders of the race, drove this luxurious straight-eight 7.3-litre Tipo 8A Isotta Fraschini, partnered by Bindo Maserati, who was still chief test driver for Isotta. Sixth place established that this big, lolloping car, with its high fuel consumption and three-speed gearbox, was not a suitable mount for the Mille Miglia. (Spitzley-Zagari Collection)

had believed that the 90mph (145kph) Isotta would have good prospects of success when the lightweight competition cars fell by the wayside. In fact this approach, as the results reveal, was totally wrong.

'Frate Ignoto'/Sozzi were the first Alfa Romeo drivers to finish, in seventh place. Eighth was the 2-litre Itala of young Franco Cortese and Baroncini. This and the other two Itala team cars were outpaced by the Alfa Romeo and OM opposition. Built in Turin, the Itala Tipo 61 was a handsome beast with six-cylinder, seven main-bearing engine and four-speed gearbox. Tipo 61s sold in insufficient numbers and a 21-million lire loss in 1929 hastened the company's demise. In the 1960s there were a couple of these cars in the UK and the one that the writer drove was a very satisfactory piece of machinery.

Still very much the apprentice racing driver, Nuvolari's tenth-place with an underpowered 2.3-litre, 59bhp Bianchi 20 was not a bad result. Fiat Tipo 519s took first two places in the 5,000cc class. These were very uninspiring 4.8-litre six-cylinder cars with flat radiators and hydro-mechanical, servo-assisted brakes that were in production from about 1921 through to 1929.

In the 1,500cc class Binda/Belgir drove a magnificent race with their Type 40 Bugatti, finishing 12th overall, winning the class and beating the leading Ceirano by just over ten minutes. The Peugeots that won the 750cc class were the 719cc Quadrilette model that had first appeared shortly after the end of the First World War with fixed L-head 668cc engines. The class-winner spent almost 1½ days on the road.

Results:
General classification:

1st	F. Minoia/Morandi (OM),	21hr 4min 48 sec (47.99mph/77.22kph)
2nd	T. Danieli/Balestrero (OM),	21hr 20min 53sec
3rd	M. Danieli/Rosa (OM),	21hr 28min 27sec
4th	Strazza/Varallo (Lancia Lambda),	21hr 42min 48sec
5th	Pugno/Bergia (Lancia Lambda),	21hr 55min 14sec
6th	Count A. Maggi/B. Maserati (Isotta Fraschini Tipo A),	22hr 0min 35sec
7th	'Frate Ignoto'/Sozzi (Alfa Romeo RLSS),	22hr 6min 11sec
8th	Cortese/Baroncini (Itala Tipo 61),	22hr 45min 00sec
9th	Guttermann/Nunaron (Alfa Romeo RLSS),	22hr 53min 57sec
10th	Nuvolari/Capelli (Bianchi 20),	23hr 12min 2sec

Class results:

750cc: Cazzulani/Moneferroi (Peugeot Quadrilette), 33hr 51min 33sec (29.8mph/47.9kph)
1,100cc: Moali/Ferrari (Fiat 509), 22hr 23min 41sec (41.4mph/66.61kph)
1,500cc: Binda/Belgir (Bugatti Type 40), 23hr 18min 23sec (43.3mph/69.7kph)
2,000cc: Minoia/Morandi (OM Tipo 665), 21hr 4 min 48sec (47.9mph/77.22kph)
3,000cc: Strazza/Varallo (Lancia Lambda), 21hr 42min 48sec (46.5mph/74.8kph)
5,000cc: Silvani/Minozzi (Fiat 519), 24hr 52min 54sec (40.7mph/65.5kph)
8,000cc: Count A. Maggi/B. Maserati (Isotta Fraschini Tipo 8A), 22hr 0 min 35sec (45.8mph/73.7kph)

1928

31 March-1 April
Starters: 83; Finishers: 40; Distance: 1018 miles (1,638km).
Circuit: See page 242.
Weather: fine, dry throughout.

Main contenders for victory:

21	Carlo Tonini/Luigi Parenti (Maserati Tipo 26, 1,493cc)
25	Bruno Presenti/Canavesi (Alfa Romeo 6C 1500 Turismo 1,487cc)
26	Attilio Marinoni/Batista Guidotti (Alfa Romeo 6C 1500 Turismo, 1,487cc)
30	Giuseppe Campari/Giulio Ramponi (Alfa Romeo 6C 1500 Super Sport 1,487cc)
33	Bornigia/Guatta (Alfa Romeo 6C 1500 Turismo 1,487cc)
39	Count Aymo Maggi/Ernesto Maserati (Maserati Tipo 26B 1,980cc)
44	Giuseppe Morandi/Vincenzo Coffani (OM Tipo 665 Superba 1,991cc)
51	Franco Cortese/Ciffi (Itala Tipo 61, 1,991cc)
61	Archimede Rosa/Franco Mazzotti (OM Tipo 665 Superba, 1,991cc)
63	Ferruccio Radice/Lissoni (Lancia Lambda 2,370cc)
66	Scarfiotti/Lasagna (Lancia Lambda, 2,370cc)
70	Gildo Strazza/Varallo (Lancia Lambda, 2,370cc)
71	Gismondi/Valsania (Lancia Lambda, 2,370cc)
83	Count Gastone Brilli Peri/Lumini (Bugatti Type 43 2,262cc)
84	Tazio Nuvolari/Bignami (Bugatti Type 43 2,262cc)
85	Pietro Bordino/De Gioannini (Bugatti Type 43 2,262cc)

The list of serious contenders in the 1928 race was substantial and was a reflection of the success of the 1927 event. Alfa Romeo had now entered a team of eight of the latest Vittorio Jano-designed six-cylinder cars. The main difference between the 6C 1500s raced by the factory and the production cars was that the competition cars had the engine set back in the frame about eight inches to increase traction. The Campari/Ramponi car was an experimental version with single Memini carburettor and a Rootes-type supercharger. There had been little opportunity to test this car and there were doubts about its endurance.

The entry of the Bugattis was especially interesting and these were Type 43 cars that combined a slightly shorter version of the Type 38 touring car chassis and other mechanical components with the supercharged 2,262cc engine of the Type 35B Grand Prix car. These cars first appeared in 1927, they were intended for long-distance sporting events and fast touring, and maximum speed was 100mph (161kph). There is little doubt that

By 1928, Ing. Vittorio Jano's 6C 1500 twin overhead camshaft engines were ready to race. This car, driven by Campari/Ramponi, was fitted with a supercharger and won by a tight margin of just under eight minutes from the OM of Rosa/Mazzotti. (Spitzley-Zagari Collection)

OM had been optimistic about winning the race for the second time in 1928, but the 'Superba' was no longer a match for the Alfa Romeo opposition. Morandi/Coffani, seen here on the unmetalled streets of Modena, drove this car into tenth place.

Pietro Bordino is seen with the Type 43 Bugatti that he drove in the 1928 race. He fell out of contention because of brake problems and an engine misfire. Note the covers over the headlamps and spotlights. These did not, of course, protect against stone damage as effectively as the celluloid covers introduced the following year by Alfa Romeo. (Author's Collection)

the Bugatti factory was disappointed by the poor showing of these cars and no full team from Molsheim ever ran in the race again.

In addition to the three works OMs, there were ten private cars, again a reflection of the success of the marque the previous year. Another make entered in substantial numbers was Lancia and a total of 15 Lambdas was entered. One was driven by two of the Benelli brothers (there were six brothers who had started building Benelli motorcycles just before the First World War).

Despite his disdain for other forms of motor racing, Vincenzo Lancia was very enthusiastic about the Mille

Miglia, mainly because of the close link between the competing cars and standard production models. In January 1928 he had accompanied Lancia test driver Gildo Strazza on a complete lap of the circuit. Strazza was said to be Vincenzo Lancia's favourite test driver.

Young Achille Varzi was at the wheel of another private Bugatti. Among other, later well-known drivers, Franco Cortese led an Itala team as in 1927 and at this stage the Itala company thought that it could do very well with these 2-litre cars designed by ex-Fiat engineer Ing Cappa. Luigi Fagioli again drove his French Salmson, but he was young and inexperienced and stood very little chance against the Fiat 509s.

Two American makes, La Salle (a new marque introduced in 1927 by General Motors as a cheaper alternative to Cadillac) and Chrysler contested the race. They believed that the very considerable potential for sales in Europe could be exploited by competition success and teams of both Chrysler and Stutz had already contested the Le Mans 24 Hours race. The Chryslers were of especial interest as they had hydraulic braking on all four wheels. Unfortunately, these big heavy cars were not suitable for the race and performed badly.

Initially the Bugattis set the pace in the 1928 race and at Bologna the leader was Nuvolari, five minutes ahead of Brilli Peri, and then came Bordino. Next was Campari (Alfa Romeo), two Lancias, Morandi (OM), another Lancia and the Chrysler of Materassi. It had become obvious at this early stage in the race that OM had lost the margin of supremacy that it had possessed in 1927.

Despite their greater speed, the Bugattis ran into mechanical problems; both Nuvolari and Bordino ran out of brakes and were delayed while new shoes were fitted. All three cars suffered from engine misfires that necessitated plug changes, and Brilli Peri's car started to overheat. By Rome the Bugattis had ceased to be a threat and although Brilli Peri was still running strongly, he had lost too much ground. Campari/Ramponi now led from Lancia test driver and development engineer Gismondi partnered by Valsania; Gismondi had driven a fast and furious race to bring himself through to a position in which he could challenge for the lead.

Campari still led as the cars reached Bologna for the second time and Gismondi was only three minutes behind. After a comparatively slow race up until this point, Rosa (OM) began his charge, albeit too late to win the race, but he finished second after the retirement of Gismondi's Lancia. All three Bugattis finished, but apart from Brilli Peri they were way down the field. Although Minoia/Balestrero won the 5,000cc class, the American entries were generally unsuccessful. They were 'soft' touring cars and not really suitable for an event of this kind.

Maserati made its first appearance in the Mille Miglia in 1928. Count Maggi/Ernesto Maserati drove a 2-litre straight-eight car, while this 1.5-litre car was driven by Bruno Tonini/Luigi Parenti. The 2-litre car retired but, despite mechanical problems, Tonini and Parenti finished the race, albeit in 23rd place. (Spitzley-Zagari Collection)

The Maserati of Tonini/Parenti finished well down the field in 23rd position. Although never in the lead, Ernesto Maserati had set a good pace with the 2-litre Bologna car, but this retired early because of unknown mechanical problems. Overall, the leading cars were much more tightly bunched at the finish than in 1927.

Results

General classification:

1st	Campari/G. Ramponi (Alfa Romeo), 19hr 14min 5sec (52.2mph/84.0kph)
2nd	Rosa/Mazzotti (OM), 19hr 22min 0sec
3rd	Strazza/Varallo (Lancia), 19hr 37min 37sec
4th	Marinoni/Guidotti (Alfa Romeo), 19hr 38min 13sec
5th	Bornigia/Guatta (Alfa Romeo), 19hr 42min 0sec
6th	Brilli Peri/Lumini (Bugatti), 19hr 45min 44sec
7th	Scarfiotti/Lasagna (Lancia), 19hr 52min 2sec
8th	Presenti/Canavesi (Alfa Romeo), 20hr 10min 55sec
9th	Radice/Lissoni (Lancia), 20hr 13min 17sec
10th	Morandi/Coffani (OM), 20hr 26min 4sec

Class Results:

1,100cc:	Gilera/Menenti (Fiat 509), 23hr 59min 2sec (41.8mph/67.3kph)
1,500cc:	Campari/Ramponi (Alfa Romeo), 19hr 14min 5sec (52.2mph/84.0kph)
2,000cc:	Rosa/Mazzotti (OM), 19hr 22min 0sec (51.6mph/83.0kph)
3,000cc:	Strazza/Varallo (Lancia), 19hr 37min 37sec (51.1mph/82.2kph)
5,000cc:	Minoia/Balestrero (La Salle), 21hr 17min 24sec (47.5mph/76.4kph)

Brescia Grand Prix (team prize):

Presenti/Canavesi, Marinoni/Guidotti, Marcinello/Bruno (Alfa Romeo)

1929

13–14 April
Starters: 72; Finishers: 44; Distance: 1,018miles (1,638km).
Circuit: see page 242.
Weather: heavy showers at the start, but later fine and dry.

Main contenders for victory:

37	Ernesto Maserati/Baconin Borzacchini (Maserati Tipo 26B 1,980cc)
39	Giuseppe Campari/Giulio Ramponi (Alfa Romeo 6C 1750 Gran Sport 1,752cc)
41	Gismondi/Valsania (Lancia Lambda, 2,570cc)
42	Ferdinando Minoia/Attilio Marinoni (Alfa Romeo 6C 1750 Gran Sport 1,752cc)
46	Count Aymo Maggi/Count Franco Mazzotti (OM Tipo 665 Superba 2,221cc)
47	Count G. Brilli Peri/Canavesi (Alfa Romeo 6C 1750 Gran Sport 1,752cc)
61	Giuseppe Morandi/Archimede Rosa (OM Tipo 665 Superba 1,991cc supercharged)
73	Achille Varzi/Colombo (Alfa Romeo 6C 1750 Gran Sport 1,752cc)
75	G. Foresti/Coffani (OM Tipo 665 Superba 1,991cc supercharged)
79	Gildo Strazza/Varallo (Lambda 2,370cc)
83	Truco/Cip (Lancia Lambda 2,370cc)
84	Luigi Arcangeli/Bassi (OM Tipo 65 Superba 2,221cc)
85	Tazio Nuvolari/Greggio (OM Tipo 665 Superba 1,991cc supercharged)
86	Pietro Ghersi/Guerrini (OM Tipo 65 Superba 2,221cc)
90	Scarfiotti/Lasagna (Lancia Lambda 2,570cc)
102	Franco Bornigia/Carlo Pintacuda (Alfa Romeo 6C 1750 Gran Sport 1,752cc)

This is a line-up of the works 6C 1750 Alfa Romeos entered in the 1929 race. Photographed at the Portello factory are (from left) the cars of Pintacuda/Bornigia, Cortese/Guatta, Campari/Ramponi (the winners), Pirola/Guidotti and Varzi/Colombo. It has not been possible to identify the drivers of the car nearest the camera. (Centro Documentazione Alfa Romeo)

Although the number of starters was down – and lower than that in the first race – the number of entries had risen to 108, but there were 27 non-starters. The cause is not entirely clear, but economic conditions in Italy were worsening, just as in the rest of Europe, and it is likely that a number of companies and individuals decided that they could not afford to run in the race.

Alfa Romeo offered a special, subsidised preparation service for entrants of their cars and this proved very popular – the result was that more than 25 per cent of the starters were Alfa Romeos. Likewise around 25 per cent of the starters were Fiat 509As, still quite an advanced design and destined to dominate the results in the 1,100cc class.

By 1929 Alfa Romeo was racing the Jano-designed 6C 1750 cars with 1,752cc (62 x 88mm) engine and a power output of 105bhp. These latest competition versions had a fixed cylinder head cast with the block (Testa Fissa), which eliminated the problem of gasket failure, but also allowed the use of a higher compression ratio. They were fitted with Roots-type superchargers, while the three 'back-up' 6C 1750s were unsupercharged. Twenty 6C 1500 and 6C 1750 cars ran in the race, the majority prepared at the works.

All works-prepared cars had three main headlamps, of which the outer headlamps turned slightly outwards so as to broaden the area caught by the lights, while a central headlamp was set up to achieve maximum depth of vision. All three headlamps had wire-mesh grilles to prevent glass damage by stones thrown from the still dreadful roads, unmetalled for much of the race distance. These cars also had for the first time half-sphere red celluloid covers that fitted over the headlamps during the daytime.

Jano's six-cylinder (and, later, eight-cylinder) cars were the product of a steady development at Portello and Alfa Romeo richly deserved the many successes that they achieved. In contrast OM, still struggling to regain superiority in the race, was to bodge ad hoc modifications that turned the standard sweet-handling cars into ill-handling brutes that were too powerful for the chassis. In all there were nine OMs in the race, of which three 1,991cc supercharged models were works cars and three 2,221cc unblown cars were works-supported. Like the Alfa Romeos, the OMs had celluloid headlamp covers.

There were 13 Lancia Lambdas, of which four were works-entered, in fact if not name. As in the previous year, with 85bhp and a maximum speed of 90mph (145kph), they were strong contenders for good placings, but unlikely to win. Although there was also a mixed bag of Bugatti, Buick, Lorraine-Dietrich and Voisin entries, the only other serious contender was the Maserati Tipo 26B of Baconin Borzacchini/Ernesto Maserati.

The starting arrangements had changed and now the small-capacity cars started first and the first was away at 11am. The cars left at three-minute intervals, save where there was a non-starter and there was an additional pause of three minutes for each. The late start in the morning meant of course that all the competitors had to drive for longer in the dark towards the end of the race than would have been the case with an early start.

After the 22 cars in the 1,100cc class had departed, the organisers had a break of, supposedly, half an hour (it was in fact 34 minutes) before the next classes started at one-minute intervals. It was not long before disaster struck one of the competitors and after only five miles the Baroness Avanzo overturned her Alfa Romeo.

Initially, Borzacchini/Maserati set the pace, but few spectators were confident that the Tipo 26B would last the distance. They averaged close to 80mph (129kph) on the fast stretch to Bologna where they had a lead of four minutes over Campari and then came Varzi, Brilli Peri, Bornigia, Morandi (OM) and Strazza (Lancia). Already some well-known names were out of the race: Maggi/Mazzotti had retired their OM because of transmission problems and Nuvolari had gone off the road with his OM.

By Rome the Maserati still led by four minutes from Campari/Ramponi and then came Minoia/Marinoni some 20 minutes behind. Varzi had lost 40 minutes because of a small on-board fire, while Brilli Peri was out because of valve trouble. Borzacchini was pushing hard to increase his lead, but as he was approaching Terni the gearbox failed. So at Ancona the leaders were Campari/Ramponi 22 minutes ahead of Strazza/Varallo (Lancia). Minoia/Morandi had lost their second place after a collision with an Alsatian dog and apart from damaged front and bonnet, they were delayed while the

Alfa Romeo won for the second year in succession and the winners were Giuseppe Campari and Giulio Ramponi at the wheel of this 6C 1750. The car had a body by Zagato and, for the first time, Alfa Romeo used the distinctive red celluloid covers to protect the headlamp glass. The 6C 1750 is seen in dreadful weather and appalling road conditions on the Raticosa Pass. (Author's Collection)

front axle was repaired (some sources say, rather improbably, replaced).

When the cars passed through Bologna for the second time on the return leg of the race, Campari/Ramponi had held on to their lead of 22 minutes, but Morandi/Rosa in second place with their OM were starting to make a late charge; Strazza/Varallo were still in third place and, fourth on time, Varzi/Colombo were steadily catching up after their earlier problem and were now 36 minutes behind the leading Alfa Romeo. The race still had dramas before the finish and Campari/Ramponi were delayed by two punctures.

At the finish they were still ten minutes ahead as they took the flag for their second successive victory in this race. Morandi/Rosa finished second and so, if OM was down, it was certainly not out. After setting record after record along the various sectors of the course from Bologna onwards, Varzi/Colombo took third place overall. Campari/Ramponi were over an hour faster than in 1928, a feat attributable in the main to the greater speed of the 6C 1750 Alfa Romeos, but also to a small improvement in the atrocious Italian roads. The first eight cars to finish had all beaten the 1928 winning speed.

Especial heroes in 1929 were Tamburi/Ricceri who crashed their class-leading Fiat 509 into the parapet of a

Although an OM took second place, Achille Varzi, partnered by Colombo, drove this 6C 1750 to third place, 12 minutes behind the winner, but only two minutes behind Morandi/Rosa with the OM. Winter is just over and in the Italian mountains the snow is still heaped up by the roadside. (Spitzley-Zagari Collection)

bridge not much more than a mile from the finish. They were victims of an excess of enthusiasm, coupled with sheer exhaustion after a full 24 hours of racing. Both car and drivers were severely battered, but with the help and support of spectators, they were able to trundle to the finish to win the 1,100cc class from another Fiat 509 by just under eight minutes.

One commentator, F. A. Shepley, wrote in *The Autocar*, "As late as April 6th the roads at Gubbio, on the course [north of Perugia and on the road to Ancona], were impassable, and cars endeavouring to force a way through were blocked by the snow and had to be dug out. In some parts during the race the roads were atrocious, due to rain, while some of the mountain passes are nothing but semi-deserted tracks of land where hairpin bends have been scattered in heedless prodigality." However deplorable the roads were, they were gradually improved during the years that the race was held and a major factor causing their improvement was the holding of the race.

Results:

General classification:
1st	Campari/Ramponi (Alfa Romeo),	18hr 4min 25sec (55.73mph/89.67kph)
2nd	Morandi/Rosa (OM),	18hr 14min 14sec
3rd	Varzi/Colombo (Alfa Romeo),	18hr 16min 14sec
4th	Strazza/Varallo (Lancia),	18hr 17min 41sec
5th	Ghersi/Guerrini (OM),	18hr 55min 8 sec
6th	Minoia/Marinoni (Alfa Romeo),	19hr 1min 44sec
7th	Natale/Zampiera (Alfa Romeo),	19hr 4min 37sec
8th	Carraroli/Munaron (Alfa Romeo),	19hr 7min 42sec
9th	Cortese/Guatta (Alfa Romeo),	19hr 16min 47 sec
10th	Bornigia/Pintacuda (Alfa Romeo),	19hr 17min 17sec

Class results:
1,100cc: Tamburi/Ricceri (Fiat 509), 24hr 13min 32sec (41.59mph/66.92kph)
1,500cc: Pirola/Guidotti (Alfa Romeo), 19hr 40min 36sec (51.20mph/82.38kph)
2,000cc: Campari/Ramponi (Alfa Romeo), 18hr 4min 25sec (55.74mph/89.69kph)
3,000cc: Strazza/Varallo (Lancia), 18hr 17min 41sec (55.07mph/88.60kph)
5,000cc: Leonardi/Barbieri (Chrysler), 22hr 43min 25sec (44.33mph/71.33kph)

Brescia Grand Prix (team prize):
Campari/Ramponi, Minoia/Marinoni, Priola/Guidotti (Alfa Romeo)

Opposite: At the 1929 Mille Miglia, Baconin Borzacchini and Ernesto Maserati led as far as Terni, shortly after Rome, when the gearbox on their Maserati failed. (Officine Alfieri Maserati)

1930

16–17 April
Starters: 135; Finishers: 73; Distance: 1,018 miles (1,638km).
Circuit: see page 242.
Weather: fine and dry until the final stages when heavy rain fell.

Main contenders for victory:

69	Giuseppe Campari/Attilio Marinoni (Alfa Romeo 6C 1750 Gran Sport, 1,752cc)
74	Achille Varzi/Canavesi (Alfa Romeo 6C 1750 Gran Sport, 1,752cc)
84	Tazio Nuvolari/Battista Guidotti (Alfa Romeo 6C 1750 Gran Sport, 1,752cc)
138	Count Franco Mazzotti/Count Aymo Maggi (Alfa Romeo 6C 1750 Gran Sport, 1,752cc)
	(All the above were entered by the works, but there was an additional and less competitive team entered by the newly formed Scuderia Ferrari)
71	Ferdinando Minoia/Giuseppe Morandi (OM Tipo 665 Superba, 2,327cc supercharged)
80	Archimede Rosa/Coffani (OM Tipo 665 Superba, 2,327cc supercharged)
101	Gildo Strazza/Gismondi (Lancia Lambda, 2,570cc)
118	Bassi/Gazzabini (OM Tipo 665 Superba, 2,327cc supercharged)
128	Rudolf Caracciola/Christian Werner (Mercedes-Benz SSK, 7,069cc supercharged)
150	Luigi Arcangeli/Pastore (Maserati Tipo 26B, 1,980cc)

These 12 Alfa Romeos, lined up at Portello before the 1930 race, belonged to private owners. All had been prepared at the works and they were in receipt of full works support during the race. (Centro Documentazione Alfa Romeo)

Despite a greater number of entries, there were few serious challengers to Alfa Romeo supremacy and even the OMs were no longer able to put up much of a fight. Despite this, there were no fewer than 23 OM entries. The only car capable of challenging the Portello entries was the Maserati, which was reckoned to have a maximum speed of 112mph (180kph), and the Mercedes-Benz in its 1930 form was simply not quick enough. This was not clear until after the race and it was seen very much as a dark horse, the potential of which was unclear.

The SSK was without doubt very fast, but it was also very heavy, the handling was ponderous and its reliability in such an arduous event was an unknown factor. What in fact Mercedes-Benz was doing was to make a trial entry and to use the experience gained in a serious challenge in 1931. Other entries came from Ceirano, Chrysler, Itala and Jordan. The last-named was a now-forgotten marque built in Cleveland, Ohio, between 1916 and 1931 when the company became a victim of the Great Depression. It is believed that the car that ran in this race was the 5.3-litre straight-eight Speedway model.

Because the most competitive cars were highly modified, the organisers included a class for 'utilitarian cars' and this helped to boost the number of starters. These had to be standard production cars (of which at least 50 had been built before the race); they had to have standard bodywork and unmodified engines of greater than 1,100cc in capacity and to cost no more than

Left: *The starter at the 1930 race, believed to be the Duke of Spoleto, President of the Royal Italian Automobile Club.* (LAT)

Above: *The Fiat 509 of Savelli/Nardi has just crossed the famous pontoon bridge over the River Po at Casalmaggiore. Note the sign 'PASSAGIO PERICOLOSO' (dangerous causeway). This car finished 70th.* (Author's Collection)

Below: *Seen before the start of the race are the eventual winners, Tazio Nuvolari and Batista Guidotti, with their special works 6C 1750 with larger than standard supercharger, fixed cylinder head, strengthened chassis and Zagato body.* (Centro Documentazione Alfa Romeo)

Sixty-two mph for 1,000 miles on the road

An Interview with Tazio Nuvolari, the Winner of the Classic Italian Event (Reproduced from The Motor *of 22 April 1930)*

When some of the applause had died down and Tazio Nuvolari, the winner of the Italian 1,000-mile race which finished at Brescia last Sunday week, was seated in the café at the finishing point, surrounded by a group of admirers, we succeeded in evading the watchful eyes of the gendarmes and crossed the finishing enclosure in order to offer our congratulations.

We found a young man, sunburnt, dirty, and with the dust of 30 provinces of Italy still matting his eyebrows and lying deep in the wrinkles about his eyes and mouth. He looked remarkably fresh; indeed, one would have thought that he had not done anything more strenuous than participating in a 24-hour reliability trial. Yet he had actually covered over 1,018 miles in 16hr 18min 59sec, equal to a speed of 62.41mph [The writer reckons 62.43mph] over ordinary roads left open to the public and including all stops for replenishment and refreshment and the natural difficulties caused by dense clouds of dust and several hours driving in the dark.

"It was a good race," Nuvolari told us, "and from Rome onwards I never had any doubt that I should win. The car was wonderful and never gave a moment's trouble. I could have driven it much faster had I wished to do so. The hardest part of the race for me," he continued, "was when Signor Jano locked me up in a room at Bologna on the return journey and compelled me to rest for five minutes or more and had me washed and fed. I was in such a frenzy

24,000 lire (the equivalent of £270). There were 17 cars in this class, the majority being Fiat 514As with 37bhp engine, wire-spoked wheels and open two-seater bodywork. Also running in the class, however, were two Bianchi S.5s in sports form and six four-cylinder Citroën roadsters.

Of the scene in Brescia before the start of the race, *The Motor's* Special Representative wrote, "Saturday came, and with it hot, drowsy weather, with the sun half veiled by the haze. The starting point, half a mile from the heart of Brescia, was a section of road closed to the public, and barricaded each end with an imposing gateway made to the best Drury Lane standard of painted canvas and wood. Black-shirted Fascisti soldiers in field grey, smartly uniformed policemen and gendarmes in swallow-tailed coats, cocked hats and much silver braid, kept all trespassers severely away from the select enclosure."

At 11am before the first car left, tribute was paid to Brilli Peri, who had been killed a week before the race while practising with Materassi's Talbot for the Tripoli Grand Prix. Then first the Utility class and subsequently the 1,100cc class left at minute intervals. The first starter left three minutes after the hour. When the last 1,100cc car had departed at 12 noon, the starter broke off and everyone, officials and competitors alike, went off for lunch. The departure of the cars resumed at 1pm and the last 43 starters were dispatched at half-minute intervals.

The big guns set a cracking pace and at Bologna Arcangeli, who had averaged 87mph (140kph), led by 13 seconds from Nuvolari, a further 18 seconds behind was Caracciola, then Varzi and Campari. It was significant that the fastest OM, driven by Rosa/Coffani, was in an unpromising sixth place and that Minoia/Morandi, the most rated of the drivers of the Brescia-built cars, were already out because of a cracked supercharger casing. By the time that the leaders reached Florence, Arcangeli had retired the Maserati because of a broken piston and the Mercedes was dropping back on worsening roads.

So the Alfa Romeo supremacy was becoming increasingly dominant; Varzi reached Rome in exactly six hours at an average of 64mph (103kph) and at this stage led Nuvolari by one minute, with Campari/Marinoni ten minutes behind the leader. Ghersi/Cortese with a Scuderia Ferrari-entered Alfa Romeo held fourth place. Ing Vittorio Jano directed the works cars from Rome and according to *The Motor*, "So afraid was [Jano] that his three drivers would start scrapping among themselves for first place, that with pardonable duplicity he told Varzi that he was winning and could therefore slacken his speed a trifle."

After the race Varzi complained that he had been misled in this way, but it is rather mysterious because he had been leading at Rome, albeit only by a margin of one minute. It may be that Jano exaggerated the extent of

After that first victory in 1927, OM gradually faded in importance and Alfa Romeo became dominant. Here are the 1930 winners, Tazio Nuvolari partnered by Batista Guidotti (later Alfa Romeo racing manager) with their 6C 1750. They are on the stretch of road shortly after Florence. For the first time, the winners' speed topped 100kph and they averaged 100.45kph (62.43mph). (Author's Collection)

to get off that I almost fought with the pit attendants. I was much too excited to listen to the arguments that I had the race in the hollow of my hand and could afford to take it easy."

Nuvolari then went on to tell us of the extraordinary good service given by the new buttressed Pirelli tyres which never gave a moment's trouble. He used the same front tyres throughout the race and the rear tyres, which looked absolutely unworn at the finish, were only changed purely as a precaution.

Varzi, who finished second, on another Alfa Romeo, was almost inarticulate with rage when we sought him out. He was furious because all along the route and at every control he had been told that he was leading. He was, in fact, the first of the fast cars to arrive from Rome onwards, but was not actually leading on a time basis, because Nuvolari, who had started ten minutes behind him, was fast catching him up.

However, thinking that he was leading by a very comfortable margin, he slackened speed so as to nurse the engine over the last 100 miles or more, and was horrified suddenly to find Nuvolari on his heels. Insufficient time then remained, however, for him to regain his position, and he had to be content with second place.

Campari arrived looking thoroughly fed up. He would not say much except that he was bitterly disappointed at not winning. Indeed, he seemed almost in tears. He had quite a number of minor and easily remedied troubles which just sufficed to lose him time. Moreover, rounding a bend at considerable speed, he found that owing to the presence of a stationary car, he was unable to take the corner properly and shot off the road. As it was not improbable that there might be similar obstructions round other corners which he might not so luckily escape hitting, he cut down his speed a shade, so that the ultimate result was that he finished third.

In the 1930 Mille Miglia, co-driver Carraroli is seen at the wheel of this Alfa Romeo 6C 1750, while driver Scarfiotti waves to the photographer. Scarfiotti was a member of the Lower Chamber of the Italian Parliament, and the father of works Ferrari driver Ludovico Scarfiotti. (Author's Collection)

Rudolf Caracciola, accompanied by Christian Werner, drove this Mercedes-Benz SSK in the 1930 Mille Miglia. The SSK weighed close to a formidable 4,000lb (1,777kg) and had a power output of around 250bhp. Although Caracciola had proved unbeatable on many circuits with his works SSK, the Mille Miglia made special demands. The Stuttgart team treated the 1930 race as a trial run and Caracciola finished sixth. Note the sheer enormity of the steering wheel. (Spitzley-Zagari Collection)

Varzi's lead and, if he did this, it would have been clear favouritism to Nuvolari. In any event, Nuvolari had the advantage that he started ten minutes after his rival; he could be informed of their relative positions at every control.

As darkness closed in, so Fascisti with torches lined the road at particularly dangerous points and in many villages flares were ignited. Campari was delayed by a collision with a dog (or went off the road to avoid a parked car – take your pick) and, plagued by headlamp failure and other problems Caracciola with the big Mercedes was steadily losing ground. At Ancona, Nuvolari led Varzi by one minute and by the time the leaders passed through Bologna for the second time the gap had increased to seven minutes, mainly because Varzi had to stop to change wheels after two punctures.

By the Sunday morning Nuvolari had gradually closed upon Varzi, still leading on the road and at Feltre swooped past his rival to lead on the road as well as time. Rain had begun to fall and Nuvolari crossed the torrentially wet finishing line just under 11 minutes ahead of his arch-rival. A demoralised Varzi was unable to fight back and settled for second place. OM retained some prestige by a fifth place and a class win, while Caracciola was a disappointed sixth.

Results:

General classification:

1st	Nuvolari/Guidotti (Alfa Romeo), 16hr 18min 59.2 sec (62.43mph/100.45kph)	
2nd	Varzi/Canavesi (Alfa Romeo), 16hr 29min 51.0sec	
3rd	Campari/Marinoni (Alfa Romeo), 16hr 59min 53.6sec	
4th	Ghersi/Cortese (Alfa Romeo), 17hr 16min 31.0sec	
5th	Bassi/Gazzabini (OM), 17hr 18min 34.4sec	
6th	Caracciola/Werner (Mercedes-Benz), 17hr 20min 17.4sec	
7th	Rosa/Coffani (OM), 17hr 22min 58.0sec	
8th	Mazzotti/Maggi (Alfa Romeo), 17hr 46min 45.4sec	
9th	Ferrari/Foresti (Alfa Romeo), 17hr 55min 16.4sec	
10th	Fontanini/Minozzi (Alfa Romeo), 17hr 57min 14.0sec	

Class results:

Utilitarian: Mazza/Pezzoni (Fiat), 23hr 14min 31.0sec (speed not available)
1,100cc: Periccioli/Apollonio (Fiat), 21hr 30min 42.0sec (47.35mph/76.19kph)
1,500cc: Pirola/Guatta (Alfa Romeo), 18hr 30min 46.0sec (55.02mph/88.53kph)
2,000cc: Nuvolari/Guidotti (Alfa Romeo), 16hr 18min 59.2sec (62.43mph/100.45kph)
3,000cc: Bassi/Gazzabini (OM), 17hr 18min 34.4sec (58.85mph/94.69kph)
5,000cc: Leonardi/Barbieri (Chrysler), 21hr 24min 43.0sec (47.56mph/76.52kph)
Over 5,000cc: Caracciola/Werner (Mercedes-Benz), 17hr 20min 17.4sec (58.75mph/94.53kph)

Brescia Grand Prix (team prize):

Varzi/Canavesi, Ghersi/Cortese, Mazzotti/Maggi (Alfa Romeo)

This 2-litre straight-eight Maserati was driven in the 1930 race by Luigi Arcangeli, partnered by Pastore. It was a highly potent Grand Prix car with sports equipment, but retired because of a broken piston. Arcangeli was the leading works Maserati driver in 1930, but he joined Scuderia Ferrari for 1931 and was killed at the wheel of a twin-engined Tipo A car at Monza. (Spitzley-Zagari Collection)

Well, the hood does fit after a fashion. This is the four-cylinder 1,100cc Salmson of Fagioli and Lauri. It was Fagioli's fourth appearance in the race and there were three other four-cylinder 1,100cc Salmsons entered. The car looks decidedly tatty even before the start, and there seems precious little tread on the front tyres. Small wonder it failed to finish. (Author's Collection)

1931

11–12 April
Starters: 99; Finishers: 59; Distance: 1,022 miles (1,644km).
Circuit: see page 243 (slightly modified from 1928–30).
Weather: fine throughout.

Main contenders for victory:

70	Gazzabini/Guatta (Alfa Romeo 6C 1750 Gran Sport Berlinetta, 1,752cc)	
71	Franco Cortese/Balestrieri (Alfa Romeo 6C 1750 Gran Sport Berlinetta, 1,752cc)	
86	Giuseppe Campari/Attilio Marinoni (Alfa Romeo 6C 1750 Grand Sport, 1,752cc)	
87	Rudolf Caracciola/Wilhelm Sebastian (Mercedes-Benz SSKL, 7,069cc supercharged)	
89	Luigi Arcangeli/Bonini (Alfa Romeo 8C 2300 Spider Corsa), 2,336cc	
90	Piero Taruffi/Matrullo (Itala Tipo 61, 1,991cc supercharged)	
102	Giuseppe Morandi/Archimede Rosa (OM Tipo 665 Superba, 2,327cc supercharged)	
104	Tazio Nuvolari/Battista Guidotti (Alfa Romeo 8C 2300 Spider Corsa), 2,336cc	
105	Maino/Gildo Strazza (Mercedes-Benz SSK, 7,069cc supercharged)	
106	Baconin Borzacchini/Eugenio Siena (Alfa Romeo 6C 1750 Gran Sport, 1,752cc)	
135	Achille Varzi/Unknown (Bugatti Type 50, 4,972cc supercharged)	

Caracciola crosses the finishing line at Brescia to win the 1931 race. Caracciola scrawled this message with his signature across the original print. It is very difficult to read, but basically it is a congratulatory note to the organisers. (Author's Collection)

Apparently, the original plan was to run four SSKLs under Neubauer's management, but as only the one appeared at the start, the works team took under its wing the private SSK. At this time Daimler-Benz lacked the finances to fund the sort of racing effort made in later days, so the SSKL duo were on their own for much of the race and had to refuel at roadside garages. In contrast Alfa Romeo had crews at every control and they looked after both the works cars and private entries.

The new 8C 2300 Alfa Romeos are discussed in some detail on pages 42–43, and it suffices to say here that these cars were not yet ready to race and they proved too fast for their Pirelli tyres. They were entered to counter the threat from the SSKL and although they failed in the Mille Miglia, they were soon raceworthy and highly competitive. The Alfa Romeo team also entered four 6C 1750s, two open cars with supercharged engines and two unblown cars with Zagato berlinetta bodies. The total number of Alfa Romeo entries was 32, just short of a third of the starters.

Although there were other apparently potent cars, only Morandi/Rosa with their OM was able to offer a serious challenge for outright victory. Apart from Taruffi's blown Itala, there were a number of near-enough standard Tipo 61s. Both Varzi (whose partner is unknown) and the Baroness Avanzo/Count Castelbarco drove 5-litre Bugatti Type 50s of American Miller

influence in design. These cars had supercharged twin overhead camshaft, straight-eight 4,972cc engines.

They were reckoned to have a power output in excess of 200bhp and a maximum of over 100mph (161kph) in standard form. As raced in the Mille Miglia they were very potent contenders, with the handling, steering and braking to match the sheer performance. The other entries included two Lancia Lambdas of normal engine capacity and one powered by the V8 3,960cc DiLambda engine. The only American runner was a Graham-Paige saloon (strictly speaking known as Graham from 1930) and this is believed to have been the 5.3-litre straight-eight version.

In the smaller-capacity classes there were two cars of especial interest: Tuffanelli raced a straight-eight 1,100cc Maserati with Guerino Bertocchi, the Bologna company's head mechanic as passenger; in addition there was the first ever British entry, the 747cc Austin Seven of Charles Goodacre partnered by Trevisan. It ran in the 1,100cc class in which it gave away 350cc, but it attracted great interest.

The cars did not begin to leave the start until 1pm and once again the Utilitarian class was away first, followed by the other classes in ascending order of capacity. In the Utilitarian class there was a team of blue Bianchis entered by the Italian equivalent of the Flying Squad; the team hoped to do well, but failed to achieve success.

There were a significant number of retirements very early in the race. Varzi's Bugatti had an engine change

OM was still persevering in 1931, even though their moment of glory was long past. Morandi, who had been Minoia's riding mechanic in the 1927 race, was now the driver and he was partnered by Rosa. They took third place on the marque's last works appearance in the Mille Miglia. (Author's Collection)

In a cloud of dust on the unmetalled road, the new 8C 2300 of Luigi Arcangeli, partnered by Bonini, has just swept over the summit of the Futa Pass. In the background is the famous Albergo & Ristorante Futa *at the summit of the Pass. Mainly because of tyre troubles they failed to finish the race. (Author's Collection)*

before the start. "He worked day and night, was wakened from sleep in a nearby café just in time to jump into his seat, and came to a stop with a broken water pipe after covering 12 miles, according to his friends, a broken connecting rod according to his critics." He had lost around 45 seconds at the start because the engine failed to fire up and his maniacal driving may have resulted in premature and terminal engine failure.

Maino proposed to drive his SSK Mercedes for only ten kilometres ("for the sake of his amour propre"), but before he had stopped to hand over to Strazza, "the great white Mercedes" blew a cylinder head gasket and was out of the race. One of the blue flying squad Bianchis crumpled itself against the parapet of a bridge and De Laurentis crashed at the same spot, causing a broken rib for his reserve driver Foresti (there is no way of knowing whether this was the great Jules Foresti who drove Ballots, Bugattis, Sunbeams, et al).

Yet another wheel-change for Nuvolari/Guidotti in the 1931 Mille Miglia. Tyre failures and other problems cost Alfa Romeo the race and this pair eventually finished a poor ninth with their new 8C 2300 car. The engine is running and the headlamps and spot lamp are on while the wheels are changed. (Centro Documentazione Alfa Romeo)

Right from the start Caracciola set a tremendous pace with the SSKL. W. F. Bradley, who had chosen a vantage point on top of the Raticosa Pass, "dominated by the slightly higher Futa Pass, which precedes the descent to Florence", wrote in *The Autocar*: "Dust on the opposite ridge, a few musical notes from a trumpet, a shriek from an exhaust-operated horn, and a white car plunged into the hollow and climbed up to us, with its supercharger in full blast.

"It was Rudolf Caracciola's Mercedes. In 1hr 48min it had covered 158 miles [254km], of which 30 miles consisted of mountain climbing. The car must have gone like the wind, but the impression given by Caracciola as he worked his way along the mountain ridge was that he was driving very cautiously and nursing his tyres. Later information showed that he had made the run of 129 miles [208km] from Brescia to Bologna at an average of 95.8mph [154.1kph] and had beaten last year's record, made by Arcangeli, by eight minutes.

"True, the road comprises some very fast stretches, including the ten-kilometre run near Cremona, on which the world's ten-kilometre record was once established [the 'Sedici Cilindri' 4-litre Maserati of Borzacchini timed in September 1929 at 152.9mph/246.02kph] but there are half a dozen towns, at least a dozen villages, some

particularly nasty turns, and a long pontoon bridge across the River Po."

By the time Caracciola reached Brescia, the Alfa Romeos were already in trouble and in second place, seven minutes behind was the OM of Morandi/Rosa. Behind them came Campari/Marinoni with their six-cylinder Alfa Romeo. The two eight-cylinder Alfa Romeos were next, but they were proving too fast for their Pirelli tyres and frequent stops to change wheels were necessary. Just how many wheel-changes Arcangeli and Nuvolari made is uncertain, but the number was certainly imperial, some sources say nine tyres for the two cars by the time they reached Rome.

According to Bradley, Alfa Romeo switched from Pirelli to Dunlop tyres at Rome. All the Alfa Romeo drivers were under the strictest directions from Jano to drive their hardest to beat the Mercedes-Benz (they needed little encouragement). By Florence, Nuvolari was in second place five minutes behind Caracciola. Caracciola lost ground on the slower sections of the course and Borzacchini, driving on roads that he knew intimately, took the lead by Terni and was still holding it at Perugia ahead of Campari and Arcangeli. By Ancona the order of the Alfa Romeos had changed to Campari-Arcangeli-Borzacchini with Caracciola fourth.

In the early hours of the morning the fastest cars tackled the mist-enveloped plains to the north of Bologna. Caracciola exploited the power of the Mercedes-Benz to the full and by Treviso the German car led once more. Nuvolari had been delayed by clutch trouble, Arcangeli crashed into a wall at Verona and Borzacchini, too, went off the road very close to his team-mate. Running on British Dunlops, Caracciola won the race at a speed 8min 49sec faster than the winner in 1930. Campari finished second and Morandi/Rosa took third place in the OM factory's last attempt in the race. Less than 20 minutes covered the first three cars.

There were few unexpected results in the classes, but two works Zagato-bodied Alfa Romeo berlinettas ran especially well. Gazzabini/Guatta with their 6C 1750 berlinetta took eighth place and won both the closed and unsupercharged categories. Franco Cortese with the second of these very light berlinettas had windscreen wiper failure and had to drive for some distance, sticking his head out of the window to see where he was going. Fiat 514s took the first nine places in the Utilitarian class.

Tuffanelli drove superbly with the little, jewel-like eight-cylinder Maserati to win the 1,100cc class. Remarkably, Goodacre/Trevisan with the Austin Seven finished second in the class, but their time of 21hr 34min 34.2sec was just over 1hr 45min longer than that of the Maserati. Third in this class was a French Rally, a delightful little sports car with a surprisingly exhilarating performance from a maker that died in 1933. The sturdy,

In 1931 the Alfa Romeo works team included two 6C 1750 Sport cars with Zagato berlinetta bodywork. Gazzabini/Guatta drove this car to eighth place overall and wins in both the closed car and unsupercharged categories. (Centro Documentazione Alfa Romeo)

This OM, driven in the 1931 race by Zanmorani/Colla, finished 37th overall. Note the member of the Fascisti and the soldier in the foreground. (Author's Collection)

but sluggish Graham-Paige survived the course to take fifth place in the over 3,000cc class and fourth in the closed-car category.

There was an immense, national difference between the approach of Mercedes-Benz in building the SSKL and that of Jano and his colleagues at Portello. In essence, the SSKL was a much-developed and modified touring car with an engine of sufficient capacity to give it brute-force power. The 8C 2300 represented automobile engineering in its most advanced and sophisticated form and it was one of the greatest cars of all time.

That the German victory shook the Italian public is undoubted, but, in reality, it was in the long-term interests of the race. The Mille Miglia was a very expensive event to stage and it could not have been done without the support of Mussolini's government. It was not a question simply of money, but the immense manpower of Fascisti, military and police required to administer the race and ensure, in relative terms, its safety.

After the defeat by Mercedes-Benz, the race had to continue to give the opportunity for Alfa Romeo to re-assert its supremacy. This victory also encouraged the entry in the race of many more foreign teams, some of which achieved a good measure of success. Mussolini's greatest achievement was not to get the trains to run on time (they never did and still don't), but his successful support for the Mille Miglia.

Results
General Classification:

1st	Caracciola/Sebastian (Mercedes-Benz), 16hr 10min 10sec (63.06mph/101.46kph)	
2nd	Campari/Marinoni (Alfa Romeo), 16hr 21min 17.0sec	
3rd	Morandi/Rosa (OM), 16hr 28min 35.0sec	
4th,	Klinger/Saccomanni (Alfa Romeo), 17hr 7min 57.8sec	
5th	Gerardi/Gerardi (Alfa Romeo), 17hr 8min 6.2sec	
6th	Scarfiotti/Bucci (Alfa Romeo), 17hr 27min 36.4sec	
7th	Tadini/Siena (Alfa Romeo), 17hr 39min 50.0sec	
8th	Gazzabini/Guatta (Alfa Romeo), 17hr 47min 8.0sec	
9th	Nuvolari/Guidotti (Alfa Romeo), 17hr 48min 25.6sec	
10th	Cornaggia/Premoli (Alfa Romeo), 17hr 48min 50.0sec	

Class results:

Utilitarian: Di Liddo/Ricceri (Fiat), 20hr 12min 18sec (50.31mph/80.95kph)

1,100cc: Tuffanelli/Bertocchi (Maserati), 19hr 48min 40sec (51.31mph/82.56kph)

1,500cc: Caniato/Sozzi (Alfa Romeo), 18hr 30min 34.0sec (54.92mph/88.36kph)

2,000cc: Campari/Marinoni (Alfa Romeo), 16hr 21min 17.0sec (62.16mph/100.02kph)

3,000cc: Morandi/Rosa (OM), 16hr 28min 35.0sec (61.69mph/99.26kph)

Over 3,000cc: Caracciola/Sebastian (Mercedes-Benz), 16hr 10min 10.0sec (62.86mph/101.14kph)

Unsupercharged: Gazzabini/Guatta (Alfa Romeo), 17hr 47min 8.0sec (57.15mph/91.95kph)

Closed cars: Gazzabini/Guatta (Alfa Romeo), 17hr 47min 8.0sec (57.15mph/91.95kph)

Charles Goodacre's race with an Austin Ulster

(From an interview conducted by Julian Hunt in 1981)

I was born in Cheshire in 1906 and I joined the Austin Motor Company in 1926. I started straightaway in the experimental department, which was housed in a rat-infested corrugated shed on the old flying ground. It was freezing cold in winter and boiling hot in summer. I remember that in 1931 I was paid 38s 0d per week, plus a bonus of £2 for my job at the experimental car road test centre at Dollgellau in North Wales. On that sort of wages, life was good for a young man out of his apprenticeship.

It was during the middle of 1930, while the mechanics were busy preparing the cars for the Ulster TT to be held on 23 August, Sir Herbert Austin came and told us that he had decided to enter the Mille Miglia to demonstrate to Agnelli of Fiat that the Austin Seven was the best small car in the world. He then set out what he wanted. The car was to be based on the Ulsters being prepared for the TT. Raleigh Appleby and I were to build it and it was to be ready by January.

As prepared for the race, the Mille Miglia Ulster had a roller-bearing, pressure-fed crankshaft, an Austin-modified Number 4 Cozette supercharger gear-driven from the front of the engine and with a 9psi boost. We used a Solex carburettor, a Blic magneto [this company later became Lucas], KLG 356 mica plugs and on a compression ratio of 6:1, power output was 46bhp at 5,000rpm. Maximum revs were 5,800.

There was an alloy body, a 14-gallon fuel tank above the driver's knees and a ten-gallon tank in the tail. The gearbox was the usual three-speed. Maximum speed was about 95mph [153kph] and it was a very flexible and easy car to drive. The car was painted cream with black wings and it had black upholstery. In Italy someone added a third Guertz headlamp between the standard pair.

The car was to be driven out to Italy and the race driver was to travel out nearer the time. On 18 January 1931 I carefully drove the Ulster from Longbridge down to Brighton and the following morning I drove on along the coast to Newhaven in high winds – at one point I thought that I'd be blown off the cliffs. At Newhaven the car was loaded on to SS *Worthing* and the crossing was very rough. It was my first trip abroad and I felt ill all the way across the Channel.

In Dieppe I met Arino and Pino Gandolfi from Mr Nicholls's Rolls-Royce agency in Milan. They had driven from Italy in an unblown Ulster, which I was to take back to Austin's London service department in Oxford Street. So the Gandolfis took the race car through the Simplon Tunnel to

Milan, not exceeding 3,000rpm, which gave 68mph [110kph] and I returned to England with the unblown car.

Back at the Longbridge factory, Sir Herbert sent for me. He told me that he wanted me to go over to drive the car in the race. He said that he couldn't see any point in employing a professional driver, because I had done well as a mechanic in the TT, in the 500-mile race at Brooklands as co-driver to 'Sammy' Davis and in setting a number of records at Brooklands at the end of the season. I would have to travel out two weeks before the race to check the car and make sure that it was in top condition for the race. My co-driver would be Trevisan, an Italian motorcycle racer who had experience of Italian road races.

I travelled out to Italy by train and arrived on Easter Sunday. It was not until the Tuesday that Mr Nicholls arrived, full of apologies after spending the holiday weekend at his villa in the Alps. During the week he lived in a flat above his Rolls-Royce showrooms and he made a good living selling about six cars a year. At Nicholls's premises I met my co-driver Francesco Trevisan. He was a pleasant gentleman and as he spoke a little English and some French, we were able to understand one another.

On test the car would not pull more than 3,500rpm, so I took off the cylinder head. The valves were perfect, but a further look revealed that the pressure relief spring on the supercharger had broken, so I used an inner clutch spring as a replacement. The car was now back to full revs, but when I borrowed a boost gauge it showed 17psi, so it was no surprise that there was a feeling of increased power. We

drove the car down to Bologna as a reconnaissance and we agreed that Trevisan would drive in the mountains and I would take the easier lowland sections of the route.

While I was in Milan, I went to a number of parties and at one of these I met Signore Aldo Giovannini, who was manager of the Alfa Romeo works team and he had been in Ulster for the TT the previous year. Giovannini gave me some advice about the race and urged me to fix minor troubles enough to get to the next control where more help would be available. Alfa Romeo offered a preparation service to all competitors, whether driving Alfas or not, and set up supply pits at all controls where Shell fuel and oil were supplied, plus Pirelli tyres, refreshments and mechanical assistance.

At 1.54 on the hot afternoon of Saturday, 11 April I was at the wheel as the Austin bearing number 50 left Brescia. We planned to change drivers at Bologna, Rome and Ancona. Within five miles the Boyce motometer was boiling, but I could not ease off too much as the Tuffanelli/Bertocchi 1,100cc Maserati was behind us, and it

This Austin Seven Ulster was driven by Charles Goodacre, who is seen perched against the cockpit. It was the first British entry in the Mille Miglia and its performance was outstanding. Another, better-known, photograph, reproduced in Motor Sport *for May 1931, misleadingly shows Goodacre as mechanic in the 1930 Double Twelve race, riding in the passenger seat of the car.* (Julian Hunt Collection)

was running in the same class. I backed off a little and this lowered the temperature. We were soon passing the Fiats running in our class and when we reached Cremona, we were leading the class. After checking in at the control, we waved to Giovannini in the Alfa Romeo pit and drove on.

Trevisan took over at Bologna and drove the car over the Futa and Raticosa passes, which, like many of the roads, were loose surface over a compacted base. The Austin was going well and we made good time to Siena, but Trevisan was feeling unwell and I was faced with roads that I had never seen before. I set off in the gathering dark across the Radicofani pass towards Viterbo where we were due to refuel. By this time the faster cars were overtaking us, covering the car and us in dust. Nuvolari with a new 8C 2300 Alfa Romeo came by and as the dust cleared I saw the road clearly in front of me.

However, Nuvolari had missed the proper road and he, together with the other Alfa Romeo drivers, who were chasing him and following the dust that we had thrown up, were rushing up a track that led to a farmyard. With much cursing and waving of arms the Alfa drivers turned round and roared back to the main road followed by the Austin. Soon afterwards, Caracciola, partnered by Wilhelm Sebastian in the big Mercedes-Benz SSKL, roared past. We arrived in Viterbo, still ahead of the 1,100cc Maserati, and pulled into the Alfa pit where we filled up with Shell and changed drivers.

Shortly after Viterbo, Tuffanelli and Bertocchi in the Maserati overtook us, as they pressed on towards Rome. I thought that to have stayed for so long ahead of the supercharged Maserati driven by two experienced road-racers was no mean achievement. About 15 minutes after we had left Viterbo, we came across the big white Mercedes at the side of the road and we stopped to see if we could help. The bonnet was open and Rudi Caracciola was pacing up and down, swearing. Sebastian, who acted as navigator for Caracciola and was also a first-class mechanic, came over and asked whether we had a strong elastic band.

My pockets were stuffed with bits and pieces and I searched around, found one and passed it to him. Sebastian thanked me and ran back to the Mercedes. We drove on and shortly afterwards the Mercedes came rushing past, with the supercharger wailing. We checked into the Rome control just before 10pm, after 8hr 1min on the road. In the Alfa Romeo pit Nuvolari was having a blazing row with Giovannini about his tyres, which were throwing treads and spoiling his chances of holding the Mercedes. After we had refuelled, Trevisan took over and, as arranged, drove through the bitterly cold mountains, where Nuvolari – going like hell – passed us again, and down to the control at Ancona.

Here I took the wheel again and set out along the fast coast route to the flatlands of the lower Po Valley and onwards to Bologna. When we pulled into the pits at Bologna, I was about all in. It was early on the Sunday morning and we had been travelling for over 14 hours. Giovannini gave me some concoction to buck me up. [Julian Hunt makes the point that Giovannini must have been using an aircraft to move around the course, as the Alfa Romeos, which were his prime concern, must have been faster than all but the fastest trains. He suggests that this may have been the first time that aerial support was used in racing or rallying.]

After my 'pick-me-up', I climbed back into the passenger seat and Trevisan set off to drive the last major section through Ferrara and Padua, then up to Trento in the foothills of the Dolomites. The Austin was whirring along merrily when suddenly everything went quiet. The engine had stopped and Trevisan put the clutch out and pulled into the side of the road, making 'well, that's it!' gestures. I had a quick look under the bonnet and spotted that the Simms coupling to the magneto had broken. I searched through my pockets for the spare, found it and replaced it with no problems in timing the engine.

We restarted and had an uneventful run from then on, passing through Verona and following the road round Lake Garda before the final stretch into Brescia. We arrived 21hr 34min 34.2sec after the start, second in our class and 1hr 46min behind the Maserati, which had broken the class record, and we were 34th overall. I passed out after the race and woke up 36 hours later. After a short holiday I returned to England by train and ship. I left the Ulster in Italy and I believe that it broke its crankshaft the following year.

In his report of the race in The Autocar W. F. Bradley commented that one Italian newspaper described the Austin Seven as having an exhaust like a dog being run over. According to Orsini and Zagari (The Scuderia Ferrari) the Scuderia had taken over a supercharged Austin Ulster, which was probably the Goodacre/Trevisan car and entered it in the 1932 Mille Miglia. It was prepared by Nicholls, but although the crankshaft had exceeded its 40 hours racing life, it was not replaced and broke. As a result the car failed to start the race. Francesco Trevisan was killed in a motorcycle accident during the early months of the Second World War. He should not be confused with Bruno Trevisan who became responsible in the late 1930s for the development of touring Alfa Romeos.

Charles Goodacre remained part of the works Austin racing team throughout the 1930s and he was one of the most successful drivers of the Murray Jamieson-designed twin-cam single-seaters along with Pat Driscoll and Bert Hadley. He left Austin in 1938 to become a consulting engineer and following the outbreak of the Second World War joined the Royal Air Force. He became an Engineer Officer in Fighter Command. In post-war days he resumed his career as a consulting engineer and spent some eight years working in Italy with Fiat. He died on 7 August 1989.

1932

9-10 April
Starters: 88; Finishers: 42; Distance: 1,022 miles (1,644km).
Circuit: see page 243.
Weather: fine throughout, but strong winds.

Main contenders for victory:

82	Pietro Ghersi/Giulio Ramponi (Alfa Romeo 8C 2300 Spider Corsa, 2,336cc, Scuderia Ferrari entry)
83	Count Felice Trossi/Marquis Antonio Brivio (Alfa Romeo 8C 2300 Spider Corsa, 2,336cc, Scuderia Ferrari entry)
85	Eugenio Siena/Piero Taruffi (Alfa Romeo 8C 2300 Spider Corsa, 2,336cc, Scuderia Ferrari entry)
88	Strazza/Gismondi (Lancia Lambda fitted with 3,960cc V8 DiLambda engine)
90	Broschek/Sebastian (Mercedes-Benz SSKL, 7,069cc)
98	Giuseppe Campari/Sozzi (Alfa Romeo 8C 2300 Spider Corsa, 2,336cc, works entry)
102	Achille Varzi/Count Castelbarco (Bugatti Type 55, 2,262cc)
105	Tazio Nuvolari/B. Guidotti (Alfa Romeo 8C 2300 Spider Corsa, 2,336cc, works entry)
106	Baconin Borzacchini/Bignami (Alfa Romeo 8C 2300 Spider Corsa, 2,336cc, works entry)
115	Rudolf Caracciola/Bonini (Alfa Romeo 8C 2300 Spider Corsa, 2,336cc, works entry)

From now on not only would Alfa Romeo win every pre-war Mille Miglia up to and including 1938, but at no time during this period did any other make lead the race, apart from Dreyfus (Delahaye) for a short while in 1937. When both the Alfa Romeo works and Scuderia Ferrari entered teams, it always leads to an element of confusion, but in this case it was indicative of the immense power of Alfa Romeo in sports car racing during the 1930s. It was however not too difficult to distinguish the cars of the two teams. The works cars were fitted with Touring two-seater bodies characterised by a horizontally split windscreen that was adjustable.

The Scuderia Ferrari cars had Zagato two-seater bodies with cut-down windscreens and there was no 'break' running across it. In addition the Zagato bodies had cut-down mudguards and tails. There were many other Alfa Romeos in the race, more in 2,336cc form, some 6C 1750 and 6C 1500 cars and in all 35 of the entries were Alfa Romeos.

Varzi was still a works Bugatti driver and his mount was a very formidable and highly competitive Type 55 with

The 1932 race was won by Baconin Borzacchini, partnered by Bignami, driving this Alfa Romeo 8C 2300. Alfa Romeos now won every pre-war race until the event was banned after 1938. The first ten cars were all Alfa Romeos, save for a Lancia in eighth place. (Author's Collection)

Tazio Nuvolari was partnered by Battista Guidotti in the 1932 race. They went off the road several times with their new and underdeveloped 8C 2300 Alfa Romeo and were finally eliminated from the race when Nuvolari crashed heavily at Florence. Note the horizontally-split windscreen of the Touring body, which could be adjusted to suit the height of the driver. (Centro Documentazione Alfa Romeo)

The 1932 race was Giuseppe Campari's last Mille Miglia before he was killed in an accident at Monza. He drove a fine race in his 8C 2300, leading at Ancona, but mechanic Sozzi crashed the car. (Centro Documentazione Alfa Romeo)

Type 51 Grand Prix twin overhead camshaft, straight-eight 2,262cc engine. The Type 55 had the Type 54 chassis (also a Grand Prix car, but powered by a 4.9-litre engine) and a very handsome two-seater body that was probably designed by Jean Bugatti. The Bugatti's engine developed a claimed 135bhp and the Type 55 was reckoned to be good for 112mph (180kph). There were no other potential race-winners, apart from the Lancia and the SSKL mentioned above. The Hon Brian Lewis (later Lord Essendon), one of two British entries, drove a 2,976cc Talbot 105.

Although the day of the OM was over and these cars were no longer being built, four ran in this year's race. Tuffanelli, again partnered by Bertocchi, drove a 1,100cc Maserati and running in the same class was the D-type MG Midget of Lord de Clifford, partnered by Selby. The D-type, of which 250 were built in 1931–32, had a four-cylinder single overhead camshaft, 746cc engine. De Clifford's car was a rather special supercharged competition version. Fiat had introduced a more powerful 'Mille Miglia' version of the 514 and this was eligible for the Utilitarian class, which attracted 24 entries, 18 of them Fiats and six very outclassed Bianchis.

The start had been brought forward to 8am, which meant that so much more of the race was run in daylight. The 8C 2300 Alfa Romeos set a tremendous pace. By Bologna the order was Nuvolari/Guidotti, Caracciola/Bonini and Varzi/Castelbarco with only five seconds covering the three cars. Again the record for this first stage had been smashed and the leaders had covered the 130 miles (209km) at around 101mph (163kph).

W. F. Bradley watched the race from the summit of the Futa Pass and wrote: "A few yards up the hillside was a roadmender with a huge red flag which he waved frantically as each car approached. A Fascisti officer warned the people on the bend by the cry of 'una macchina, due macchine,' as the case might be; the village grocer kept a score sheet, the proprietress of the hotel rushed out excitedly every few minutes in the hope of seeing Nuvolari, Campari or some other Italian favourite.

"In the warm sunshine we watched the cars come down from the summit of the pass, saw the drivers change gear, and almost felt the brakes go on in preparation for the swing round a blind turn, often clouded by the dust of a preceding car. It was thrilling, and yet it was only one of the hundreds of such that drivers had to negotiate in that run of one thousand miles across Italy.

"The champions came closer together. Nuvolari, as we timed him, had a lead of only 30 seconds over Caracciola, while Varzi was two minutes behind, followed by Campari 2½ minutes behind. The order in which they passed us, however, was Campari first, followed a minute later by Varzi, and by his great rival, Nuvolari.

"The most impressive car was the big white Mercedes, driven by its owner Herr Broschek. Explosions came from its supercharger, its brakes screeched and it skidded round the bend in a cloud of dust. A Bugatti driver clashed in a lower gear a dozen yards from the bend. Nuvolari was grim; Varzi was precise, while Campari swung round with a most scientific skid. In comparison with the others Brian Lewis on the Talbot was almost sedate.

"Running into the Piazza Michel Angelo at Florence, under the gaze of several thousand spectators, Ghersi [underestimated] his speed, skidded wildly as he attempted to take a right-angle bend, and hit a post with fatal results to his machine and with slight injuries to himself and Ramponi. A few minutes later cheers arose at the approach

Caracciola, winner for Mercedes-Benz in 1931, drove this works 8C 2300 Alfa Romeo the following year. Partnered by Bonini, he was leading at Florence but later retired because of mechanical problems. This photograph was taken in the Piazza Michelangelo, not far from the Florence control. Note the tramlines in the foreground. (Author's Collection)

In 1932 Count Lurani, partnered by Caverni, finished ninth overall with this 6C 1500 Alfa Romeo, and second in the 1,500cc class. Lurani achieved much press comment because of the elegance of his bright red overalls. Whether this had anything to do with the obvious enthusiasm of the female spectators is unknown. (LAT/The Autocar/Fumagalli)

An interesting contender in the 1932 race was this Lancia Lambda driven by Strazza and Gismondi. As was usual with Lambdas built for the Mille Miglia, it had a shortened chassis but, also, it was powered by a V8 4.9-litre engine from the luxurious DiLambda model introduced by Lancia in 1929. They finished eighth. (Spitzley-Zagari Collection)

In 1932 German privateer Broschek entered this SSKL Mercedes-Benz that was almost identical to the car in which Caracciola won the previous year. He was partnered by Wilhelm Sebastian, who had been Caracciola's mechanic. Broschek drove a determined race, but was not sufficiently able to squeeze the best out of the Grosser Mercedes-Benz. At one stage he was in second place, but he dropped back and retired. (Spitzley-Zagari Collection)

of Nuvolari. The national champion looked up, turned his head to glance at the wreckage of Ghersi's machine, and as a result of that infinitely brief moment of inattention had commenced a skid which brought him up with a crash only a few yards from the wrecked companion car."

So Caracciola/Bonini led from Campari/Sozzi and Siena/Taruffi. That behemoth, the SSKL, was in fourth place and Varzi, whose Type 55 was not going as well as might be expected was fifth. Somehow Varzi's Bugatti holed its fuel tank; Broschek moved up to second place, but by Rome the German car had dropped back to sixth. Soon the SSKL was out of the race. By Perugia the order was Siena-Campari-Caracciola (who had lost time having his brakes adjusted)-Borzacchini, but the first three of these were destined to retire.

The Hon Brian Lewis (later Lord Essendon) was a very capable Bugatti and Talbot driver. He drove this 3-litre Talbot 105 with mechanic Barnard. It was rather less rorty-torty than most of the sports cars competing, but Lewis rose as high as fourth place overall before going off the road. After the car was pushed back on to the road by willing spectators, he carried on to finish 25th. In the background of this photograph is the famous wall, with its memorial to drivers from Florence who had been killed in motor racing. (Spitzley-Zagari Collection)

As the cars departed from Macerata, Campari let his co-driver take the wheel while he replaced his goggles – Sozzi stretched across to take the wheel, but promptly lost control and crashed. Some sources report that a near-demented Campari, furiously waving a wheel mallet, chased his co-driver down the road. Then the Siena/Taruffi car broke a piston near Ferrara and not far from the finish Caracciola was forced to pull out of the race because the engine of his Monza dropped a valve.

Borzacchini had been pushing hard and he won the race with a time 1hr 15min faster than that of Caracciola in 1931. After Trossi/Brivio crossed the finishing line in second place with their 8C 2300, Scarfiotti/D'Ippolito were third with their 6C 1750 and Minoia/Balestrieri in fourth place won the class for closed cars. Although the British MG seemed at one stage to be offering a threat to the Maserati in the 1,100cc class, Tuffanelli/Bertocchi won with a time substantially quicker than they had achieved in 1931.

With one headlamp out of action, Lewis crashed the Talbot heavily near Feltre, ending up at the bottom of a ten-foot embankment. Some 50 inhabitants from a nearby village pulled the car back on to the road with ropes. Damage to the car was slight and consisted only of a leaking fuel tank (temporarily repaired with chewing gum) and a broken windscreen. Up until this point the Talbot had been in fourth place. Neither Lewis nor his mechanic was badly injured and they resumed the race to finish 25th. At Le Mans two months later, Lewis partnered by Tim Rose-Richards finished third overall with a Talbot 105.

Results:
General classification:

1st	Borzacchini/Bignami (Alfa Romeo), 14hr 55min 19.4sec (68.29mph/109.88kph)	
2nd	Trossi/Brivio (Alfa Romeo), 15hr 10min 59.0sec	
3rd	Scarfiotti/D'Ippolito (Alfa Romeo), 15hr 44min 41.6sec	
4th	Minoia/Balesteri (Alfa Romeo), 16hr 54min 37.4sec	
5th	Carraroli/M. Ghersi (Alfa Romeo), 17hr 4min 3.8sec	
6th	Giulay/Venturi (Alfa Romeo), 17hr 9min 14.4sec	
7th	Santinelli/Berti (Alfa Romeo), 17hr 10min 55.2sec	
8th	Strazza/Gismondi (Lancia), 17hr 14min 22.6sec	
9th	Lurani/Canavesi (Alfa Romeo), 17hr 22min 54.4sec	
10th	Gazzabini/Dias (Alfa Romeo), 17hr 26min 21.8sec	

Class results:
Utilitarian: Gilera/Sartori (Fiat), 19hr 53min 25.4sec (51.23mph/82.44kph)

1,100cc: Tuffanelli/Bertocchi (Maserati), 18hr 35min 2.2 sec (54.83mph/88.23kph)

1,500cc: Giulay/Venturi (Alfa Romeo), 17hr 9min 14.4 sec (59.41mph/95.59kph)

2,000cc: Scarfiotti/D'Ippolito (Alfa Romeo), 15hr 44min 41.6sec (64.30mph/103.66kph)

3,000cc: Borzacchini/Bignami (Alfa Romeo), 14hr 55min 19.4sec (68.29mph/109.88kph)

Over 3,000cc: Strazza/Gismondi (Lancia), 17hr 14min 22.6sec (59.13mph/95.14kph)

Closed cars: Minoia/Balestrieri (Alfa Romeo), 16hr 54min 37.4sec (60.26mph/96.96kph)

Brescia Grand Prix (team prize)
Minoia/Balestrieri, Borzacchini/Bignami (Alfa Romeo)

Lord de Clifford's race with his MG D-Type Midget

(From an interview conducted by Julian Hunt in the Peers' Bar, Houses of Parliament, Summer 1981)

Lord de Clifford was born in 1907 and read engineering at University. The 1932 Mille Miglia was his first race. He had experience of long-distance rallying and had finished 46th in the 1930 Monte Carlo rally at the wheel of a Bentley powered by a Gardner diesel engine. He had close connections with the original Lagonda company, and drove a 3-litre Lagonda into 20th place in the 1932 Monte Carlo event.

I thought that I would like to run in the Mille Miglia and I wanted to beat the time achieved by the Austin Seven in the 1931 event. I went to Ulster to watch the 1931 Tourist Trophy on the Ards circuit and when I saw the performance of the MGs, I was convinced that one could beat the

The MG C-Type of Lord Edward de Clifford and Selby is seen on the Raticosa Pass. This MG had a 746cc single overhead camshaft engine. There were three different versions of these cars and this unblown model probably had the cross-flow cylinder head. They were second in their class at Rome, albeit 44 minutes behind the leading 1,100cc Maserati, but failed to make it to the finish. (Andrew Morland Collection)

Austin's time. I bought the 746cc D-type Midget that Norman Black had used to win the 1931 Tourist Trophy.

Because I knew very little about the Mille Miglia, I entrusted preparation of the Midget to the MG works at Abingdon. I shared the car in the race with Vivian Selby [he raced a 2-litre Bugatti at Brooklands and in post-war days was competition manager of the Bristol 450 team]. We towed the MG to Italy behind my 3-litre Lagonda and I had complete faith in Abingdon's preparation of the car. We started the car for the first time on the Milan Autostrada and drove from there to the Alfa Romeo works for them to check the car over before the race.

They laughed at the Brooklands silencer and fishtail, which the MG works had fitted, and asked us what they were for! They assured us that they were completely unnecessary and a new exhaust was made up with a straight pipe and a fishtail 'silencer' held in place by a single through bolt that had a small hole bored in the bolt head. The fishtail was purely for scrutineering and the start of the race. As they pointed out, a piece of wire was threaded through the hole in the bolt head and led to the cockpit. After the start we could easily withdraw the bolt and the fishtail would fall off in its own time.

While the MG was being finished off at Portello, we decided to do a lap of the course in the Lagonda. We completed the course in one go and we found the experience was very valuable when it came to the race. We took notes and these were especially detailed over the last section, as it would be covered in the dark. [JH commented to de Clifford that this lap was no mean drive in itself, but he simply shrugged and said he was used to long journeys in rallies.]

We took the MG from the Alfa Romeo works to Brescia for scrutineering and the Royal Automobile Club had sent

over Hugh P McConnell, who spoke good Italian, to represent us, and afterwards we put the MG in the parc fermé. The night before the race we got into a friendly argument with a gang of Fiat drivers. One of them held that the British showed a lack of spirit racing downhill – we decided to look out for this bloke!

We left Brescia at 8.18am and decided to take it easy to begin with. However, we had a puncture and after stopping to change the wheel we decided to speed up. Just before reaching Bologna for the first time, we caught up with around 15 Fiats. As the road seemed wide, we pulled out to overtake, but discovered that we had strayed right on to the tramlines and just managed to squeeze between two converging trams. We caught up with 'our' Fiat man on a downhill section, passed him on the inside of a right-hand bend and gently pushed the Fiat into a wall.

At the Bologna control in the Piazza Re Enzo we asked the British consul to telegraph 'Dunlop Mac' that we would need a new tyre at Rome. The crowd control was surprisingly good, as Fascisti boys would blow bugles to warn the crowd of an approaching car. We found that the larger the crowd, the dicier were the bends. At Siena, Selby was able to swipe a bottle of wine from the officials' table. We continued to make good progress to Rome where we arrived in 7hr 24min 17sec; third in class [the Austin took 8hr 1min 4sec]. Thanks to the Alfa organisation, who were supplying fuel and support as part of their package, 'Dunlop Mac' was ready with a new tyre.

The route from Rome took us along the slow, rough and twisting roads over the Apennines and then wound towards the Adriatic Sea at Ancona. Soon after Tolentino the engine stopped and we realised that the vertical drive to the camshaft was not moving. We discovered that the drive-key had sheared. Fortunately, we managed to find a blacksmith who made up a new one and after a delay of about 45 minutes we were off again. This key didn't last as long as the first and the second key broke in the early hours of Sunday morning on the way to Ravenna and we were some distance from help.

Although we managed to get two new keys made and fitted and then drove the MG back to Brescia, we were too far behind to be classified. We were bitterly disappointed not to have finished because the car had been going very well. After we had returned to England, I went to see Cecil Kimber at Abingdon. He queried why we had not been given any spare keys, as it was a known weakness of the engine. He commented, "We could have given you some of our specially hardened ones." I was very annoyed about this, as they could have tipped me off and put half a dozen in a matchbox, so when the sodding things broke we could have slipped another in place. The whole race cost £400–£500.

Subsequently de Clifford continued rallying in Lagondas and Lagonda Rapiers. In 1934 he entered into partnership with Charles Dobson and traded in Staines as Dobson & de

Both de Clifford and Selby were well over six feet in height and towered out of the MG, for which they were really too big. (Andrew Morland Collection)

Clifford Limited. They specialised in Lagonda Rapiers and built the de Clifford special. He drove a Lagonda Rapier with Charles Brackenbury at Le Mans in 1934. The works built the special 1,100cc engine and the valves stretched. "I told them they would, but they knew better." They finished 16th, running on three cylinders. This was de Clifford's second and last race.

In 1935 he became the last peer tried by the House of Lords when he was charged with manslaughter following a motoring accident – he was acquitted. During World War Two he served in the army and became colonel in REME (Royal Electrical and Mechanical Engineers). At the end of the war he became town Governor of Milan.

He later ran a quarantine kennel in Somerset, and worked as a door-to-door dog food salesman. It seems that finally he lived on his attendance fee at the House of Lords.

Lord de Clifford, seen here at the wheel of the 1,100cc Lagonda Rapier that he co-drove with Charles Brackenbury at Le Mans in 1934. They finished 16th overall. (Author's Collection)

1933

8–9 April
Starters: 85; Finishers: 52; Distance 1,022 miles (1,644km).
Circuit: see page 243.
Weather: fine throughout.

Main contenders for victory:

78	Hans Ruesch/Kessler (Alfa Romeo 8C 2300 Spider Corsa, 2,336cc)
80	Battaglia/Bianchi (Alfa Romeo 8C 2300 Spider Corsa, 2,336cc)
85	Scarfiotti/D'Ippolito (Alfa Romeo 8C 2300 Spider Corsa, 2,336cc)
87	Count Felice Trossi/Marchese Antonio Brivio (Alfa Romeo 8C 2300 Spider Corsa, 2,336cc)
90	Piero Taruffi/Lelio Pellegrini (Alfa Romeo 8C 2300 Monza, 2,336cc)
91	Franco Cortese/Count Castelbarco (Alfa Romeo 8C 2300 Corto, 2,336cc)
94	Baconin Borzacchini/Lucchi (Alfa Romeo 8C 2300 Spider Corsa, 2,336cc)
97	Gazzabini/D'Alessio (Alfa Romeo 8C 2300 Spider Corsa, 2,336cc)
98	Tazio Nuvolari/Compagnoni (Alfa Romeo 8C 2300 Spider Corsa, 2,336cc)

Scuderia Ferrari now took responsibility for the official entry of Alfa Romeo cars in all categories and these 8C 2300s had Touring bodies. On the eve of the race an

Nuvolari, partnered by Decimo Compagnoni, are about to leave the Scuderia Ferrari works for a practice run with their Touring-bodied 8C 2300 before the 1933 Mille Miglia. Compagnoni is at the wheel. (Author's Collection)

electric spark set fire to Cortese's Alfa Romeo while it was being refuelled in the company's works at Portello and an electrician was still working under the car. The damage was extensive and the fuel tank and pipes, the tail, the tyres and electrics were all badly damaged. Mechanic and test driver Bonini suffered severe burns. It seems that no one bothered to tell Cortese about the fire immediately and he did not find out what had happened until four hours before the start of the race.

Cortese insisted that the car be repaired in time for the start and a frantic rush ensued. Most of the damage was to the rear of the car and a combination of industry and frenzy ensured that it was repaired. Further problems followed when a mechanic poured a can of water into the fuel tank an hour before the start. Despite this near-catastrophe, Cortese made the start only a few seconds late, after being called while the car was still being refuelled, and he insisted driving for the entire race. The results proved that all the effort had been worthwhile.

It was a sad fact that there was not a serious challenger to the Alfa Romeos in this race. The works Mercedes-Benz driver Manfred von Brauchitsch had entered an SSKL, but these cars were now outdated and uncompetitive. Carlo Pintacuda entered one of the new V8 2,604cc Lancia Asturas, but it was a touring car with no special competition modifications. Strazza/Gismondi had their now familiar DiLambda-powered Lambda, but it was even less of a serious proposition than it had been in 1932.

An unusual entry was an 8C 2300 Lungo Alfa Romeo entered by General Agostini and Professor Mario Ferragutti. It had a charcoal burner which produced the

gas that powered the car while it was running. At the time it was more weightily described as 'propelled through carbon-gas.' It was totally impracticable as a competition car as there was an enormous tank that extended up to the level of the driver's head. A smaller tank below it and another two bolster-shaped tanks recessed into the running boards. Maximum speed barely exceeded 30mph (48kph).

This experiment represented one of a number of attempts supported by the Italian government to find an alternative fuel to petrol. With some prescience the Fascist government recognised the possibility of isolation accompanied by embargoes. This was not a successful experiment.

Perhaps the greatest interest was in the 1,100cc class in which a team of MG Magnettes, the first British works team to run in the race, discounting the single Austin Seven in 1931, battled with the Maseratis of Tuffanelli/Bertocchi and Tabanelli/Borgnino. After Tuffanelli had raced an eight-cylinder Maserati in 1931–32, both drivers now had the latest four-cylinder model.

There were also four Fiats in the class. To provide back-up and carrying an inventory of MG spares Lord Howe, who was financing the MG team, entered his personal Mercedes-Benz SSK driven by Penn Hughes/Thomas. (The full story of the MGs in the race is told in the Sidebar on pages 109–112.)

A new model from Fiat was the Balilla and the specification included a four-cylinder, side-valve 995cc engine, three-speed gearbox, cruciform chassis and hydraulic brakes. Balillas became a popular option for

Nuvolari drove immaculately to win the 1933 race, with the second-place car of Castelbarco/Cortese over 25 minutes behind. (Centro Documentazione Alfa Romeo)

Borzacchini/Lucchi, driving an 8C 2300 Alfa Romeo, lead Balestrero/Battilana in a similar car. Borzacchini had started eight minutes after Balestrero. This street in Modena looks virtually unchanged today. (Author's Collection)

An unsuccessful experiment: this 8C 2300 Lungo ('long wheelbase') Alfa Romeo, driven in the 1933 race by General Agostini and Professor Ferragutti, was propelled by carbon gas produced by an on-board carbon burner. As its maximum speed was only around 30mph, the drivers showed great patience in managing to complete the course. (Author's Collection)

the Utilitarian category of the Mille Miglia and in the 1933 event one was driven by the Villoresi brothers, Emilio and Luigi, both of whom were to become famous racing drivers.

At the start of the race a Fascist band played stirring music and the first cars were now flagged away from 7am onwards. First off was the 1,100cc Utilitarian class, all Fiat Balillas mostly red, then the over 1,100cc Utilitarian class, a mixture of Fiats and Bianchis. When the MGs appeared in the 1,100cc class, someone turned on a gramophone which blared out a rather scratchy recording of *Soldiers of the King*.

At last the big-capacity cars were dispatched. *The Motor* stated that "Nuvolari, who had, as usual, been embraced for luck by a hunchback on arrival, was last away to terrific cheering." Starting last was a great advantage and Nuvolari was able to monitor the position of his rivals throughout the race.

Soon there were casualties. Only 19 miles (30km) from the start Trossi took the Ponta sul Mella at Sanzeno

much too fast, overturned his Alfa Romeo and ejected a rather surprised Brivio. Injuries were restricted to Brivio suffering a badly cut eyebrow, but the car was said to be a complete wreck. Von Brauchitsch burst three tyres in the first 25 miles (40km), retired and telephoned Brescia to send out a tyre so that he could return there.

There was so little opposition that in reality Scuderia Ferrari did not need tactics, but the strategy was that Borzacchini would act as the hare. He averaged a record 101mph (163km) to Bologna where he led Nuvolari by 40 seconds and Cortese was in third place a minute behind Nuvolari. Borzacchini still led at Florence with an average of 77mph (124kph), two minutes ahead of Nuvolari. The Magnettes were thrashing the Maseratis in the 1,100cc class and Tuffanelli retired his Maserati with gearbox problems.

Borzacchini retired because of a cracked cylinder head just before he reached Terni and Nuvolari now took the lead. Then came the 16-mile (26km) tortuously winding section of road between Spoleto and Terni over the Somma Pass. Nuvolari still led, but his average speed had dropped to about 68mph (109kph). Behind him came Cortese/Castelbarco and Taruffi/Pellegrini.

At Bologna a water cart was sprinkling the pavée surfaces of the road, despite the coming and going of competitors. This took a number of competitors by surprise and an unexpecting Pietro Ghersi, at the wheel of a low two-seater Ford V8, lost control and crashed into a wall. It was here that Enzo Ferrari asked Nuvolari to ease his pace so as to conserve his car and, astonishingly, Nuvolari complied with his wishes. There was a new section of concrete-surfaced road between Bologna and Padua, one of the improvements brought to Italian roads by the Mille Miglia.

The first car to cross the finishing line at Brescia was Pintacuda's Lancia; he had led his class at one stage, but mechanical problems had halted his fast run and so he had returned to Brescia by the shortest route. At 2.33am Nuvolari took the chequered flag to win the race and he was 26 minutes ahead of Franco Cortese. The first ten finishers were Alfa Romeos and the Magnettes took the first two places in the 1,100cc class, with the very special modified Fiat of Ambrosini/Menchetti third, almost 40 minutes behind the class winner.

The Maserati of Tabanelli/Borgnino did finish the race and took fourth place in the class. They were, however, a long, long way behind after a collision with a fixed and immovable object that necessitated the removal of the front axle at Ancona so that it could be heated and straightened, an operation that took something over an hour. Penn Hughes partnered by Thomas in Howe's Mercedes-Benz 'tender car' actually finished 24th overall and took second place in the over 3,000cc class.

Results
General classification:

1st	Nuvolari/Compagnoni (Alfa Romeo), 15hr 11min 50sec (67.48mph/108.58kph)	
2nd	Castelbarco/Cortese (Alfa Romeo), 15hr 38min 02sec	
3rd	Taruffi/Pellegrini (Alfa Romeo) 16hr 0min 57sec	
4th	Battaglia/Bianchi (Alfa Romeo), 16hr 19min 40sec	
5th	Scarfiotti/D'Ippolito (Alfa Romeo), 16hr 22min 10sec	
6th	Santielli/Berti (Alfa Romeo), 16hr 25min 39sec	
7th	Ruesch/Kessler (Alfa Romeo), 16hr 25min 46sec	
8th	Gazzabini/D'Alessio (Alfa Romeo), 16hr 31min 28sec	
9th	Foligno/Comotti (Alfa Romeo), 16hr 41min 48sec	
10th	Peverelli/Dell'Orto (Alfa Romeo), 16hr 51min 55sec	

Class results:

Utilitarian cars under 1,100cc: Ricci/Maggi (Fiat), 19hr 1min 36sec (53.90mph/86.72kph)

Utilitarian cars over 1,100cc: Marinelli/Tragella (Bianchi), 18hr 54min 15sec (54.24mph/87.27kph)

1,100cc: Eyston/Lurani (MG), 18hr 1min 4sec (56.91mph/91.57kph)

1,500cc: Berrone/Carroli (Alfa Romeo), 17hr 38min 35sec (58.12mph/93.52kph)

2,000cc: Foligno/Comotti (Alfa Romeo), 16hr 41min 48sec (61.46mph/98.89kph)

3,000cc: Nuvolari/Compagnoni (Alfa Romeo), 15hr 11min 50sec (67.48mph/108.58kph)

Over 3,000cc: Strazza/Gismondi (Lancia), 16hr 58min 20sec (60.42mph/97.22kph)

Closed cars: Sperti/Donnini (Alfa Romeo), 17hr 49min 58.0sec (57.51mph/92.53kph)

Brescia Grand Prix (team prize):

Eyston/Lurani, Lord Howe/Hamilton (MG)

Count 'Johnny' Lurani and his first year with the MG Magnette team

(Adapted from Mille Miglia, 1927–57 *by Giovanni Lurani, Edita SA, 1981)*

My friend, Lord Howe, was persuasive to my requests that official British teams should compete in the Mille Miglia. He succeeded in persuading the MG company to prepare an official team. The MG team turned out to be well organised and efficient.

I met my future team mates in London in 1932 and helped plan the British Mille Miglia attempt. The MG team was to consist of three new K3 Magnette cars with 1,100cc six-cylinder engines having overhead camshafts, Powerplus superchargers, SU carburettors and Wilson preselector, epicyclic gearboxes. These cars were very fast, exceeding 100mph [161kph], but were rather heavy and lacking powerful brakes.

The crews were better than could be imagined. Lord Howe was partnered by the young Hugh Hamilton, one of the great hopes in British motor racing, who was killed shortly afterwards on the Bern circuit. Sir Henry 'Tim' Birkin, a top British driver, was one of the so-called Bentley Boys who had been successful at Le Mans and Brooklands. For this race, his crewmate was another Bentley Boy, Bernard Rubin, who had won the Le Mans 24 Hours race with Barnato. The third couple was George Eyston, one of the most skilled drivers in Europe and future land speed record holder, and me.

The political aspect of the MG entry was underlined when we stopped in Rome during our practice tour in January 1933. We were officially received by the King of Italy [Vittorio-Emanuele III], by Mussolini and by the British ambassador. We were made honorary members of the Italian Automobile Club. The entry was interpreted as an important sign of the friendly relations between Italy and Britain. [Eyston, a member of one of Britain's oldest Catholic families, was a descendant of Sir Thomas More and while he was in Italy received an audience with the Pope.]

We started at 8.03 on the morning of 8 April with George Eyston at the wheel and I at his side. Tim Birkin and Rubin followed two minutes after us, and Lord Howe and Hamilton three minutes after. Eyston had prudently fitted 'soft' plugs, fearing that 'hard' plugs would foul up. In any event he didn't believe it possible to drive the car at its maximum speed for very long. Fewer than three miles from the start, the engine started to misfire and we had to change all six plugs. A fine start!

Just as we were finishing, a roar announced the arrival of the MG driven by Tim Birkin, which flashed past at more than 100mph [161kph]. Nevertheless George Eyston rapidly caught Birkin and trailed him until Bologna. For 120 miles [193km] we were never more than 20 or 30 yards apart. It was an exciting duel at 100mph with the engine running like a turbine at more than 6,000rpm.

At Bologna, Birkin was first in the 1,100cc class in 1hr 28min 35sec at the fantastic average of 88mph [142kph]. Lord Howe followed in under two minutes and we were 20 seconds behind at an average of about 87mph [140kph]. If we hadn't stopped for plug changes, we would have led our class.

Birkin left immediately from the Bologna control and Eyston and I changed seats. Because of my previous experience, it was decided that I should drive over the mountainous part of the course as far as Perugia, crossing the Raticosa, Futa and Somma passes, as well as the Radicofani valley. I had rehearsed this critical part of the road well, and so was able to begin the hill climb towards Lojano at full speed. I soon managed to catch Tim Birkin

Seen at the Scuderia Ferrari premises in Modena before the 1933 race is one of the K3 MGs and, behind it are (from left) Eugenio Siena, Lord Howe, Tazio Nuvolari, Enzo Ferrari, Giovanni Lurani (looking surprisingly demur) and George Eyston. Nuvolari drove a K3 to a win in the 1933 Tourist Trophy. (Author's Collection)

and resume our duel. We were forced to stop again twice to change plugs and Birkin passed us each time. However, he soon lost his slender advantage, when we overtook him changing his own plugs.

Near Florence we were neck and neck. We descended Pratolino at more than 100mph [160kph], brushing past the houses, grazing the walls and skimming past the footpaths. We reached the Viale dei Colli elbow to elbow. I managed to overtake Birkin right on the corner before the Piazza Michelangelo, and stopped at the control with a five-yard lead. The race officials, ready to stamp our carnets, scattered like panic-stricken goats, as they saw both cars arriving together with all wheels locked in frenzied braking. Birkin left the confusion with a 20-yard start. I caught him again and our struggle continued.

The contest with Birkin continued on the Siena road, but finally Tim's MG started to smoke. It slowed down and our very sporting companion and rival waved us past. We arrived first in our class at Siena and seventh in general classification. We refuelled for the first time along the walls of Siena. We had carefully studied the refuelling problem and had decided to have only three refuelling points, as against Alfa Romeo's four, because of the larger capacity of the MG's tank. We took on fuel quickly, had our brakes adjusted, drank some orangeade and stuffed our pockets with bananas and rolls.

Birkin's MG arrived in a cloud of smoke just as we were leaving. A glance convinced us that our team-mate was out of the race. After Siena we continued to overtake many of the cars that had started before us, as we drove towards Buonconvento, San Quirico and Radicofani. The

One of the hazards on the mainly very fast section of the course between Bologna and Brescia was the famous pontoon bridge over the River Po at Casalmaggiore. Crossing here is the K3 Magnette of Eyston and Lurani. (Author's Collection)

MG continued to perform well towards Rome. We were among the first to arrive at the Rome control at Ponte Milvio. We only had time to acknowledge the applause and greetings with a wave. We were clearly first in our class, having reached the capital in 6hr 16min 30sec at an average of 60.9mph [98.0kph].

The stretch from Rome to Terni was particularly suited to our little car, and we made a splendid run. I took 59min 53sec to cover the distance at an average of 61.4mph [98.8kph]. Only Nuvolari, who took the lead on Borzacchini's retirement, had bettered our time. I handed over the wheel to Eyston at our second refuelling stop at Perugia, after having driven continuously for more than 400 miles of the toughest part of the course. I had taken over when we were third in our class and handed back to my companion with a 22-minute lead.

When we left Perugia, the brakes had nearly vanished, we had to change a couple of plugs, but we still went very fast. Once again, the starting order made its influence felt. We had started three minutes ahead of Lord Howe and started to lose ground to him without being aware of it. Eyston was still first in the class at Ancona, but Lord Howe was only 16 minutes behind. Shortly after Ancona, lights were needed. We were a little concerned to discover that the dynamo wasn't working and the battery was nearly flat. The feeble light given by our two enormous headlights made full speed dangerous and our passage through Pesaro, Rimini, Forli and Faenza was more terrifying than usual.

Crowds parted at the last moment as we plunged into the mass of people at about 100mph [160kph], hoping not to decapitate spectators foolhardy enough to emerge into the dimly lit passage to shout their encouragement. We arrived in Bologna at about 9pm. Our third and final refuelling stop was at Porta Mazzini, immediately after the

control. We had taken 12hr 56min, averaged 58.6mph [94.3kph] and had passed all the cars that had started before us. Besides filling up with petrol and oil, the mechanics adjusted our shock absorbers and tried to change the dynamo. Unable to dismantle it, they decided to replace the battery.

It seems that at certain times, objects conspire to be as obstructive as possible. It happened that the spare battery, apparently similar to the first one, refused to enter the battery box. Precious minutes ticked away as the mechanics struggled to install it. The roar of an engine interrupted their work, and the MG driven by Lord Howe and Hamilton arrived. Once again, the advantage accumulated in 750 miles [1200km] of hard racing had been wiped out. In reality, we were only two minutes ahead of Lord Howe when we arrived at Bologna and here he was, before we could leave.

The sight of the MG spurred our efforts, in seconds the battery was somehow dealt with and George was off like a rocket, leaving me to climb aboard the moving car. Our MG was going extremely well, but the electrical system was decidedly bad – only one headlamp was working. Yet Eyston, at his best on the fast Veneto roads, drove flat out, knowing that Lord Howe and Hamilton behind us would certainly not let up.

Fortunately, my companion had rehearsed this stretch of the road well, but it was far from pleasant for me. It was terrifying to fly through the darkness at high speed with bad lights, but Eyston refused to slacken the pace. Having

In 1933 the MG Magnettes won the team prize, this magnificent sculpture of … well, anyway, it was a very well deserved victory. There is a view that each year, shortly before the race, the organisers went out on a spending spree and purchased trophies in job lots. (LAT)

passed every car that had started before us, we were the first car to pass through the towns and villages. We were also ahead of the expected time. So we often found the road full of vehicles and people who were not very convinced by our poor headlamps that a Mille Miglia car was on its way.

I was not enjoying it. As we crossed a gulley at full speed, I almost flew out of the car and banged my knee most painfully on the dashboard. At every moment I thought that our race would come to a sudden end. At Treviso we still had three minutes' advantage over Lord Howe, but at Feltre this had been reduced to only three seconds. I kept turning round to see if I could make out the lights of the other MG through the dust. Near Vicenza I made out the powerful beam from the lights of our pursuers.

Then we were at Verona where an enormous crowd packed the streets and the cafés were brilliantly lit. We took the by-pass and just as we entered the Brescia road, the car suddenly lost stability and spun. A nail had punctured our left rear tyre. Before the car had stopped, I was out to change the wheel. Fortunately, we were still in the town and the street lights were very useful. We searched frantically and without success for the jack.

The tools and spares had originally been stowed near the mechanic's seat, but after the numerous stops to change 18 plugs and the laborious refuelling at Bologna, my place had become a depository for old iron, where plugs, spanners, tyre levers, bananas, rags, and bread rolls soaked in oil made an exhibition of their own. But no trace of the jack! Luckily, there were some young men around and I asked them to lift the car, which they did promptly and enthusiastically. I changed the wheel in an instant and we

restarted at full speed with encouragement from our helpers.

I was still clutching the wheel hammer when we arrived in sight of the street lights of Brescia. We were the first drivers to finish the seventh Mille Miglia and everyone cheered us as winners of our class; but I knew from sad experience how often such applause can change to bitter disappointment. It was still probable that Lord Howe and Hamilton would beat us.

Lord Howe had started three minutes after us, and if he arrived within the next three minutes, we would be beaten. I anxiously scanned the finishing straight for the distant lights of the other MG and counted the seconds that passed inexorably. Over four minutes after our arrival, a glare of lights and a distant roar announced the arrival of our pursuers. Lord Howe and Hamilton shot through the finishing line, but we had beaten them by 90 seconds – an exciting finish and a microscopic margin of time after 18 hours of racing. Hugh Hamilton had driven well from Bologna to the finish, chasing us with great daring. He nearly caught us near Vicenza.

I couldn't think why they had not taken advantage of our puncture to pass us. It later emerged that the two Englishmen also had a puncture outside the city and had been unable to use a human jack that had saved us so much time. The 90 seconds that divided us were entirely due to our faster wheel change. Eyston and I won the 1,100cc class in 18hr 1min 4sec at an average speed of 56.9mph [91.5kph]. We broke the class record by 34 minutes. Lord Howe and Hamilton were second and Ambrosini/Menchetti third in a Fiat-Siata, 43 minutes later.

NOTE: The K3 Magnette was a single overhead camshaft, supercharged straight-six of 1,087cc (57 x 71mm) and it had a power output of 114bhp at 7,000rpm. The rival four-cylinder 4CS-1100 Maserati's power output was said to be 90bhp at 5,300rpm, but it probably developed somewhat more in Mille Miglia form. Transmission was through a four-speed Wilson pre-selector gearbox and the point has been made that this was the first occasion on which a pre-selector gearbox was used in a long-distance road race.

The Autocar reported that the MGs' equipment in the race included Lucas ignition, Bosch lamps, Dunlop tyres, Rudge-Whitworth wheels, KLG plugs, TFT fuel cap filler, Thomson and Taylor radiator cap filler, Hartford shock absorbers, SU carburettor, Powerplus blower, Wilson gearbox, Moseley Float-on-Air cushions.

Later successes achieved by K3 Magnettes included wins by Tazio Nuvolari in the handicap 1933 Tourist Trophy on the Ards circuit and in the 1933 and 1934 Coppa Acerbo Voiturette race at Pescara (Whitney Straight in 1933 and Hugh Hamilton in 1934). Eddie Hall and C. E. C. Martin took first two places in the 1933 handicap BRDC 500 Miles race at Brooklands. There were only 33 of these cars built.

1934

8 April
Starters: 57; Finishers: 29; Distance: 1,009 miles (1,623km).
Circuit: see page 243.
Weather: heavy and sustained rain.

Main contenders for victory:

Scuderia Ferrari entries:

48	Achille Varzi/Guido Bignami	(Alfa Romeo Monza, 2,632cc)
46	Louis Chiron/Archimede Rosa	(Alfa Romeo Monza, 2,632cc)
45	Mario Tadini/Barbieri	(Alfa Romeo Monza, 2,632cc)
58	Pietro Ghersi/Carraroli	(Alfa Romeo Monza, 2,336cc)
47	Minozzi/Soffietti	(Alfa Romeo Monza, 2,336cc)
63	Hans Ruesch/Maag	(Alfa Romeo Monza 2,336cc)
44	Tazio Nuvolari/Eugenio Siena	(Alfa Romeo Monza, 2,336cc, entered by Scuderia Siena)

The number of entries in the 1934 race was much reduced because there was now a separate race, the Coppa d'Oro del Littorio held over three days and over a distance of 3,534 miles (5,686km) for cars that had previously run in the Utilitarian classes of the Mille Miglia and other touring cars. So, as it has been expressed by more than one writer, the Mille Miglia was now a race for Italy's 50 top drivers. That is, of course an exaggeration, and the number of entries tended to fluctuate over the next few years, but they were vastly less numerous than in the past.

Of the 57 starters, 31 were Alfa Romeos; 19 of them 2.3 or 2.6-litre straight-eight cars and another ten were 6C 1750s. The 2.6-litre cars were all Scuderia Ferrari entries, but it is impossible to be absolutely certain just how many of these cars were entered; there were 16 Fiat Balillas with various modifications and certain of them were side-valve cars with Siata overhead valve cylinder head conversions; three MG Magnettes (and once more their full story is told on pages 117–118) faced two four-cylinder 1,100cc Maseratis (the strength of which the MG team personnel tended to underrate).

The field was completed by a works Lancia Astura, a private Lancia DiLambda, an old Itala running on diesel or naphtha (a coal tar derivative) according to which source you believe, the Aston Martin of the Maharajah Manesh Dinshaw/Esson-Scott and a private Magnette for

In the 1934 race Achille Varzi was partnered by Bignami, who was to remain his mechanic until the great driver's death. Varzi's 8C 2300 Monza was fitted with the new Pirelli Pneugrippa tyres that gave much greater adhesion in the wet than the Dunlops fitted to Nuvolari's car – and it was a very wet race. (Spitzley-Zagari Collection)

Germans Fork and Charley (it was Nuvolari's 1933 Tourist Trophy car).

There were significant changes in the Alfa Romeo team of drivers since 1933; both Borzacchini and Campari were dead, killed in their heat of the Monza Grand Prix in September; Count Trossi's Scuderia Ferrari Duesenberg had broken a connecting rod and, it is believed, dropped oil that was not cleared up properly between heats. The track was damp, it was virtually impossible for either Borzacchini or Campari to see the oil and both drivers went over the top of the retaining wall at Monza's Curva Sud; Campari was killed instantly, but Borzacchini survived for a few minutes after the crash.

After two seasons with Bugatti, Achille Varzi returned to Alfa Romeo and Scuderia Ferrari who prepared for him a special Monza, a racing car for the road, with what was probably the standard enlarged Grand Prix engine of 2,632cc and a Weber carburettor. It was said to develop 180bhp at 5,400rpm and had a maximum speed of 120mph (193kph).

The great Tazio Nuvolari had fallen out with Enzo Ferrari and so he drove a car with 2,336cc engine entered and prepared by Scuderia Siena which was based at Como. Siena had been head of the tuning shops at Portello, but according to Lurani modifications to the car were the work of Vittorio Jano. While Scuderia Ferrari used Pirelli Pneugrippa tyres (they were the normal tyres

Nuvolari and Eugenio Siena are seen here at the start of the 1934 race. Nuvolari, known as 'The Flying Mantuan', was running as an independent and his car could not match the performance of Varzi's works entry. He did well to finish second. (Centro Documentazione Alfa Romeo)

Opposite: The Scuderia Ferrari-entered Monzas of Swiss drivers Hans Ruesch/Maag and Italians Battaglia/Bianchi fight between themselves through the streets of Rome. Ruesch/Maag retired, but Battaglia/Bianchi took an excellent fourth place. (Spitzley-Zagari Collection)

with cross-cuts to facilitate drainage and a little extra grip), Nuvolari was on Dunlops, which certainly lacked grip in the wet. Listed above are only the most competitive of the 8C 2300 entries.

The MGs were also running on Dunlop tyres and although Lurani urged that the team should switch to Pirelli Pneugrippas, they declined and this may have been for contractual reasons. There is little doubt that Taruffi partnered by Bertocchi in the 1,100cc Maserati represented very serious opposition and it is unlikely that whatever the MG team did, they would not have beaten him in 1934.

Important changes had been made to the course. The first section had been extended to include Piacenza; in the latter stages there was now a control in Venice, reached by a bridge from Mestre. At Treviso the circuit no longer followed the winding route north to Feltre, but instead took the Autostrada to Vicenza and Verona. The course was now much faster, partly because of steadily improving roads – now even the Raticosa Pass had a metalled surface.

In 1934 the start was brought forward to 4am and although this meant that most of the cars started in the dark, the faster speeds resulting from technical development and road improvements enabled the race to be completed, by the fastest contenders at least, in daylight and all the finishers completed the course in the one day. *The Motor* described the lead-up to the start:

"The pessimists had prophesied correctly. An hour before the start at the Venetian Gate a steady rain was falling and the downpour continued throughout the two hours during which the [57] cars were being dispatched one by one on their 1000-mile journey.

"The scene at the start is the road leading into Brescia, and the cars set off actually facing the town, but swing left within the first 100 yards, then left again over the tramlines and out on the road to Cremona.

"As 4am draws near the populace of Brescia begin to arrive, standing patiently in the rain. Everywhere are lanterns and flares reflected on the glistening helmets of the Fascisti, who, rifles on hand, guard every corner of the lined streets. Despite the heavy downpour, all is enthusiasm."

Nuvolari started before Varzi, which gave the latter an advantage, and the last away was Hans Ruesch. Although the roads were treacherous, not all drivers were proceeding with caution. Dinshaw lost control of the

One of the finest performances in the 1934 race was that of Piero Taruffi with a four-cylinder 4CTR 1,100cc Maserati. Partnered by Guerino Bertocchi, he defeated the MG Magnettes to win the 1,100cc class. Here Taruffi is seen in foul, wet and very misty weather on the Futa Pass. (Spitzley-Zagari Collection)

Among the luckiest drivers were Pintacuda and Nardilli who, in a particularly wet and miserable race, drove this comfortable, snug Lancia Astura saloon. Seen here at Modena, they finished tenth overall and won the over 3,000cc class. As Asturas had an engine of under 3 litres in capacity, this car probably had a non-standard power unit. The arrow in the background could not have been clearer, but outside the towns the road directions were often vague or absent. (Spitzley-Zagari Collection)

Aston Martin after mistaking the route in the village of Pontevico. He went off the road, uprooted a stone post and hit a wall. Neither driver nor co-driver was injured, but Argentiero, partnered by one Ferrari at the wheel of a 6C 1500 Alfa Romeo, slid off the road and crashed into a house in Pontevico, injuring both himself and his co-driver. Borelli with an Alfa Romeo Monza collided with the wrecked Aston Martin.

By Bologna, Tadini, a hill-climb specialist and a partner in Scuderia Ferrari, had averaged 95.8mph (154.1kph) for the 145 miles (233km). Privateers Bonetto/Negri were in second place with their 8C 2300, Varzi was third, seven minutes in arrears and Nuvolari was back in seventh place. The deficiencies of Nuvolari's Dunlop tyres were obvious. As the race progressed, the rain eased and finally stopped, but the roads remained wet. At Florence Tadini still led, with Varzi a minute in arrears and Nuvolari four minutes behind the leader.

It is reported that as the field roared over the Futa Pass, they passed Enzo Ferrari and some mechanics who were manning the service depot there before moving on to Bologna for the return journey. Felice Bonetto, competing in his first race, was driving an older 2.3-litre Alfa Romeo, loaded with spares and tyres. He was leading Varzi on the road. Seeing the red car approaching at speed and believing it to be Varzi's car, Enzo Ferrari ran into the road, waving his arms. Bonetto kept his foot down and Ferrari had to throw himself into the ditch. Bonetto later hit a tree and did not make it to Rome. He did not race again until after World War Two.

The positions remained unchanged at Rome. Tadini, who turned in what was probably the best drive of a long racing career, slowed because of gearbox trouble, Varzi and Nuvolari passed him at Macerata close to the Adriatic coast. By Ancona Varzi led Nuvolari by 40 seconds and Tadini was grimly holding on to third place despite having the use of only two gears but was forced to retire. There was now a fast run to Bologna but when Varzi suffered a puncture, Nuvolari went ahead and arrived at Bologna three minutes ahead of him.

Heavy rain began to fall again after the leaders left Bologna and once again Nuvolari's tyres put him at a major disadvantage. Varzi reached Venice eight minutes ahead on time and the race was over barring an accident. The drivers took the same bridge to the control in the Piazza Venizia and back out again to join the road to Treviso. Varzi and Nuvolari passed in opposite directions on the bridge after the race-leader had left the control and they had time to give each other a quick wave.

It was dusk when Varzi reached Brescia and he was nine minutes ahead of Nuvolari. The weather conditions had become worse and worse and third-place man Louis Chiron, a relatively inexperienced road-race driver with a great career ahead of him, was over an hour behind Nuvolari. The top ten finishers was not an unbroken list of Alfa Romeos. Taruffi had turned in an incredible, brilliant drive to take fifth place with the 1,100cc Maserati and finishing tenth dry and having raced in some luxury were Nardilli/Pintacuda with their elegant Lancia Astura saloon, the only closed car in the event.

Results:
General classification:

1st	Varzi/Bignami (Alfa Romeo), 14hr 8min 5sec (71.04mph/114.30kph)	
2nd	Nuvolari/Siena (Alfa Romeo), 14hr 16min 58sec	
3rd	Chiron/Rosa (Alfa Romeo), 15hr 24min 0sec	
4th	Battaglia/Bianchi (Alfa Romeo), 15hr 29min 35sec	
5th	Taruffi/Bertocchi (Maserati), 15hr 39min 1sec	

6th,	Sanguinetti/Balestrero (Alfa Romeo), 16hr 21min 31sec
7th	Dusio/Ajmini (Alfa Romeo), 16hr 38min 10sec
8th	Auricchio/Berti (Alfa Romeo), 16hr 43min 17sec
9th	Pertile/Jonoch (Alfa Romeo), 16hr 55min 29sec
10th	Nardilli/Pintacuda (Lancia), 16hr 58min 56sec

Class results:

1,100cc: Taruffi/Bertocchi (Maserati), 15hr 39min 1sec (64.16mph/103.24kph)
1,500cc: Marocchina/Comotti (Alfa Romeo), 17hr 32 min 55sec (57.22mph/92.070kph)
2,000cc: Pertile/Jonoch (Alfa Romeo), 16hr 55min 29sec (61.20mph/98.47kph)
3,000cc: Varzi/Bignami (Alfa Romeo), 14hr 8min 5sec (71.04mph/114.30kph)
Over 3,000cc: Nardilli/Pintacuda (Lancia), 16hr 58min 56sec (59.13mph/95.14kph)

Count Lurani and his second year with the MG Magnette team

(Adapted from Mille Miglia, 1927–57 *by Giovanni Lurani, Edita SA, 1981)*

The three official MGs arrived in Milan with the team manager, Hugh McConnell and mechanics who had previous Mille Miglia experience. MG expected to repeat its victory. The three cars were substantially the same as those entered in 1933, except that Roots superchargers had replaced the Powerplus and the compression ratio was lowered. This resulted in reduced power, but the inconvenience of plug fouling had also been eliminated. Our cars were safer and stronger than in 1933, but also slower and heavier. All in all they were not an improvement on the previous year's model, and I could not help being concerned at the threat presented by Piero Taruffi and his 1,100cc Maserati.

Our team was also weaker and less unified in its drivers. Lord Howe led the team and drove with his mechanic, Thomas. The second car was in the hands of E. R. Hall and his wife. They were from the north of England and kept themselves to themselves. The third car was entrusted to C. Penn Hughes who with Thomas had driven the Mercedes in the 1933 race, and I partnered Penn Hughes. Penn Hughes was a splendid chap, an excellent driver and a great friend.

We used the same refuelling points as in 1933, except that the Bologna point had been moved to opposite the Maserati factory in the Via Emilia Levante. There was a new process designed to make tyres more stable in the wet. Known as the Pneugrippa process, this consisted in cutting fine grooves across the tread. We had not been hindered by wet weather in 1933, but we couldn't be sure of racing in the dry this year, so I suggested we carry out the Pneugrippa process. The English didn't want to experiment and did nothing about it. Moreover, our tyres were big with narrow sections and high pressure – suitable for high speeds, but notoriously unstable in the wet.

It was still night when we arrived at the start. There were 21 starters in our class. Penn Hughes drove off with extreme caution on roads glistening in the persistent rain. Lord Howe overtook us as dawn came up. He was driving at full speed and snaking on the slippery roads. A little later, Taruffi and then Hall overtook us. Lord Howe arrived at the first control, Bologna, in 1hr 50min 29sec at an average of 79.3mph [127.6kph] and was eight minutes ahead of Taruffi. Taruffi was only one minute ahead of Hall and the private MG of Fork/Charley. Gilera (Fiat) was fifth in the class and we were sixth in 2hr 2min 35sec.

I took the wheel at Bologna and tried to improve our position in the class. Taruffi, who had Pneugrippa processed tyres, launched an attack on Lord Howe, and caught him on the Raticosa road. A duel between the two drivers began, but the Maserati, with its better braking, acceleration and handling, was clearly the superior car. Lord Howe, nevertheless, entered the battle with dash, taking risks on every corner.

The battle could not last long. It ended when the MG aquaplaned on the Pratolini descent near Florence, skidded several times and crashed into a large pylon. Lord Howe hit his head against an iron spike, but was saved from certain death by his helmet. Thomas also escaped serious injury, and when we passed them a few minutes later, they signalled that they were out of danger. The sight of the MG wrapped around the pylon had a sobering effect on other drivers who passed the scene and encouraged prudence.

The MG Magnettes returned to the Mille Miglia in 1934. This car, driven by Count 'Johnny' Lurani and Penn Hughes, was the sole survivor of the three-car MG team and finished second in the 1,100cc class, well over an hour behind the Maserati of Taruffi/Bertocchi. (Author's Collection)

From then on, the way was clear for Taruffi to start the fantastic drive that took him ahead of the pack of pursuers to final victory. At the Florence control, Taruffi had averaged more than 62mph [100kph] for a time of 3hr 24min 18sec. This was slower than our average in 1933. Behind Taruffi in the 1,100cc class came Hall, two minutes later, followed by Gilera in third place. I had moved up to fourth place. The rain had stopped when we arrived at our refuelling point at Siena. Hall was forced to retire near Buonconvento because of engine trouble and a minor crash, while I overtook Gilera and found myself in second place.

Our MG, by now the sole survivor of the British team, had to finish at all costs. The Maserati had decisively outdistanced us and only an accident to my friend Piero Taruffi could change the race order. Luckily there was no such accident, but Taruffi risked running out of petrol because of an error in the siting of the refuelling points. He overcame this by having a telephone call made to arrange an improvised refuelling point at Civitacastellana.

At Rome, Taruffi's average time was 6hr 25min at an overall speed of about 60mph [97kph]. We took 6hr 58min 26sec, averaging 57.5mph [92.5kph]. Penn Hughes and I were 16th in general classification, and the roads were perfectly dry. I had a good drive to Terni, and

was delighted to have driven this section at the best time in the class – 57min 4sec [64.4mph/103.6kph] – improving my 1933 time by about three minutes. Taruffi took about three minutes longer. I had the satisfaction of being fastest on this section only; thereafter I had to resign myself to the monotonous job of holding our second place.

Taruffi was 33 minutes ahead of us when we made our second refuelling stop at Perugia. Penn Hughes took over from there, and we set off towards Ancona without excitement or incident. Our race continued uneventfully. We refuelled again at Bologna, I resumed driving and it started to rain again. We continued to lose ground to Taruffi on this last stretch. He was using the Maserati's qualities to the full, while we had to exercise maximum caution on the rain-wet roads and with our uncut tyres. Moreover, 600 miles of racing had worn the treads, making our progress even more dangerous.

Penn Hughes took over again at Venice, and we finally arrived at Brescia without further incident. The race was a triumph for Taruffi in the 1,100cc class. His superb Maserati had completed the course in 15hr 39min 1sec at an average of 64.5mph [103.8kph]. Penn Hughes and I were second in 17hr 1min 14sec. We were 11th overall out of the 29 survivors of that gruelling race.

We were satisfied with our race, because we could not have gone faster in the circumstances. We had also improved our 1933 time by exactly one hour, increasing our average speed from 57mph [91kph] to 59mph [95kph]. Lord Howe remained in Florence to recover from his severe bruising and the Halls were somewhere in Tuscany. Thus the MG team was dispersed.

1935

14 April
Starters: 86; Finishers: 47; Distance 1,009 miles (1,623km).
Circuit: see page 243.
Weather: fine at the start, rain later.

Main contenders for victory:

106 Carlo Pintacuda/Marchese della Stufa (Alfa Romeo Tipo B Monoposto, 2,905cc)
     entered by Scuderia Ferrari

In addition Scuderia Ferrari prepared and entered a large number of 8C 2300 cars in both 2.3- and 2.6-litre forms, but although they were likely to finish high up the field, they were unlikely to win. Nuvolari did not compete in 1935, mainly because the Monaco Grand Prix was the following weekend. The only other serious contenders were:

98. Achille Varzi/Guido Bignami (Maserati Tipo 34, 3,724cc entered by Officine Alfieri
     Maserati)

The Coppa d'Oro del Littorio had not proved a success and was abandoned, so unsupercharged production cars were once again admitted provided that at least 100 had been built. This boosted the number of starters to 86, but of course rather more cars were entered and then failed to appear. Of the 86 starters, 26 were Alfa Romeos and there were 40 Fiat Balillas, the majority the new

production model with overhead valve engine. Details of the Monoposto Alfa Romeo and the Grand Prix Maserati are on page 120-121.

In addition to Varzi's car, the Maserati entries included five four-cylinder cars: a 1,500cc driven by Scarfiotti/Penati and four 1,100 cc cars. That driven by Bianco partnered by Bertocchi was the most likely to win the class. Among the Fiat Balillas was a very handsome little coupé driven by Ambrosini, who was the head of the Siata tuning company that later built its own cars, and Nuccio Bertone, who was to found the Bertone coachbuilding company. At the wheel of a more standard car were the Villoresi brothers, Emilio and Luigi. In the 1,500cc unsupercharged class were nine 1,196cc Lancia Augusta saloons, but even in tuned form they were not fast enough to be competitive.

There were two British Aston Martins entered. After finishing tenth at Le Mans in 1934 sharing the wheel of an Aston Martin Ulster with Reggie Tongue, Maurice Falkner ordered one of these cars for 1935. He entered it in the Mille Miglia with T. G. Clarke, his friend from Cambridge University where they were both undergraduates. Clarke reconnoitred the course with a

Mario Tadini, partnered by Chiari, drove this Alfa Romeo Monza in the 1935 race. They took the lead in the early stages of the race and eventually finished second, 42 minutes behind the Alfa Romeo Monoposto of Pintacuda and the Marchese della Stufa. Here Tadini is making a quick routine refuelling stop at Rome. (Spitzley-Zagari Collection)

Grand Prix cars on the road

The Alfa Romeo Tipo B Monoposto and the Maserati Tipo 6C 34

Milan

An interesting phenomenon in the 1935 race was the entry of Grand Prix cars by Scuderia Ferrari and Officine Alfieri Maserati. It has been written that Ferrari decided to adapt and enter a Monoposto after he heard that Maserati were running the 6C 34. There is no evidence to support this contention.

The winning car in 1935 was a 2.6-litre Alfa Romeo Monoposto with the bodywork extended to accommodate two people, skimpy cycle wings and electrics. Carlo Pintacuda was the driver and his mechanic, the Marchese della Stufa, a very small man, could just squeeze into the cockpit, but hung out into the airstream. This Monoposto, chassis number B5001, was subsequently rebuilt as a single-seater (Centro Documentazione Alfa Romeo)

The Alfa Romeo was chassis and engine numbers B5001 (Scuderia Ferrari numbers SF33) and, again, contrary to what has been written, it had a 2,905cc Grand Prix engine. This was detuned to run on Shell Dynamin commercial fuel. The car was one of three sold by Scuderia Ferrari and not updated for the 750kg Grand Prix Formula of 1934 onwards. These cars retained narrow cockpits (wider cockpits were needed for the new Formula). This particular Monoposto was sold to Puccinelli Sanini Lucca of Pescia, near Pistoia on 27 March 1935.

Although not owned by Scuderia Ferrari, this team prepared it for the race. Modifications included the installation of two small seats and a new cowl in front of the cockpit to permit the installation of two aero-screens. Despite being, in reality, a single-seater, the car was accepted under the very loose Mille Miglia regulations. Like the 1934 winner, this car ran on a methanol-based alcohol fuel mix. It has been claimed that Carlo Pintacuda was the only driver slim enough to fit the car and his friend and passenger Marchese della Stufa was an amateur jockey of diminutive statue. As narrated in the main text, they won the race.

Lucca sold the Monoposto back to Ferrari on 10 October 1935. The registration became MO 8463 and in

hired Fiat Balilla over a period of several weeks, but Falkner was only able to travel out a few days before the race. A second Ulster was driven by Eddie Hall partnered by Marsden. Yet another British car was a MG Magnette driven by Pellegrini/Gazzabini.

There were a number of new awards in 1935. Il Duce, Mussolini, presented a cup for the fastest time from Brescia to Rome. There were also prizes for the first ten Fiats to finish and for the youngest and oldest drivers in the race. Another innovation was that all drivers who

finished the race had their entry fee refunded and were given a gold medal.

Present at the race were Hon. Morigi (Under-Secretary of the Fascist Party), the Duke of Spoleto (President of the Royal Italian Automobile Club) and Lionel Martin (representing the British Royal Automobile Club). Once again the start was at 4am and the cars left at half-minute intervals. Pintacuda's Monoposto, which bore the number 106, was the last car to leave and during the race he was to pass 80 cars on the road.

1936 Ferrari sold it to Scuderia Maremmana of Grossetto. With this car Clemente Biondetti partnered by Cerasa finished fourth in the 1936 Mille Miglia behind a trio of three 8C 2900A Alfa Romeos. This team continued to race through 1937, but then it disappeared for a while.

It has been ascertained that this Monoposto was in Rome in 1939 and during the war its then owner shipped it to Buenos Aires where it was impounded by customs. It remained in customs until 1960 when it was sold for a nominal sum at auction. By the time that Alain de Cadenet bought it and brought it back to Britain in 1972, it was back in single-seater form. The car remains in his ownership and is exhibited in the Donington Collection.

Bologna

However early the Maserati brothers had planned their entry for the 1935 race, it was only too typical of the Bologna concern that work started late, was finished only shortly before the race, and there was no time left for anything approaching proper testing. This 6C 34 was built on chassis 3026, which had the wider 850mm-wide chassis to comply with the requirements of the 750kg Formula and it was powered by the 3,729cc (84 x

112mm) engine detuned to run on Shell commercial fuel. The very handsome body had a width of only 960mm (3ft 2in) and resembled that of the 4CS production cars.

The driver was Achille Varzi who was accompanied by his mechanic, Bignami. They ran swiftly to begin with, but the shoddily built body began to disintegrate and the car retired because of lubrication problems (of what nature precisely is unknown) shortly before the San Casciano refuelling stop after the Raticosa pass. The factory then rebuilt the car to single-seater form and sold it, as originally intended, to Scuderia Subalpina. As far as can be ascertained, the car has not survived. Tony Merrick built a copy for the late Anthony Mayman and it is believed that this is now in the United States.

Directly confronting the Alfa Romeo Monoposto was this Grand Prix Tipo 34 3.7-litre Maserati. It was driven by the great Achille Varzi, partnered by his faithful mechanic, Bignami. The Maserati had more than adequate speed to beat the Monoposto, but had been completed hastily, lacked testing and retired because of mechanical problems. (Spitzley-Zagari Collection)

In a performance that matched his 1934 drive, Tadini led by 54 seconds from Varzi, who in turn led Pintacuda, delayed by three wheel-changes, by 18 seconds. But Pintacuda was biding his time and, of course, at every control, was informed of the gap between him and the leader. As the leaders had crossed the Raticosa and Futa Passes, so Tadini extended his lead and by Florence Tadini was three minutes ahead of Pintacuda, while Varzi was dropping back because of mechanical problems.

Rain began to fall and by Rome the Monoposto had forged a significant advantage on the fast roads leading to the Eternal City and Pintacuda, despite Enzo Ferrari cautioning him at Siena to slacken his pace, led Tadini by 17 minutes. Behind the leaders came Macchia/Danese and Hans Ruesch/Guatta. Seventh at Rome was Scarfiotti with his 1,500cc Alfa Romeo and by Ancona he was in a remarkable third place.

Here he handed over to co-driver Baldani, but within three miles Baldani skidded into a crowd of spectators;

M. TADINI

two young girls were killed and several other young people were injured. Clarke/Falkner now led the 1,500cc class, but they were quite slow and much slower than the 1,100cc Bianco/Bertocchi Maserati. Hall had already retired shortly after Siena because of a blown cylinder head gasket.

On the run back north rain began to fall and Pintacuda eased off further, confident that he would win easily, provided that he did not make a mistake or the car broke. When he took the chequered flag in Brescia, he was three minutes faster than Varzi's winning time in 1934 and 40 minutes ahead of Tadini. Perhaps the greatest performance was that of Bianco/Bertocchi with the class-winning 1,100cc Maserati who finished seventh

Enrico Bianco was a very fast, but rather erratic, driver who seemed unaware of the dangers of motorsport. It was Bertocchi's lot to accompany the less responsible drivers, maybe because it was believed that he had a calming influence. Bianco finished seventh overall in the 1935 race and won the 1,100cc class. It is easy to forget how often Maseratis ran in the Mille Miglia. (Spitzley-Zagari Collection)

overall and were two hours ahead of the second finisher in the class, the Villoresi brothers with their Fiat Balilla.

Alfa Romeo's domination of the Mille Miglia was becoming boring and this would not change until after the race was banned in its traditional form following a bad accident in 1938.

Results:

General Classification:

1st   Pintacuda/della Stufa (Alfa Romeo), 14hr 4min 47sec (71.32mph/114.73kph)
2nd   Tadini/Chiari (Alfa Romeo), 14hr 46min 38sec
3rd   Battaglia/Tuffanelli (Alfa Romeo), 15hr 4min 8sec
4th   Ruesch/Gatta (Alfa Romeo), 15hr 5min 8sec
5th   Macchia/Danese (Alfa Romeo), 15hr 10min 58sec
6th   Sanguinetti/Balestrero (Alfa Romeo), 15hr 12min 47sec
7th   Bianco/Bertocchi (Maserati), 15hr 12min 56sec
8th   Cortese/Severi (Alfa Romeo), 15hr 26min 45sec
9th   Gurgo Salice/Laredo (Alfa Romeo), 15hr 39min 1sec
10th Rosa/Comotti (Alfa Romeo), 15hr 56min 43sec

Class results:

1,100cc: Bianco/Bertocchi (Maserati), 15hr 12 min 56sec (65.70mph/106.19kph)
1,500cc: Clarke/Falkner (Aston Martin) 17hr 52min 35sec (56.17mph/90.38kph)
2,000cc: Crivellari/Ferraro (Alfa Romeo), 15hr 59min 23sec (62.80mph/101.05kph)
3,000cc: Pintacuda/della Stufa (Alfa Romeo), 14hr 4min 47sec (71.32mph/114.73kph)
1,500cc unsupercharged: E. Villoresi/L. Villoresi (Fiat), 17hr 15min 26sec (58.21mph/93.66kph)

1936

5 April
Starters: 69; Finishers: 37; Distance 998 miles (1,606km).
Circuit: see page 244.
Weather: fine, dry throughout.

Main contenders for victory:

75	Marquis Antonio Brivio/Ongaro	(Alfa Romeo 8C 2900A, 2,905cc)
79	Carlo Pintacuda/Stefani	(Alfa Romeo 8C 2900A, 2,905cc)
82	Giuseppe Farina/Meazza	(Alfa Romeo 8C 2900A, 2,905cc)
84	Clemente Biondetti/Cerasa	(Alfa Romeo Tipo B Monoposto, 2,905cc)

In 1936 Scuderia Ferrari fielded a strong team of the latest 2.9-litre 8C 2900A sports cars, based on the Monoposto chassis, but with proper two-seater bodywork and slightly smoother lines. Brivio/Ongaro won the race with this 8C 2900A, but at the finish they were only half a minute ahead of the similar Scuderia Ferrari team car driven by Farina/Meazza. *(Centro Documentazione Alfa Romeo)*

Both the overall number of runners and the number of serious contenders were in decline, and although it would be higher in 1937 and 1938, starters would not be really numerous until the rebirth of the race in post-war days. Much of the shortage of runners in 1936 was attributable to the fact that Italy had invaded Abyssinia (with the Italian troops blessed by Pope Pius XI) on 2 October 1935. The result was a resolution for sanctions from the French-influenced League of Nations and although this did not include an oil embargo, there were very real fears in Italy that such an embargo would follow.

It was an all-Italian entry with one exception. Scuderia Ferrari entered three new Alfa Romeo 8C 2900A cars that were developments of the Monoposto Grand Prix car, but purpose-built for sports car racing. There was the usual miscellany of earlier Alfa Romeos and this year a particularly effective team of Maseratis. The fastest of these was a 4CS four-cylinder 1,496cc car driven by racing motorcyclist Ombono Tenni partnered by the great Bertocchi.

There was also a 2-litre four-cylinder Maserati in the hands of Rocco/Filippone from Naples and, more significantly, the rather wild, press-on regardless Bianco was again at the wheel of a 1,100cc car, but this time

partnered by Boccali. Encouraged by their 1935 success, Clarke had bought a new Ulster for 1936 and again shared it in the 1,000-mile race with Falkner. As usual, Fiats were the most numerous make.

In 1937 Venice was eliminated from the course, so the length was reduced to 998 miles (1,606km), the shortest before the Second World War. Road improvements had continued and the course was properly metalled throughout. The result was yet another increase in speeds. The government supported experiments with alternative fuels and six cars were running with charcoal burners. One of these was Professor Ferragutti's 8C 2300 Alfa Romeo that had run in the 1933 race.

Their performance was abysmal and the fastest averaged only 30mph or so and took nearly a full day longer to complete the course. The fastest cars, however, were running on alcohol-based fuel as used in the cars that had won the last two 1,000-mile races. There were now classes for supercharged and unsupercharged cars.

In 1936 the first car left Brescia at 5am, reasonable because of the rising speeds. Biondetti, who was destined to be the most successful of all Mille Miglia drivers, set the pace and led at Bologna, having averaged 104mph (167kph), and was 90 seconds ahead of Pintacuda, 80 seconds behind came Brivio and Farina was some way back in fifth place. On the difficult part of the course between Bologna and Florence the fastest driver was Farina who moved up into third place behind Biondetti and Pintacuda.

By Rome the leader was still Biondetti who had averaged a record 75mph (121kph); Farina was three minutes behind and then came Brivio. Pintacuda had lost 30 minutes – and the race – because of a blocked carburettor. At Rome, Biondetti had to refuel and fit new tyres. It was a slow stop and he left with only a few seconds in hand. Shortly after they left Rome both Brivio and Farina passed Biondetti, who had shot his bolt and gradually fell back.

Clarke/Falkner had run well again, leading their class at Rome, but they retired at Fano on the Adriatic Coast

The Alfa Romeo Monoposto that had won the race in 1935 reappeared as a private entry driven by Biondetti/Cerasa. Biondetti drove a strong race to finish third, around 37 minutes behind the winner. (Centro Documentazione Alfa Romeo)

Maserati entries did especially well in 1936 and a four-cylinder 1,500cc car was driven by racing motorcyclist Ombono Tenni, accompanied by the wonderful Maserati head mechanic, Guerino Bertocchi. Tenni was a wild driver who crashed at least once, but he won the 2,000cc class by a margin of nearly two hours from another Maserati driven by Rocco/Filippone. (Spitzley-Zagari Collection)

because of fuel-feed problems. Showing tremendous form were the Maseratis, with Tenni/Bertocchi in sixth place, despite a minor off-road excursion by Tenni in a fit of excess exuberance, while Bianco/Boccali were seventh. Both had moved up a place by the finish. Pintacuda had been making up lost time and he moved into third place ahead of Biondetti, who seemed to have lost his will to fight. It is likely that Biondetti, who was a big fellow, was suffering badly from the cramped cockpit of the Monoposto.

During the last 200 miles of the race, as darkness began to close in, Brivio had lighting problems on his Alfa Romeo, but at the finish still led by 32 seconds from Farina who had set a new record over the final Bologna-Brescia section of the course. Brivio was still around 57 minutes faster than Pintacuda's record winning time in 1935. Pintacuda finished third and Biondetti took an

unhappy and dispirited fourth place. The first of the unsupercharged cars was the 6C 2300 berlinetta Alfa Romeo that Cattaneo/Donati drove into ninth place.

Results:
General classification:

1st	Brivio/Ongaro (Alfa Romeo),	13hr 7min 51sec (75.59mph/121.62kph)
2nd	Farina/Meazza (Alfa Romeo),	13hr 8min 23sec
3rd	Pintacuda/Stefani (Alfa Romeo),	13hr 44min 17sec
4th	Biondetti/Cerasa (Alfa Romeo),	13hr 59min 21sec
5th	Tenni/Bertocchi (Maserati),	14hr 18min 40sec
6th	Bianco/Boccali (Maserati),	14hr 55min 10sec
7th	De Rahm/Banti (Alfa Romeo),	15hr 35min 35sec
8th	Gurgo Salice/Laredo (Alfa Romeo),	15hr 45min 27sec
9th	Cattaneo/Donati (Alfa Romeo),	15hr 59min 7sec
10th	Rocco/Filippone (Maserati),	16hr 14min 32sec

Class results, supercharged cars:

1,100cc: Bianco/Bocalli (Maserati), 14hr 55min 10sec (66.53mph/107.05kph)
2,000cc: Tenni/Bertocchi (Maserati), 14hr 18min 40sec (69.35mph/111.59kph)
Over 2,000cc: Brivio/Ongaro (Alfa Romeo), 13hr 7min 51sec (75.59mph/121.62kph)

Class results, unsupercharged cars:

1,100cc: Biagini/Periccioli (Fiat), 16hr 18min 31sec (59.64mph/95.96kph)
2,000cc: Jacazio/Gramolelli (Fiat), 18hr 31min 20sec (53.60mph/86.24kph)
Over 2,000cc: Cattaneo/Donati (Alfa Romeo), 15hr 59min 7sec (62.09mph/99.90kph)

1937

4 April
Starters: 124; Finishers: 65; Distance: 1,009 miles (1,623km).
Circuit: see page 243.
Weather: heavy rain throughout.

Main contenders for victory:

139	Guido Cattaneo/René Lebègue	(Talbot T150, 3,994cc)
140	Laurie Schell/René Carrière	(Delahaye 135 CS, 3,557cc)
141	Clemente Biondetti/Count Franco Mazzotti	(Alfa Romeo Tipo 8C 2900B, 2,905cc)
144	Giuseppe Farina/Meazza	(Alfa Romeo Tipo 8C 2900B, 2,905cc)
146	René Dreyfus/Pietro Ghersi	(Delahaye 135 CS, 3,557cc)
149	Gianfranco Comotti/Archimede Rosa	(Talbot T150, 3,994cc)
150	Carlo Pintacuda/Mambelli	(Alfa Romeo Tipo 8C 2900B, 2,905cc)

The 1937 Mille Miglia was held in torrential rain, so speeds and safety suffered. The latest Alfa Romeo 8C 2900B sports cars, still with stark, unstreamlined bodywork, took the first two places ahead of a French Delahaye. Here are the winners, Pintacuda/Mambelli, whose speed was over an hour slower than that of the 1936 winners, Brivio/Ongaro. (Centro Documentazione Alfa Romeo)

The circuit incorporated the Venice control once more and the length was restored to 1,009 miles. There were changes in the race regulations and the entry was now split into two categories: International Sports that included any car that complied with the very loose sports car regulations and the National Touring category; the latter became known as the National Sport category and was run to rules drawn up by Count 'Johnny' Lurani and his friend Corrado Filippini. Lurani described the rules as follows: "[the class] required a series production engine and chassis fitted with a regular sports body. Reasonable modifications to the engine and chassis were allowed to improve performance."

In the International Sports category Scuderia Ferrari fielded three of the improved 8C 2900B cars and in real terms there was little doubt that one of these would win. There were four French cars in this class and they performed well. The Delahayes, semi-works cars entered by Écurie Lucy O'Reilly Schell (husband and wife team of American heiress Lucy O'Reilly and husband Laurie Schell), were competition versions of the pushrod ohv straight-six 135 cars with 3,558cc (84 x 107mm) engines; they developed around 150bhp and they had enjoyed a very successful racing history from 1935 onwards.

There were also two Talbots, built at Suresnes in what had been the S-T-D Group's Darracq factory; Italian Antony Lago had taken over the company and

introduced a range of larger-capacity, upmarket cars and built the T150 sports-racing cars with six-cylinder push-rod, overhead valve, engine with long and short rockers and supplementary cross-over push-rods – much the same thinking as that of Fritz Fiedler at BMW; the capacity of these cars was 3,989cc (90 x 104.5mm), they developed around 180bhp and were fitted with Wilson pre-selector gearboxes. The drivers were Cattaneo/Lebègue and Comotti/Rosa.

In the National Sports category the leading contenders were three Jano-designed 6C 2300B Alfa Romeos with independent suspension front and rear and with twin overhead camshaft 2,309cc engines. As raced, power output was about 105bhp. Two cars were Scuderia Ferrari entries with lightweight Ghia bodies and driven by Siena/Luigi Villoresi and Severi/Righetti, while the third with Touring body was entered by Benito Mussolini in person and driven by his chauffeur Ercole Boratto and Battista Guidotti. Nominally, Guidotti was second driver; Boratto was at the wheel at the start and drove round the corner where Guidotti took over. The process was reversed just before the finish.

There were another ten 6C 2300 Alfa Romeos entered by private owners, but these were the earlier type with rigid axles front and rear. Eighty of the starters were Fiats and among them, running in the International Sports category, was a very streamlined 1,500cc car

driven by Il Duce's eldest son Vittorio Mussolini partnered by Vitiliani. Other Fiat drivers included Enrico Nardi, Ermini and Piero Dusio, all of whom founded their own car manufacturing companies. Dusio's Cisitalias were very successful in post-war days.

In the 1,100cc International Sports category Lurani/Emilio Villoresi drove a Maserati and seemed all set to win the class. Two British cars ran in the race. Dutchman Eddie Hertzberger had bought the ex-Dick Seaman Aston Martin 2-litre Speed Model that had run in the 1936 Tourist Trophy and, partnered by Pijl, he drove like a madman. The other British entry was an MG saloon which Tom Wisdom raced accompanied by his wife 'Bill'.

The start took place in torrential rain that persisted throughout the race. Cars left Brescia at what can only be described as very erratic intervals; four minutes for the slower cars, but there was a gap of 22 minutes after car number 33 (the Fiat of Dusio/Basadonna) left at 3.28am and when the start resumed at 3.50am, the interval was usually, but not always, two minutes. After two other long intervals, the last starter did not get away until 9.26am.

From the start Pintacuda drove at the fastest possible speed in the very bad weather conditions and he reached Bologna in the lead at a record average of 105.9mph (170.4kph). Next on time was Giuseppe Farina, seven minutes in arrears, followed by Dreyfus/Ghersi

Continued on page 137

Giuseppe Farina, destined to be the first Formula 1 World Champion in 1950, is seen with his co-driver Meazza in the cockpit of the Tipo 8C 2900B that they drove to third place in the 1937 race. (Centro Documentazione Alfa Romeo)

The usual pattern of Alfa Romeo supremacy was challenged by a team of two 3,558cc Delahayes. René Dreyfus and Pietro Ghersi, who put up a strong fight with this Delahaye, held second place for a while and eventually finished third, a little over 37 minutes behind the winner. (Spitzley-Zagari Collection)

In 1956 a young Australian, John Thompson, was travelling round Europe with a friend, watching the motor racing. At Brescia for the Mille Miglia, he was granted a press pass and joined the press photographers during scrutineering and at the starting ramp. John used a cheap East German Pentacon 35mm camera (not the usual Leica or Contax favoured by the professionals) and Kodachrome transparency film. The Pentacon was not of the single-lens reflex type, and he was unaware that, because of a fault, it had slipped out of focus. The result was images with strong colour, still unfaded after 50 years, but lacking good focus. A selection of his atmospheric images is reproduced on the first four pages of this colour section, published here for the first time.

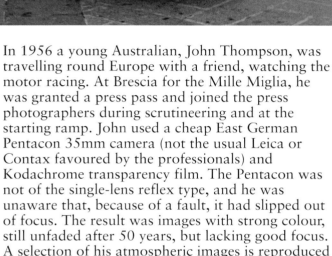

Top left: The Stanguellini team arrives at Brescia for scrutineering. Although these cars were popular in the 750cc and 1,100cc classes, the marque was virtually unknown outside Italy. In the 1956 Mille Miglia, Stanguellinis took second and third places in the 750cc class, behind an OSCA.

Top right: Ferrari driver Eugenio Castellotti at scrutineering. The young Italian drove his Tipo 290MM V12 car solo to win an outstanding victory ahead of team-mates Collins, Musso and Fangio. It was the greatest win of his very short career. Castellotti was killed in a testing accident at Modena Aerautodromo in March 1957.

Above right: Throughout the season Musso, who had previously driven for Maserati, and Castellotti battled to prove which of them was the greater driver – and both suffered lurid crashes through trying too hard. Musso took third place in 1956. He had a fatal accident in the 1958 French Grand Prix at Reims.

Right: Piero Taruffi arrived at scrutineering in his 3-litre Tipo 300S Maserati and began to talk to a young admirer. Although he led the race at one stage, Taruffi retired because of brake problems. In 1957, on his 14th attempt, the 'Silver Fox' finally won the Mille Miglia.

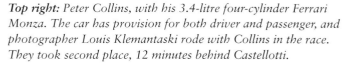

Top left: In 1956, Stirling Moss, partnered by Denis Jenkinson, drove a six-cylinder 3.5-litre Maserati. It was hastily prepared, handled badly and crashed. Here, at scrutineering, Moss discusses problems with Maserati chief mechanic Guerino Bertocchi.

Top right: Peter Collins, with his 3.4-litre four-cylinder Ferrari Monza. The car has provision for both driver and passenger, and photographer Louis Klemantaski rode with Collins in the race. They took second place, 12 minutes behind Castellotti.

Above left: Sheila Van Damm and Peter Harper shared this Sunbeam Rapier. Two of these cars were entered by the Rootes Group works team: they had been prepared in the ERA works at Dunstable. Van Damm/Harper finished 72nd overall and second in their special series class.

Above: A Maserati mechanic has changed the plugs on one of the 300S cars, probably Taruffi's.

Left: Driving this Austin-Healey 100S in the 1956 race, Leslie Brooke/Astbury were eliminated when they went off the road at Siena and hit the parapet of the bridge. They were unhurt, but both the car and bridge were badly damaged.

Top left: *It wasn't easy getting into and out of the otherwise-magnificent works Mercedes-Benz 300 SL coupés. In the very bad conditions in which the 1956 race was run, the Mercedes team manager, Alfred Neubauer, believed that one of the 300 SLs could win outright, but he was sadly disappointed, especially as a Ferrari defeated them in the GT class. Behind this 300 SL, driven by Helmut Busch and Wolfgang Pifco, is a Porsche 356 Carrera.*

Top right: *Porsche works driver Hans Herrmann at the wheel of his 550 Spyder. He had won the 1,500cc sports class in 1954, Wolfgang Seidel had won the class in 1955, but in 1956 both works entries were eliminated by valve failure.*

Above: *Castellotti at the start.*

Above right: *John Heath, driving an HWM-Jaguar, was an early starter in the class, but crashed on the rain-soaked road near Rimini and suffered fatal injuries.*

Right: *Ferrari had the noses of their Mille Miglia cars painted different colours for identification purposes and, appropriately, that of Collins' Ferrari Monza, number 551, was green. Under hard acceleration, departing cars had deposited an incredible amount of rubber on the starting ramp.*

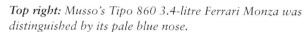

Top left: *Number 554 was the Maserati 350S of Moss and Jenkinson. Moss, at the wheel, cannot be seen because he is masked by the start-line official to whom he is talking. The 350S was a sad disappointment to both the Maserati team and the drivers.*

Top right: *Musso's Tipo 860 3.4-litre Ferrari Monza was distinguished by its pale blue nose.*

Above left: *This Maserati 300S, number 557, was driven by Cesare Perdisa, another great Latin hopeful. He ran very well in the opening stages.*

Above and left: *Fangio's 3.5-litre V12 Ferrari Tipo 290MM, number 600, bore a dark blue noseband. He finished fourth. The Argentinean was at the height of his powers and would that season win his fourth Formula 1 World Championship, but he was not an exceptionally talented sports car driver.*

Opposite: *An 1,100cc OSCA seen in 1957 in front of the Maserati brothers' works, just outside Bologna. The company had moved to this new factory three years earlier. In the post-war years, despite the appearance of the Porsche 550 Spyder, OSCA largely dominated the smaller-capacity classes of the Mille Miglia. (James M. Sitz)*

Above: *In the torrentially wet 1956 race Peter Collins, partnered by photographer Louis Klemantaski, drove this Tipo 860 Monza Ferrari to second place, just over 12 minutes behind Eugenio Castellotti with a V12 Ferrari. Maranello faced little opposition, but even so, getting the first five places was a remarkable performance. (Klemantaski Collection)*

Right: *Seen here at the Rome Control is Gregor Grant, editor of Autosport, who drove this 1957 Lotus Eleven borrowed from the works. Already the scuttle-mounted additional fuel tank has developed a leak and, although Grant turned in a fine drive, the fuel leak forced his retirement 70 miles (112km) from the finish. (Klemantaski Collection)*

Overleaf: *Peter Collins, partnered by Klemantaski, came close to winning the 1957 race, but retired at Parma because of transmission failure on his 4-litre Tipo 335S Ferrari. On his thirteenth assault on the Mille Miglia, Piero Taruffi, seen here with his 3.8-litre Tipo 315S, won, three minutes ahead of von Trips with another Ferrari. (Klemantaski Collection)*

(Delahaye). Biondetti had engine problems that would lead to his retirement and at no time did he appear on the leader board. Already, Vittorio Mussolini was out of the race because his Fiat had broken its engine.

Pintacuda was still leading at Florence, but Dreyfus/Ghersi were now in second place, the result of Farina easing off because of fuel-feed problems. Schell/Carrière held fourth place with the other Delahaye and then came the Talbots of Cattaneo/Lebègue and Comotti/Rosa. The French were putting up a remarkable performance. The rain continued unabated and Pintacuda still led at Rome, but his time was slower than the winner's in the preceding two years. At Florence Wisdom crashed heavily after swerving to avoid a pedestrian and both he and his wife were injured, albeit not too seriously.

At Rome the order was unchanged among the leaders, but as the field swept across the foothills of the Apennines, Dreyfus, one of the greatest of French drivers in the 1930s, moved into the lead and pulled out a five-minute advantage over Pintacuda. Then Dreyfus went off the road, the result of a spray of mud temporarily unsighting him; the car was badly damaged and although he was able to carry on to Bologna, he was forced to retire there. Lurani/Villoresi also retired their Maserati in the Apennines because of engine failure. It was on this section of the race that both Talbots retired. By the time the cars reached Bologna for the second time, Farina was back in second place ahead of Schell/Carrière.

Both of the leading Alfa Romeos had problems; Farina's car was still running badly because of fuel-feed problems and because of electrical problems Pintacuda's headlamps failed to work. The much later start meant

In 1937 El Duce, Benito Mussolini, personally entered this 6C 2300 in the name of Scuderia Parioli. The car was driven by Battista Guidotti (except at the start and the finish) and Mussolini's chauffeur, Ercole Boratto. They took fourth place overall and won the over 1,500cc National Touring category. Not much is known about Boratto, save that in post-WW2 days he wrote his memories of the Dictator. (Centro Documentazione Alfa Romeo)

This very handsome Fiat 1500 coupé was driven in the 1937 race by Vittorio Mussolini, second son of the dictator, and Vitalini (Fiat). They also ran as part of the Scuderia Parioli, which won the Brescia Grand Prix team prize. The third members of the team were Ceschina/Guagnelli with another Fiat. (Spitzley-Zagari Collection)

Seen passing through Modena in heavy rain is the ex-Seaman, somewhat modified 2-litre Speed Model Aston Martin of Hertzberger/Pyl. After a hectic, exciting race Hertzberger took second place behind an Alfa Romeo in the 2,000cc Sports category. (Spitzley-Zagari Collection)

that the cars were finishing the race in the dark and Pintacuda had no alternative, but to tuck in behind Farina and rely on the leading car's headlamps to show him the way. At the finish Pintacuda led Farina by over 17 minutes on time. The Schell/Carrière's third place was the best performance by a foreign car since 1931.

Hertzberger had an exciting race with his orange-painted Aston Martin. He had not practised over the course and the only way he knew to race was flat out all the way. His companion/mechanic Pijl was either very brave or totally moronic. For mile after mile Hertzberger held the Aston Martin at 5,000rpm in top gear on roads that were 'as slippery as soap.' He lost an hour while a broken valve-spring was changed and after a near-miss in the dark with a car coming the other way, the Aston Martin ended up in a ditch. Onlookers helped to get it back on the road and Hertzberger continued at unabated speed to finish 16th overall and second in the 2,000cc class, 46 minutes behind an Alfa Romeo.

Results:

General classification:

1st	Pintacuda/Mambelli (Alfa Romeo), 14hr 17min 32sec (71.32mph/114.75kph)	
2nd	Farina/Meazza (Alfa Romeo), 14hr 35min 11sec	
3rd	Schell/Carrière (Delahaye), 14hr 54min 55sec	
4th	Boratto/Guidotti (Alfa Romeo), 15hr 40mim 1sec	
5th	Ventidue/Ventuno (Alfa Romeo), 16hr 19min 45sec	
6th	Cortese/Guatta (Alfa Romeo), 16hr 21min 20sec	
7th	Crivellari/Ferraro (Alfa Romeo), 17hr 4min 25sec	
8th	Teagno/Barbieri (Alfa Romeo), 17hr 4min 33sec	
9th	Severi/Righetti (Alfa Romeo), 17hr 9min 20sec	
10th	Contini/Salvadori (Alfa Romeo), 17hr 9min 35sec	

Class results, International Sports Category:

750cc: Dusio/Basadonna (Fiat), 21hr 0min 9sec (48.53mph/78.09kph)
1,100cc: Colini/Prosperi (Fiat), 18hr 26min 15sec (55.90mph/89.95kph)
2,000cc: Contini/Salvadori (Alfa Romeo), 17hr 9min 35sec (59.40mph/95.57kph)
Over 2,000cc: Pintacuda/Mambelli (Alfa Romeo), 14hr 17min 32sec
 (71.32mph/114.75kph)

Class results, National Touring Category:

750cc: Spotorno/Besana (Fiat), 21hr 25min 6sec (47.64mph/76.66kph)
1,100cc: Braida/Jesi (Fiat), 18hr 0min 18sec (56.61mph/91.09kph)
1,500cc: Minnio/Castagnaro (Fiat), 17hr 22min 48sec (58.65mph/94.36kph)
Over 1,500cc: Boratto/Guidotti (Alfa Romeo), 15hr 40min 1sec
 (65.06mph/104.68kph)

1938

3 April
Starters: 141; Finishers: 72; Distance: 1,013 miles (1,630km).
Circuit: see page 244.
Weather: fine throughout.

Main contenders for victory:

141	Giuseppe Farina/Meazza (Alfa Romeo 8C 2900B, 2,905c)
142	Carlo Pintacuda/Mambelli (Alfa Romeo 8C 2900B, 2,905cc)
143	Clemente Biondetti/Stefani (Alfa Romeo 8C 2900C, 2,994cc)
145	Piero Dusio/Boninsegni (Alfa Romeo 8C 2900B, 2905cc)
146	Mazaud/Quinlin (Delahaye Type 145, 4,490cc)
148	Eugenio Siena/Emilio Villoresi (Alfa Romeo 8C 2900B, 2905cc)
149	René Carrière/Vanderpyl (Talbot T150, 3,994cc)
152	René Dreyfus/Varet (Delahaye Type 145, 4,490cc)

For 1938 the route was significantly altered in that at Florence it now swept west along the Autostrada to Pisa and then followed the coast south along the Via Aurelia as far as Tarquinia before veering east and taking the very fast road to Rome. From Rome the route was unchanged as far as Terni, but it then took a much more direct route to the Adriatic coast, joining this at Fano, north of Ancona; from this point the route was unchanged from 1937.

The class rules had changed again. There were two basic categories, for International Sports cars, supercharged and unsupercharged, and National Sports cars (the previous year's unsupercharged National Touring category by another name). There were 155 entries of which 119 were in the National Touring category. As indicated above, by the time the cars left Brescia, the number of starters had dropped to 141.

Because of the continuing failure of Alfa Romeo to beat the German Mercedes-Benz and Auto Union cars in Grand Prix racing, significant changes influenced by the Fascist government had been made at the Milan company. While it was only too obvious that Alfa Romeo was inadequately funded to effectively challenge the German teams, with the benefit of hindsight it is not unreasonable to conclude that recent Jano design work simply followed his previous thinking and lacked any real innovation. Jano went to Lancia and the new head of the experimental department was Spaniard Wifredo Ricart.

Scuderia Ferrari was bought out by Alfa Romeo and there was a new works team, Alfa Corse. This was still headed by Enzo Ferrari until he left in 1939, and had Luigi Bazzi as chief technician and Nello Ugolini as competitions director. For the 1938 Mille Miglia the company built new 8C 2900Bs with light spider bodies

This important photograph shows off so well the superbly balanced lines of the Touring spider body of the 1938 8C 2900B as raced by Alfa Corse. The works entered four of these cars, but the one driven by Biondetti/Stefani is often referred to as an 8C 2900C because it had a slightly larger 2,994cc engine. (Centro Documentazione Alfa Romeo)

Biondetti/Stefani at the wheel of their 8C 2900C Alfa Romeo. It was in this 1938 race that Biondetti scored the first of his four Mille Miglia victories. (Centro Documentazione Alfa Romeo)

Piero Dusio, founder of the Cisitalia company which was so successful just after the war, was partnered by Boninsegni and they drove this ex-works Alfa Romeo 8C 2900B into third place. It had been the winning car in 1937. (Author's Collection)

by Touring. The car driven by Biondetti, is described above as an 8C 2900C because it was powered by the latest 2,994cc derivative of the Monoposto engine that powered the eight-cylinder Grand Prix cars built for the formula of 1938 onwards. This designation is not recognised by Luigi Fusi and other experts. Piero Dusio's private 8C 2900B was one of the 1937 works cars.

Following their encouraging performances in 1937, both Delahaye and Talbot again entered cars in 1938. The Tipo 145 Delahayes had unsupercharged V12 engines of 4,490cc (75 x 84.7mm). The specification included aluminium-alloy cylinder heads, magnesium-alloy cylinder block, crankcase, timing and valve covers, and the crankshaft ran in roller bearings. Despite this sophistication, there were pushrod-operated overhead valves, but there was twin-plug ignition. By 1938 the power output of these cars was about 245bhp.

The V12 Delahayes competed in Grand Prix racing (pretty well all that was necessary was to remove the cycle wings) and for 1938 Écurie Bleue run by Lucy O'Reilly and Laury Schell had six of these cars, plus a single-seater. A week after the 1938 Mille Miglia, René Dreyfus scored a remarkable victory with one of these cars in the Pau Grand Prix, defeating the Mercedes-Benz of Caracciola/Lang. If neither Delahaye nor Talbot was to prove capable of defeating the red army of Alfa Romeos, they would, nevertheless give their drivers quite a fright.

Significant in the 2,000cc unsupercharged class was a team of works BMW 328s driven by Fane/James,

Lurani/Schaumburg-Lippe and Richte/Wernick, backed up by the private German entry of von der Mühle/Holtzschuh. A.F.P. Fane was regarded as one of the most promising British drivers of his era, but he failed to achieve greatness because of his death in the RAF during the war. The BMW team was managed by Ernst Loof, who had at one time been in charge of BMW's motorcycle-racing programme and in post-war days was responsible for the Veritas.

The irrepressible Hertzberger was again at the wheel of his Aston Martin, but he had no prospects of defeating the Teutonic efficiency of the BMW team and the speed of their 328s. In the National Sports category there were many interesting cars and among the most significant. were the newly introduced Fiat 508CMMs with 1,089cc four-cylinder overhead valve engines developing 42bhp, with very slippery coupé bodies and a maximum speed of around 95mph (153kph).

Piero Taruffi, partnered by Carena, had a conspicuously fast Fiat in the 1,100cc class and of especial interest were several of the Lancia Aprilias running in the 1,500cc class. Marazza had an especially aerodynamic Aprilia berlinetta, but there seems to be no record of who built the body. Another Aprilia variant was the car driven by Luigi Villoresi/Forti which had a well-streamlined Spider body by Zagato, completed so late that it was unpainted.

The first car left Brescia at 2am and it was not until 6am that the last car was away. It meant that fastest cars would complete the course in daylight, even if the start – for most competitors – took place in darkness. By Bologna, Pintacuda had averaged a record 112mph

Cortese came from Leghorn where he is seen in the 1938 race with the Alfa Romeo that he shared with Fumigalli (Alfa Romeo). Their car was a modified 6C 2300 model with special body by Touring, the leading Italian coachbuilder at this time. Cortese and Fumigalli finished ninth overall and won the National Sport category. (Centro Documentazione Alfa Romeo)

In 1938 the rather bizarrely-styled V12 4.5-litre Delahayes put up a strong challenge. Gianfranco Comotti/Roux, drove this car, but the French team brought insufficient tyres and they had to retire. Dreyfus/Varet finished fourth with their V12 Delahaye. (Author's Collection)

(180kph), six mph faster than the record and had built up a lead of two minutes over the Delahaye of Dreyfus/Varet, followed by Biondetti and Dusio; Farina was already out of the race because of a crash and Siena/Emilio Villoresi had also retired.

All the French cars were suffering excessive wear of their Dunlop tyres and it became clear that Écurie Bleue had brought along insufficient tyres to enable both cars to complete the course. The decision was made, very reluctantly, that Comotti would retire at Florence to enable Dreyfus to carry on to the finish. After he left Florence, Dreyfus started to have overheating problems caused, Lurani says, by failure of 'a small gasket', whatever that may mean in precise terms.

Pintacuda still led at Rome, having averaged just under 89mph (143kph), closely pursued by Dusio,

Dreyfus, Carrière (Talbot) and Mazaud (Delahaye). Dreyfus was forced to stop on a number of occasions to top up the radiator and then the faulty gasket was changed. It was a remarkable feature of the Mille Miglia that a driver could spend a lot of time, more than an hour on occasion, resolving mechanical and other problems and still finish well up the field. After Rome Pintacuda was slowed by brake problems, and although he thought about retiring, he decided to carry on.

After repairs to his brakes, Pintacuda began to make up lost ground, and at Venice he passed Biondetti on the road as they crossed the bridge. When they reached Brescia Biondetti still led on time by two minutes, with Dusio third (all of 40 minutes behind the winner) and Dreyfus fourth. One of the more remarkable performances was that of the BMW 328s, which took the first four places in their class. The eighth place of Fane was an outstanding achievement, but Lurani said that in winning the class Fane broke team orders laid down by Ernst Loof at Bologna on the return run to maintain station, but did so inadvertently.

Lurani, always the smooth diplomat, also wrote that the car he was sharing with Schaumburg-Lippe punctured a tyre because Forti, Luigi Villoresi's mechanic, carelessly threw a bottle out of the cockpit of their class-winning Lancia in front of the BMW. Hertzberger had a poor race and retired the Aston Martin because of a blown cylinder head gasket. Other notable performances in the National Sports category were Cortese with a unsupercharged 6C 2300 Alfa Romeo (winner of the category and ninth overall) and Taruffi who led the 1,100cc class throughout and was 30 minutes ahead of his nearest rival at the end of the race.

Everyone was congratulating themselves on having run a really good race with no serious accidents, when terrible news came through. On the Bologna ring road as the cars raced north to the finish, two Italian amateurs, Bruzzo and Mignanego, lost control of their near-enough standard Lancia Aprilia as they crossed the railway lines at a level crossing just after the control.

Most of the other drivers felt a bad jolt when they went over this crossing, but nothing more. The Aprilia crashed into the crowd, killing ten people (seven of them children) and injured another 23. What caused this terrible accident is unknown, but in any event the Italian government issued the equivalent of a D-Notice, putting an embargo on publication of the details. Inevitably and swiftly, the Mille Miglia was banned.

Results
General classification:

1st	Biondetti/Stefani (Alfa Romeo), 11hr 58min 29sec (84.47mph/135.91kph)	
2nd	Pintacuda/Mambelli (Alfa Romeo), 12hr 0min 31sec	
3rd	Dusio/Boninsegni (Alfa Romeo), 12hr 37min 31sec	
4th	Dreyfus/Varet (Delahaye), 12 hr 39min 53sec	
5th	Carrière/Vanderpyl (Talbot), 12hr 59min 3sec	
6th	Ventidue/Ventuno (Alfa Romeo), 13hr 28min 53sec	
7th	Mazaud/Quinlin (Delahaye), 13hr 33min 41sec	
8th	Fane/James (BMW), 13hr 36min 19sec	
9th	Cortese/Fumagalli (Alfa Romeo), 13hr 38min 11sec	
10th	Lurani/Schaumburg-Lippe (BMW), 13hr 38min 52sec	

Class Results, International Sports Category:

2,000cc unsupercharged: Fane/James (BMW), 13hr 36min 19sec (74.06mph/119.16kph)

2,000cc supercharged: Bellandi/Vagelli (Alfa Romeo), 14hr 57min 42sec (67.35mph/108.36kph)

3,000cc supercharged: Biondetti/Stefani (Alfa Romeo), 11hr 58min 29sec (84.47mph/135.91kph)

4,500cc unsupercharged: Dreyfus/Varet (Delahaye), 12hr 39min 53sec (79.56mph/128.01kph)

Class Results, National Sports Category

750cc: Baravelli/Sola (Fiat), 17hr 19min 25sec (58.16mph/93.58kph)

1,100cc: Taruffi/Carena (Fiat), 14hr 28min 55sec (69.58mph/111.95km)

1,500cc: L. Villoresi/Forti (Lancia), 14hr 9min 25sec (71.18mph/114.53kph)

Over 1,500cc: Cortese/Fumagalli (Alfa Romeo), 13hr 38min 11sec (73.89mph/118.89kph)

A. F. P. Fane's report to the BMW factory after practice

Letter to Mr Schleicher, Messrs BMW (Note: surviving copies are in draft form only)

Dear Mr Schleicher
I would first of all like to thank you for letting me once again drive one of your cars and tell you how much I enjoyed this. I would also very much like to thank Herr Loof and his mechanics for the hard work they put in on the car and the efficient way in which the whole of the Mille Miglia practice was carried out.

As promised you when I was in Munich, I am setting out below some points that arose during practice, some of which I did not mention to you.

My first impression of the cars was that they all behaved remarkably well. I think that this race is in many ways a greater test to gearbox, differential and back axle, etc, than perhaps even the engine.

I agree with you that during the race the three cars should in no way be over-stressed and be driven with the utmost consideration in view of the length of this event and bearing in mind that the team speeds are more important than the individual speeds. I think the maximum revolutions should be 4,500 and that all gear changes should be done reasonably slowly and not crashed through as might be done in a short event where every fraction of a second counts.

In respect of the behaviour of the cars, the actual criticisms you know already, but the points in my own car were: failure of an experimental gasket, lack of sufficient oil pressure and the very bad front wheel patter. It is worth remarking that the self-starter on my own car became disengaged from the engine owing to the retaining belt loosening through vibration. The retaining screw to this belt should be locked to prevent this or any such other parts from working loose.

All these troubles can be quite easily overcome and apart from that I was very satisfied with the behaviour in general. The performance is absolutely sufficient for a race of this distance, the maximum speed obtainable being 4,700rpm, which is more than necessary for the race. The rear suspension appeared to be perfect, brakes were always very good, although inclined to become very hot on the section between Bologna and Florence which is very twisty. They cooled very quickly and the [sic] two or three hundred metres straight was sufficient for them to operate once again very effectively.

I also drove for a very short distance the car that was being driven by Herr Loof. On this the steering was good,

Fane in his 328 BMW before the 1938 Mille Miglia. Alongside him is Frazer Nash mechanic Bill James, who later worked for Aston Martin, and then Cooper, before emigrating after the end of the 1959 season. James was a notorious chain-smoker and later became very bald. He would tuck a lighted cigarette behind one ear, forget about it, light another and pop this behind the other ear. The result: nicotine stains up both sides of his head. By the car are H. J. Aldington and Mrs Fane. (Frazer Nash Archives)

Fane at the wheel of the works BMW 328 with which he won his class. He is seen on a twisting section of road on the Adriatic coast. Note the swastika on this side of the bonnet – on the other side the Briton had stuck a Union flag. (Frazer Nash Archives)

though it was immediately apparent that the clutch was not good and made the gear-change very difficult. It was also apparent that the brakes were not in the same class as those on my car. Metzeller tyres as fitted to my car gave better road adhesion than the Continentals on Herr Loof's car.

Reverting once more to the car I used, the seat position, windscreen and general equipment were absolutely satisfactory and I do not think these [should] be altered. However, the seat for the mechanic or passenger should be lowered as much as possible, as this at the moment is very high and the passenger may experience difficulty in keeping himself in the car.

I think that it would be a very good idea and would be appreciated by the drivers, if you would make a list of notes for this race – and for that matter all events – of the instructions that you would like us to obey and points which you would particularly ask us observe and if I might suggest a few:-

On the Autostrada [Fane wrote 'Autostrahder'], the occasional closing of the throttle which gives certain relief to the engine – say, once every kilometre – can only affect the total time taken over the Autostrada by a matter of 15 seconds and, therefore, if you consider this a good idea, it can hardly have any effect on the result.

Secondly, should the cars close up on one another and run together, as may be likely, it is dangerous and not advisable as very often we did in practice. It must be remembered that the Italian Autobahns are not double-track roads as in Germany – where a bridge has to be crossed, the other side of which the driver cannot see an obstruction that might possibly arise, if the three cars were running in close proximity the second two could not fail to run into the first car, should it have to brake suddenly. This of course applied throughout the whole course.

Thirdly, it should be realised at the pit stops that there is a possibility of two or even all three of the cars arriving at about the same time; an arrangement should be made in case of this arising.

With reference to the question of an English mechanic, unfortunately, the only mechanic that I would like to bring is at the moment ill and it is very doubtful whether he will be able to come in time for the race. Perhaps, therefore, you would be so kind as to arrange for me to have a German in case I am unable to bring my mechanic.

[Note: Fane's mechanic, Bill James, later of the Aston Martin and Cooper works teams, was fit and rode with him in the race.]

With reference to Dunlop tyres, it looks as if it will be extremely unlikely for me to arrange to use these as there is likely to be a considerable amount of trouble in getting these tyres either into Germany or Italy. I shall, however, write to you again on this subject and if it is impossible to arrange for the use of Dunlops I should prefer to use the Metzellers as I used in practice.

Lastly, I would like to thank you once again and I sincerely hope I will be able to help BMWs to obtain the team prize, as I know that you will be doing your utmost to ensure success in the preparation of the cars.

Yours sincerely,
A. F. P. Fane

A. F. P. Fane's report to the BMW factory after the race

Letter to Mr Schleicher, Messrs BMW (Note: surviving copies are undated), very slightly amended.

Dear Mr Schleicher
As usual, I am writing a report on any observations in the Mille Miglia, which may be of use to you.

First of all, let me thank you once again for letting me drive one of your cars in this event. I can only say that I enjoyed doing so very much. Perhaps you would also be so kind as to also convey my thanks to everyone who helped in obtaining such a marvellous result.

As you know, the car suffered from no serious trouble whatsoever, the only actual work done to it being the changing of a dynamo at Pisa owing to the fact that it had not been charging. After changing the dynamo no further trouble was experienced in this direction.

From Brescia to Bologna after the start, 4,000 revolutions were seldom exceeded allowing the lively engine to become thoroughly warmed up and throughout the race the maximum revolutions on any gear were 4,500 and I frequently lifted my foot off the throttle on Autostradas and long straight stretches.

The only one feature of the car which began to worry me, and which appeared just before Rome, was a vibration in the transmission. It felt as if it was something to do with either the gearbox or the propeller shaft. This – although it worried me considerably at the time – did not appear to get any worse although there was a considerable amount of oil being thrown up from some part of the transmission.

The engine ran absolutely perfectly throughout the race, the oil pressure invariably at 5 atmospheres and the oil temperature rose to 110 only on one occasion whereas normally it stayed at 100 degrees. I feel that the reason for it rising as high as 110 is the fact that the centre light partly obstructed the airflow on [to] the oil side.

The suspension and steering of the car [were] remarkably good and the brakes, although they started losing their efficiency when they were very hot between Terni and the coast, where the road is extremely twisty, immediately they cooled the full efficiency returned.

About 30 kilometres from the finish of the race, I

A. F. P. Fane poses with a works BMW 328 in Brescia. This is not the car that he drove in the 1938 race. Note his two-tone shoes – they were very fashionable at the time. (Frazer Nash Archives)

noticed that the oil pressure fell on left-hand corners, indicating that the sump was getting empty of oil. I therefore reduced speed considerably on left-hand corners and about ten kilometres from home, the oil pressure dropped to 3 atmospheres on the straight. This again showed the sump was getting empty, but I did not stop to put any oil in as I thought it was better to drive into the finish at a reduced speed because here the crowds were so thick it was not possible to drive at high speeds in any event.

I do not think that the car used more oil on this last section, but I feel it is quite probable that the sump was not completely filled at the Bologna check although no doubt you will be able to discover whether this was so.

In closing, I would like to congratulate [you] once more on the marvellous success of the team and to say how very pleased all of us here are for your sake and for the sake of everyone who has worked so hard to make this success possible.

Yours sincerely,
A. F. P. Fane

1940

28 April
Starters: 88; Finishers: 33; Distance: 927 miles (1,492km), nine laps of 103-mile
    (166km) circuit; cars in the 750cc and 1,500cc classes had to complete only
    eight laps (824miles/1,326km).
Circuit: see page 244.
Weather: fine and dry throughout.

Main contenders for victory:

70	Baron Huschke von Hanstein/Baümer (BMW 328 coupé, 1,971cc)	
71	Wenscher/Scholz (BMW 328 open two-seater, 1,971cc)	
72	Briem/Richter (BMW 328 open two-seater, 1,971cc)	
73	Count Giovanni Lurani/Franco Cortese (BMW 328 coupé, 1,971cc)	
74	Brudes/Röse (BMW 328 open two-seater, 1,971cc)	
76	Count Felice Trossi/Lucchi (Alfa Romeo 6C 2500 berlinetta, 2,443cc)	
77	Piero Taruffi/Luigi Chinetti (Delage D6, 2,973cc)	
79	Clemente Biondetti/Stefani (Alfa Romeo 6C 2500 spider, 2,443cc)	
82	Carlo Pintacuda/Consalvo Sanesi (Alfa Romeo 6C 2500 spider, 2,443cc)	
84	Giuseppe Farina/Mambelli (Alfa Romeo 6C 2500 spider, 2,443cc)	
86	Gianfranco Comotti/Archimede Rosa (Delage D6, 2,973cc)	

This special BMW coupé was driven by Baron Huschke von Hanstein and Baümer. It was very light, very fast and more than a match for the Alfa Romeo opposition. The coupé won the race at 103.60mph (166.70kph). (Spitzley-Zagari Collection)

After the Mille Miglia was banned, Count 'Johnny' Lurani proposed that the race be continued on a circuit of around 100 miles (161km), but initially this proposal came to nothing. Then it was announced that the Brescia Auto Club was organising the Gran Primo Brescia (it was also described as the First Grand Premio della Mille Miglia) and it has become accepted that it is one of the Mille Miglia series. The organisers chose a high-speed course with a distance of 103 miles (166km) running from Brescia to Cremona and then on to Mantua before turning north again and running back to Brescia.

The Italian government had banned races passing through the centre of towns and so it was necessary to build a new link road in order that the course did not pass through the centre of Mantua. There was a level crossing over the circuit, but race organisers Mazzotti and Castagneto managed to persuade Italian railways that trains should stop for the competing cars. As there were 88 cars competing and the race lasted over 11 hours, very few trains can have run that day.

There were no longer any Grand Prix cars in sports car clothing competing, as the entry was limited to cars built to the Italian 'National Sports' regulations. The race was held over nine laps, but 750cc and 1,500cc cars completed only eight laps. Cars in the 1,100cc class had to cover the full distance. The rationale behind this seems to have been that the 1,100cc cars were much-modified Fiats and the majority of them sports-racing cars, while the 1,500cc class was mainly, but not completely, Lancia Aprilia saloons.

Fiat entries monopolised the two smallest classes with 19 in the 750cc class and 25 in the 1,100cc class. In the 1,500cc

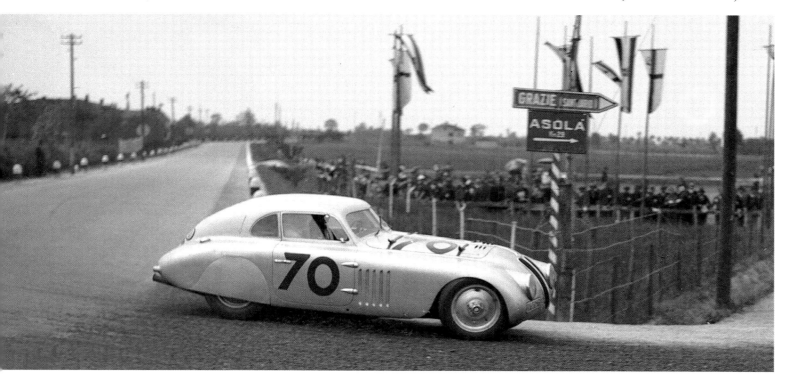

class there were 12 Lancia Aprilias, a solitary Fiat and the two AutoAvia Tipo 815s entered by the new company formed by Enzo Ferrari since his departure from Alfa Corse. Designed by Alberto Massimino, these cars had 1,496cc (63 x 60m) engines based on Fiat cylinder blocks, and they incorporated a number of other Fiat components. The bodies of the 815s were the work of the Touring company.

Outright victory was a straight fight between Alfa Romeo and BMW and although the BMWs were of smaller capacity, they were lighter and more powerful. There was one other team competing that in more favourable political conditions could have been a force to reckon with: Écurie Watney, run by Paris-based, English-nationality Delage dealer Walter Watney (at one time, when Delage was on the rocks, before the Delahaye take-over, he funded Delage production).

War had been declared on Germany by Great Britain and France on 3 September 1939, Germany had not yet invaded the Benelux countries and France (but was about to occupy Denmark and Norway). Italy did not declare war on the Axis side until 10 June 1940. So the race was held in 'phoney war' conditions.

The Écurie Watney entry was not popular with the Germans (especially as an Écurie Watney Delage had

finished second at Le Mans in 1939), nor was the French government too keen on it. Almost all French drivers had been conscripted into the armed forces and Watney was not allowed to take French mechanics to Brescia.

Watney had to recruit Italian mechanics to help and the cars were to be driven by Italians Taruffi/Chinetti and Comotti/Rosa. BMW tried to get the Delage team disqualified and Watney was quoted as saying, "I have a rhinoceros hide. The more you try to get me out, the more determined I am to start." Only the Comotti/Rosa car made it to the starting line, but it was in second place at the end of the first lap and lasted five laps before retiring. One report said that the car caught fire, but that seems not to be the majority view.

The circuit was almost completely flat, there were no bends and the faster cars were lapping at well over 100mph (161kph). Von Hanstein partnered by Baümer set the pace and led throughout; he also drove the whole race, apart from one lap when Baümer took the wheel. Lurani/Cortese with what was in theory the fastest of the BMWs, the works-designed coupé, took second place on lap two, but it covered only six laps and retired after a succession of pit stops.

Wenscher/Scholz drove this works BMW 328, known as the 'Bügelfalten', to sixth place. The bodywork was very distinctive, but there is no reason to suppose that it had possessed any aerodynamic advantages over the other open 328s in the race. (Spitzley-Zagari Collection)

The Alfa Romeos were no match for the BMWs but Giuseppe Farina, partnered by the faithful Mambelli, finished second in this 6C 2300 car with Touring spider body. It is noticeable that the styling of the Touring body on this car was vastly inferior to the styles used for the Touring-bodied BMWs running in the race. (Author's Collection)

Above: One of the Tipo 815 cars built by AutoAvia Costruzioni is seen here during initial testing on a straight stretch of the San Venanzio road, just outside Modena. Watching, on the left immediately under the road sign, is Ernesto Maserati, and it is almost certainly his Fiat 1,100 on the right of the picture. (Author's Collection)

Below: Touring made an excellent job of the aerodynamics of the 6C 2300 berlinetta that Count Felice Trossi, partnered by Lucci, drove to eighth place. (Centro Documentazione Alfa Romeo)

In practice this car had been plagued by mixture problems and according to Lurani, the fuel mixture was too rich at low revs and too lean at high revs. It was apparent that the problem had not been cured. The Alfa Romeos fought hard to stay with the BMWs, but even Farina at his most determined could not overcome the excessive weight and aerodynamic shortcomings of the 2.5-litre Alfa Romeo and finished second, 14min 21sec in arrears. Fastest lap was set by von Hanstein/Baümer in 56min 51.4sec (108.21mph/174.11kph). The winning car had completed the race on one set of tyres and averaged 16mpg.

Neither of the AutoAvia cars finished, but they did show considerable promise. Ascari led the 1,500cc class on the first lap, but retired at the end of the lap. The Marquis Rangoni then assumed the lead in the class, ahead of a streamlined Lancia Aprilia driven by Major Leoncini and Batista Guidotti (the services of the latter by courtesy of Alfa Romeo). Both of these cars retired because of mechanical maladies at the end of lap seven and victory in the class went to D'Ambrosio/Guerrini with a much more standard Aprilia who had been around an hour behind the leaders in the class.

The 'Ersatz' Mille Miglia was a success, but not a great one. The attitude of the Germans, especially that arch-Fascist Huschke von Hanstein who wore the SS insignia on his overalls, was revolting, especially towards British people present at the race, while the majority of the Italians were greatly embarrassed and the last thing they wanted was any hostilities with Great Britain.

Count 'Johnny' Lurani, a strong anglophile who was an honorary member of the British Racing Drivers' Club, wore blue Italian racing overalls with a BMW badge sewn on, but wore his BRDC badge underneath. According to *The Autocar*, the German national anthem was not played after the race and when an attempt to run up the swastika flag was foiled by it winding itself round the flagpole, the crowd made 'ironic cheers and catcalls'.

Results:
General classification:

1st	Von Hanstein/Baümer (BMW), 8hr 54min 46.3sec (103.62mph/166.72kph)	
2nd	Farina/Mambelli (Alfa Romeo), 9hr 10min 16.2sec	
3rd	Brudes/Röse (BMW), 9hr 13min 27.3sec	
4th	Biondetti/Stefani (Alfa Romeo), 9hr 13min 37.2sec	
5th	Briem/Richter (BMW), 9hr 16min 8.4sec	
6th	Wenscher/Scholz (BMW), 9hr 17min 15.4sec	
7th	Pintacuda/Sanesi (Alfa Romeo), 9hr 25min 47.2sec	
8th	Trossi/Lucchi (Alfa Romeo), 9hr 36min 55.3sec	
9th	Fioruzzi/Cavanna (Fiat), 11hr 11min 47.1sec	
10th	Bertani/Lasagni (Fiat), 11hr 16min 46.1sec	

Class results:
750cc: Venturelli/Ceroni (Fiat), eight laps, 11hr 34min 52.2sec (70.90mph/114.08kph)

1,100cc: Fioruzzi/Cavanna (Fiat), 11hr 11min 47.1sec (82.49mph/132.73kph)

1,500cc: D'Ambrosio/Guerrini (Lancia), eight laps, 10hr 27min 35.1sec (78.42mph/126.18kph)

2,000cc: Von Hanstein/Baümer (BMW), 8hr 54min 46.3sec (103.62mph/166.72kph)

3,000cc: Farina/Mambelli (Alfa Romeo), 9hr 10min 16.2sec (100.70mph/162.03kph)

Fioruzzi and Cavanna drove the beautifully styled, streamlined 1,100cc Fiat in the 1940 race. They finished ninth overall and won their class at 82.49mph (132.73kph) from two other Fiats. (Spitzley-Zagari Collection)

BMWs and Frazer Nash

The cockpit of the 1940 car after Frazer Nash had converted it to right-hand drive and announced it to an unsuspecting public as the Frazer Nash Grand Prix. Although the 1940 race was held after the outbreak of the Second World War (but not yet involving Italy), it was widely reported in British magazines. Even so, in post-war days no one (or almost no one) realised that the Grand Prix was one of the 1940 Mille Miglia cars. (Tony Haynes)

The engine bay of the 1940 Mille Miglia BMW that H. J. Aldington brought to the UK after the Second World War. Note the oil cooler mounted above the water radiator – a feature seen only on 1940 cars. (Tony Haynes)

BMW's 328 was a development of the company's first six-cylinder car, the 303 introduced in 1933 when the Munich company was still very much a fledgling motor manufacturer. In 1936 the 326 was the first BMW with a 1,971cc (66 x 96mm) engine and later the same year came the 328 sports two-seater and for this engineer Fritz Fiedler designed an expedient that provided additional engine power without resorting to twin overhead camshafts. There was still a chain-driven camshaft mounted on the cylinder block and the inlet valves were operated in the conventional way by pushrods and rockers, but bell-cranks actuated supplementary cross-over pushrods that operated the exhaust valves.

In standard form these cars with twin-tubular chassis and centre-lock disc wheels had a power output of 80bhp in original form and were good for over 100mph (161kph). This was gradually increased and it is reckoned that the 1940 Mille Miglia cars had a power output of close to 140bhp. They carried very aerodynamic bodywork and of the cars that competed in the 1940 race three were open two-seaters and two were coupés. All these cars had bodywork built by Touring, but one of the coupés was designed at the BMW factory.

Of these cars, *The Autocar* wrote, "Although not a definite figure, it seems likely that the BMW weighed not more than 12cwt [1,344lb/609.5kg] empty. At Le Mans last year these cars were known to weigh a little over 15cwt [1,680lb/762kg], and this shows how the Germans have got down to the weight reduction question by the very extensive use of light alloys. As far as could be found out under the prevailing conditions, the chassis was of light alloy, the disc wheels being probably of duralumin, and the duralumin-magnesium all-metal body is said to weigh only 95lb.

"The saloon body of the winning car is a very interesting type, it being in size a four-seater, though only the two front seats were in use, the rear being taken up with fuel tank. There were no excrescences at all, the petrol filler being internal and reached through a trap-door, and even projecting hinges and handles had been avoided." In fact, this description appears to relate to the car driven by Lurani/Cortese which was fastest but retired.

What is perhaps remarkable is that four of the cars survive and one of them had a long and distinguished racing career in post-war British races. The example that came to Britain was brought over by H. J. Aldington then a Lieutenant-Colonel. Aldington controlled AFN Limited, manufacturers of Frazer Nash cars and British BMW concessionaires. In 1939 he had left his own BMW for repair at the Munich works after he had crashed it at a race meeting at Hamburg. The outbreak of war meant that it stayed there for the duration.

When he went to Germany to locate it after the cease of hostilities, he was given one of the 1940 Mille Miglia cars and decided to take it away without further discussion. In Britain this car was converted to right-hand-drive steering and the front was modified so that an air intake of the type to be used on post-war Frazer Nash cars was fitted. This car was then shown to the press as the post-war Frazer Nash prototype. What the car was typed is somewhat arguable and the writer has seen at least one publication that referred to it as the 'Frazer Nash Grand Prix 2-Litre Sports model'.

Frazer Nash sold the car on to Liverpool motor trader, Gillie Tyrer, who raced it for some seven years until he acquired a Jaguar C-type. Some years later Michael Bowler, one-time Technical Director of Aston Martin and latterly editor of *The Automobile* magazine, raced it in historic events. When Bowler moved on to a Lister-Jaguar, the car was sold to the BMW museum.

The 1940 Mille Miglia BMWs

Race number 70. Coupé bodied by Touring. It was driven by von Hanstein/Baümer to a win in the 1940 Mille Miglia. Hermann Lang drove in the Ruhestein hill climb in 1946 and thereafter it went to the United States. It joined BMW's Mobile Tradition (the BMW Museum) in 2002 and ran in the Mille Miglia Storica in 2006.

Race number 71. Open roadster known as the Bügelfalten ('trouser crease') because of its wing shape. The front wing line was drawn in a straight line or crease from above the wheel-arch back to the door rather than being formed in a curve; the contemporary BMW Z4 sports two-seater replicates this front wing-line but is different at the rear; number 71 was driven in the 1940 Mille Miglia by Hans Wencher and Rudolf Scholz and finished sixth. It is now in a private collection in Munich.

Race number 72. At the present research has not established precisely which car this is; as it and number 74 had almost identical bodies and there are no chassis records relating to the cars in the 1940 race, the confusion is understandable; it was driven by Briem and Richter. It is believed that this was the car that H. J. Aldington brought to Britain.

Race number 73. This was the aerodynamic coupé that resembled a saloon, designed by Professor Wunibald Kamm, director of the research institute for automotive engineering at Stuttgart's Technical University and pioneer user of wind tunnels. It was driven in the 1940 Mille Miglia by Johnny Lurani and Franco Cortese, but retired because of fuel mixture problems; somehow Ernst Loof managed to hold on to this car; Karl Kling drove it to its only win at Hockenheim in 1947; Loof used it as a road car until it was involved in an accident in the early 1950s and scrapped.

Race number 74. See number 72 above; this was probably the third-place car of Brudes/Röse in the 1940 Mille Miglia; this car is also in a private collection in Munich.

The BMW 328, moved to Britain by Aldington, is seen here in 1953, by then in the ownership of Gillie Tyrer. The radiator grille is post-war Frazer Nash style and the badge, reading 'Bristol 2-litre', was as seen on production Bristol 401 cars. The wheels are the standard Kronprinz disc-type designed to circumvent Rudge-Whitworth patents. (Guy Griffiths)

1947

21–22 June
Starters: 155; Finishers: 54; Distance: 1,139 miles (1,833km).
Circuit: see page 245.
Weather: fine at the start, but strong winds and heavy rain later.

Main contenders for victory:

222	Luigi Villoresi/Guerino Bertocchi (Maserati A6G Coupé, 1,954cc)	
150	Piero Taruffi/Buzzi (Cisitalia 202 Spider, 1,089cc)	
172	Eugenio Minetti/Piero Facetti (Cisitalia 202 Spider, 1,089cc)	
175	Inico Bernabei/T. Pacini (Cisitalia 202 Coupé, 1,089cc)	
179	Tazio Nuvolari/Carena (Cisitalia 202 Spider, 1,089cc)	
219	Franco Cortese/Marchetti (Ferrari Tipo 125S Spider, 1,497cc)	
230	Emilio Romano/Clemente Biondetti (Alfa Romeo 8C 2900B berlinetta, 2,905cc)	

The decision to run the Mille Miglia again as a proper road race after a nine-year interval and after a war that had seen the downfall of the Fascist government, much of the country occupied by German forces and widespread

Stormy weather in the mountains. Biondetti speeds up the Raticosa Pass with Romano's 8C 2900B Lungo Alfa Romeo. He defeated Tazio Nuvolari (Cisitalia) by a margin of about a quarter of an hour. Other Cisitalias finished third and fourth. (Centro Documentazione Alfa Romeo)

industrial devastation, captured support and enthusiasm at all levels. Although Italy had ended the war on the Allied side fighting the Axis, it was at this time under American military government.

In fact, the American authorities did not seem too interested one way or the other whether the race was restored – it seems that they failed to understand what it was all about. Only three of the original organisers Count Maggi, Canestrini and Castagneto had survived. Mazzotti had been a volunteer pilot in the Reggia Aeronautica and had been killed on a sortie to Tunisia. The three survivors had a relatively free hand in reviving the race with local government and trade support. It was, however, a purely National race and there were no overseas entries. As a tribute to Mazzotti, the title of the race was changed to '[number of the race] 1,000 Miglia Coppa Franco Mazzotti.'

One of the biggest problems was the state of the roads, for these had deteriorated badly during the war years, partly because of tracked military traffic, and many bridges had been destroyed by bombing and replaced by temporary Bailey bridges. In many places works to restore damaged buildings interfered with the passage of traffic. These poor road conditions made it necessary to use a new course and the organisers settled on one with a longer distance of 1,000 nautical miles (1,833km).

This ran in a clockwise direction from Brescia through Verona, Vicenza, Padua and southwards to Fano. From there it began, approximately, to follow the

old route in the opposite direction to Rome via the Furlo Pass and Terni. After Rome it swung across to the west coast and passed on the Via Aurelia through Leghorn and on to Pisa. It then turned east to Florence, passed through Bologna just the once and routed west to Turin and returned to Brescia via Milan and the Autostrada.

It became clear that neither entrants nor the authorities responsible for repairing the roads would be ready by the date originally proposed, 27 April, so the decision was made to postpone the race until June. Two of the biggest problems were fuel and tyres. At this time petrol was still rationed, but with a bit of wangling the organisers obtained the release of sufficient supplies of fuel. According to one source, the quantity of fuel needed was 91,000 litres (19,800 gallons). So far as tyres were concerned, Pirelli stepped into the breach and made available a set of tyres to each entrant at a very favourable rate.

Originally, there were 245 entries in the race, a vast number and it soon became clear that many of these simply wanted the tyres and the actual number of starters was 155. It was still an immense number and it was clear that enthusiasm to compete was much higher than in pre-war days.

The regulations for the race divided the runners into the International Sports category with four capacity classes and the International Touring category with three classes. Superchargers were now banned. Cars running in the touring classes had to be to strict manufacturers'

specification, but the organisers soon realised that this was impossible to police and a blind eye was turned to minor modifications.

More than 90 of the starters were Fiats and of these, running in the Sports category, over 40 were 508CMM coupés of the type that had first raced in 1938. There were also a number of new and very streamlined Fiat berlinettas that put up a good fight against the Cisitalias. The rest of the Fiats were saloons, many of them pre-war. Lancias were also very numerous, with a total of 20; the 1,091cc Ardeas running in the 1,100cc International Touring class and the 1,486cc Aprilias in the 1,500cc class. There was one British car in the race, the pre-war MG of Cenacchi/Moretti, but this retired without making any impression.

New Cisitalias dominated the International Sports category. Industrialist Piero Dusio, who had been a successful Mille Miglia competitor in pre-war days, owned the company and it was to build some of the exquisitely styled coupés and Spyders with Pinin Farina bodies. Dante Giacosa of Fiat had designed these cars in broad outline during 1944 and later development work was carried out by Giovanni Savanuzzi and Piero Taruffi.

The only British car in the 1947 race was the pre-war MG of Cenacchi/Moretti. It failed to finish. The other MG in the photograph is the YA 1,250cc saloon of John Dugdale, who had driven out to report the race for The Autocar. *(LAT/The Autocar/De Zardo)*

Fiat was always a great supporter of the Mille Miglia. Post-war, there were numerous Fiat cars, and Fiat engines powered a myriad of small-capacity cars. These are two of the latest streamlined 1,100cc cars before the 1947 race. On this occasion they proved no match for the Cisitalias. (LAT/The Autocar/ De Zardo)

The basis of these cars was a multi-tubular chassis built from chrome-molybdenum tubing, with transverse leaf spring independent front suspension and a rigid rear axle suspended on both coil and quarter-elliptic springs (the latter also serving as radius arms). The power unit was the familiar 1,089cc four-cylinder push-rod ohv Fiat engine developing about 60bhp. Not only did these cars have more than adequate power in the engine-capacity class, but they handled superbly. Five of these cars ran in the 1947 race and of particular significance was that one of them was driven by Nuvolari. The Mantuan was seriously ill and it was expected that he would be forced to retire.

There were three other significant entries in the International Sports category. Franco Cortese was at the wheel of the new Ferrari Tipo 125S and Luigi Villoresi was at the wheel of the Tipo A6G Maserati and both of these are described in some detail earlier. One of the 1940 AutoAvia cars was entered for Beltracchini and Matta, but failed to start. There were also six Alfa Romeos, but there was only one of significance.

Emilio Romano had entered his pre-war 8C 2900B Alfa Romeo Lungo (long-chassis) with Touring berlinetta body (it was said to be the 1938 Paris Show car). To comply with the race regulations, he had removed the superchargers and fitted a new inlet manifold together with four carburettors (reports vary as to whether these were Solex or Weber instruments).

Power output was a modest 140bhp, not much on a power to weight ratio.

Apparently, Biondetti could not afford his own entry and was only offered a drive at the last moment. This is how it came about according to *The Motor*: "He was not down to drive at all, but went to watch the final scrutineering and ran into his old friend Romano. 'Look,' said the latter, 'I've entered a streamlined 2.9 Alfa saloon. I've taken off the twin blowers and fitted four carburettors instead. She's heavy and not terribly well tuned, but would you care to share the driving with me.'"

The first car, the Fiat of Caratti/Navone, left Brescia at 8.11pm on the Saturday and thereafter they departed at intervals of one minute, with odd gaps here and there, until the last car, the Alfa Romeo of Baggio/Rossini departed at 3.03am the following morning. Romano/Biondetti were among the last to leave and were flagged off at 2.53am. Nuvolari/Carena had left at 1.56am and although, before the start, the 8C 2900B Alfa Romeo was not considered a likely winner, its crew had the major advantage of being able to monitor the progress of their rivals.

Apart from the Alfa Romeo, the race was fought out between the 1,100cc Cisitalias and Fiats. Among the early retirements were Cortese (Ferrari) because of cylinder head gasket failure, Villoresi (Maserati) because of bearing failure and Taruffi (Cisitalia) was eliminated by engine problems. At Padua and on to Pesaro Gilera/Minozzi and Bassi/Morandi held the first two places with their streamlined Fiats, then came Nuvolari/Carena with the first of the Cisitalias, Scagliarini/Annovi with another Fiat, Lanza/Pelassa with a 6C 2500 Alfa Romeo and, back in sixth place, the thunderous 8C 2900B of Romano/Biondetti.

Then Nuvolari asserted his vast ability and by Rome led at an average of 70mph (113kph) and a margin of seven minutes from Romano/Biondetti. Both were beginning to pull away from the rest of the opposition. Gilera/Minozzi were dropping back and retired. While Bassi/Morandi finished the race, they had problems and dropped back to 21st place after losing a great deal of ground because of mechanical trouble.

By Florence, Nuvolari's lead had shrunk to two minutes, but at Asti, not far short of Turin, he had extended his advantage once more to seven minutes. Then driving rain inundated the circuit and high winds caused problems for all the drivers. The story of Nuvolari's drive is recounted in emotional tones on pages 155–156, but the sick Nuvolari in an open car had difficulty in coping with these conditions, while Romano/Biondetti were snug in their big berlinetta. The last, fast section of the race over the Autostrada also favoured the Alfa Romeo and at the finish Romano/Biondetti led by nearly 16 minutes.

Cisitalias were second, third and fourth and took the first three places in the 1,100cc Sports category. Fiats took the first three places in the 750cc Touring and Sports categories, while Lancia was almost equally dominant with three class wins that included first three places in the 1,500cc Touring category with Aprilia saloons. The Aprilia was a technically advanced saloon with excellent performance, superb handling and good braking. One can but lament the downfall of this once great marque. The fastest car on the final stretch of the Autostrada was the closed Cisitalia of Bernabei/Pacini which was timed at 94.8mph (152.5kph).

Results:
General classification:

1st	Romano/Biondetti (Alfa Romeo), 16hr 16min 39sec (69.76mph/112.24kph)	
2nd	Nuvolari/Carena (Cisitalia), 16hr 32min 35sec	
3rd	Bernabei/Pacini (Cisitalia), 16hr 38min 17sec	
4th	Minetti/Facetti (Cisitalia), 17hr 0min 40sec	
5th	Capelli/Gerli (Fiat), 17hr 17min 38sec	
6th	Della Chiesa/Brandeli (Fiat), 17hr 26min 4sec	
7th	Ermini/Quentin (Fiat), 17hr 27min 37sec	
8th	Comirato/Comirato (Fiat), 17hr 27min 45sec	
9th	Balestrero/Bracco (Fiat), 17hr 31min 44sec	
10th	Gurgo Salice/Cornaggia (Alfa Romeo), 17hr 51min 55sec	

Class Results, International Touring Category:
750cc: Capelli/Nosotti (Fiat), 24hr 1min 5sec (46.00mph/74.01kph)
1,100cc: Coda/Dana (Lancia), 21hr 16min 4sec (53.39mph/85.90kph)
1,500cc: Tullini/Rossi (Lancia), 18hr 42min 16sec (61.95mph/99.68kph)

Class Results, International Sports Category:
750cc: Avalle/Prina (Fiat), 22hr 12 min 35sec (51.13mph/82.27kph)
1,100cc: Nuvolari/Carena (Cisitalia), 16hr 32min 35sec (68.64mph/110.44kph)
2,000cc: Meschi/Bianchi (Lancia), 18hr 26min 28sec (61.57mph/99.07kph)
3,000cc: Romano/Biondetti (Alfa Romeo), 16hr 16min 39sec (69.76mph/112.24kph)

Nuvolari in the 1947 race

(Adapted from Nuvolari *by Count Giovanni Lurani, Cassell & Co, 1959)*

Because of chest problems Nuvolari returned to Gardone Riviera in late 1946. He got used to the idea of competing only in sports car races, where the exhaust fumes contained no alcohol. The quiet winter by Lake Garda was most beneficial for Nuvolari's lungs, and above all his nerves benefited by the peace. After it was announced that the Mille Miglia would be held again in 1947, Nuvolari agreed to drive a Cisitalia for Piero Dusio.

When Nuvolari's entry was announced, the news was received with scepticism in view of his precarious physical condition, and an early withdrawal was anticipated. He could not last those deadly roads for 16 or 17 hours without respite: the idea was folly. On the other hand, what prospect of winning had he on such a tiny vehicle as the little open Cisitalia with its engine capacity of no more than 1,100cc?

If the technicians had little confidence in Nuvolari's prospects, the crowd at least accorded him a moving tribute when he presented himself in the Piazza della Vittoria at Brescia for the scrutineering. He went to bed early, and started under a dark and menacing sky, typical of the Mille Miglia, which has rarely been run in good weather. One by one, during the night and into the dawn, the hundred competitors emerged from the Viale Rebuffone. The

Mantuan's Cisitalia was an open car, no higher than three feet above the ground, very light, and with a nose like a shark.

He shot out of the Viale Rebuffone like lightning and disappeared around the corner, as behind him was soon to follow the big Alfa Romeo of Biondetti and Romano. The pace immediately showed itself killing and the roads although repaired, still presented a thousand dangers; long tracts of asphalt remained untouched, signposts were scarce and the sky continued to pour out cascades of water with only brief pauses. In spite of all this, the little Cisitalia arrived at Pesaro high in the general classification. Carena, Tazio's companion, having commended his soul to God, was gripping the safety handles or the dashboard and yelling warnings to his driver on dangerous corners.

This was a real surprise in the true Nuvolari style. How did that man in his precarious condition of health, who had received such a severe spiritual blow [the death of a son at the age of 18 in 1946], keep the old foxes at bay in their much more powerful cars? From Pesaro, across the Abruzzi by Aquila and on to Rome, Tazio produced his fabulous best. The result was that at the Ponte Milvio, the Rome control point, he found that he had a lead over Biondetti of seven minutes. Nuvolari was playing with death, teasing him, laughing at him – he could take him now if he wished.

Instead, death refused him at every bend that he took, when he skimmed the trees and kerbstones or each time the wet surface caused fearsome skids. Nuvolari was once again the old devil of 20 years before and the Alfa's extra 50 horsepower were useless against the precise, nervous touches of the Mantuan's hands. They steadied the car over the tortuous Raticosa and Futa Passes, where the fog was so

Nuvolari made a brilliant, determined effort with his 1,100cc Cisitalia in the 1947 race and, but for minor problems with his car, he would have won. The Cisitalia spider was beautifully styled by Pinin Farina, even if it was not quite as blindingly beautiful as the maestro's berlinetta body on the same chassis. (Author's Collection)

thick that no light pierced it. It was not raining now, but the fog was worse than the rain. This did not worry Nuvolari, who was able to drive over these two passes with his eyes closed, having fought and won some of his most spectacular battles here.

From Rome to Florence, Biondetti had been able to reduce Tazio's advantage by three minutes, but after the two Apennine passes found he had to make up time all over again. Nuvolari arrived at Bologna with nine minutes' lead. Enormous crowds thronged the Emilian capital's control point, where Tazio stopped for a few seconds. He was glued to his seat, his legs dead, hands painful, and a dull ache in his chest making his ears buzz; but he would not give in. No one could stop him; the race already seemed won by the resuscitated Mantuan who had led from the beginning.

It started raining again, and then came another setback. The diversion from Bologna to Asti was over roads in poor condition, but this did not worry Nuvolari, who had made the greatest aces eat dust on much worse roads. The bad weather finally let him down. The little Cisitalia crossed a dip, which was submerged under a vast puddle like a miniature lake. Throwing up waves on either side, the machine coasted through in silence. The engine had cut out as the distributor was swamped. The rain began to pour

down as Tazio took advantage of his momentum to coast to the shelter of a nearby bridge.

Fuming, he jumped out with Carena, who believed that it was valve trouble and immediately began to remove the valve cover. By the time that they had found out that it was the distributor, 15 minutes had been lost. Biondetti had caught up and had gone ahead, flying towards Turin. Tazio was not dismayed, and did not even contemplate retiring. Carena succeeded in remedying the fault and they set off once more flat-out, to learn at the Turin control that Biondetti was leading them with five minutes to spare.

There were still over 150 miles to go along the reasonable surface of the Autostrada, where the Alfa could easily use its full power. Nuvolari put his foot down to the floorboards and kept it there until he reached Brescia. Soon after leaving Turin the rain had turned to hail, flaying their faces. A tremendous welcome awaited them. Tazio felt his strength leaving him. Water had invaded the seats, making him sorry that he had not chosen the closed model, which would at least have sheltered him from the hailstones. Even under these conditions, if it had not been for the puddle incident he would have won just the same.

Nuvolari stopped just over the finishing line, which despite the inclement weather was very crowded. The public broke through the police cordon and surrounded the small car. It contained two very exhausted men, soaked to the marrow. Nuvolari's face was unrecognisable, pale and cadaverous under the black coating of smoke, grime and mud. His eyes looked dead. It was necessary to lift him out of his seat and help him to walk. The loudspeakers announced that Biondetti and Romano had won by a margin of just [under] 16 minutes.

1948

1 May
Starters: 167; Finishers: 64; Distance: 1,139 miles (1,833km).
Circuit: see page 245.
Weather: fine and dry initially, rain in the later stages of the race.

Main contenders for victory:

3	Alberto Ascari/Guerino Bertocchi (Maserati A.6GCS, 1,978cc)
7	Piero Taruffi/Rabbia (Cisitalia 202 Coupé, 1,246cc)
10	Franco Cortese/Adelmo Marchetti (Ferrari Tipo 166S spider, 1,995cc)
16	Clemente Biondetti/Giuseppe Navone (Ferrari Tipo 166S Allemano berlinetta, 1,995cc)
20	Franco Rol/Alessandro Gaboardi (Alfa Romeo 6C 2500 Experimental, 2,443cc)
22	Piero Dusio/Carlo Dusio (Cisitalia 202 Spider, 1,089cc)
53	Bonetto/Maritano (Cisitalia 202 Spider, 1,089cc)
86	Inico Bernabei/Sari (Cisitalia 202 Coupé, 1,089cc)
1047	Consalvo Sanesi/Zanardi (Alfa Romeo 6C 2500 Experimental, 2,443cc)
1049	Tazio Nuvolari/Sergio Scapinelli (Ferrari Tipo 166S Ansaloni spider, 1,995cc)

Maserati's industrial problems made it difficult for them to compete with their sports cars on a consistent basis and, as anticipated, the preparation of Ascari's A.6GCS

was less than satisfactory. The two Alfa Romeos, based on the post-war production 6C 2500 Freccia d'Oro ('Golden Arrow') saloons could have been serious contenders, but like the Maserati, preparation was inadequate, mainly because the company was committed on limited funds to racing their very successful Tipo 158 Grand Prix cars. Two Alfa Romeo-based specials were the Nardi-Danese cars with 6C 2500 engines and built by Enrico Nardi and Renato Danese. Both of these unsuccessful cars retired.

All three Ferraris were very serious contenders, but there were doubts about Nuvolari's stamina and his ability to finish a long race. He had badly damaged lungs, supposedly caused by the inhalation of exhaust fumes from racing cars that burned alcohol-based fuels, and both his sons had now died. Although he lived until 1953, he was obviously close to death. Nuvolari had

Before the start of the 1948 Mille Miglia, the great Tazio Nuvolari looks on as an elderly woman presents his mechanic, Scapinelli, with a bouquet of flowers. During the race Nuvolari's Ferrari Tipo 166 came close to disintegration as the result of his excessively hard driving. Count Lurani wrote: "His white-faced mechanic swore that never again would he sit beside this devil incarnate." (Author's Collection)

There have been few more beautiful cars than the Pinin Farina-bodied Cisitalia Gran Sport coupé. The New York Museum of Modern Art describes it as 'movement in sculpture'. Scagliarini/Maffiodo drove this car into fifth place overall in the 1948 race. (Author's Collection)

spent the winter of 1947–48 in a sanatorium on Lake Como attached to a convent and the condition of his lungs improved slightly. He travelled to the Ferrari factory at Maranello, and there arranged with Enzo Ferrari to drive one of his cars.

Of the three works Ferraris entered in the race, the favourite to win was the coupé driven by Biondetti. The 50-year-old Sardinian had already won the race twice and although not the most popular of drivers, especially so far as Enzo Ferrari was concerned, he was vastly experienced in the race and, following his drive with the Alfa Romeo berlinetta in 1947, he insisted that Ferrari should provide him with a closed car. A fourth, private Ferrari 166S spider with Ansaloni spider body was driven by Soave and Gabriele Bessani.

There were a total of ten Cisitalias entered in the race and at least four of them (listed above) were serious contenders for victory, despite giving away nearly a litre to the Ferraris and Maseratis. There were a vast number of Fiats and Fiat specials in the smaller-capacity classes, which was just as well in view of the high level of attrition among the faster runners. There were three British entries, Healey Elliot saloons driven by

Lurani/Sandri and Haines/Haller in the Touring category and a Westland tourer with Donald Healey at the wheel, partnered by son Geoffrey, running in the Sports Category.

The circuit was unchanged from 1947. The racing numbers allotted to the various cars seemed to be on a random basis; they certainly had no relationship to the starting order. The cars left at minute intervals from a minute past midnight and the first car away was car number 257 the Fiat Metano of Bevilacqua and Carboni. The last departure at 4.39am was number 364, the Lancia Aprilia of Coletti and Theodoli.

Initially Ascari led from Cortese, Sanesi, Nuvolari and Taruffi, but soon there was attrition amongst the leaders. Taruffi (Cisitalia) retired because of engine problems and both Sanesi and Rol crashed their Alfa Romeos; Cortese retired for reasons unknown. Nuvolari averaged 78mph (126kph) to Rome where he led Ascari by 12 seconds. Ascari retired his Maserati shortly after Rome because of a broken gearbox. Already Nuvolari had lost the left front wing damaged in a minor collision and he set off from Rome without the bonnet which would not fit back on properly.

In another crash near Leghorn the left rear spring was damaged and the mechanic's seat worked loose. Despite all these problems he led Biondetti by 29 minutes at Bologna. Nuvolari disciplined himself to continue at a reduced speed, well aware that if he could keep going then Biondetti would never catch him. Not far out of Modena, the brakes failed completely and there was no

In 1948 Clemente Biondetti scored his third Mille Miglia win. He was partnered by Navone in a 2-litre Ferrari Tipo 166, with fixed head coupé body by Allemano. This was Ferrari's first win and it broke Alfa Romeo's stranglehold on the race – Milan never won it again. (Author's Collection)

alternative but retirement. Nuvolari was catatonically exhausted. Now that he was out of the race almost all interest was lost.

Biondetti won by a margin of just under an hour and a half. Fiat 1,100cc cars took the next three places. The results represented a turning point in motor racing history. Alfa Romeo, despite continued efforts, never again won the 1,000-mile race. There were to be nine more races before the Mille Miglia came to an end and Ferrari was to win seven of them.

NOTE: *It is just as difficult to obtain an objective description of Nuvolari's drive in this race, as it is, say, of the travels of Jason and the Argonauts. I have endeavoured to give a straightforward objective account. Earlier accounts have included such claims as:*

"While speeding along the bonnet became unfastened, and a gust of wind blew it over Nuvolari's head and down the mountainside. 'That's better,' shouted Tazio to his mechanic, 'The engine will cool more easily.'"

"His seat began to come adrift. Nuvolari did not hesitate to jettison the seat. He continued the race seated practically on the frame, using a bag of lemons and oranges as a cushion."

"At Modena Enzo Ferrari begged Nuvolari to retire from the race."

"At Modena, Enzo Ferrari saw him fly past; he wept as he realised that the machine could not possibly hold out."

"A priest, fearful for Nuvolari's well-being, stepped into the road to try to stop him as he sped past."

Results:
General classification:
1st	Biondetti/Navone (Ferrari), 15hr 5min 44sec (75.34mph/121.22kph)	
2nd	Comirato/Dumas (Fiat), 16hr 33min 8sec	
3rd	Apruzzi/Apruzzi (Fiat), 16hr 52min 30sec	
4th	Terigi/Berti (Fiat), 16hr 57min 10sec	
5th	G. Scagliarini/Maffiodo (Cisitalia), 17hr 0min 5sec	
6th	Bianchetti/Cornaggia (Alfa Romeo), 17hr 2min 43sec	
7th	C. Scagliarini/Masi (Fiat), 17hr 17min 4sec	
8th	Christillin/Nasi (Fiat), 17hr 17min 4sec	
9th	D. Healey/G. Healey (Healey), 17hr 26min 10sec	
10th	Colnaghi/Pozzoni (Fiat), 17hr 27min 56sec	

Class Results, International Touring Category:
1,100cc: Capelli/Nosotti (Fiat), 20hr 5min 42sec (56.60mph/91.076kph)
Over 1,100cc: Lurani/Sandri (Healey), 17hr 32min 12sec (64.74mph/104.17kph)

Class Results, International Sports Category:
750cc: Fiorio/Avalle (Fiat), 19hr 37min 29sec (57.95mph/93.24kph)
1,100cc: Comirato/Dumas (Fiat), 16hr 33min 8sec (68.71mph/110.56kph)
2,000cc: Biondetti/Navone (Ferrari), 15hr 5min 44sec (75.34mph/121.22kph)
Over 2,000cc: Bianchetti/Cornaggia (Alfa Romeo), 17hr 2min 43sec (66.72mph/107.36kph)

Count Lurani's race with a Healey Elliot

(Adapted from The Autocar *for 14 May 1948)*

The only foreign team was the British Healey entry, with two Elliot saloons competing in the Standard Touring Category (a sort of stock car category) in which 61 cars started, mostly Fiats and Lancias and the third Healey was a normal roadster competing in the open sports category. The drivers of the saloons were myself together with the motorcycle ace G. Sandri (my original co-driver Serafini had been taken seriously ill a week before the race) and Nick Haines and R. Haller. Donald Healey, partnered by his son, drove the third car.

It had rained for days and days, but now the night was calm and the sky filled with stars. The Healeys all sported the Scuderia Ambrosiana badges and the Union Jack. On the 'Rebuffone Alley' where 15 'Thousand Mile' races have

Donald Healey's Healey Motor Company was a stalwart supporter of the Mille Miglia throughout the post-war years. Count Lurani, partnered by Sandri, drove this Elliot saloon in the 1948 race. They won the over 1,100cc Touring category, despite sustaining a broken Panhard rod, which meant that the rear axle was moving and the rear tyres rubbed against the bodywork. (Author's Collection)

started, the lights were shining bright and gay bunting added festivity to the scene, while huge crowds watched the proceedings. Punctually at midnight the first car, an 1,100cc Fiat, was dispatched and the race had started.

Our car, carrying the same number 76, as it had in the Targa Florio, duly started at 1.35am on the Sunday morning. Sandri was driving for the first section on the fast roads towards Verona and Padua. It was a glorious run. The engine hummed perfectly. We had added an extra and powerful light to help us on the night run and we knew the road well. We soon passed some of the cars that had started in front of us, all Lancia Aprilia entries in our class, and among these was Bracco, the daredevil driver who had beaten us in the Targa Florio. When we passed him, we felt that we were doing well.

Soon came the outskirts of Padua and the Healey had averaged over 78mph [126kph], beating the previous best speed by a big margin. From Padua, still in the dark, we drove on to Ferrara (all towns and villages were crowded with thousands of enthusiasts and were brilliantly lit) and through Ravenna, finally reaching Forli, the first control and pit stop. We were glad to have reached Forli because for some time we had been running on reserve and were getting nervous about our petrol supply. A quick stop, a hasty refilling and off we went towards Pesaro and the Adriatic coast.

It was still dark and only near Fano, where we left the sea and pointed towards the heart of Italy on the Rome road, did we start to see the first lights of dawn. Up to now the car had gone splendidly and we were in high spirits. But suddenly came trouble. An ominous clatter at the back and a sudden swerve showed that something was wrong. Before stopping and jumping out of the car to inspect the trouble I realised what it was – the fracture of the brake

torque rod between the rear axle and chassis, the same trouble as had marred our run in Sicily. So, after only 280 miles [450km], and with over 850 miles [1,370km] of fast and slow, straight and winding roads to cover, our car was badly maimed.

On the Terni-Rome section at last the battered rod broke away completely and the hammering ceased. We reached the Rome control and filling station still thinking of retiring from the race, but by now it was morning, the sun was shining and we felt more optimistic. We learned that we were among the leaders and that we had broken the previous touring record by 26 minutes. When we were leaving, we saw that Bracco, driving his Lancia, had caught up with us.

On I drove on the winding road towards Civitavecchia and somewhat to my horror I suddenly saw in the mirror the Bracco car right on my tail. Immediately I pushed the Healey hard. The car responded well and we drew away. But it was a long fight. On and on we pushed towards Grosseto, often reaching 100mph [160kph] and then we lost precious time on the twisty road near Leghorn where our car was almost undriveable, but at the Leghorn control we were still in front of Bracco and he arrived at the pits only just when we leaving towards Pisa.

What a race! By then we knew that we were leading our category, that the fight was a very close one and that we might win the touring category if the car could take it for the full distance. We reached Florence, the first entry to pass the control, and with no Bracco in sight. Then we started for the dreaded Futa and Raticosa passes towards Bologna, the twistiest section of the whole race and the most difficult one for the Healey in the circumstances. I tried to get the most out of the engine on the steep hills, pushing it to boiling point and Sandri kept looking back in case Bracco should catch up.

Instead it was a red car, a sleek Cisitalia driven by Bonetto, the first and only car to pass us in the whole race. On the Futa pass the red car overtook us, leaving black tyre marks on the concrete road as it accelerated away. After a painful and dangerous drive we reached Bologna where it was pouring with rain. The mountains were behind us and Bracco arrived at speed at the control while we were hastily refuelling the Healey. We thus had five minutes' lead again (on time) when we left Bologna level with the Lancia.

But it was raining, the road was very slippery and we could not take immediate advantage of the greater power of the Healey's engine. We kept level with Bracco, but our alligator bonnet opened (it had not been properly closed) and we had to stop twice to fix it. It was enough for Bracco to vanish in the spray and Sandri had to drive very fast, skidding on the wet road, before catching him up and passing him near Parma.

For almost 450 miles [724km] we had been fighting this ding-dong battle with the game Lancia. Steadily we drew away, nursing the Healey, which was getting worse

and worse, until we safely reached Piacenza, Tortona and Asti, where we had a control stop. The showers were now developing into minor cloudbursts and slowed our speed considerably. The last winding corners of the Pino hill near Turin were negotiated with great care and we finally reached the control and refilled for the last time.

Then we saw Bracco and another Lancia reaching the pit area almost on our tail. So once more, 120 miles [193km] from the finish and after 16 hours of gruelling racing, we were all together. At Turin our Healey had a lead of four seconds over Bornigia's Lancia, followed at four minutes by Bracco, also with a Lancia. But now came the final fast section on the Autostrada, over 100 miles [160km] flat-out on which the Healey would come into its own.

Almost at once we reached the 100mph [160kph] mark and realised that we were actually (on the road and not on time) the first car in the race. Since the Healey is quiet and normal-looking, the thousands of spectators who lined the Autostrada did not find out until the very last second that we were a racing car in a very great hurry. The Autostrada was also packed with unruly cars and buses and the going was very dangerous indeed. We sped along at almost 105mph [170kph] in quite heavy traffic with people and cars missing us by fractions of inches.

We knew that we had not a second to spare and we pushed very hard. It continued to rain and the road was skiddy. Now and then we felt as if we were in a traffic block, but we extricated ourselves and pressed on. Near Milan we had to slow down among a bunch of cars and go down to second gear to get away. How long are the last miles! We left the Autostrada having covered the last section in 1hr 33min under bad conditions at an average of 87.4mph [140.6kph]. With our gallant Healey saloon our time on this section was among the best six of the race.

Now we were in Brescia, the crowd cheering, and we were strained and nervous, but finally saw the coveted finishing straight, the stands and the chequered flag waved by the corpulent Castagneto, the famous Mille Miglia organiser. We slowed down, were stopped amid thunderous applause and were literally dragged from the car. One by one the other cars finished and we learned of the fortunes of the other Healey drivers.

After a good start Haines and Haller with the other saloon Healey had the same trouble as us at almost the same spot: the torque rod broke. They took the Healey to a garage and the rod was welded and refitted in less than 50 minutes. They then restarted at full speed, but the repair was useless because after another 50 miles [80km] the rod broke again. The battered Healey carried on gamely to beyond Florence, where on the Futa pass a leak in the gearbox allowed all the oil to escape and the main-shaft seized, so they had to retire. In the unlimited sports class, the failure of the Alfa Romeos allowed Donald and Geoff Healey to finish second [in their class] with their standard-looking Westland roadster.

1949

24 April
Starters: 303; Finishers: 182; Distance: 996 miles (1,603km).
Circuit: see page 245.
Weather: mist in the early hours of the morning, but thereafter bright sunshine
    throughout.

Main contenders for victory:

624	Clemente Biondetti/Salani (Ferrari Tipo 166MM, 1,995cc, Touring Barchetta)	
627	M. P. Tenbosch/Peter Monkhouse (Frazer Nash High Speed, 1,971cc)	
629	Giovanni Bracco/Umberto Maglioli (Ferrari Tipo 166SC, 1,995cc, Ansaloni spider)	
630	Franco Cortese/Gabriele Besana (Ferrari Tipo 166SC, 1,995cc, Ansaloni spider)	
632	Piero Carini/Budriesi (Maserati A.6GCS, 1,978cc)	
634	Dorino Serafini/Haller (Frazer Nash High Speed, 1,971cc)	
641	Felice Bonetto/Pasquale Carpani (Ferrari Tipo 166MM, 1,995cc, Touring Barchetta)	
642	Piero Taruffi/Sergio Nicolini (Ferrari Tipo 166MM, 1,995cc, Touring Barchetta)	
648	Rol/Richiero (Alfa Romeo 6C 2500 Experimental, 2,443cc, berlinetta)	

In 1949 Clemente Biondetti, partnered by Salani, drove this Tipo 166MM 2-litre Ferrari with Touring 'Barchetta' spider body. The Ferraris dominated the race and these outstandingly reliable V12 2-litre cars took the first two places. It was Biondetti's fourth and last Mille Miglia win. Second place went to the Barchetta-bodied Tipo 166 driven by Felice Bonetto and Carpani. (Author's Collection)

The circuit had been completely changed so that it ran anti-clockwise (for the only time post-World War Two), eliminating Modena and Bologna, together with both the Futa and Raticosa passes, as well as stretches of Autostrada. It did, however, have a new and very fast stretch along the Adriatic coast from Pescara to Ravenna. It has been suggested that the organisers eased the route because of the large number of inexperienced drivers. Although the organisation was to improve, in 1949 it was totally chaotic and the officials were unable to cope with 300 starters.

Conditions were especially difficult for the faster competitors who faced, sometimes under very difficult road conditions, overtaking a succession of Fiats, mobile chicanes, with slow, erratic and purblind drivers at the wheel. With the benefit of hindsight, it can be seen that the organisers had lost control of the event and that the lack of proper spectator control could result in a terrible accident. In subsequent years the organisers exercised much greater control over both the entries and the race.

There were nine Ferrari Tipo 166 cars entered, but the winner was most likely to come from the three works Touring barchetta-bodied cars driven by Biondetti, Bonetto and Taruffi. It was only if all three works cars retired that anyone else had a serious chance of winning. Additional runners in this class were three A.6GCS Maseratis in the hands of Aprile Palmer/Bofatti, Gianfranco Comotti/Romano and Piero Carini/Budriesi.

Franco Rol was at the wheel of the very fast Alfa Romeo that he had driven in 1948 and there were two

British Frazer Nashes that were not really fast enough, together with the Healey Elliot of Cohen/Hignett. Another uncompetitive runner in this class was John Gordon/Lewis with a pre-war, special-bodied 2,972cc Lancia Astura. By 1949 Piero Dusio was in severe financial trouble and had shut down the Cisitalia operation in Italy and moved it to the Argentine.

There were, however, two new Italian marques competing in the 1,100cc class. The rise of the OSCA concern run by the Maserati brothers in Bologna is told on pages 70–73. In 1949 these cars still lacked development and the three driven in the race by private owners were not competitive. Much the same can be said of Stanguellini whose Fiat-based cars were still too fragile for long-distance road racing.

All the cars in the Touring Category were supposed to run on 80-octane petrol supplied by the organisers, but this did not suit many of the cars, so entrants were surreptitiously pouring additives into their fuel tanks. The Touring category included the works Alfa Romeo 6C 2500 Freccia d'Oro of Consalvo Sanesi/Venturi, but in the same class there were also two very serious British contenders, the Healey Elliot of Geoffrey Healey/Tom Wisdom and a Bristol 400 driven by H. J. Aldington and Count 'Johnny' Lurani. Journalist Tom Wisdom was to become Britain's most experienced Mille Miglia driver and competed in a total of ten races, all with one exception post-war.

Dorino Serafini, partnered by Rudi Haller, drove this Frazer Nash 'High Speed' in the 1949 race. The car was chassis number 421/100/006, registered TME 924 in the UK. It had been loaned to Count Lurani's Scuderia Ambrosiana. Serafini had led the Tour of Sicily with this car until he hit a kerbstone. He retired again in the Mille Miglia, before half-distance. Later the 'High Speed' model became known as the 'Le Mans Replica'. (Frazer Nash Archives)

The Bristol was a BMW-based combination of the 328 1,971cc engine with cross-over pushrods and a 327/80 BMW chassis with Autenreith-style body. Originally, Frazer Nash had merged with Bristol Aviation's car division, but the two sides soon found that they could not work together and rapidly demerged! H. J. Aldington owned Frazer Nash Cars and ran it with his two brothers. Despite the split, relations were still good and Bristol supplied engines for Frazer Nash cars, all of which helps explain why Aldington was driving a works-owned Bristol 400 saloon in this race.

As usual, there were vast numbers of Fiats and Lancias in the race. There were 45 Fiats in the 750cc Touring class and in the 1,100cc Touring class there were 51 Fiats and a mere four of Lancia's small, but very attractive Ardea saloons. Among the Fiat 508S production sports cars was one driven by 50-year-old Luigi Fagioli, pre-war Alfa Romeo, Maserati, Mercedes-

Benz and Auto Union Grand Prix driver. Fagioli was making a quiet, low-profile return to racing accompanying his nephew, one Leopardi, and made it clear that he was there only for the ride. In fact the arthritis that had crippled him in pre-war days had abated and he was to reappear in the Alfa Romeo Grand Prix team in 1950.

The over 1,100cc class included 40 Aprilias and despite engines of only 1,452cc they battled strongly with the two British cars and Sanesi's Alfa Romeo. The most significant Aprilia entries were the cars of brothers Giannino and Umberto Marzotto; these had their numbers painted on the roof so that the team's supporting light aircraft could spot and report back to those running their service depots.

An important change in the way that the race was run was that the cars now carried numbers that represented their starting time. The first car to depart, the Fiat of Andreini/Del Moro, bore the number 001 and left at one minute past midnight. The entry list included a Healey number 649 that failed to appear, so the last starter was Alfa Romeo Rol/Richiero numbered 648 and this left the start at 6.48am.

Journalist Gordon Wilkins decided to stick some numbers on his Bristol 400 and with Count Maggi he left after the last runner to experience the race at first hand. Only 12 miles (19km) from the start they came to the bridge at Manerbio which had a gap in the iron railings. Cohen and Hignett, garage proprietors from Manchester in their first race, had skidded on to the footpath; their Healey Elliot had spun round and demolished the parapet. Hignett was killed instantly, but Cohen was catapulted 25 feet on to the bank of the river. His injuries left him paralysed, but he lived for some years. This accident led to the organising club requiring that national clubs must endorse all foreign entries.

Bonetto set the pace for much of the race and had the advantage of being one of the last drivers to start. By Parma he had averaged a little over 105mph (close to 170kph) and he was still ahead at Rome at a speed of just short of 83mph (134kph). Behind him were Taruffi (lagging by four minutes) and Biondetti (seven minutes).

H. J. Aldington entered this works Bristol 400 saloon in the 1949 race and co-opted Count Lurani to accompany him. 'H J' did almost all the driving with this 2-litre British-built but BMW-originated car. It was not really fast enough and in the 2,500cc Touring car class they finished third, behind two 2.5-litre cars, a Healey and an Alfa Romeo. (Author's Collection)

In fourth place was Rol with the very fast Alfa Romeo. Early retirements included Cortese and Serafini. Bonetto had been pushing his Ferrari too hard and when he was delayed by clutch and brake problems, Taruffi was able to move up into the lead.

By Ancona, Taruffi had extended his lead and had averaged around 80mph (close to 130kph), Biondetti was in second place, then came Rol and Bonetto was fourth. At Ancona, with just over two hours to the finish, Taruffi's transmission failed and he dropped out of the race. Rol was delayed by overheating problems that were eventually cured. With a proper, full team and an element of organisation and backing Alfa Romeo could have won the race, but lacked the resources and determination to tackle it fully. So Biondetti took the lead and went on to win the race for the fourth time, something no other driver achieved. Bonetto took second place and Rol was third with the Alfa Romeo.

The high level of retirements among the fastest cars meant that there were four very swift, streamlined Fiats in the top finishers. After a tremendous battle Geoffrey Healey and Tom Wisdom took tenth place and won the over 1,100cc Touring category. The climb of the marque Ferrari from nothing in 1947 to winner of the Mille Miglia in 1948–49 was truly remarkable.

Ferrari also won the Paris 12 Hours race at Montlhéry in 1948, won at Le Mans in 1949 and covered the greatest distance in the Belgian 24 Hours race in 1949. (There was no outright winner, only class winners.) Enzo Ferrari had captured the role of supremacy amongst Italian competition sports car manufacturers that Alfa Romeo had occupied for so many years.

The Villoresi brothers, Emilio and Luigi, first drove this streamlined Lancia Astura Spider in the 1938 race. It had been entered the previous year but non-started after a road accident. Lance Macklin (seen here at the wheel) and John Gordon (who lived in Italy) drove it in the 1949 race. The car was running very late by the time it reached Rome and ultimately retired because of engine problems. (Author's Collection)

Results:
General classification:

1st	Biondetti/Salani (Ferrari), 12hr 7min 5sec (81.70mph/131.46kph)
2nd	Bonetto/Carpani (Ferrari), 12hr 35min 7sec
3rd	Rol/Richiero (Alfa Romeo), 12hr 51min 10sec
4th	V. Auricchio/Bozzini (Fiat), 13hr 57min 52sec
5th	G. Scagliarini/Maggio (Cisitalia), 14hr 9min 42sec
6th	Basi/Brambilla (Fiat), 14hr 12min 43sec
7th	P. Aprile/Bofatti (Maserati), 14hr 17min 51sec
8th	Adanti/Mallucci (Fiat), 14hr 18min 59sec
9th	D. Capelli/Veronese (Fiat), 14hr 21min 49sec
10th	G. Healey/Wisdom (Healey), 14hr 24min 3sec

Class Results, International Touring Category:

750cc: Ferrraguti/Ferraiolo (Fiat), 18hr 47min 6sec (52.70mph/84.80kph)
1,100cc: Segre/Valenzano (Fiat), 16hr 34min 12sec (59.75mph/96.14kph)
Over 1,100cc: G. Healey/Wisdom (Healey), 14hr 24min 3sec (68.75mph/110.62kph)

Class Results, International Sports Category:

750cc: Maggiorelli/Maggior (Fiat), 16hr 53min 30sec (58.61mph/94.31kph)
1,100cc: V. Auricchio/Bozzini (Fiat), 13hr 57min 52sec (71.32mph/114.75kph)
2,000cc: Biondetti/Salani (Ferrari), 12hr 7min 5sec (81.70mph/131.46kph)
Over 2,000cc: Rol/Richiero (Alfa Romeo), 12hr 51min 10sec (77.03mph/123.94kph)

H. J. Aldington's race with a Bristol 400

(From an interview conducted by Julian Hunt with John Aldington, Managing Director of Porsche Cars Great Britain Ltd at Reading in June 1982.)

AFN entered a Bristol 400 saloon for my father, H. J. Aldington, to drive in the 1949 Mille Miglia partnered by Count 'Johnny' Lurani. My father accompanied by my mother, Ivy, and a Bristol works engine specialist drove out from England in a 400 saloon. They were in company with another Bristol 400 and two Frazer Nash High Speed competition two-seaters which, after my father and Norman Culpan drove Culpan's car to third place at Le Mans in June, were renamed the 'Le Mans Replica'.

One of these was a works car, entered by Count Lurani for Dorino Serafini, and driven out by Ronnie Hovenden, who was at that time AFN's works manager, and my cousin, Tim, accompanied him. Dickie Stoop, who was to co-drive Culpan's new car, drove that out and I, 14 years old at the time, accompanied him.

After some problems with the oil temperature on the new car, we stopped before St Dizier and propped open the rear of the bonnet with a piece of rubber hose to

The BMW 335 which W. H. Aldington (brother of H. J. Aldington) drove to France to meet the Frazer Nash équipe on the N4 near St Dizier. Behind the BMW is the Bristol 400 saloon that H. J. Aldington/Lurani drove in the race. (Frazer Nash Archives)

improve the cooling of the engine compartment. When we set off again, Dickie was driving the car as fast as possible to see whether there was any reduction in temperature. On the fast, open roads before St Dizier, we were running at around the car's maximum of 115mph (185kph). I was watching the gauges and I signalled to Dickie that the temperature was now all right, but, of course, he had to have a look for himself and leant over to peer at the gauge.

Stoop looked up again to see that we were heading for a large boulder lying out in the road. He swerved, missed it with the front wheels, but caught it with one of the rear wheels. This blew the tyre and sent the car sideways; it hit the edge of the road and threw me out into the ditch. The Nash turned over, Stoop ducked down in the cockpit and the car landed on top of me. As I lay in the ditch unable to move, with fuel pouring over me, I could hear Stoop, who was still inside the car, moaning that he had injured his thumb, as the car turned over. I shouted, 'Bugger your thumb, get the car off me!'

My father, driving the Bristol, arrived at the scene. He stopped the 400, jumped out to assist, but failed to put the handbrake on. The Bristol began to roll down the road, much to the alarm of my mother, who was left trying to find the handbrake, which was positioned between the front seats. Ronnie Hovenden pulled up with the other Frazer Nash, dashed after the Bristol and stopped it running away.

In his haste, my father grabbed the exhaust pipe to try to turn the crashed Frazer Nash over. The car didn't move, but he severely burnt his hand. When we crashed the road had been completely deserted, but other vehicles soon appeared, including a bus, and the Nash was quickly rolled back on to its wheels. I was pretty badly shaken and while, much to my disgust, I had a large amount of brandy poured down my throat, Stoop, who was teetotal and a non-smoker, fortified himself with a whole bottle of Kia-Ora orange squash. I would much rather have shared that.

After the crash, it was concluded that Culpan's Frazer Nash was drivable, but not fit to race, so Hovenden drove it gently back to England. A still shaken Stoop, Tim and I then squeezed into the Bristol and in company with the Lurani Nash, now with Smith at the wheel, we drove on to St Dizier where we telephoned my Uncle Bill (W. H. Aldington) who was in Geneva with Norman Culpan who had flown out. WHA drove his BMW saloon to Dijon to meet us, Tim accompanied my parents, plus all the luggage, in the Bristols, while Stoop and I travelled on to Dijon by train.

From Dijon, we drove the four cars to Count Maggi's house at Calino. There we met Basil Cardew of the *Daily Express* and when he learned of the accident, he filed a dramatic account with his newspaper. When I returned to school at Harrow, I found copies of the 'English Schoolboy Escapes Death' headlines plastered all over my study door. The Healey team and all the other British competitors stayed at Calino.

Norman Culpan's Frazer Nash Le Mans Replica, chassis number 421/100/008, after Dickie Stoop had crashed it driving to the 1949 race. On the left behind the car, young John Aldington nurses his injured nose. (Frazer Nash Archives)

I remember that scrutineering was fairly casual, although there were various people muttering about the poor standard of fuel available. I recall that 'lead' in small phials was being added directly to the tanks of cars. The Bristol engine specialist was very closely involved with this and a lot of testing had to be done to determine how many phials made the optimum dose. Strictly speaking, the Bristol and all the other touring cars should have been running on standard fuel.

M. P. Tenbosch, who despite his name lived in Fulham, had a new Frazer Nash with the Fox & Nicholl body from the first post-war Nash and his co-driver was Peter Monkhouse. Instead of reconnoitring the course, Tenbosch just blasted up and down at racing speed. He retired from the race just after Rome and the general view was that he cooked his chances by his odd behaviour at Brescia.

On the day of the race Cohen/Hignett took me into Brescia in their Healey Elliot, which seemed tractor-like compared to the Bristol. I had an uncanny feeling of fear as we drove into town. It was so strong that before the start I felt compelled to go and wish them luck and added, "I think you're going to need it." Sadly, I was proved right, as the car crashed only 12 miles after the start and one of the men was killed and the other badly injured.

My father hated being driven, so in spite of his very painful hand he installed Count Lurani in the passenger seat for most of the race. Lurani, for his part, spent the greater part of the race sounding the extra horn fitted on the passenger glove locker lid, and crossing himself. Lurani later wrote, 'I

recall before La Spezia, while Aldington was at the wheel, Venturi in the Alfa [which finished second in the class] tried to pass us downhill as we were approaching a narrow bridge'.

Neither of the drivers wanted to give way. According to my father, when he looked across at the Italian, he knew that the Alfa driver had decided that it was death or glory, so he took his foot off the throttle. [There was a similar Mexican stand-off between Aldington and Tom Wisdom with the Healey Westland at another bridge and again Aldington gave way.]

At Rome they quickly refuelled the car, which was fitted with twin fillers and an extra-large tank, and while my father was checking the car over, Lurani disappeared. When the car was ready to leave, he looked around, but there was still no Lurani. Time was slipping by so he went to look for him and found the Count recounting his adventures into a microphone for a radio broadcast.

My father grabbed his partner and hustled him back into the car. Geoff Healey/Tom Wisdom won the class with their Healey, just under two minutes ahead of Sanesi/Venturi (Alfa Romeo 6C 2500 Golden Arrow), and my father and Lurani finished third in the class, just over another two minutes behind.

1950

23 April
Starters: 375; Finishers: 213; Length: 1,022 miles (1,644km).
Circuit: see page 246.
Weather: sustained rain.

Main Contenders for victory:

711 Giovanni Bracco/Umberto Maglioli (Ferrari Tipo 166MM, 1,995cc, Touring Barchetta)

720 Franco Rol/Richieri (Alfa Romeo 6C 2500 competition model, 2,443cc)

722 Vittorio Marzotto/Paolo Fontana (Ferrari Tipo 166SC/with Tipo 195 2,341cc engine, Fontana Barchetta)

724 Giannino Marzotto/Marco Crosara (Ferrari Tipo 195 Sport, Touring berlinetta 2,341cc)

728 Alberto Ascari/Senesio Nicolini (Ferrari Tipo 275 Sport, 3,322cc, Touring Barchetta)

730 Juan Fangio/Zanardi (Alfa Romeo 6C 2500 competition model 2,443cc)

731 Luigi Villoresi/Pasquale Cassani (Ferrari Tipo 275 Sport, 3,322cc, Touring Barchetta)

732 Felice Bonetto/G. Casnaghi (Alfa Romeo Tipo 412, 4,492cc, spider)

733 Dorino Serafini/Ettore Salani (Ferrari Tipo 195 Sport, 2,341cc, Touring Barchetta)

740 Consalvo Sanesi/Bianchi (Alfa Romeo 6C 3000 competition model, 2,955cc, berlinetta)

Once again the route was changed, so that it ran clockwise once more with a very fast stretch early in the race along the Adriatic coast from Ravenna to Pescara. The return leg from Rome ran north along the Mediterranean coast to Leghorn, turned inland to Florence and then north to Bologna, incorporating once more the Futa and Raticosa Passes. At this time the organisers were having great difficulty in selecting a consistent route, but there may have been pressures from local and regional authorities and also, quite possibly, financial encouragement through certain areas. The cars had to run on 80-octane fuel supplied by the organisers.

In 1950 there were 375 competitors and their cars had to be scrutineered during a period of 2½ days and this explains why the race attracted a reputation for the most casual scrutineering – except, of course, when the scrutineers were determined to be difficult. Of this enormous entry 116 were Fiat 500 Topolinos of all types

Giannino Marzotto takes the chequered flag at Brescia in 1950 to win his first Mille Miglia. The car is a Ferrari Tipo 195S with Touring berlinetta body. Marzotto did not know that he had won until Serafini crossed the finishing line with his Ferrari, seven minutes 33sec behind on time. At 22 years of age, Marzotto was the youngest driver ever to win the race. (Author's Collection)

Partnered by Casnaghi, Felice Bonetto drove a 1939 Tipo 412 4.5-litre V12 Alfa Romeo. In the terribly wet conditions he kept this very powerful car up with the leaders until he retired at Pescara because of mechanical problems. (Foto Locchi)

and ages, but theoretically to standard specification. Those running in the 750cc sports class were in the main highly developed and a considerable number of them were the work of such constructors as Dagrada, Ermini, Giannini, Stanguellini, Taraschi and Testadoro.

Different were the Morettis which had the company's own backbone chassis and 750cc single overhead camshaft engines. It was the same in the 1,100cc sports class where Fiats dominated, but there were 13 Cisitalias, although the marque was very much on the wane. Of the three OSCAs Luigi Fagioli partnered by Diottalevi had a new version with 1,093cc twin-cam engine.

In the up to 2,000cc and over 2,000cc sports classes, there was a strong field. The growth of the marque Ferrari was spectacularly demonstrated by the fact that 17 of these cars started the race including those listed above. With an entry of 11 Tipo 166MM cars, Ferrari seemed destined to win the 2,000cc sports class easily. Ferrari hopes were pinned on the 275 Sport cars with Touring Barchetta bodies, the first V12s to appear under Lampredi's name.

They were, however, a poor and temporary combination of the existing chassis with the first of the so-called 'long block' Ferrari V12 engines. They handled badly, they were too powerful for the existing Ferrari transmission and they had more than their fair share of tyre problems. As we shall see, the failure of the cars driven by Ferrari's lead drivers gave a fine opportunity for other drivers to make their mark.

Alfa Romeo had still not passed the baton of Italian pride in sports car racing to Ferrari, for, not without reason, those in control at Alfa Romeo and Enzo Ferrari had a peculiarly Italian love-hate relationship. Alfa Romeo was still trying to retain its supremacy, but it did so in a very half-hearted way. For both entrants the challenge was even greater and more important in Grand Prix racing where the blown 1,500cc Tipo 158 Alfa Romeo cars that dated back to 1938 had maintained an unbroken record of success since 1946, but were under increasing pressure from Ferrari.

It would not have been so bad from Portello's point of view if they had adequate resources to fight off Ferrari. The two 2.5-litre cars entered in the 1950 Mille Miglia were obsolescent and because of pressure from the

Clemente Biondetti, partnered by Bronzoni, drove one of three Jaguar XK 120s entered in 1950. The car was fitted with a radio (the aerial can clearly be seen) so that Biondetti could listen to race bulletins. Here, in torrential rain, he accelerates along the road from the start, leading out of Brescia. Despite a broken rear spring he took eighth place. (LAT/The Autocar)

Italian communist unions, egalitarian in theory, oppressive in behaviour, the latest 3-litre car was driven by chief tester Consalvo Sanesi, who was no match for Fangio and could barely match the performance of Franco Rol. The Alfa Romeo with the best prospects was the 4.5-litre V12 car of private entrant Felice Bonetto and this is discussed in some detail on pages 176–77.

In the larger-capacity classes there were a number of British cars that displayed various degrees of performance. Perhaps the most significant was the 2-litre Frazer Nash Le Mans Replica of Franco Cortese/Taravessi entered by Count 'Johnny' Lurani's Scuderia Ambrosiana. Sadly, a Bristol-engined Le Mans Replica was no match for a competently driven Tipo166MM Ferrari.

Jaguar had introduced their brilliant XK 120 with twin overhead camshaft 3,442cc engine in 1948. Early versions had aluminium-alloy bodywork, as the model was originally intended only as a limited production model for proving the engine before it was installed in the Mark VII saloon. Five early production XK 120s with aluminium-alloy bodywork were entered in the 1950 Mille Miglia and one was driven by four-times race winner Clemente Biondetti partnered by Giancarlo Bronzoni. Another XK 120 was driven by ERA owner Leslie Johnson, partnered by Jaguar engineer John Lea. These were works entries, but nominally entered privately.

As three of these cars were running with hoods, it was believed that they would be eligible for the Gran Turismo class. The scrutineers, however, thought differently and determined that they should run in the sports category, because, apparently, the distance between the pedals and the rear axle was ten cm (3.9 inches) too short. Biondetti's car was fitted with a radio to pick up news bulletins en route.

Among the Healeys in the race was an example of the latest 3.8-litre Nash-powered sports car with Nash three-speed gearbox and overdrive. With only 138bhp compared with the XK 120s, coupled with excess weight, they were never going to achieve anything in the Sports category of the Mille Miglia. In 1950 the car was driven by Donald and Geoffrey Healey, but the slight chance of success disappeared after Donald indulged in an off-road excursion, following which the overdrive no longer worked. Nor were the Healey saloons eligible for the GT class, as the scrutineers maintained that the bodywork was an inch too narrow.

Once again, the first car departed at a minute past midnight under a sky with bright moon and stars – despite forecasts of rain. All the touring cars and sports cars had a dry run in the early hours of the morning, but then there was heavy mist and by dawn heavy rain enveloped the start and badly affected the fastest cars. Weather conditions over the first 150 miles (241km) were appalling and there were many crashes.

Local driver Bassi lost control of his Tipo 166 Ferrari at a bridge not long after the start; he died shortly after the crash and his co-driver was seriously injured. Just ten miles short of Padua, Prince Lanza, who was one of the organisers of the Targa Florio, lost control of his Cisitalia on a flyover at Barbando di Zocco, the car rolled over several times and he and his mechanic were lucky to escape with minor injuries. This car was hauled back on to the road and Lanza drove it back to Brescia.

Before the Cisitalia was retrieved, Wood crashed at the same spot with the Healey that he was sharing with Peter Monkhouse. Wood broke a leg, but Monkhouse was hurled into a hoarding that bore the words 'Good Luck' in English and was fatally injured. There were quite a number of serious accidents at this point which were largely attributable to little or no knowledge of the circuit because of lack of training before the race.

Sanesi, who had been delayed by plug trouble, crashed the 3-litre Alfa Romeo near Ferrara and both he and Bianchi were seriously injured. Robin Richards crashed his Healey at the same spot and both Umberto and Paolo Marzotto crashed their Ferraris. Umberto hit a tree and his Ferrari was torn in two.

On wet roads Giannino Marzotto had set an unbeatable pace and led at Ravenna at an average of 89mph (143kph), but the greater power of the 3.3-litre Ferrari came into its own on the fast run to Pescara and there Villoresi led at an average of 92.5mph (149kph). Ascari lost 11 minutes in changing a punctured tyre; he had no spare wheel that fitted and was forced to flag down Serafini and borrow one. Villoresi also had tyre trouble and dropped back. Not long after Pescara both 3.3-litre Ferraris retired because of transmission failure and another retirement was Bonetto with the 4.5-litre V12 Alfa Romeo.

By Rome the order was Giannino Marzotto, followed by Serafini, Fangio and Bracco. The order of the first four remained unchanged at the finish and for 22-year-old Marzotto it was a truly remarkable performance. He was the youngest driver ever to win the 1,000-mile race. Leslie Johnson drove a very good race to finish fifth with his XK 120 ahead of Cortese (Frazer Nash) and Fagioli who won the 1,100cc class with his OSCA. Ferrari was now a major force and it was to continue to dominate the race over the next three years.

Veteran driver Luigi Fagioli, partnered by Diotallevi, drove this 1,100cc OSCA with twin overhead camshaft engine and rather odd full-width body in the 1950 Mille Miglia. He turned in a superb performance to finish seventh overall and win his class ahead of a Fiat and a Stanguellini. (Spitzley-Zagari Collection)

Results:

General classification:

1st	G. Marzotto/Crosara (Ferrari), 13hr 39min 20sec (76.57mph/123.20kph)	
2nd	Serafini/Salani (Ferrari), 13hr 46min 53sec	
3rd	Fangio/Zanardi (Alfa Romeo), 14hr 2min 5sec	
4th	Bracco/Maglioli (Ferrari), 14hr 7min 23.3sec	
5th	Johnson/Lea (Jaguar), 14hr 29min 27sec	
6th	Cortese/Taravassi (Frazer Nash), 14hr 33min 59sec	
7th	Fagioli/Diotallevi (OSCA), 14hr 34min 44.2sec	
8th	Biondetti/Bronzoni (Jaguar), 14hr 38min 39.4sec	
9th	V. Marzotto/Fontana (Ferrari), 14hr 39min 2.3sec	
10th	Schwelm/Colonna (Alfa Romeo), 14hr 45min 51.1sec	

Class results, International Touring Category:

750cc: Piodi/Citterio (Fiat), 18hr 43min 57sec (55.82mph/89.82kph)
1,100cc: Mancini/Renzi (Fiat), 17hr 8min 29.0sec (61.00mph/98.15kph)
Over 1,100cc: Cornaggia/Mantegazza (Alfa Romeo), 15hr 48min 37sec
  (66.14mph/106.42kph)

Class results, Grand Touring:

Schwem/Colonna (Alfa Romeo), 14hr 45min 51.1sec (70.82mph/113.95kph)

Class results, International Sports Category:

750cc: Leonardi/Prosperi (Fiat-Patriarca), 15hr 55min 40.0sec
  (65.75mph/105.79kph)
1,100cc: Fagioli/Diotavelli (OSCA), 14hr 34min 44.2sec (71.72mph/115.40kph)
2,000cc: Bracco/Maglioli (Ferrari), 14hr 7min 23.3sec (74.04mph/119.13kph)
Over 2,000cc: G. Marzotto/Crosara (Ferrari), 13hr 39min 20sec
  (76.57mph/123.20kph)

Robin Richards's race with a Healey Silverstone

(Richards was a motor trader and race commentator and this account is based on an interview with him at his home in Cranleigh, Surrey by Julian Hunt in April 1982)

I only competed the once, in 1950 with a Healey Silverstone. It was entered with the connivance of the Healey Motor Company (it was long before the Austin tie-up). I drove in the race because it was a challenge. I had won a Coupe des Alpes in the Alpine Rally with an HRG in 1948 and I had finished fourth with an Allard in the 1950 Monte Carlo Rally. Both results were very pleasing. I made two more attempts on the Monte, which resulted in 54th and 104th after which I thought enough was enough.

But I do think that there was a resemblance between the Mille Miglia and rallying as it was then, not as it is now. In the 1948 Alpine we went flat out virtually all the time, just like the Mille Miglia. Another similarity was that none of the roads repeated themselves.

The Mille Miglia was a wonderful event and the main thing about it was the tremendous enthusiasm of the whole of Italy. At Brescia, for the scrutineering before the race, all the schools closed and the children went to the scrutineering. That gives a tremendous feeling of atmosphere; it is more than a Cup Final and more of an event than Le Mans, which in its heyday attracted over 300,000 spectators. To the Italians, the Mille Miglia was what Le Mans was to the French. The numbering system, with the times of departure as the numbers, helped spectators to follow the event as the race progressed.

In 1950 it was very wet, really pelting down. It was pouring down when we got there. My co-driver was Rodney Lord, an Australian, whom the Italians insisted on referring to as 'Lord Rodney' and treating him as if he were an aristocrat. We drove the whole way out to Brescia. We were amateurs. We arrived absolutely sodden – the Healey had no side screens and a pretence of a hood. It was a very nice car with a 2.5-litre Riley engine. It was a reliable motorcar, but it didn't handle too well in the wet. It was a good reliable old slogger.

We arrived at the Maggis' house at Calino, which was an eye-opener to me because I spent some of the war in Italy and I had been horrified at the devastation of the towns and villages. So it was a tremendous surprise to arrive at Calino and see 50 or so well-fed, clothed and healthy-looking servants of all kinds, who collected our sodden clothes from the Healey and took us, with green umbrellas (which we hardly needed because we were soaked already) into the Casa. When we had bathed and changed, we found our clothes had been cleaned and dried, our shoes polished like new and the Healey put away cleaned and polished, all of which was a revelation to me.

The race itself had the order of starting by engine size and further split into sports or touring cars. Fairly simple distinctions were applied, though not very well defined distinctions. The Healey was in the over 2,000cc Sports class. I was told that there would be a ballot for starting times, in which I would have to make a draw. But, in fact, I was never asked to draw; all that happened was that I was told that I would be Number 736, which was six positions from the end.

I wasn't very happy about this, not only because

Robin Richards was a very well-known and professional commentator for the BBC. He was also a very successful motor trader and a partner in the company, Richards & Carr Ltd., who in the 1950s had premises in Kinnerton Street, London SW1. (Author's Collection)

Here Robin Richards is seen at the wheel of the 1,100cc HRG sports car that he shared with John Beaumont in the 1948 Alpine Rally. They won their class and also a Coupe des Alpes for a penalty-free run. (Author's Collection)

someone else had drawn the time for me, but also because most of the Italian heroes were getting away in front of me, and Sanesi's fast Alfa Romeo was only a few minutes behind. I was anxious not to be overtaken by him until I had overtaken a number of cars myself and built up a cushion of cars behind. So I went fast from the start to build up a barrier behind.

Going along the road it was appalling; there were so many cars in the ditch or up the bank that it was obvious that I couldn't get enough cars behind me to hold up Sanesi. The Silverstone, with a little bit of tuning done by Healey's, had a maximum speed of about 110mph [177kph]. I knew that the Alfa could go a lot faster. As we went along, it was difficult to see out of the rear-view mirror with the rain and mud flying about. The Healey had a let-down screen and I had a visor on, so that I could see quite well ahead, but I could not see well behind.

I was fairly pleased with my progress because I saw Leslie Johnson's Jaguar ahead of me; I knew he was a good driver and he had started a minute before me. I reckoned if I was catching Leslie, then I wasn't doing too badly. After a bit, I could see a little red dot in the mirror that got bigger and bigger. I thought, "Christ! That's Sanesi." He finally came past me going so very fast on a flat stretch of road just outside Ferrara on the Adriatic.

After Sanesi passed me, the whole picture of the race changed. Everyone who had been held back for hours,

saw the last of their heroes go through and started to stream out on to the road. It was then about ten in the morning and buses began to appear on the roads, so, although I was lying about tenth at the time, the roads were completely blocked.

We had to avoid the buses, but the people could be made to stand back by weaving the car from side to side. It takes a hell of a lot of courage to keep your foot down on the loud pedal, approaching a wall of spectators, so I started to lift off and I think I lost a lot of time. Sanesi was getting further ahead, which made things worse.

The race was becoming more difficult too, because without having previewed the course, I didn't know what was ahead and I began to rely on the marshals with yellow flags. There were a lot of these to warn of dangerous corners, or other hazards and they would wave, or hold up flags, to warn of something ahead. This was fine, but they were inconsistent in their positioning, so you would see a flag, put on the anchors and then you would find that you were 300 yards from the bend, so you had to accelerate again, all of which lost time.

Some 10–20 kilometres further on you would see another yellow flag and you would think, "I wonder if it's right" and then find yourself on top of a corner and have to brake really hard to get round. As the race went on, I was still trying to press on and I found myself approaching what looked like a fairly fast left-hander with another fast right-hander beyond it. There was no flag, so I thought, "This must be okay." But it wasn't.

The right-hander wasn't fairly fast, it was a right angle. So I was in trouble, approaching in third gear at about 85–90mph (140kph or so). I tried to spin the car on the handbrake, but this didn't work and I went straight off the edge of the road into a cabbage field. It was interesting to find that I landed up alongside Mr Sanesi, who was being consoled by the yellow flag marshal. The accident was caused by relying on the flags and not doing a thorough reconnaissance.

If I was going to do the Mille Miglia again, it would have been much better to choose a car that ran in the middle of the field, rather than being at the back with the fast stuff. It was very exciting to see the tremendous enthusiasm for the Mille Miglia, but also depressing to learn how the population didn't care for anyone but their own heroes.

After the accident Richards and Lord got the Healey back on the road and Rodney Lord drove it back to England. Robin Richards had injured a leg, which had previously been hurt in a testing accident with an HRG before Le Mans in 1949. He was taken to hospital and his leg was put in plaster as a precaution before he returned to England by train. The plaster came off Richards in a fortnight and he raced a Healey Silverstone again in the Tourist Trophy at Dundrod in September 1950. It was a handicap race and he finished 11th.

1951

28-29 April
Starters: 325; Finishers: 175; Distance: 978 miles (1,574km).
Circuit: see page 246.
Weather: initially dry, but thereafter driving rain.

Main contenders for victory:

315 'Ippocampo' (Castiglione)/Mori (Lancia Aurelia B20 GT, 1,991cc)
325 Luigi Grolla/Monteferrario (Lancia Aurelia B20, GT, 1,991cc)
332 Giovanni Bracco/Umberto Maglioli (Lancia Aurelia B20 GT, 1,991cc)
334 Piero Valenzano/Maggio (Lancia Aurelia B20 GT, 1,991cc)
357 Paolo Marzotto/Marino Marini (Ferrari 166MM, Touring Barchetta, 1,995cc)
405 Luigi Villoresi/Pasquale Cassani (Ferrari 340 America, Vignale berlinetta, 4,101cc)
410 Giannino Marzotto/Marco Crosara (Ferrari 212 Export, Fontana berlinetta, 2,562cc)
411 Vittorio Marzotto/Ottelo Marchetto (Ferrari 340 America, Touring Barchetta, 4,101cc)
416 Alberto Ascari/Senesio Nicolini (Ferrari 340 America, Touring Barchetta, 4,101cc)
419 Franco Rol/Gino Munaron (Alfa Romeo 6C 2500 Experimental, berlinetta, 2,443cc)
422 Franco Bornigia/Mario Bornigia (Alfa Romeo 6C 2500 Experimental, berlinetta, 2,443cc,)
427 Felice Bonetto/Casnaghi (Alfa Romeo 412, 4,492cc, Vignale spider)
428 Dorino Serafini/Ettore Salani (Ferrari 340 America, Touring Barchetta, 4,101cc)
434 Piero Scotti/Amos Ruspaggiari (Ferrari 212 Export, Motto Spider, 2,562cc)
437 Clemente Biondetti/Cortini (Biondetti special combining Ferrari 166MM chassis with 3,442cc Jaguar engine)

British Entries:

352 Franco Cortese/Tagni (Frazer Nash Le Mans Replica, 1,971cc)
359 Ernest Stapleton/Betty Stapleton (Aston Martin Speed Model, 1,949cc)
406 Donald Healey/Geoffrey Healey (Nash-Healey, 3,848cc)
421 J. Gatty/Fantuzzi (Jaguar XK 120, 3,442cc)
425 Tom Wisdom/Tony Hume (Aston Martin DB2, 2,580cc)
429 Leslie Johnson/John Lea (Jaguar XK 120, 3,442cc)
432 Stirling Moss/Frank Rainbow (Jaguar XK 120, 3,442cc)
435 Sydney Allard/Tom Lush (Allard J2, 5,420cc)

Yet again the course had been changed and although it was the same from Brescia to Ravenna, it then went inland to Forli and joined the Adriatic coast at Rimini. From Pescara it went north only as far Rieti, and then routed to Rome. From Rome it followed a route well inland to Florence via Siena. The remainder of the course was unchanged. There were now more classes to reflect the demands of entrants.

A very large number of competitive cars included 26 Ferraris, the majority of them 2-litre Tipo 166MM cars.

In 1951, for the second year running, Franco Cortese drove 'Johnny' Lurani's Le Mans Replica. Although early starters had left on dry roads, heavy rain soon began to fall and Cortese, together with 'mechanic' Tagni, were already soaked at the start. Cortese was faster than in 1950, despite a broken pushrod, but could manage only ninth place and a class second. (Frazer Nash Archives)

Bonetto and the Tipo 412 Alfa Romeo

In the 1950–51 Mille Miglia races Felice Bonetto drove a very fast 4.5-litre Alfa Romeo. It was in fact a private entry in the 1,000-mile race, although its origins were as a works car and dated back to 1936. In that year Alfa Romeo introduced for Grand Prix racing a 60° V12 engine with a capacity in its original form of 4,064cc (70 x 88mm). With twin overhead camshafts per bank of cylinders gear-driven from the rear of the crankshaft, a single large supercharger mounted at the front of the engine and twin Weber carburettors, the power output of this engine, known as the 12C36, was around 370bhp at 5,800rpm on a compression ratio of 7:1.

For 1937 the capacity of the engine was increased to 4,495cc (72 x 92mm) and on a raised compression ratio of 7.25:1 it developed 430bhp at 5,800rpm. Like all Alfa Romeo engines of the period its design was the work of the great Vittorio Jano. The engine was raced for two seasons only and became obsolete at the end of 1937 with the introduction for the coming year of a Grand Prix formula that had capacity limits of 3,000cc supercharged and 4,500cc unsupercharged.

Alfa Romeo built two sports cars using modified versions of this engine for the 1939 season. It has been said that there may have been as many as four of these V12 sports cars, but there is no evidence to support this contention. The chassis was very similar to that of the 1938 Tipo 8C 2900B and the body, once again the work of Touring, was very similar to that of the 2.9-litre cars, but the tail was smoother and the headlamps were more deeply nacelled into the front wings.

As used in the sports car, the supercharger was removed from the V12 engine, three twin-choke downdraught carburettors were fitted and the compression ratio was raised to 8.15:1. Weight was around 1,000kg (2,205lb) and maximum speed was claimed as 220kph (137mph).

Race debut for the new car, typed the 412, was at Antwerp at the end of May 1939 and in the face of weak opposition Farina and Sommer took the first two places. Five days later Biondetti drove one of these cars into second place behind Wimille's Bugatti in the Luxembourg Grand Prix. Farina and Biondetti practised with 412s at Liège in Belgium for a race to be held on 20 August, but this event was cancelled by the imminence of war and Belgian mobilisation. The final appearance of one of these cars while in works ownership was the one car used in practice only at the 1940 Mille Miglia.

After the war, two cars were sold off to private owners. Swiss hill climb exponent Willy Daetwyler bought one (believed to be the second chassis). Over a period of years it was extensively modified by fitting a supercharger and two twin-choke Weber carburettors, together with a lighter body. The car was offered for sale by a Zurich dealer in late 1954 and although its immediate history thereafter is not known, it passed into the ownership of what is now known as the French National Motor Museum/Collection Schlumpf at Mulhouse.

The first of these cars (believed to be chassis number 412151) was sold to Felice Bonetto who first raced it in the 1950 Targa Florio held as the Circuit of Sicily. He drove the Alfa Romeo down from the north of Italy on snow-covered roads and took with him on the car, spare wheels, tools and a passenger. During this race he went off the road, resumed the race, but retired.

Partnered by Casnaghi, he then drove the car in the 1950 Mille Miglia. He was well up with the leaders in very

One of these 2-litre cars was driven to 50th place overall by one Eugenio Castellotti, then a novice driver and later one of Italy's great aces. The Alfa Romeo entry was rather pathetic, as it consisted of the two six-cylinder Experimental cars with berlinetta bodies running in the race for the third time, without any development work carried out in the interim, and Bonetto's pre-war V12 4.5-litre car which had now been fitted with a new body. Of much greater significance were the new and very beautiful 2-litre Lancia Aurelia GTs.

The British entries are set out in full, as the numbers were steadily growing. Cortese's Frazer Nash was the Scuderia Ambrosiana car that he drove later in the year to unexpected wins in the Targa Florio and the Enna Cup, both in Sicily. For the second year running, Stapleton drove his pre-war Aston Martin, this time

accompanied by his wife. It was an enthusiast's entry in search of excitement and fun and could not be regarded seriously.

Another and much more serious Aston Martin entry was the DB2 shared by Wisdom and Hume. This car, VMF 64, was a hard-raced example that had finished fifth at Le Mans the previous year; it was used as a road car by Aston Martin owner David Brown and had been prepared for the Mille Miglia in the Service Department, as opposed to the Racing Department at Feltham. Later in 1951 it was to finish third at Le Mans. The Healeys' entry was an open two-seater prototype of the Nash-Healey, but it was rather outpaced in the Mille Miglia.

Of the Jaguar entries, the cars of Johnson and Moss were works-supported (in fact works cars in everything but name and who was footing the bills); Gatty was a

wet weather conditions, but retired after Pescara because of unknown mechanical reasons. Later that year Bonetto took the car to Portugal where he won the 193-mile (311km) Circuit of Porto. The opposition was rather thin and Piero Carini (OSCA) and Tom Wisdom (Jaguar XK 120) finished in second and third places.

Over the winter of 1950–51 Bonetto had the car rebodied by Vignale. The new body was a typical Vignale Spider body, with 'portholes' along the front wings, but it also had a streamlined headrest and a vertical Alfa Romeo intake that looked as if it had come straight off a 6C 2500 saloon. Bonetto drove the car in

Felice Bonetto had his 4.5-litre Tipo 412 Alfa Romeo rebodied by Vignale over the winter of 1950–51. The result was this very handsome spider distinguished, with its Vignale 'portholes' in the front wings. In 1951 Bonetto drove a good race to finish sixth. (Author's Collection)

the Mille Miglia and in very bad weather took sixth place. This seems to have been the car's last race. It was offered for sale in 1952–53 and, again, in late 1954 when Franco Cortese was trying to dispose of it. Its ultimate fate is unknown.

fruiterer at Convent Garden and his car, which made absolutely no impression in the race was a bona fide private entrant. Sydney Allard's J2 Allard with push-rod Cadillac V8 engine was a pure competition car and these sold well in the United States to amateur racers, even if, generally, they made little impression in Europe. An exception was the 1950 Le Mans race in which one of these cars shared by Sydney Allard and Tom Cole finished third.

As 'Johnny' Lurani pointed out, "An official publication declared the number of starters as 428, whereas in reality there were 325, while official communiqués gave the number as 319." In this writer's opinion there can be no absolute certainty as to the number of cars that started the race. As usual, the great majority of the entries were in the small-capacity classes.

The 750cc Utilitarian category attracted 80 entries, the majority of them Fiats, but there were also air-cooled twin-cylinder front-wheel-drive Dyna Panhards and rear-engined Renault 750s.

There were 57 starters in the 1,100cc Utilitarian class; again the majority of them were Fiats, and 40 in the 1,500cc class, the majority of them Lancia Aprilias. Another marque that was becoming more prolific was OSCA and there were six of these 1,100cc cars and also 14 Cisitalias. The first car left the start at 11.01pm on the Saturday and the last car away was Biondetti's Jaguar-engined Ferrari at 4.37am on the Sunday morning.

The weather remained dry for most of the early starters, but all the powerful cars left in torrential rain on treacherous roads. Within a few miles of the start many cars in the hands of experienced drivers had crashed. Ascari went off the road with his 4.1-litre Ferrari and killed a spectator. He reported that the crash was caused by a spectator who temporarily blinded him when he shone a powerful flashlight on the Ferrari to read the race number. Understandably, Ascari formed an aversion to the race and only drove in it once more, in 1954.

Johnson and Moss also crashed their Jaguars. In his book *My Cars, My Career*, Stirling Moss set out his diary entry for the day of the race: "Today is Mille Miglia day so up at 3am. Cold and wet. Went to start, tremendous set-up, with thousands of bods organizing things. Pouring rain when I left at 4.32am, 3 minutes after Leslie Johnson. Caught the Ferrari saloon which started 1 minute ahead in about 4 miles [Checcaci/Gentili with a Motto-bodied 2,562cc 212 berlinetta]. Car going well considering, getting along at about 115mph, in darkness!

"Then after 15 miles it happened. Chap waved me down, applied brakes, nothing happened, turned wheel, same effect. On oil! Hit Fiat which Leslie had done and bent wing on to wheel. Went to garage and reversed, gearbox jammed in reverse, took 2 hours to repair. Also bonnet wouldn't close, so had to retire, damn it."

Yet another retirement was Biondetti with his Jaguar-powered Ferrari. Flexing of the chassis on the bumpy roads caused the fan to cut through a water hose and the car was withdrawn because of an overheated engine. Sydney Allard also went off the road near Ravenna,

hitting a kilometre post and bending the front suspension; when he retired he was well up with the leaders. Giannino Marzotto went into the lead with his 2.6-litre Ferrari and was driving superbly in near-impossible conditions. Young Sergio Sighinolfi, who later became a Ferrari test driver, crashed his Cisitalia near Ferrara, uprooted three kerbstones and handed victory in the 1,100cc class to the OSCAs.

Luigi Villoresi was struggling with the handling of his 4.1-litre Ferrari which was very difficult and primitive in the wet. An off-course excursion where Siginholfi had crashed on the road near Ferrara wrecked the left front wing, together with the headlamp and pushed the radiator grille back. Fortunately, the radiator was undamaged and he was able to continue. Another victim of the terrible weather was Dorino Serafini who crashed on a bend that he knew well near his home town of Pesaro because his line through the corner was obscured by spectators encroaching on the road. Serafini's Ferrari mounted a bank and crashed through trees before dropping into a field; he suffered a broken arm and leg.

On the Adriatic coastline, just south of Pesaro and close to Fano, Giannino Marzotto became disconcerted because of a bad rumbling and vibration from the rear of his Ferrari. He thought that a bearing in the transmission was breaking up and decided that there was no alternative but to retire from the race. He has been criticised on the basis that he was too inexperienced to diagnose that the Ferrari had a chunked rear tyre. This is ridiculous; the complete Aston Martin team was unable readily to diagnose the same problem at Le Mans in 1959. Vittorio Marzotto also retired his Ferrari for unknown mechanical reasons and another mysterious retirement was Stapleton with his Aston Martin.

Villoresi/Cassani, drove this 4.1-litre Ferrari America berlinetta in the very wet 1951 race and won from Giovanni Bracco (Lancia). The photograph was taken after an off-road diversion that demolished the left headlamp and wing. (Foto Locchi)

Villoresi was having more and more trouble with his gearbox and by the time that he reached Florence he had only fourth gear usable and was merely two minutes ahead of the much less powerful, but superb handling and brilliantly driven Lancia Aurelia of Bracco, partnered by Maglioli. In third place was the 1,100cc OSCA of World War Two fighter pilot Franco Bordoni. On the Futa Pass the Experimental Alfa Romeo driven by the Bornigia brothers slid off the edge of the road and dropped 60ft (18m) and came to rest on top of two other cars that had crashed. The brother who was driving at the time suffered a fractured pelvis.

Over the final, fast stretch back to Brescia, Villoresi was able to extend his lead to just under 20 minutes, but there is no doubt that the moral winners were Bracco and the Lancia in second place, with 90bhp or so compared with the winner's 230bhp. Bordoni stopped because of fuel pump failure and after losing 40 minutes while the pump was changed, finished in tenth place. Third place went to portly Sicilian mineral water bottler Piero Scotti, who was accompanied by former Alfa Romeo test driver Ruspaggiari.

Paolo Marzotto upheld the family tradition with fourth place; other Lancia Aurelia GTs were fifth and seventh and Bonetto did well to finish sixth with a car that on a power/handling basis was totally unsuitable for the conditions. Somewhere on the route the Alfa Romeo had shed its boot lid. A particularly pleasing result was the 11th place overall and class win by trilby-wearing Wisdom and Hume with the Aston Martin DB2. The Healeys had a poor race and took a rather miserable 30th place overall.

One of the sensations of the 1951 race was the drive by Bracco in a works Lancia Aurelia B20 GT car. The wet conditions favoured less powerful cars but, even so, his second place overall, at an average speed of nearly 74mph (118.50kph), was an outstanding achievement. In standard form, the B20 was one of the best road cars of the 1950s. It had good performance, especially on long journeys, and wonderful road-holding and steering. (Author's Collection)

2,000cc: Bracco/Maglioli (Lancia), 13hr 10min 14sec (73.80mph/118.75kph)
Over 2,000cc: Wisdom/Hume (Aston Martin), 14hr 7min 41sec
    (68.80mph/110.70kph)

Class results, Sports Category:
750cc: Zanini/Bertozzo (Giannini), 15hr 25min 28sec (63.02mph/101.40kph)
1,100cc: Fagioli/Borghi (OSCA), 13hr 52min 35sec (70.05mph/112.71kph)
2,000cc: P. Marzotto/Marini (Ferrari), 13hr 30min 48sec (71.93mph/115.74kph)
Over 2,000cc: Villoresi/Casani (Ferrari), 12hr 50min 18sec (75.71mph/121.82kph)

Luigi Fagioli drove a 1,100cc OSCA again in the 1951 race, but this year he was partnered by Borghi. The car had cycle-wing bodywork. Fagioli, seen here passing through Modena, finished eighth overall and won the 1,100cc class from two other OSCAs, driven by Bordoni and Cabianca. (Spitzley-Zagari Collection)

Results:
General classification:

1st	Villoresi/Casani (Ferrari), 12hr 50min 18sec (75.71mph/121.82kph)	
2nd	Bracco/Maglioli (Lancia), 13hr 10min 14sec	
3rd	Scotti/Ruspaggiari (Ferrari), 13hr 22min 4sec	
4th	P. Marzotto/Marini (Ferrari), 13hr 30min 48sec	
5th	'Ippocampo'/Mori (Lancia), 13hr 47min 30sec	
6th	Bonetto/Casnaghi (Alfa Romeo), 13hr 49min 35sec	
7th	Valenzano/Maggio (Lancia), 13hr 50min 0sec	
8th	Fagioli/Borghi (OSCA), 13hr 52min 35sec	
9th	Cortese/Tagni (Frazer Nash), 14hr 5min 28sec	
10th	Bordoni/Serbelloni (OSCA), 14hr 6min 49sec	

Class results, Utilitarian Category:
750cc: Descollanges-Gignoux (Dyna Panhard), 17hr 27min 17sec
    (55.67mph/89.57kph)
1,100cc: Andreini/Quericoli (Fiat), 16hr 3min 49sec (60.51mph/97.36kph)
1,500cc: Anselmi/Gianni (Lancia), 14hr 42min 45sec (66.07mph/106.30mph)

Class results, Fast Category (Gran Turismo Cars):
750cc: Ferraguti/Faido (Fiat Zagato), 16hr 31min 32sec (58.82mph/94.64kph)
1,100cc: F.Musitelli/G. Musitelli (Cisitalia), 14hr 34min 34sec
    (66.68mph/107.29kph)

1952

4–5 May

Starters: 501; Finishers: 275; Distance: 978 miles (1,574km).

Circuit: see page 246.

Weather: dry initially for the first starters, but there was sustained heavy rain from early morning while the faster cars were still leaving Brescia.

Main Contenders for victory:

427	T. Anselmi/Semino (Lancia Aurelia B20 GT, 1,991cc)
428	Amendola/Pinzero (Lancia Aurelia B20 GT, 1,991cc
437	Luigi Fagioli/Borghi (Lancia Aurelia B20 GT, 1,991cc)
500	'Ippocampo'/Mori (Lancia Aurelia B20 GT, 1,991cc)
611	Giovanni Bracco/Alfonso Rolfo (Ferrari 250 Sport, Vignale berlinetta, 2,953cc)
613	Rudolf Caracciola/Kurrle (Mercedes-Benz 300 SL, 2,996cc)
614	Piero Taruffi/Mario Vandelli (Ferrari 340 America, Vignale spider, 4,101cc)
615	Paolo Marzotto/Marino Marini (Ferrari 225 Sport, Vignale spider), 2,715cc)
619	Stirling Moss/Norman Dewis (Jaguar C-type, 3,442cc)
622	Clemente Biondetti/Ercole (Jaguar-engined Ferrari)
623	Karl Kling/Hans Klenk (Mercedes-Benz 300 SL, 2,996cc)
626	Hermann Lang/Grupp (Mercedes-Benz 300 SL, 2,996cc)
629	Eugenio Castellotti/Annibale Broglia (Ferrari 225 Sport, Barchetta spider, 2,715cc)

British Entries:

523	Ernest Stapleton/Betty Stapleton (Aston Martin Speed Model, 1,949cc)
545	Sergio Mantovani/Callerio (Frazer Nash Le Mans Replica, 1,971cc)
546	Tom Meyer/O'Hara Moore (HWM-Alta, 1,970cc)
550	Donald Healey/Geoffrey Healey (Nash-Healey, 4,138cc)
551	Nigel Mann/Mortimer Morris Goodall (Aston Martin DB2, 2,580cc)
554	Reg Parnell/Serboli (Aston Martin DB2, 2,580cc)
556	George Abecassis/Pat Griffith (Aston Martin DB2, 2,580cc)
600	Tom Wisdom/Fred Lown (Aston Martin DB2, 2,580cc)
619	Stirling Moss/Norman Dewis (Jaguar C-type, 3,442cc)
624	Leslie Johnson/Bill McKenzie (Nash-Healey, 4,138cc)

The circuit was unchanged for the 1952 race and despite the even larger number of entries, the race organisation had improved since 1951. The organisers had increased the number of classes, mainly because of the great number of entrants. There was a total of 26 Ferraris and for the first time in post-war days there was a very serious foreign challenge, three works Mercedes-Benz 300 SL Gullwing coupés. The specification of these cars included a space-frame chassis and delightfully anachronistic coupé bodies with the famous Gullwing doors necessitated by the complex chassis design. The mechanical components were mainly those of the production Mercedes-Benz 300 saloon.

That the larger-capacity Ferraris were the quickest cars in the race was undoubted, for the 300 SLs were heavy and had a lower power output. Bracco's Ferrari, for example, weighed about 2,000lb (907kg) and had a

power output of 220bhp at 7,000rpm, together with a five-speed gearbox. This 2,953cc (73 x 58.8mm) version of the Colombo V12 engine was to be the classic Ferrari unit, powering a number of cars over the next 12 years, including the 250GT series, the Testa Rossa sports-racing cars and the GTO model that dominated GT racing in 1962–4.

By way of contrast the 1952 300 SLs weighed 2,340lb (1,060kg), had a power output of 170bhp at 5,200rpm and were fitted with a four-speed gearbox. Inevitably, the Ferrari power output was exaggerated, but even so there was a big Maranello advantage. Where the 300 SL entries scored was firstly by vastly superior aerodynamics, but more importantly, the most careful preparation, exceptional organisation and a thorough knowledge of the course as it was possible for a foreigner to possess.

The team had strong connections with the Mercedes-Benz racing outfit of pre-war days, in that the team manager was Alfred Neubauer and the drivers included aces from pre-war days Rudolf Caracciola and Hermann Lang. Caracciola was not the fittest of drivers after a crash at Indianapolis in 1946, but his 300 SL was slightly less powerful than that of his team-mates. The German team had practised on the circuit for a month. The drivers of each car had lapped the entire circuit at least ten times and it was reckoned that the fuel costs amounted to £2,000 (some £40,000 at today's monetary values).

Scrutineering for the Mille Miglia was normally very brief because of the large number of cars, but it took four hours for the 300 SL's unconventional gull-wing doors to be approved. The officials went through the rules over and over again trying to find grounds on which to disqualify the cars, but finally conceded that they were legal. There was still a lot of anti-German feeling because of the Second World War and the arrogance of the Mercedes-Benz team offended many.

The Lancia Aurelia GTs, now with more power and lightweight bodies, were in with a chance as in 1951. There was also a 'wild card' in the pack, the C-type Jaguar with experimental Dunlop disc brakes in the hands of Stirling Moss and Jaguar chief tester Norman Dewis. With a power output of at least 200bhp and a dry weight of about 2,070lb (940kg) it represented a very serious threat to both the leading teams. That is subject to certain caveats, namely, the drivers had done virtually no practice and the back-up was minimal. This was mainly because of the strict financial restrictions imposed by the British government on overseas expenditure.

In 1952 Alfa Romeo had been developing the aerodynamic Disco Volante sports-racing cars, but these were not raced until 1953 by when they had been substantially modified. So Portello had settled for a team of 1900 saloons, the company's first mass-produced saloon that had appeared in 1950, with a strong team of drivers that included Fangio, Cortese and Sanesi. Another new model to appear was the Fiat 8V sports coupé with V8 2-litre engine. As well as Fiat's own rather odd-looking cars, the Siata company had built a number of cars on this chassis and both versions ran in the 1952 race.

As usual, the smaller-capacity classes were dominated in numbers by Fiat, but in the 750cc category they faced strong opposition from French Dyna Panhards and Renaults. The Porsche factory entered the race for the first time with cars running in both the 1,500cc and 1,100cc GT categories. There was also a military cars category in 1952. The aim was to attract entries from armed forces personnel and their staff cars. The result was an entry of two Fiat Campagnolas and two Alfa AR51s, both Jeep-type vehicles. These were numbered 1M to 4M. One of the Alfa Romeos completed the course at 57.5mph (92.5kph) and was classified 114th at the finish.

A starting ramp was used for the first time in 1952, but rather oddly not by all cars and some still left from the road as in the past, either because they were running a few seconds late and could not be bothered to waste time in ascending the ramp, or because the driver was worried about wheelspin in the torrential rain. Another concern was the cars grounding on the ramp.

The military vehicles were first away from 11.01pm and the departures went on through the night until the last car, Castellotti's Ferrari was off at 6.29am. Bracco with his Ferrari was soon leading, and by the first

control at Ravenna he had averaged 90mph (145kph) and had built up a lead of 5½ minutes over Karl Kling. Then came Paolo Marzotto, Fagioli and Anselmi. Behind them the order was Biondetti, Taruffi, Castellotti, Caracciola and Moss.

There is confusion about Biondetti's Jaguar-powered Ferrari, which is sometimes referred to as a Ferrari and sometimes as a Jaguar. This car now had a full-width body that vaguely resembled that of a C-type. It ran with the number 620, but in the official list this number was allotted to a Jaguar driven by Pezzoli/Cazzulani and the Biondetti car is listed as number 622. It failed to finish and retired at Siena where it caught fire.

Already out of the race was Lang who had crashed his 300 SL near Ferrara. Donald Healey had a tyre burst, slithered into a bridge and wrecked his car. Another retirement was Abecassis because of clutch failure (he was always excessively heavy on his clutches), but he had been leading Caracciola. Stirling Moss also had problems with his C-type Jaguar and wrote in *My Cars, My Career*:

This is the 300 SL Gullwing of Hermann Lang/Erwin Grupp, at Brescia in 1952. They are starting from alongside the ramp. It was the first year in which the ramp was used and, however much the organisers objected, some drivers insisted on starting from the road. This was either because they were running a few seconds late or, in Lang's case, to avoid the furious wheelspin that the surface of the ramp was causing. (DaimlerChrysler)

"The only car modifications for the race were a full-width screen, and a tool-kit and drinking flask in the cockpit. After a couple of hours the rain eased and finally stopped and we'd overtaken several good runners when a thump and lurch announced a thrown rear tyre tread. While we were changing it Karl Kling's Mercedes went by, and he had started four minutes behind us, which was worrying …

"I trailed him into the Ravenna control, and passed him soon after, then caught Caracciola's 300 SL and passed him only to catch myself out going into a right-hander. We knocked down some posts on the verge before I was able to gain the road, and Norman used up a whole box of matches trying to light a cigarette."

Moss had damaged the C-type's exhaust system and both he and Dewis were reeling and unsteady on their feet when they arrived at Rome in seventh place.

Bracco's Ferrari was using up tyres at a phenomenal rate and by L'Aquila, 455 miles from the start he had dropped to fifth place, 13½ minutes behind race-leader Kling who had averaged just under 93mph (150kph). Castellotti was now second, Taruffi was third with his 4.1-litre Ferrari and Moss, eighth and rapidly making up ground. Castellotti crashed near Rieti and damaged his

The 300 SL of Caracciola/Kurrle, seen just after the start. Conditions were wet and difficult throughout much of the race. Caracciola was a little 'over the hill' as a driver, and he did well to finish fourth with a car that was slightly less powerful than those of his team-mates. (DaimlerChrysler)

Opposite: Piero Taruffi, seen in Vicenza at the wheel of the 4.1-litre Ferrari America that he drove in the 1952 race; following him is René Cotton's old Delahaye. Taruffi retired just before Florence because of transmission problems. The Ferrari America survives and is now fitted with a 4.5-litre engine. (Author's Collection)

car too badly to continue. By Rome Kling had a lead reduced to a still healthy 6 min 17sec over Taruffi and had averaged 85mph (137kph).

From this point onwards the race gradually slipped from Kling's grasp, as Bracco, fortified by brandy, chain-smoking and driving at a maniacal pace, began to close the gap and then pull ahead. All Bracco's co-driver had to do, it was said, was to light him cigarette after cigarette and keep passing him the flask of brandy. It all went wrong for Kling at Siena where he lost six minutes while the mechanics tried to free a jammed rear spinner and eventually he had to leave the control without changing the rear tyres. There were more problems as the rain intensified and Kling lost time over the Futa and Raticosa Passes, in particular, because of fading brakes.

Taruffi dropped out of the race when the transmission failed at Poggibonsi. Now Fagioli was in third place with the leading Lancia and turned in a superb drive that matched Bracco's efforts in 1952. At the finish at Brescia, Bracco led Kling by a margin of 4min 27 sec and Fagioli was 26min 48sec behind.

Stirling Moss seemed on course to take fourth place until he understeered into a rock at Raticosa, only 145 miles (233km) from the finish. Sadly, only a few weeks after the Mille Miglia, Fagioli crashed in practice for the 2,000 Prix de Monte Carlo (the accompanying race for smaller-capacity cars to the sports car Monaco Grand Prix) and suffered injuries, in particular a very serious head injury, that proved fatal.

Johnson's seventh place with the Nash-Healey was the best performance in the race ever by a British car. Yet again Tom Wisdom won the over 2,000cc Grand Touring category and Reg Parnell finished second in the class with his DB2 despite a delay following a collision with a stone post and running out of fuel. Another superb drive was that of Umberto Maglioli with a Lancia Aurelia saloon in the over 1,500cc division of the National Touring Category. He won the class and thrashed the Alfa Romeos.

Both OSCA and Porsche had also performed exceptionally well. Cabianca, Pagani and Venezian took the first three places with OSCAs in the 1,100cc International Sports Category. Porsche was racing mildly modified versions of the original 356 model powered by four-cylinder, horizontally opposed, air-cooled engines of similar configuration to that of the Volkswagen beetle (and in passing it is worth mentioning that the same configuration was adopted for the majority of post-1945

The truly outstanding drive in the 1952 Mille Miglia was that of Giovanni Bracco. Bracco drove a brave, alcohol-fuelled race with his Ferrari Tipo 225 Sport to win by a margin of just over four minutes from Kling/Klenk in a Mercedes-Benz 300 SL Gullwing. Bracco, who was partnered by Rolfo, is seen here passing through Modena. (Spitzley-Zagari Collection)

light aircraft engines). Porsche entries took the first three places in the 1,500cc class of the International GT category and also won the 1,100cc Sports class.

What happened subsequently to the leading marques in this race is of material interest. Bracco's Ferrari was the prototype of the Tipo 250MM that appeared for 1953 and was one of the most copacetic of all Ferrari V12s of the 1950s; it was a car that handled delightfully, that had an excellent performance and, together with the 1953 Le Mans coupés, was the first of the long line of Pinin Farina-bodied cars. As mentioned above, the engine was the most famous of all Ferrari power units.

It was the first race for the 300 SL Gullwings and although, subsequently, Mercedes-Benz won the Le Mans 24 Hours race (through the failure of faster cars) and the Panamericana Road Race (lack of serious opposition) with these cars, they cannot be regarded as a great success. Caracciola's racing career came to an end when he crashed heavily with a 300 SL at Bremgarten in May.

The C-type Jaguar had performed surprisingly well. In one major respect, however, the Jaguar did suffer badly because of the Mille Miglia. Moss, who was Jaguar's number one driver in 1952, had been impressed, too much so, by the straight-line speed of the 300 SLs in the Mille Miglia. He sent a telegram to William Lyons that said "Must have more speed at Le Mans." Jaguar broke their own rule for racing – only what was thoroughly tried and tested – by fitting the Le Mans cars with longer nose and tail sections that were untested. All three Jaguars retired very early in the race.

Results:
General classification:
1st   Bracco/Rolfo (Ferrari), 12hr 9min 45sec (79.92mph/128.59kph)
2nd   Kling/Klenk (Mercedes-Benz), 12hr 14min 17sec
3rd   Fagioli/Borghi (Lancia), 12hr 40min 5sec
4th   Caracciola/Kurrle (Mercedes-Benz), 12hr 48min 29sec
5th   Anselmi/Semino (Lancia), 12hr 54min 6sec
6th   'Ippocampo'/Mori (Lancia), 13hr 5min 39sec
7th   Johnson/Mackenzie (Nash-Healey), 13hr 11min 59sec
8th   Amendola/Pinzero (Lancia), 13hr 12min 18sec
9th   Brivio/Cassani (Ferrari), 13hr 14min 22sec
10th   Bordoni/Geronimo (Ferrari), 13hr 19min 58sec

Class results, National Touring Category:
750cc: Recordati/Bigi (Fiat), 17hrs 42min 50sec (54.87mph/88.29kph)
1,100cc: Mantrullo/Conti (Fiat), 16hrs 18min 26sec (59.61mph/95.91kph)
1,500cc: Manaco/Ferraguti (Fiat), 15hrs 49min 6sec (61.44mph/98.87kph)
Over 1,500cc: Maglioli/Monteferraio (Lancia), 13hr 58min 35sec (69.55mph/111.90kph)

Class results, International Grand Touring Category:
750cc: Gignoux/Touzot (Dyna Panhard), 15hr 20min 24sec (63.37mph/101.97kph)
1,500cc: Lurani/Berckheim (Porsche), 14hr 53min 3sec (65.31mph/105.08kph)
2,000cc: Fagioli/Borghi (Lancia), 12hr 40min 5sec (76.73mph/123.46kph)
Over 2,000cc: Wisdom/Lown (Aston Martin), 13hr 29min 40sec (72.03mph/115.90kph)

Class results, Sports Category:
750cc: Rédelé/Pons (Renault), 15hr 46min 15sec (61.63mph/99.17kph)
1,100cc: Metternich/Einsiedel (Porsche), 15hr 35min 59sec (61.14mph/98.37kph)
1,500cc: Mazzonis/Marsaglia (Lancia), 15hr 27min 10sec (62.90mph/101.21kph)

Class results, International Sports Category:
750cc: Marchese/Palverini (Dyna Panhard), 15hr 35min 17sec (62.36mph/100.33mph)
1,100cc: Cabianca/Roghi (OSCA), 13hr 32min 50sec (71.78mph/115.49mph)
2,000cc: Brivio/Cassani (Ferrari), 13hr 14min 22sec (73.42mph/118.13kph)
Over 2,000cc: Bracco/Rolfo (Ferrari), 12hr 9min 45sec (79.92mph/128.59kph)

Hans Klenk, co-driver with Karl Kling in the 1952 race

Hans Klenk was born on 28 October 1919. He learned to fly at an early age and when he went solo in a glider at the age of 11, he was probably the youngest pilot ever. His original intention was to study medicine, but he met Willy Messerschmitt and under his influence went to Munich to study aircraft and automobile engineering.

During the Second World War he was a pilot in the Luftwaffe and flew Messerschmitt Bf109s. Afterwards, in about 1950, he set up his own engineering company. He raced the ex-Kling Veritas Meteor single-seater, for which he built two different bodies, an unstreamlined body weighing 19kg (42lb) and a fully streamlined body that weighed 65kg (143lb). Both were constructed following aircraft principles.

There are arguments that the 'space-frame' chassis of the Veritas influenced Mercedes-Benz engineers when they designed the 300 SL chassis and the streamlined body of Klenk's Veritas and those of other private German entrants were a factor in the Mercedes decision to use streamlined bodies on the 1954–55 W196 Grand Prix cars.

I entered my Veritas in unstreamlined form in the 1952 Eifelrennen at the Nürburgring. I was slow in practice and failed to qualify. The organisers allowed me to start; there were 26 starters on the grid and I spent the race working

Seen on the starting ramp at the 1952 Mille Miglia is the 300 SL of Karl Kling/Hans Klenk. Mille Miglia founder Renzo Castagneto, clad in his famous grey bowler hat, watches proceedings. (DaimlerChrysler)

my way through the field. I set fastest lap and I passed 21 cars to finish fifth. I preferred long races and this event over 99 miles [160km] was too short for me to do really well.

After the race Alfred Neubauer, Mercedes-Benz racing manager, and engineer Rudi Uhlenhaut came over to talk to me and asked me if I would drive works cars for the company in 1952. I said, maybe I would, but I wanted to think about it. What I did think about was the dangers of long-distance racing over roads that the drivers did not know well. And these races were so long that it was impossible for any driver to remember every corner.

I did join Mercedes-Benz for 1952 and I was paired with Karl Kling in the Mille Miglia. I believed that I had found a way of reducing danger in these long races. I devised a road book whereby the whole course was set out, showing the distance at each corner, the shape of the corner and the speed in kmh at which the corner could be taken. It took the form of a coil spring notebook. This is a sample ('Kuppe' means in English the brow of a hill):

I was able to prepare this in training for the race in which we used Mercedes saloons initially and then our race car. We told no one, not even Neubauer, about the road book, as we did not wish to give away our advantage. So we used my road book and I shouted instructions at Kling through a small megaphone.

You asked me how I maintained my concentration. Well, I was a young man then and I chewed gum all the time. I could not be sure about the exact distance covered, because tyre wear and wheelspin made the odometer inaccurate. It didn't matter, though, provided I kept a clear reckoning of every corner.

We were leading the race by 5min 40sec when we reached Rome. It was, I think, at the next control after Rome, that we needed new rear tyres. When we stopped, the mechanics found that the spinner of the right centre-lock rear wheel had jammed and despite bashing away at it with their wheel hammers, they could not free it. Eventually Kling decided that we had to continue on the old, well-worn tyres. The stop cost us over six minutes, Kling was forced to drive slower on the very wet roads and we were also suffering from fading brakes.

Bracco had started 12 minutes before us and it was a very great disappointment when we learned that he had

This photograph, taken immediately after the finish of the 1952 race, shows (from left) Frau Kling, Karl Kling, Hans Klenk, Frau Klenk and Mercedes-Benz rennleiter (race director) Alfred Neubauer. Note the megaphone slung round Klenk's neck – the means of communicating instructions to the driver. (Hans Klenk)

passed us on time on the last section between Verona and Brescia. At the finish he was about 4½ minutes ahead of us. We met and talked after the finish. Was he drunk? Bracco was a great sportsman and you never saw him without a bottle of cognac. He had a special mounting for it in all his cars.

The Mercedes-Benz team after the 1952 Mille Miglia with (from left) Karl Kling, Rudolf Uhlenhaut, Hans Klenk at the back, Frau Kling at the front, Dr Fritz Nallinger, Frau Nallinger and Alfred Neubauer. (Author's Collection)

Later that year I co-drove with Kling at Le Mans, but we retired because of dynamo failure. Then Kling and I drove in the Panamericana Mexico Road Race, which we won. Our biggest rival was again Bracco. The race was run in eight stages and just before the start of the seventh stage, Bracco said to me, "Take it nice and gently Klenk, there is no need to hurry, I'll be retiring soon; I've noticed some peculiar noises in the back axle." He retired because of transmission problems and we went on to win from team-mates Hermann Lang/Fritz Riess.

We used my 'road book' system in the 1953 Mille Miglia and also supplied a copy to Hans Herrmann, who used it when he and Erwin Bauer drove a 356 Porsche to a 1,500cc Sports Car class win that year. It was, of course, a system that only worked with closed cars and when Daimler-Benz raced the open 300 SLRs in 1955, the works devised a version of my road-book system on a roller and Denis Jenkinson gave hand instructions to Stirling Moss.

During 1952–53 Klenk continued to race his Veritas and he also shared an Alfa Romeo 6C 3000 CM coupé with Kling in the Mille Miglia (see page 190–191). In July 1953 he was driving a 300 SL in tests at the Nürburgring, but he failed to take a curve and was flung out of the car, which rolled over several times. He suffered injuries that brought his racing career to an end. He became racing manager and later head of public relations at the Continental Tyre Company.

Of Klenk, German journalist Günther Molter wrote, "His driving style is elegant and despite the ruthlessness of modern racing his attitude is rather that of the 'gentleman' driver. His approach to technical problems, however, is serious in the extreme ..." This section is based on an interview with Hans Klenk at Untertürkheim on 31 March 2005 and the contents have Herr Klenk's approval.

Bob Berry and Moss's Jaguar in the 1952 race

Bob worked in the publicity department of Jaguar Cars Ltd, which he had joined in 1951. In 1952 he ran a Mark VII saloon in the Monte Carlo Rally as a support car, with Alan Currie from the sales department, and then he was involved in the Mille Miglia. Stirling Moss had persuaded Jaguar Chairman William Lyons (later Sir William) to run a C-type in the 1,000-mile race that year. Moss was very persuasive, for there was no real enthusiasm by the company for the race. Bob went out as a sort of 'team leader'. Stirling drove chassis number XKC 003, the car with Dunlop disc brakes that he had first appeared with at Goodwood on Easter Monday.

On this international debut of the C-type with disc brakes, Moss's co-driver was Jaguar chief tester Norman Dewis. The Jaguar support team consisted of just four people (one of whom was Harold Hodkinson, a Dunlop engineer working with Jaguar on the disc brake programme), a Jaguar Mark VII and the race car, which they drove out. Moss stayed in the house of Count Maggi, a founder of and driving force behind the Mille Miglia, on his estate at Calino near Brescia; the others were in a little chalet on the estate. Moss and Dewis used the Mark VII for reconnaissance, but they covered only sections of the circuit, and used the race car on only one occasion.

The back-up team discussed what they were going to do. Bob said, "If Stirling gets halfway round, that's the time to start showing some interest. We can't possibly do the entire circuit, so he's on his own to Rome [the southernmost point]. We'll do what work we can on the car at Rome and then he's on his own again." So on the Saturday night they handed the car over – Dewis knew the C-type so well that he could deal with any minor problems – and drove off into the night en route to Rome.

During his turn at the wheel, mechanic Frank Rainbow fell asleep and hit a huge stone marker post, knocking it out of the ground and damaging the Mark VII's front suspension. The team crawled into a garage that was closed; Bob decided that the mechanics who were responsible for the accident, should repair it, and went to sleep. They managed to get the suspension roughly safe and the team carried on. They arrived in the huge square in front of St. Peter's in Rome at about 5am and none of them had any idea where the control-point was.

They had a rather basic map of the southern outskirts of the city and this showed the control point, but they had absolutely no idea how to get there. A police car noticed them, and after some interrogation, they were ordered to follow it. With its blue light flashing, the police car tore

through Rome with Bob and his crew in (just about) hot pursuit. The control point made Bob feel as though he was in the Coliseum.

The organisers had built huge grandstands on two sides of a square and for each car there was a kind of stall with the car's racing number. In Bob's words, "It was absolute, total chaos. I had never seen anything like it in my life. There were several hours to wait before the first cars arrived and they did so at very high speed. They were screaming into the square at enormous speed, there were people everywhere and drivers trying to find their stall. There was going to be complete disaster, if we weren't careful."

Many British people were there and one came over to Bob and told him that he was the commercial attaché at the British Embassy in Rome. Bob learned that there were eight or nine from the embassy and told him, "Right! I've got a job for you. When the Moss car arrives, I want you to rush over here, link arms and make a cordon round the car. Anyone in the cordon, throw him out."

Moss and Dewis were in seventh place when they arrived at Rome and it was learned that there had been a number of high-speed excursions: one on the Ravenna

Bob Berry worked in the PR department of Jaguar for many years and eventually became Director of Public Relations. Between 1955 and early 1957 he raced an ex-works 1954 Jaguar D-type for 'Jack' Broadhead. Here Bob (right) is seen talking to Jaguar stalwart Duncan Hamilton at the 1955 Portuguese Grand Prix at Porto. Berry also attended races in an official capacity for Jaguar and became reserve driver, although he never actually raced for the works. (Author's Collection)

Although the Jaguar entry in the 1952 race was badly organised, Stirling Moss, partnered by Norman Dewis, turned in the best performance ever by a British car and driver combination. As the Jaguar retired because of damaged steering, it failed to finish, but Moss was well on his way to third place. (Foto Locchi)

straight when Moss had gone off the road into a ditch and run down the ditch for several hundred yards before he could haul the Jaguar back on the road. The incident had flattened the underside of the car and deranged the exhaust pipe. Fumes had been coming into the cockpit, Dewis was slowly being asphyxiated and he was very confused.

"Moss was jumping up and down in a very high state of excitement," recalled Bob, "and it was very difficult to understand what it was he was trying to say to me." So they made their own decisions, they changed the tyres, wired up the exhaust pipe and had a look underneath the C-type, but decided not to look too carefully. Already (according to Moss) the dampers were shot and the fuel tank was leaking, another result of the off-course excursions. With a slap on the back, Moss roared off again.

Bob and his crew were chatting to the people from the embassy and about to pack up, when former Jaguar driver Leslie Johnson with his Nash-Healey came along the row of pits and was looking for somebody to help him. Bob waved him into their area, the cordon went back in place and they refuelled the Healey, fitted the wheels off the Moss car with the least worn tyres and 'fettled it up' as best they could. Johnson departed and Bob thought no more of the incident.

By Siena, just under halfway between Rome and Brescia, Moss was in fifth place behind Bracco, Kling, Caracciola and Fagioli. On the descent to Ravenna, Moss lost front-end adhesion, understeered into a rock and damaged the steering rack. On early C-types the rack was rubber-mounted in blocks and as Moss had sheared the blocks, the rack was moving loosely and the car was barely drivable. So there was no alternative but retirement.

After Moss had departed from Rome, the crew started to make their way back along the course to Brescia. When they arrived at the assembly area in Brescia, there was no Moss, no Dewis and no Jaguar. Nobody knew what had happened to them and it was several hours later when Moss arrived back in a taxi at Count Maggi's house and gave Bob the bill to pay. "Several tens of thousands of lire were paid by me to bail Mr. Moss out of his taxi," Bob recalls. Moss and Dewis had left the car in a garage near Siena and it was collected afterwards. Moss flew home and the small team did what they could to make the C-type fit enough to drive back to Coventry.

By this time Bob was running out of money, for Jaguar were never over-generous and, despite the fact that Count Maggi had paid all their living expenses, he had run-up heavy expenditure, apart from the taxi. They got as far as Lyon on the way home, by when he had not a franc left and both the C-type and the Mark VII had empty tanks. So Bob went to see the local Jaguar distributor, Henri Peignaux, whom he knew quite well. Peignaux heard the C-type and shot out. "What can I do for you?" asked Peignaux and Bob told him, "I want to sell you some tyres." Bob went on to explain that he needed some money. "But you don't have to sell me tyres to have some money," Peignaux said.

Bob explained that Jaguar would not allow him to borrow money from a distributor. He borrowed the equivalent of £250, but insisted on leaving four racing wheels and tyres, which Peignaux brought back to the factory on his next visit. Peignaux was a racing enthusiast and wanted to drive the C-type. For reasons that Bob could not recall, he let him drive the car unaccompanied and the team spent an anxious hour or so waiting his return, with the consolation that the C-type's exhaust could be heard reverberating through the streets of Lyon.

About a week after his return to the factory, William Lyons rang Bob and told him to come to his office. Bob shot up to the chairman's office and Lyons was standing behind his chair. It was a really bad sign. If you were in serious trouble, Lyons would be standing up, if he were just having a chat with you, he'd sit down. He said to Bob, "Tell me what happened at Rome on the Mille Miglia." Bob gave him a very brief account and Lyons then said, "How do you account for this?" and handed Bob a letter. It was on Healey notepaper, signed by Leslie Johnson and thanked Jaguar, Bob Berry and his team for the help they had given him.

Bob told Lyons that what the letter said was correct and explained to him what he had done. Lyons said. "It's interesting that you didn't think it worthy of note." Bob told him that, frankly, he didn't. "It seemed obvious and sensible to help a guy who had done so much for Jaguar," Bob said, hopefully. Lyons commented, "We don't normally go to races to help our competitors." Bob pointed out that Leslie Johnson driving a Nash-Healey was hardly a competitor to Moss in a C-type. "No, but the principle is there, isn't it?" Lyons pointed out. "Yes," Bob agreed, "the principle is there." "Fine," said Lyons, "That's all I wanted to establish. Thank you, Berry."

1953

25–26 April
Starters: 481; Finishers: 286; Distance: 945 miles (1,521km).
Circuit: see page 247.
Weather: Fine at the start, dry and warm, but with some rain during the race.

Main Contenders for victory:

511	Luigi Musso/Donatello (Maserati A6GCS, 1,986cc)
512	Sergio Mantovani/Palazzi (Maserati A6GCS, 1,986cc)
525	Emilio Giletti/Guerino Bertocchi (Maserati A6GCS, 1,986cc)
542	Stirling Moss/Mortimer Morris Goodall (Jaguar C-type, 3,442cc)
543	Paolo Marzotto/Marino Marini (Ferrari 250MM, Pinin Farina berlinetta, 2,953cc)
547	Giannino Marzotto/Marco Crosara (Ferrari 340MM, Vignale spider, 4,101cc)
551	Peter Collins/Mike Keen (Aston Martin DB3, 2,922cc)
554	Franco Bornigia/Viglio (Lancia D20, 2,962cc)
555	Leslie Johnson/Bill Mackenzie (Jaguar C-type, 3,442cc)
602	Juan Fangio/Sala (Alfa Romeo Tipo 6C 3000 CM, 3,495cc)
603	Karl Kling/Hans Klenk (Alfa Romeo 6C 3000 CM, 3,495cc)
606	Felice Bonetto/Peruzzi (Lancia D20, 2,962cc)
607	Franco Bordoni/Serb Cetti (Gordini, 2,262cc)
608	Tom Cole/Mario Vandelli (Ferrari 340MM, Vignale spider, 4,101cc)
609	Giovanni Bracco/Alfonso Rolfo (Ferrari 250MM, Pinin Farina berlinetta, 2,953cc)
611	Reg Parnell/Louis Klemantaski (Aston Martin DB3, 2,922cc)
612	George Abecassis/Pat Griffith (Aston Martin DB3, 2,922cc)
613	Luigi Villoresi/Pasquale Cassani (Ferrari 340MM, Touring Barchetta, 4,101cc)
615	Giuseppe Farina/Luigi Parenti (Ferrari 340MM, Touring Barchetta, 4,101cc)
616	Clemente Biondetti/Barovero (Lancia D20, 2,962cc)
619	Umberto Maglioli/Carnio (Lancia D20, 2,962cc)
625	Mike Hawthorn/Azelio Cappi (Ferrari 250MM, Vignale spider, 2,953cc)
635	Piero Taruffi/Gobbetti (Lancia D20, 2,962cc)
637	Eugenio Castellotti/Ivo Regosa (Ferrari 340 Mexico, Vignale berlinetta, 4,101cc)
638	Tony Rolt/Len Hayden (Jaguar C-type, 3,442cc)

British entries (in addition to those listed above):

406	Montadori/Fedrigoni (Jaguar Mark VII, 3,442cc)
540	John Fitch/Ray Willday (Nash-Healey, 4,138cc)
548	Bert Hadley/Bertie Mercer (Austin-Healey 100, 2,660cc)
551	Johnny Lockett/Jock Reid (Austin-Healey 100, 2,660cc)
604	Donald Healey/Geoffrey Healey (Austin-Healey 100, 2,660cc)
618	Tom Wisdom/Helliwell (Aston Martin DB2, 2,580cc)

The route was changed again for 1953, but in a relatively minor way. It now ran directly from Rieti to Rome, omitting Terni. There were changes in the classes with a 600cc International Touring Category intended of course for entrants of Fiat Topolinos. There were no Gran Turismo class awards and a 750cc International Sports Category only, but in the 'Sport Series' Category for sports-racing cars there were six classes from 750cc to over 2,000cc. Crash helmets were now compulsory, but the rule was not strictly observed and resulted in a fatal accident. The race was a round in the newly inaugurated World Sports Car Championship and continued to be so including the last race in 1957.

What was strictly observed was unofficial closure of the course to the public until 6pm on race day. Denis Jenkinson wrote in *Motor Sport*, "Although the roads are not officially closed for this race, there is no hope of driving along the course, for every man in Italy with a gun and a uniform makes it his responsibility to see that no one gets in the way of the competitors. The main road out of Bologna was very much shut off with guards at every crossing, while in the village I was at two people were 'pinched' for riding motor scooters along the grass verge. If you wanted to move, you went on foot or wheeled your push-bike or motorcycle and there was no leniency."

The list of starters above excludes a number of less competitive Ferraris and three C-type Jaguars, one Italian-entered and two French-entered. Leslie Johnson's Jaguar was fitted experimentally with overdrive, which explains some reports that it had a five-speed gearbox. Although as usual the British drivers had little opportunity to learn the course, an exception was Stirling Moss who was reckoned to have covered some 6,000 miles (9,650km) in practice.

Jaguar entered three C-type cars in the 1953 Mille Miglia. The Jaguars lined up before the start at Brescia are (from left) Leslie Johnson's car fitted with overdrive, Tom Wisdom's car driven by Moss, and the works car of Tony Rolt. In a suit, with his hand on the centre car, is Tony Rolt and, standing between the second and third cars, are Stirling Moss and Mortimer Morris Goodall. 'Mort' Morris Goodall was Jaguar racing manager in 1953, and in the Mille Miglia he rode with Moss. None of the C-types finished the race. (Louis Klemantaski)

Karl Kling and Hans Klenk in the 1953 Mille Miglia

Hans Klenk recalls: "In 1953 Alfa Romeo asked Karl Kling and myself to drive an Alfa Romeo 6C 3000 CM in the Mille Miglia and my only complaint about it was that the coachbuilder, Colli, did not make allowance for the fact that riding mechanics come in different sizes! I am tall and at first I could not sit comfortably in the car, so I redesigned the mechanic's seat so that I could sit in reasonable comfort. There were three of these Alfa Romeos in the race and they were the fastest cars competing.

"Kling and I again used the road-book system and it worked perfectly. The other Alfa Romeo drivers, Fangio and Sanesi, did not use it. It gave us an immense advantage and other drivers without a system like ours would follow us into corners, without knowing how fast they could drive in safety. The result was that they would make errors of judgement, lose time and sometimes crash."

Karl Kling wrote (*Pursuit of Victory*, with Günther Molter, The Bodley Head, 1956): "It was Saturday when I received my car for the race – as usual; it was only ready at the last moment. The engineers always find something to alter at the last minute, and you have literally to snatch the car from their hands. After I received it, we went back to the works once again and eventually arrived at Brescia at 8.15 on Saturday evening. Neubauer was already waiting and thought that I would not make it in time!

"'603' was painted on both sides of our Alfa Romeo, and was also painted on the back and front of the car; this meant that we started at 6.03 hours. The weather was miserable when Signor Castagneto gave us the starting signal. Hans, this time on my left, crouched in his seat and studied his detailed notes. We covered mile after mile. Despite the early hour, thousands of spectators were already standing at the side of the road.

"I drove with restraint, spared my car and intended to close in on my opponents quite slowly. They were apparently concerned at the works for they thought that Fangio and I might try to race each other! He had started a minute before me, so I only needed to keep him in sight and I should know that I was in front. If my lead was only a few seconds, I could always go over to the attack when I considered it necessary.

"As I arrived at the first control-point, Fangio was just driving away. I could keep calm – as long as I had him in sight there was no danger. I also had no intention of crowding the Argentinean. In my opinion, he had the greater moral right with Alfa Romeo, because he had been driving for the Milan firm for many years, and had been World Champion in the Alfetta in 1951.

"The race continued as far as Pescara without incident. The position between Fangio and myself had not changed, although I became obsessed with watching the Argentinean, and I failed to remember Sanesi driving his Alfa behind me. He had started at 6.31 and at once he had set a cracking pace. After the race I learned that he had reached Pescara well in the lead, with the extraordinary average of 109.88mph [176.80kph].

"Five minutes behind me lay Farina in a Ferrari in second place, and I lay third, a further five minutes behind him; close behind me [on time], Fangio raced towards the

Film director Roberto Rossellini shared a Ferrari 250MM Vignale spider with Aldo Tonti and made a great fuss of his plans to make a film of the race that never happened. In contrast Bill Mason directed a successful film of the race for the Shell Film Unit. In February he had toured the course with Zuccini, the Shell Italia representative. For the race, Mason took out an English cameraman and engaged one, Ventemiglia, an Italian cameraman who spoke English. Another four Italian cameramen covered the race and, at vast expense, a cameraman in an aircraft covered part of the course.

At scrutineering, Mason managed to set up to ride with amateur driver Doctor Alberico Cacciari, who had entered his works-prepared Tipo 166 Ferrari with Scaglietti spider body. As well as filming, Bill helped out by giving directions from a 200-page tear-off route sheet which marked hazards. Mason commented to Julian Hunt in 1982: "It began to rain heavily two hours after we started and everyone (except the bravest) slowed down.

"The good Dottore was a safe, sensible driver most of the time, but he was not a fan of Germans. After cutting up one Porsche, he later pushed one on to the pavement in Siena. I drove some of the route, but Cacciari, who drove sensibly for the most part, was not a happy passenger and after a couple of sporting bends, he insisted on taking over again." They finished 56th overall.

Overall, there was an immensely strong field of potential winners and the favourites were the 4.1-litre

Opposite: Giannino Marzotto, partnered as usual by Crosara, drove a brilliant race in 1953 with his Ferrari Tipo 340MM Vignale Spider. He beat Fangio's Alfa Romeo into second place and there was a lot more to the win than the fact that Fangio had steering problems. Note that Crosara is wearing a peaked cap, not a helmet, although he started the race with a helmet. Anyone who has met Marzotto will realise that Crosara must have been a very brave man. (Spitzley-Zagari Collection)

Abruzzi mountains. I caught up and reached Rome first, with a final average of 96.75mph [155.67kph]. My stable-companion, Sanesi, and Farina had dropped out. At the control-point somebody called to me in German, 'You're in front, Kling.'

"I therefore decided to drive on according to plan, and merely to increase speed a little. This is always a better policy than needlessly taking too much out of a car; no machine can stand up to high speeds for long. I was still running beautifully. Nevertheless, I was cautious for I still had to drive my engine to the limit of its capabilities, and careful to keep a little in reserve for the final burst.

"We passed Viterbo and drew near to Lake Bolsena. I increased my speed. Suddenly … what was that? When driving with a car for hours on end at racing speed, the slightest change is noticed at once. I reduced speed and then accelerated again. There was no doubt about it; something was wrong with my Alfa Romeo. There was a sharp smell of overheated oil – always an unmistakable sign that some part was no longer functioning. I tried to ignore the danger, but it was no use.

"I had to stop. Besides, there might have been a possibility of repairing the damage if I stopped at once. Climbing out of the car, I noticed that the back of the Alfa was spattered with oil. It could mean only one thing – a corroded rear axle [the actual problem was the failure of a rubber sleeve over the final drive and drive-shaft coupling and this allowed the oil in the final drive to leak out]. I tried to drive on again, but soon saw that it was pointless. Crawling under the car again, I examined the damage more carefully and saw that the oil was now pouring out!

Karl Kling and Hans Klenk, driving a 3.6-litre Alfa Romeo Tipo 6C 3000 CM, are on the starting ramp at Brescia, waiting to be flagged off. These Alfa Romeos were staggeringly fast, probably the fastest of all sports-racing cars in 1953, but they were plagued by mechanical problems. After battling for the lead, Kling and Klenk retired because of final drive failure. At the end of 1953 Alfa Romeo withdrew from sports car racing. (Centro Documentazione Alfa Romeo)

"This would happen to me on my first entry with the new Alfa Romeo! We pushed our car hard over to the right and waited till the rest of the field was past. Despite my bad luck, Alfa Romeo were satisfied with my performance, and confirmed that we would be driving at Le Mans."

Juan-Manuel Fangio drives the Alfa Romeo 6CM 3,670cc coupé over the finishing line at Brescia to take second place behind a 4.1-litre Ferrari. The Argentinian World Champion was slowed, allegedly by a broken track-rod that meant only one wheel responded to the steering. The fault may have been exaggerated, but it was a very brave drive and Fangio knew just how much a good performance meant to the Portello Company. (Author's Collection)

Ferraris and the brutal-looking Alfa Romeo 3000 CMs which were making their race debut. Although the smaller classes were Fiat-dominated as ever, quite a number of Dyna Panhards and Renaults were running. There were two French Gordinis racing in the 2,000cc class, well-prepared works Porsche entries and a very strong team of Alfa Romeo 1900TI saloons. On the eve of the race Lancia withdrew from the touring category, claiming that the starting times were being fiddled. This was no revelation and most people reckoned that it had been going on for years!

The first car away, a Fiat Topolino, left at 9pm on the Saturday night and the last car away was Rolt with his C-type Jaguar at 6.38am on the Sunday morning. Sanesi set the pace from the start and averaged 108.27mph (174.20kph) to Ravenna, 20mph faster than Bracco had managed in the wet the previous year. Behind him were Farina, Kling, Bordoni (surprisingly fast with his Gordini), Fangio, Bracco, Paolo Marzotto, Bonetto and Hawthorn. Shortly after the start of the race French

driver Luc Descollanges crashed heavily with his C-type Jaguar; he was seriously injured and his co-driver, Pierre Ungon, who was not wearing a crash helmet, was killed.

Early retirements included Johnson (split fuel tank), Moss (rear axle), Taruffi (front brakes), Wisdom's DB2 (transmission) and Villoresi (rear axle). The Austin-Healeys of Lockett and Hadley retired because of clutch trouble, and the Nash-Healey driven by Fitch was also eliminated. At Pescara, after the fastest part of the course, Sanesi had averaged 109.24mph (175.77kph) and led by 4min 39sec from Farina and with the other Alfa Romeos of Kling and Fangio in third and fourth places. Rolt had been going steadily with his C-type, restricting engine speed in the lower gears to 5,500rpm and in top to 5,800rpm. Even so, a connecting rod broke, very rare on the so reliable XK engines.

Not long after he had passed through Pescara, Sanesi retired because of steering problems and Farina inherited the lead, but held it only briefly before crashing at L'Aquila, almost in sight of his refuelling point. At Rome Kling led from Fangio, Giannino Marzotto, Bracco and Bonetto with the first of the rather breathless Lancias. Peter Collins was up to seventh place, American Tom Cole driving his private Atlantic Stable 4.1-litre Ferrari with restraint was now ninth and Parnell tenth.

At Rome film star Ingrid Bergman emotionally embraced husband Roberto Rossellini for the benefit of the cameras. They were 'married' by proxy in Mexico on 24 May after her Mexican divorce came through. On the same day Bergman and Rossellini exchanged rings in an

empty church in Rome without witnesses. As a marriage that was not, it seems a complete waste of time. Rossellini and co-driver Aldo Tonti retired their 250MM Vignale Spider before they reached Siena. By Florence race-leader Kling was out and so was Bracco. So Fangio now led from brothers Marzotto, Giannino and Paolo.

Jenkinson's village in the latter stages of the race was "at the foot of the Futa Pass just before the run-in to Bologna." Of Giannino Marzotto, 'Jenks' wrote in the evocative manner that only he could manage, "While we were anticipating the 2-litre class there was a shattering roar, a screaming of tyres, a strong smell of hot oil and Giannino Marzotto went through using all the road, fighting the 4.1 in a series of juggles with steering and throttle, his passenger looking very worn and haggard.

"The time was six minutes past 3pm, which meant a total time of 9 hours 19 minutes and a higher speed than had ever been recorded before. Obviously the Ferrari-Alfa duel was forcing a terrific pace … If Fangio was to retain the lead, he had to come by at 3.21pm and at 3.24 the fierce-looking Alfa Romeo coupé with the yellow grille went by, closely followed by Paolo Marzotto, which meant that Giannino was now leading by three minutes, after nine and a half hours racing at an average of over 137kph [85mph].

Fangio wrote of his steering failure: "I began to imagine with pleasure winning this most classic of Italian races when my steering played tricks on me. There was too much play, which had the curious effect of making it impossible to steer with the left wheel. Only the right

wheel answered. Imagine taking the endless succession of Apennine curves, having to slow down to a ridiculous pace for each one! In that stretch, Giannino Marzotto passed me without trouble, showing that he was no amateur, but a front rank driver." What Marzotto thought of Fangio's steering problems is set out on page 234.

Of Marzotto's drive to victory, 'Jenks' wrote, "When Marzotto reached the Bologna control, Ferrari himself was awaiting him and told him to give the 4.1 its head on the very fast stretch to Cremona and thence to Brescia. This meant cruising at speeds which tend to make the mind boggle, for the road is wide, straight and smooth as far as the eye can see and with nearly 300bhp available it is quite likely that the estimated 270kph [168mph] was approached." Even 'Jenks' was influenced by Ferrari's power output claims and the true output of the Ferrari was around 230bhp.

Although Fangio continued to the finish over the last, fast roads at around 100mph (161kph), Marzotto won by a margin of 11min 41sec. The high level of retirements enabled Bonetto to finish third with the fastest of the Lancias. Tom Cole's steady drive with his Ferrari brought him fourth place, but sadly the American was killed in the same car when he crashed at White

Paul Frère's win in the Touring Class over 2,000cc

From 1950 to 1952 I was service and workshop manager of the Jaguar importers in Brussels. I quit the Jaguar job to become a full-time journalist and have more time for racing. As a Jaguar service manager in Brussels, I often had contact with Lofty England, who was Jaguar's service and motor sport manager. One person I had often met as a journalist was 'Johnny' Lurani, and some time at the end of 1952 he said to me: "One thing you should do is to find a car to compete in the Mille Miglia in the class for touring cars over 2 litres; I am sure you would win." My first choice was clearly a Jaguar Mark VII, so I asked Lofty if he would make a car available. His answer was "no".

Then I remembered that when I had won a two-hour race for absolutely standard cars at Spa in 1952 with a General Motors-entered Oldsmobile, the fastest cars had been the 5.3-litre Chrysler Saratogas. They had retired because both had broken their heavily stressed left front wheel. So I contacted Jo Beherman, the Chrysler importer, who immediately agreed to put a Saratoga at my disposal. The car that I was to drive had done 9,000 miles, so it was in its prime and preparation did not entail much work.

The head was removed for decarbonising and while it was off, the inlet ports were polished as much as possible. A washer was put under each valve spring so as to increase their strength slightly. We decided to take off the fan, which we put in the tool box so that it could be replaced if, during my practice run, the engine overheated in the mountain sections. One of the two silencers was removed. The springs were replaced by slightly harder ones, a catalogued modification, and the shock absorbers were modified. The brake linings were treated with Cop-Sil-Loy so as to increase their resistance to fading.

An extra fuel tank holding 46 gallons was installed in the boot and the car's equipment was completed by the indispensable screen washer, two Lucas 'flame-throwers' with their concentrated beams, and an extra-loud horn which soon refused to work. For the actual race, we also took with us many spare parts (of which not one was used), 12 sparking plugs, slightly harder than the ones normally used in the car and ten reinforced wheels with specially made Englebert tyres, which were only stowed in the car with the greatest of difficulty.

As an afterthought it was also decided to put a switch by the left foot, which would allow one to pass into third gear on the semi-automatic box at will without having to kick the accelerator pedal to the floor boards. We also placed a block on that pedal which would allow the driver to heel-and-toe when changing down to second gear while braking. I did not suspect at the time that this would be the most useful bit of equipment on the car. When the work was finished we took the car to the Jabbeke Autostrade where it was timed in pouring rain at 105.7mph [170.07kph] in one direction and 104.4mph [167.98kph] in the other.

I chose as my co-driver André Milhoux, who would be able to relieve me at the wheel should this become necessary and drive sufficiently fast without alarming me, and who would also be able to help with any repairs that we had to make during the race. Originally we were the only entry in the class, but two Jaguar Mark VIIs were late entries and provided some competition. During our reconnaissance lap of the circuit, the brake linings wore out with alarming rapidity. We had started out with new linings and, as a result, had brought along no spares.

There was some anxiety at the start as to whether the starting ramp built on scaffolding would stand up to the two-ton weight of the Saratoga, but it did and likewise we had

House during the Le Mans 24 Hours race in June.

Reg Parnell turned in a spectacular drive with the DB3 to finish fifth – it was to prove the best result by a British car in the history of the race. This was despite the crew realising that the DB3 had a broken Panhard rod mounting when it arrived at Florence and the throttle cable breaking as they crossed the Apennines. Parnell wired the throttle open and drove the car on the ignition switch. Of the other works Aston Martin drivers, Abecassis crashed near Florence because of a loose steering rack and Collins struggled to the finish and 17th place in a car that looked as if it had spent as much time off the road as on it.

Biondetti's Lancia broke down four miles from the flag and he and his mechanic started the long push to the finish. When the mechanic collapsed, Biondetti put him in the car and pushed him as well. He managed to take eighth place. Emilio Giletti partnered by Bertocchi finished sixth and won the 2,000 sports class, ahead of Sergio Mantovani with another A6GCS. Giletti was an inexperienced driver and while he no doubt benefited from having Bertocchi on board, he should have beaten

Opposite: Bruno Venezian drove an inspired race in 1953 with this 1,100cc OSCA. He finished 11th overall and won his class. Here he has the OSCA really wound up at Capelle, on the Futa Pass. Directly on the line that the Venezian was taking lay a large lump of rock that no one had bothered to remove. (Author's Collection)

no difficulty in getting the car through the narrow gates of Peschiera. By the time we reached Rome, we had averaged 75.5mph [121.5kph], but from that point onwards the brakes began to fade. There were grinding noises and a wheel began to lock under braking, but I was able to use the accelerator pedal-block to double declutch down into second gear, keeping my foot on the brake and accelerator pedals simultaneously, thereby getting extra braking from the engine.

Because of the braking problem, our speed had dropped to 69.5mph [111.8kph] by the time that we had reached Florence. Descending the Futa and Raticosa Passes, I tried not to use the brakes, so I was entering corners too fast, the car would go into a broadside and this would bring the speed down sufficiently to get round the rest of the corner. Despite this, examination of the tyres after

Paul Frère and André Milhoux drove this Chrysler Saratoga in the 1953 race and, despite brake fade, scored a very easy win in the over 2,000cc International Touring category. At the start there were concerns that the ramp would collapse under the two-ton weight of the American car, but fortunately there were no problems. It seems that no one was allowed to start from the road any more. (Author's Collection)

the finish revealed that we could have completed the race on one set if necessary. Our time for the course was 13hr 38min 03sec, an average of 68.92mph [110.90kph]. The only Jaguar to finish, driven by technical and motor book publisher Mondadori partnered by Fedrigoni, was nearly 2½ hours behind us.

Felice Bonetto ran out of fuel shortly before the finish of the 1953 race, so he and his mechanic, Peruzzi, pushed the Lancia D20 coupé until Peruzzi collapsed from exhaustion. Then Bonetto pushed both car and mechanic! His efforts were rewarded with third place overall. This photograph shows to good advantage the superb lines of the D20 coupé. (Spitzley-Zagari Collection)

Parnell. The Maserati was more powerful than the DB3, despite giving away a litre in engine capacity, it was lighter and it was still in fine fettle at the finish.

Luigi Musso crashed his Maserati and third place in the class went to Gasella/Puccini with a 2-litre Gordini. Bordoni had retired his very fast Gordini. Alfa Romeo 1900TIs took first three places in the 2,000cc Touring class, but they all looked badly battered. Paul Frère won the over 2,000cc class with his Chrysler Saratoga and his account of the race begins on page 194. Porsche entries dominated the 1,300cc and 1,500cc GT classes with first four places in both.

In his report of the race for *The Autocar*, Sports Editor John Cooper concluded; "But maybe the strangest, and in a way the most pathetic scene of all was the railway station at Brescia on Sunday evening, when dirty, despondent and bedraggled drivers, each clutching a crash helmet and various items of personal impedimenta, some with telltale bandages or strips of sticking plaster, came tumbling out of trains from every part of Italy – all part of the long trek home after trouble or accident somewhere along the way".

Results:

General Classification:

1st	G. Marzotto/Crosara (Ferrari),	10hr 37min 19sec (88.47mph/142.35kph)
2nd	Fangio/Sala (Alfa Romeo),	10hr 49min 3sec
3rd	Bonetto/Peruzzi (Lancia),	11hr 7min 40sec
4th	Cole/Vandelli (Ferrari),	11hr 20min 39sec
5th	Parnell/Klemantaski (Aston Martin),	11hr 32min 43sec
6th	Giletti/Bertocchi (Maserati),	11hr 38min 42sec
7th	Maggio/Anselmi (Lancia),	11hr 41min 7sec
8th	Biondetti/Barovero (Lancia),	11hr 49min 49sec
9th	Cabianca/Roghi (Ferrari),	11hr 51min 39sec
10th	Mantovani/Palazzi (Maserati),	11hr 51min 56sec

Class results, International Touring Category:

600cc: Brighetti/Sandrolini (Fiat), 16hr 32min 51sec (56.78mph/91.34kph)
750cc: Agelelli/Recchi (Renault), 15hr 46min 12sec (59.59mph/95.88kph)
1,100/1,300cc: Mancini/Mancini (Fiat), 14hr 5min 16sec (66.70mph/107.33kph)
1,500cc: Massi/Bendetti/Boano (Fiat), 14hr 37min 45sec (64.24mph/103.36kph)
2,000cc: Pagliai/Parducci (Alfa Romeo), 12hr 34min 5sec (74.77mph/120.31kph)
Over 2,000cc: Frère/Milhoux (Chrysler), 13hr 38min 3sec (68.92mph/110.90kph)

Class results, International Sports Category:

750cc: Touzot/Persillon (Dyna Panhard), 14hr 15min 36sec (65.90mph/106.03kph)

Class results, Sports Series Category:

750cc: Rédelé/Pons (Renault), 15hr 14min 51sec (61.63mph/99.16kph)
1,100cc: Venezian/Albarelli (OSCA), 12hr 4min 50sec (77.79mph/125.16kph)
1,300cc: Hösch/Engel (Porsche), 13hr 27min 23sec (71.31mph/114.73kph)
1,500cc: Herrmann/Bauer (Porsche), 12hr 47min 33sec (73.45mph/118.18kph)
2,000cc: Giletti/Bertocchi (Maserati), 11hr 38min 42sec (80.70mph/129.84kph)
Over 3,000cc: G. Marzotto/Crosara (Ferrari), 10hr 37min 19sec (88.47mph/142.35kph)

1954

1–2 May
Starters: 374; Finishers: 275; Distance: 998 miles (1,606 km).
Circuit: see page 247.
Weather: misty at the start, rain, wet roads for most of the race.

Main contenders for victory:
500	Luigi Musso/Zocca (Maserati A6GCS, 1,986cc)
506	Bruno Venezian/Orlandi (Maserati A6GCS, 1,986cc)
523	Vittorio Marzotto (Ferrari Tipo 500 Mondial, Scaglietti spider, 1,980cc)
536	Paolo Marzotto/Marino Marini (Ferrari 375MM, Pinin Farina spider, 4,522cc)
537	Sergio Mantovani/Palazzo (Maserati A6GCS with 250F engine, 2,493cc)
538	Giannino Marzotto/Gioia Tortina (Ferrari 375 Plus, Pinin Farina spider, 4,954cc)
539	Reg Parnell/Louis Klemantaski (Aston Martin DB3S, 2,922cc)
545	Umberto Maglioli (Ferrari 375 Plus, Pinin Farina spider, 4,954cc)
547	Piero Taruffi (Lancia D24, 3,284cc)
548	Franco Bordoni (Gordini, 2,982cc)
601	Clemente Biondetti (Ferrari 250MM, Morelli spider, 2,953cc)
602	Alberto Ascari (Lancia D24, 3,284cc)
605	Piero Valenzano (Lancia D24, 3,284cc)
606	Giuseppe Farina/Luigi Parenti (Ferrari 375 Plus, Pinin Farina spider, 4,954cc)
609	Peter Collins/Pat Griffith (Aston Martin DB3S, 2,922cc)

Other British entries:
411	Olivier Gendebien/C. Fraikin (Jaguar XK 120 Fixed Head Coupé, 3,442cc)
454	Sture Nortopp/Bratt (Frazer Nash Le Mans Fixed Head Coupé, 1,971cc)
507	Leslie Brooke/Jack Fairman (Triumph TR2, 1,991cc)
526	J. Stoddart/White (Triumph TR2, 1,991cc)
528	Maurice Gatsonides/Ken Richardson (Triumph TR2, 1,991cc)
550	Lance Macklin (Austin-Healey 100, 2,660cc)
551	Tom Wisdom/Mortimer Morris Goodall (Austin-Healey 100, 2,660cc)
557	Louis Chiron (Austin-Healey 100, 2,660cc)
612	Tom Meyer/O'Hara Moore (Aston Martin DB3 coupé, 2,922cc)
613	George Abecassis/Denis Jenkinson (HWM-Jaguar, 3,442cc)

A number of changes were made to the race for 1954. Following the death of the great Tazio Nuvolari on 10 August 1953, as a tribute to him the circuit was changed to incorporate his home town of Mantua in the last, fast run to Brescia. An additional award was the Gran Premio Nuvolari for the driver who set the fastest time from Cremona via Mantua to Brescia.

Somewhat controversial was the introduction of a rule that permitted drivers to run solo. This happened at the request of the Lancia team and upset a number of competitors, including Aston Martin and was made only about three weeks before the race. There is little doubt that some drivers liked to have on board a well-informed colleague with a decent set of 'pace notes' (in particular Kling/Klenk in 1952 and Moss/Jenkinson in 1955). Many other drivers preferred to be on their own, without

having to worry about their passenger's safety or the accuracy of the directions that he gave.

Although the number of entrants had fallen, this made the race much more manageable from the organisers' point of view. With no works Jaguars and no Alfa Romeos, the battle for outright victory was between Ferrari and Lancia, but with the slim possibility of a win by Aston Martin, Gordini or Maserati. Certainly, the Ferrari team was not at its strongest because of the loss of Ascari and Villoresi and Mike Hawthorn was unfit to drive after crashing his Formula 1 car at Siracusa and suffering burns.

Quite why Maurice Trintignant (who had joined the team after the Argentinian races) was not given a drive is far from clear. The latest 4.9-litre Ferraris were unwieldy,

Umberto Maglioli is seen at Brescia before the start of the 1954 race with his monstrous Tipo 375 Plus 4.9-litre Ferrari. Maglioli never made his mark in Formula 1, but he was an outstandingly fast and safe sports car driver. The 375 Plus cars proved an impossible handful in the Mille Miglia and Maglioli retired because of transmission problems. Not long afterwards, on the more favourable roads of the Sarthe circuit, Froilan Gonzalez/Maurice Trintignant won the Le Mans 24 Hours race with one of these cars. (Author's Collection)

ill-handling brutes and unsuitable for road racing. In contrast the Lancia D24 Spider was the epitome of the ideal road-racer: it possessed excellent handling with an engine that was not too powerful for the chassis, it was superbly balanced with exceptional traction and had a superb, precise and positive gearbox with well-spaced ratios.

Ascari's contract with Lancia excluded the Mille Miglia, but he agreed to drive after Villoresi was injured in an accident during practice. Among the red cars was an interloper, the 3-litre Gordini of Franco Bordoni, who had a penchant for buying and racing these potent, but rather fragile French cars. Bordoni was a good, above average driver, and in World War Two days he had been a notable pilot with the Reggia Aeronautica, flying Fiat CR42 biplane fighters.

The latest Aston Martin DB3S cars were much more competitive than the previous year's DB3s, but the cars were running on a very hard compound tyre and the handling of these cars was near-impossible in the wet. The HWM-Jaguar was not too serious an entry; it was rather more the case that Abecassis liked the race and wanted to drive in it a car of his team's own construction.

In the 1,500cc class young Hans Herrmann partnered by Linge drove the new and very potent Porsche 550 Spyder with four-cam 1,489cc engine. The company was also out in force in the GT classes. There was still a strong entry of Lancia Aurelias in the GT category and Piero Carini was to turn in a remarkably fast drive with an Alfa Romeo 1900TI. After all these years, 'Frate Ignoto' was still regularly competing in 1954 with a Lancia B20 GT car.

In 1954 the first car left at precisely 11pm on the Saturday evening and the first seven away were Isetta bubble-cars. The last car away was Abecassis's HWM at 6.13am. This car illustrated that being last away is not necessarily an advantage, for the HWM's speed was reduced by a suspension problem and having averaged 87mph (140kph) to shortly before Ravenna, the car was dropping well back behind others in its class and was caught by the resumption of normal traffic on the roads (see pages 202–203).

Alberto Ascari looks cheerful and optimistic as he chats to his supporters while waiting with his winning D24 at the check-in before the start at Brescia. For this race, to ensure greater reliability, Lancia built a team of new cars with slightly detuned engines. (Author's Collection)

Early race leader in 1954 was veteran Piero Taruffi, at the wheel of another Lancia D24. He is seen at Ravenna, waiting anxiously for the mechanics to finish work on his car. He retired at Vetralla while trying to avoid a much slower car that crossed his line through a corner. (Author's Collection)

The Ferraris were very disappointing in 1954 and the most successful driver for Maranello was Vittorio Marzotto who brought this 2-litre Mondial across the line in second place. It is believed to be the prototype car that Ascari/Villoresi drove to second place in the 1953 Casablanca 12 Hours race, and was the first competition Ferrari to be fitted with Scaglietti bodywork. (Author's Collection)

Mantovani retired his Maserati very shortly after the start because of transmission problems. Another early retirement was Farina who crashed his Ferrari heavily into a telegraph pole near Peschiera; he broke an arm, but mechanic Parenti's injuries were more extensive and a number of spectators were also hurt. Early in the race, at Tortoreto, Giovanni Brinci in a Vignale berlinetta-bodied Tipo 225S Ferrari was killed when he collided with the barrier of a closed level crossing.

Lancia soon had a grip on leadership of the race. Taruffi led from Ascari and Castellotti and by Pescara he had averaged 110.6mph (178.0kph), breaking the record set by Sanesi in 1953. Then came Maglioli with his Ferrari 375 Plus, Valenzano with the fourth of the D24 team cars, followed by Paolo and Giannino Marzotto

and Peter Collins (Aston Martin). Already there was a tough, slogging battle in the 2-litre class between Vittorio Marzotto with the Ferrari Mondial and Luigi Musso with his Maserati A6GCS.

Retirements reduced the number of cars battling for the lead. Valenzano crashed his Lancia very heavily and

In 1954 Luigi Musso was a promising, but far from consistent, driver. Partnered by Zocca (about to get back in the car at the Ravenna control), Musso drove a well-judged but somewhat emotional race to finish third overall and second in the 2,000cc class, behind Vittorio Marzotto. (Author's Collection)

Porsche drivers, photographed after the 1954 Mille Miglia are (from left) Heinrich Sauter, Hans Herrmann, Herbert Linge and Richard von Frankenberg (proving that Marzotto was not the only driver to wear a suit in the Mille Miglia and looking very much an unimaginative 'büroangestellter' or office pen-pusher). A bored-looking Ferry Porsche stands on the extreme right of the photograph. Von Frankenberg and Sauter drove their bashed and dented 356 Porsche to a win the 1,600cc GT class, ahead of two other 356s. (Porsche-Werkfoto)

was lucky to escape with a broken collar-bone. Between Pescara and Rome Bordoni retired the impressive Gordini with mechanical problems and Castellotti's Lancia disappeared out of the race because of gearbox trouble. Giannino Marzotto's Ferrari started to lose its bodywork and Parnell went off the road with his DB3S.

By Rome Taruffi still had a lead of 4½ minutes, but he was worried by fluctuating oil pressure; the mechanics diagnosed a broken oil pipe and spent some 40 minutes working on the Lancia. So Ascari moved up into the lead, with Maglioli in third place, Paolo Marzotto fourth and Peter Collins fifth. Not long after leaving Rome, Taruffi crashed at Vetrallo after a slower car crossed his line. The weather was now atrociously wet and the roads were slippery and treacherous.

Ascari's engine developed a misfire, but he was able to keep going steadily. Between Florence and Bologna the Ferrari of Paolo Marzotto retired because of gearbox failure, while Maglioli crashed his 375 Plus. Unchallenged, but frantically worried about his car, Ascari scored a fine victory and Ferrari's first defeat since 1948. He was also the winner of the Gran Premio Nuvolari at a speed slightly over 112mph (180kph). Vittorio Marzotto and Luigi Musso battled fiercely to the end and although Marzotto in second place was over half an hour behind Ascari, he was a mere nine seconds ahead of Musso.

Clemente Biondetti, now a seriously ill man, took a very meritorious fourth place. Carini's drive with his 1900 Alfa Romeo was one of the highlights of the race and his average speed of 77.15mph (124.14kph) would have been fast enough to win the race outright in 1950 or 1951. Porsche defeated OSCA in the 1,500cc Sports class, despite a close shave when Herrmann and Linge squeezed under the barrier of a closed level crossing by crouching down in the cockpit and just cleared the track before a train reached them.

Only six miles from the finish Mancini crashed his Maserati, killing his co-driver and a spectator. It was not the only fatal accident for Pouschol was killed when he crashed his Citroën near Vicenza; both his co-driver and spectators were injured. The sole Austin-Healey to finish was that of Macklin who lost the use of his clutch (repaired at the Healey depot at Pesaro) and he took fifth place in the Unlimited Sports class. Two of the TR2s finished, Gatsonides/Richardson 27th and Brooke/Fairman 94th. Overall it had been a very satisfactory race, but concerns about the safety aspects were growing.

Opposite: The 1954 race was run in wet weather for much of the distance and on roads that were in very poor condition after a hard winter. This is the 1,500cc class-winning Porsche 550 Spyder of Herrmann/Linge. It was a brilliant effort by a relatively inexperienced driver. Hans Herrmann tells the story of this race on page 288. (Porsche-Werkfoto)

In the 2-litre touring car class the Alfa Romeo 1900s were almost unbeatable, and variants of the model won their class in the Mille Miglia each year between 1952 and 1955. This is Piero Carini who, partnered by Artesani, won the over 1,300cc Special Touring category in 1954. (Centro Documentazione Alfa Romeo)

Results:

Overall Classification:

1st	Ascari (Lancia), 11hr 26min 10sec (86.79mph/139.65kph)	
2nd	V. Marzotto (Ferrari), 12hr 0min 1sec	
3rd	Musso/Zocca (Maserati), 12hr 0min 10sec	
4th	Biondetti (Ferrari), 12hr 15min 36sec	
5th	Venezian/Orlandi (Maserati), 12hr 27min 43sec	
6th	Herrmann/Linge (Porsche), 12hr 35min 44sec	
7th	Serafini/Mancini (Lancia), 12hr 47min 12sec	
8th	Carini/Artesani (Alfa Romeo), 12hr 51min 52sec	
9th	C. Leto di Priolo/D. Leto di Priolo (Fiat), 12hr 52min 38sec	
10th	Cabianca (OSCA), 12hr 55min 8sec	

Class Results, Special Touring Group Series:

750cc: Rédelé/Pons (Renault), 15hr 4min 33sec (65.84mph/105.93kph)
1,300cc: Maldrini/Ferrari (Fiat), 14hr 30min 46sec (68.39mph/110.04kph)
Over 1,300cc: Carini/Artesani (Alfa Romeo), 12hr 51min 52sec
(77.15mph/124.14kph)

Class Results, Grand Touring Group:

1,300cc: Hampel/Berghe (Porsche), 14hr 11min 23sec (69.95mph/112.55kph)
1,600cc: von Frankenberg/Sauter (Porsche), 13hr 53min 50sec
(71.42mph/114.91kph)
Over 1,600cc: Serafini/Mancini (Lancia), 12hr 47min 12sec (77.68mph/124.99kph)

Class Results, International Sports Category:

750cc: Faure/Storez (Panhard), 15hr 3min 16sec (65.93mph/106.08kph)
1,500cc: Herrmann/Linge (Porsche), 12hr 35min 44sec (78.80mph/126.79kph)
2,000cc: V. Marzotto (Ferrari), 12hr 0min 1sec (82.71mph/133.08kph)
Over 2,000cc: Ascari (Lancia), 11hr 26min 10sec (86.79mph/139.65kph)

No. 613 – Mille Miglia by Denis Jenkinson

(Adapted from the June 1954 issue of Motor Sport)

As the Mille Miglia is a difficult race at which to spectate and a dull one from the press grandstand, I decided that it would be more interesting to take part in the event. Also it would provide the opportunity of satisfying a schoolboy ambition, to ride as a racing mechanic in the most fantastic of all races; a desire that was born in the early days of the Ulster TT and from photographs of Mille Miglia Alfa Romeos studied avidly under cover of a history book – the real reason for utter failure in all examinations. Another desire was to sample the 150mph [240kph] speeds that are spoken of lightly by people 'in the know' these days.

Not so long ago it was 100mph [160kph], but now you can do that with all the family on board and a sports car must do 150mph [240kph]. So I was prepared to try it, not just up the by-pass, but in the Mille Miglia. By a series of coincidences and misunderstandings I finally settled to ride with George Abecassis in the HWM-Jaguar, a motor car in the true sporting tradition, no frills, no sleek coupé top, but a blood-and-thunder sports car of this present age.

[At the front there was] independent front suspension with transverse leaf spring and wishbones, tubular chassis frame, at the rear de Dion rear suspension on torsion bars, brakes from the Formula 2 cars and an all-enveloping body topped by a curved Perspex windshield. The cockpit was spacious and the closely fitting bucket seats allowed one to see just over the windscreen, but not in the airstream.

When the HWM équipe met in Brescia, a few details were added, such as drinking bottles with long rubber pipes, a bracket made to keep a tin of sweets and some oranges in place, a block of wood on the floor for me to brace my feet against, a little 'bungee' rubber padding, a second handhold on the tail of the car, and we were then ready for a trial run on the Autostrada. The only indicator for speed was the large rev counter and the position of the gear-lever, for 4,500rpm in top meant 120mph [193kph], as the car was geared for 26.9mph [43.3kph] per 1,000 revs in top gear.

As I had never travelled at more than a genuine 110mph [177kph] on the road before, I viewed '4,500' with interest; but I could not help taking a rather blasé view of the speed. Then the needle went up to 5,000 and on up to 5,400rpm – that was different. I was very conscious about being in a realm about which I had no experience and the feeling was very odd to say the least, and I began to play very close attention to all about me. Then some traffic appeared and we were back to a cruising 100mph [160kph]. Yes, I was quite certain that I was going to enjoy the Mille Miglia.

Dawn had broken and a dull grey sky was overhead as the over 2-litre sports class lined up on the main road out of Brescia, and above the general clamour I could occasionally hear the rasp of a racing engine as a Ferrari or Lancia roared away towards Verona; when we had left, at 6.13am, the organisers could go and have breakfast and the crowds go to sleep. In front of us was Tom Meyer's light green Aston Martin coupé, and as he mounted the starting ramp and was given the signal to start I set my watch at 6.12 and then we drove, surrounded by a vast sea of cheering faces and waving hands.

An official gave me our control card that had to be stamped eight times during the next 1,000 miles. It was 6.13 and we were away, gently down the ramp and then accelerating away through the gears. In front of us was a solid block of people, but Abecassis had done many Mille Miglias and he just drove straight at them with the speed rising to 80 and 90mph [128–145kph]. When they were petrifyingly close, the crowd swayed back to let us pass, and for the next 20 or 30 miles it seemed that we must sweep them down by the hundred, but they always moved aside in time.

The greatest difficulty was that it was quite impossible to see any of the corners or bends because the crowds covered everything, and I thought how infuriating it must be to learn the course on a normal day and then try to remember it under these conditions. Everyone had the same trouble, for the number of marks on the road from panic braking was unbelievable, and every corner showed signs of one of the 373 cars in front of us having had a dodgy moment, with black marks up on to pavements, signs of locking wheels and so on.

Once clear of Brescia, the road straightened up and '5,000', and more, was showing on the rev counter, as commonly as the average car shows 50mph [80kph] on its speedometer. It was not long before we saw a speck in the distance that was number 612 and we went past at nearly 130mph [210kph]. By now the crowds were thinning out, though the villages and towns were still packed. In Peschiera the crowd was nearly delirious and their attempts to slow us down were fascinating, one man even running straight at us with a chair.

Round the next corner we saw the reason for all this pandemonium. Number 606 was well and truly wrapped round a tree and a quick look at the list stuck on our dashboard showed it to be Farina. I exchanged a wry look with Abecassis just before he opened out and we got into our 130mph [210kph] stride. Out of Verona the road ran dead straight, but was lined with people, most of whom seemed to have bicycles or umbrellas, and at 140mph [225kph] we drove through this sea of 'ants' with only a three-foot space on each side of the car.

On 120mph [190kph] bends in the open country there would still be a crowd of people standing right on the apex, exactly at the point where a car would leave the road; presumably, they were all quite oblivious of the danger. Once away from Verona '5,200' came up and after a while I had the feeling of being satisfied with having done 142mph [228kph] on the open road and was quite prepared for Abecassis to ease back to a sedate 100mph [160kph], but as far as the eye could see the road ran straight and was completely clear, there was no reason to ease off and for mile after mile we cruised at 142mph [228kph].

Eventually, a blind brow necessitated the throttle being eased back and the speed dropped to around 120mph [193kph], but only for a fleeting moment and we were back to our maximum again with nothing but straight flat road in front of us. In Vicenza the road was very bad and on one corner we hit a bump, which threw us almost on to the pavement and the crowd stepped smartly backwards as one man. Out of the town we accelerated up to three figures and soon realised that something was wrong for the car was wandering about at over 120mph [193kph].

Clearly the big bump in Vicenza had broken something, probably a shock absorber or part of the rear suspension, for on corners the car was behaving most peculiarly. After a time we became used to the snaking

This is the HWM-Jaguar in which Denis Jenkinson rode with George Abecassis. It used one of the very simple HWM Formula 2 twin-tube chassis, had a steel body built specially for this race (Abecassis thought that the usual aluminium-alloy body would be too flimsy), a Jaguar engine to C-type tune and a Jaguar gearbox. An empty road emphasises that, because of mechanical problems, Abecassis had already ceased to be a serious contender. (Spitzley-Zagari Collection)

Abecassis had been racing since pre-war days and was a partner in the HWM business based at Walton-on-Thames. He ran the garage side while his partner, John Heath, raced round Europe with the HWM Formula 2 team. Abecassis had been a works Aston Martin driver until the HWM-Jaguar sports car was ready to race in 1953 and he later married Angela Brown, daughter of Sir David Brown, patron of Aston Martin. This photograph was taken in 1952, during testing with an Aston Martin DB3. (Guy Griffiths)

above 120mph [193kph] and as there was no one immediately in front of us we had all the road to play with. We had caught 612, 611 did not start, and 610 we had seen by the roadside a long way back. Number 609 was Peter Collins with the works Aston Martin and, now that we could not corner very fast, obviously we could not catch him.

After Padua a thick mist developed, which reduced visibility to less than 100 yards and limited speed to a bare 100mph [161kph] or less in places, for the HWM now had a very small safety margin and panic-braking was now

quite out of the question. This poor visibility continued for more than 15 miles [24km] and when it finally cleared the roads were in very greasy condition. We had dropped more than ten minutes behind our self-imposed schedule and being unable to motor on full throttle, the engine started to fuss and stopped working on one cylinder.

This was getting depressing and, just after Rovigo, the recent floods had completely washed away about two miles of road and a loose cart track had been built to replace it. The surface of this limited us to second gear and we took the opportunity to discuss the situation. We decided to carry on to the first control at Ravenna, about 30 minutes further on. As we had dropped speed considerably, Meyer in his Aston Martin repassed us and we followed him down to Ferrara. It was now raining spasmodically and the roads were like sheets of ice at more than 100mph [161kph]. In addition Abecassis had to cope with a car that was unstable at high speeds.

As we approached a fairly sharp right-hand bend, we both suddenly became aware that the Aston Martin in front was not going to get round it and, sure enough, the front wheels broke away and the car slid straight on. The next few seconds were very full for Tom Meyer, while all we could do was to slow down and watch. The car ran along the left bank, bouncing so high that the sump was in full view, missed all the spectators and trees, skidded back on to the road, spun gracefully round in front of us, struck a tree with its tail and fell on its side in the ditch at very low speed. As we passed, the door opened, the passenger O'Hara climbed out and helped the driver out.

Eventually, we arrived at the control at Ravenna, had our card stamped and pulled over to our pre-arranged pit. The misfire proved to be something obscure in one of the Weber carburettors, while the damage at the rear was that the complete end of one of the telescopic shock-absorbers had broken off and was quite irreparable. As we were now 20 minutes behind schedule, with no hope of making up any time, only losing more, it was decided to retire, very reluctantly, for the Mille Miglia happens only once a year and there really is nothing to equal it.

A further trouble had become obvious in the last 20 miles [32km] into Ravenna and that was that the public were considering the race finished and were quite justifiably driving off home along the road on which we had been trying to race. We were the last starter and they had allowed us a certain measure of time and then considered the event finished. We had got behind this time allowance and it was going to be impossible to regain it.

We had covered 200 miles [322km] and the race for us had hardly started. There was another 800 miles [1,290km] to cover, so we removed our crash-hats and went and had coffee. For the 200 miles [322km] from Brescia to Ravenna we had averaged 87mph [140kph] and that was too slow to justify continuing – a solemn thought indeed.

1955

1–2 May
Starters: 521; Finishers: 281; Distance: 998 miles (1,606km).
Circuit: see page 247.
Weather: fine throughout.

Main contenders for victory:

417 John Fitch/Kurt Gesell (Mercedes-Benz 300 SL, 2,996cc)
658 Juan Fangio (Mercedes-Benz 300 SLR, 2,979cc)
701 Karl Kling (Mercedes-Benz 300 SLR, 2,979cc)
702 Peter Collins (Aston Martin DB3S, 2,922cc)
704 Hans Herrmann/Hermann Eger (Mercedes-Benz 300 SLR, 2,979cc)
705 Umberto Maglioli/Luciano Monteferraio (Ferrari Tipo 118LM, 3,747cc, Scaglietti spider
718 Piero Scotti (Ferrari Tipo 375MM, 4,523cc, Pinin Farina spider)
722 Stirling Moss/Denis Jenkinson (Mercedes-Benz 300 SLR, 2,979cc)
723 Eugenio Castellotti (Ferrari Tipo 121LM, 4,412cc, Scaglietti spider)
724 Sergio Sighinolfi (Ferrari Tipo 750 Monza, 2,999cc, Scaglietti spider)
725 Paolo Marzotto (Ferrari Tipo 121LM, 4,412cc, Scaglietti spider)
726 Franco Bordoni (Gordini, 2,982cc)
727 Cesare Perdisa (Maserati 300S, 2,992cc)
728 Piero Taruffi (Ferrari Tipo 118LM, 3,747cc, Scaglietti spider)

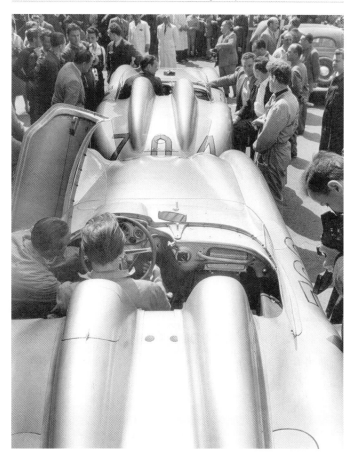

British entries (primarily those with British drivers):

347 P. Barsotti (Rover 75, 2,230cc)
418 Paul Frère/Louis Klemantaski (Aston Martin DB2-4, 2,922cc)
434 John Heath (Jaguar XK 140 fixed-head coupé, 3,442cc)
436 Tom Wisdom/Peter Bolton (Aston Martin DB2-4, 2,922cc)
441 Hermanos da Silva Ramos/J. Vidilles (Aston Martin DB2-4, 2,922cc)
609 Peter Scott Russell/Tom Haig (Triumph TR2, 1,991cc)
610 Dickie Steed/A. Bruce (Triumph TR2, 1,991cc)
611 Leslie Brooke/D. Lampe (Triumph TR2, 1,991cc)
700 George Abecassis (Austin-Healey 100S, 2,660cc)
708 Lance Macklin (Austin-Healey 100S, 2,660cc)
709 Ron Flockhart (Austin-Healey 100S, 2,660cc)
712 Donald Healey/Cashmore (Austin-Healey 100S, 2,660cc)

Because there was such a large entry, the organisers increased the number of classes and there were a total of 27, including sub-classes. Some of these were aimed at specific cars, such as the 250cc sub-class meant for Isettas. The entry included the usual vast number of Fiats, 500s in standard and a vast range of modified forms, together with many Alfa Romeos, Lancias and Porsche 356s. Renault entered a works team of 750 saloons. There were 18 Ferraris, 19 Maseratis and ten OSCAs entered. The works Ferraris consisted of four of the latest six-cylinder models, plus a 3-litre Monza driven by works tester Sighinolfi.

A significant Mercedes-Benz works entry was the 300 SL of American driver John Fitch, partnered by German journalist Kurt Gesell. This was an early

Two of the 300 SLRs in their garage at Brescia (below) before the 1955 race (left). These cars were 3-litre sports versions of the Mercedes-Benz W196 Grand Prix cars and were outstandingly quick, but also very reliable. (DaimlerChrysler)

production Gullwing built in late 1954 and to a very standard specification. Mercedes-Benz were never able to race the 'Lightweight' 300 SLs with aluminium-alloy bodies, as insufficient were built for homologation in the GT category. Other 300 SLs in this year's race were driven by Olivier Gendebien and Casella. Casella was strictly an amateur entry and he was to turn in a remarkable performance.

The Mercedes-Benz team had practised assiduously with the 300 SLRs over the course and came to the race with the best chance of success. Apart from speed and the drivers' knowledge of the course, the cars were very tough, as shown by the way in which they survived minor accidents. Lack of reliability was the shortcoming of the latest Ferraris and they also had tyre problems. In *Red Arrows* (Giannino Marzotto's definitive book on Ferraris in the Mille Miglia), Paolo Marzotto commented in relation to Englebert tyres and the 1955 race:

"The team used Englebert tyres, but we drivers did not want to know. Piero Taruffi, in particular, was very worried because they would not stand up to the stress caused by the bigger-capacity engine [sic]. All of us protested a little, Maglioli, Castellotti and I, but in the end, as I was closer to him, I said, 'Listen, Ferrari, change those tyres for us. It is

too dangerous. At the last moment, Ferrari approved and we fitted Pirelli. A decision at the last moment that did not resolve the problem. The Pirellis, evidently, were not suitable either and both Castellotti and I had to retire because of the tyres."

The cars started from 9pm onwards on the Saturday. The first starters were cars running in the newly inaugurated diesel class, ten cars in all, and then, as usual, there were vast numbers of Fiats and Fiat derivatives. The weather was to prove gloriously warm, more like summer than springtime and, in the words of one commentator, "golden sunshine." Soon after the fastest cars had left Brescia on the Sunday morning, it became clear that average speeds would be significantly higher than previously.

What Moss said of Castellotti's driving in this race (*My Cars, My Career*) is of considerable interest. In Padua Moss had hit a straw bale with the left front wing. "During our 'moment' Castellotti had roared by and grinned over his shoulder, which I didn't appreciate. He was over-driving that Ferrari terribly. I quickly realised that there was little point in racing him – he could not last long. He was slithering into kerbs and over gravelly verges, burning shards of rubber off his tyres and

Stirling Moss and Denis Jenkinson with their 300 SLR before the start of the 1955 Mille Miglia. 'Jenks', it will be noted, is wearing an old-fashioned 'pudding basin' helmet. (DaimlerChrysler)

On the starting ramp at Brescia is the Mercedes-Benz 300 SLR of Moss/Jenkinson. The corpulent figure wearing a trilby and standing behind the car is Mercedes-Benz race director Alfred Neubauer. (DaimlerChrysler)

Moss/Jenkinson are seen in the early stages of the race. In perfect weather conditions Moss set a record average of 97.90mph (157.65kph) that was not bettered during the remaining two years in which the race was held. (Author's Collection)

smashing his car through the gears so roughly we could see it twitching and bucking on every change."

After only 100 miles (161km), Paolo Marzotto was out of the race with his very potent Ferrari because a rear tyre threw a tread and the spare wheel fitted only at the front. By the first control at Ravenna, 188 miles (302km) from the start, Castellotti had averaged 119mph (191kmh) and led by over half-a-minute from Moss, followed by Taruffi, Herrmann, Kling, Maglioli, Perdisa and Fangio, whose engine some observers thought to be decidedly off-tune. At this stage, it was still any of the leaders that could win – save Castellotti and there is little doubt that he was calculatedly acting as the 'hare' in the knowledge that neither his car nor his tyres would hold up.

On the very fast section down the Adriatic coastline Moss moved ahead with his 300 SLR and by Ancona he led by over half a minute from Taruffi and Herrmann (the latter displaying an unexpectedly high turn of speed), while Castellotti had dropped back to fourth place. Next up were Kling, Maglioli, Fangio and Perdisa. In tenth place, turning in an outstanding performance, was Giardini with his 2-litre A6GCS Maserati. Both Frère and Wisdom retired their DB2-4 Aston Martins because of clutch trouble and Collins with the DB3S retired with a blown engine because of furious driving after he had been delayed by a puncture.

Near Rimini, Ron Flockhart with his Austin-Healey 100S passed team-mate Lance Macklin, but was rattled by the sight of a Lancia that had plunged into a thick crowd of spectators, lost control, misjudged the entry to a bridge and ploughed through the parapet into the river below. Macklin stopped to help and once he knew that Flockhart was shaken, but otherwise unhurt, carried on his way. It was not long before the throttle broke on Macklin's car, but he bodged it so that he could drive on the ignition switch and carried on.

By the time the fastest cars reached Pescara, Taruffi was again in the lead, but by a margin of only 15 seconds, and behind him the order was Moss, Herrmann, Kling, Fangio, Maglioli and Perdisa. Castellotti was out because of engine failure and a Mercedes-Benz victory was inevitable unless Taruffi's Ferrari held together, which seemed unlikely. At Pescara the 300 SLRs took on board 18 gallons (82 litres), just enough to reach Rome where they would be filled to the brim. In the GT class Fitch led from Gendebien and Casella and this looked like being another Mercedes-Benz clean sweep.

Isettas in the Mille Miglia

Back in 1954 seven entrants drove original Italian-built Iso Isettas with 236cc two-stroke engine in the Turismo Serie Speciale Class up to 750cc. At least one driver was well aware that the Isetta's engine could not conceivably last the race distance and so he had arranged for clandestine engine changes along the route. The leading Isetta of Cipolla/Brioschi finished 175th overall, eighth in class and took 22hr 4min 52sec to complete the circuit. Although there is no significance – or interest – attached to it, there was an Index of Performance in the Mille Miglia and in 1954 it was won by the leading Isetta.

In late 1954 BMW started manufacturing these 'bubble cars' under licence in Germany with 247cc and 297cc single-cylinder four-stroke engines. Iso themselves ceased manufacture of Isettas in Italy. It is not entirely clear which versions ran in 1955, but they were probably BMW-built, as these were faster and more reliable. There were four Isetta starters in the 1955 race and all four finished. The first was 52nd in the 750cc class in 20hr 8min 9sec. Denis Jenkinson commented to Julian Hunt that in the 1955 race he and Moss with the winning Mercedes-Benz passed an Isetta when going at around the 300 SLR's maximum speed. "We must have nearly blown him off the road."

The presence of Isetta 'bubble-cars' stressed the diversity of entry in the Mille Miglia. Cipolla, seen here at Modena, drove this Isetta to a win in the 350cc Special Touring group. It took him over 20 hours to cover the course and his average speed of 49.30mph (79.31kph), albeit on vastly improved roads, was faster than the winning speed of the OM in the 1927 race. (Spitzley-Zagari Collection)

American John Fitch and young journalist Kurt Gesell drove this works-entered, early production Mercedes-Benz 300 SL in the 1955 race; they finished fifth overall and won the over 1,300cc GT category. (Author's Collection)

By Rome, Moss had averaged 107.43mph (172.85kph) and led Taruffi by 1min 49sec. He had, however, to refuel, while the Ferrari refuelling depot was at Viterbo. Just before reaching Rome, Kling had kissed an earth bank with his 300 SLR, but it was enough for him to lose directional control and crash heavily. So, the order behind Moss was Taruffi, Herrmann, Fangio (whose car was still running roughly), Perdisa, Maglioli, Sighinolfi and then Giardini and Musso with their 2-litre Maseratis. Gendebien had moved up into the lead in the GT category.

The field rushed on through Siena to Florence with Moss, Herrmann and Fangio in the first three places. At Florence the Mercedes mechanics worked furiously on Fangio's 300 SLR in an effort to cure the fuel-injection problem. Taruffi had retired his Ferrari because of a broken transmission joint, but the oil pressure had been fluctuating and it is doubtful if the car would have lasted much longer in any event. Throughout the race Taruffi had been worried about his tyres and although he had touched 174mph (280kph) during the fast run to Pescara, he had generally been backing off every time he touched 168mph (270kph).

On the Futa Pass, Herrmann crashed with his 300 SLR and Perdisa edged into second place ahead of

Eugenio Castellotti, with the big six-cylinder 4.4-litre Ferrari Tipo 121LM, crosses the bridge in front of the Hotel Bell' Arrivo at Peschiera. Castellotti led the race briefly, driving flat out in the certain belief that his car would not last the distance and, as expected, he had to retire because of problems with his Englebert tyres. (Author's Collection)

Fangio. Perdisa was forced to retire on the final section between Bologna and Brescia when his gearbox broke. Moss won at the record speed of 97.98mph (157.65kph) from Fangio, whose car was still running roughly. Maglioli, who had not been feeling at all well because of a practice crash, finished third, 45 minutes behind the winner. It seems remarkable that the usually very unreliable six-cylinder Ferrari had lasted the distance, but it was probably because Maglioli was unwell and unable to drive the Ferrari to the limit. Ferrari had been trounced for the second year in succession.

Giardini's drive with his 2-litre Maserati into fourth place at a speed so very close to that at which Marzotto had won in 1953 was outstanding. Another fine performance was that of Seidel who was eighth overall and won the 1,500cc sports class with his Porsche 550. OSCAs took the first four places in the 1,100cc sports class. The 300 SL Gullwings of Fitch, Gendebien and Casella took the first three places in the over 1,300cc Special GT class. According to the records, Casella was resident in Tripoli and did not take delivery of his car until 19 April, a fortnight before the race.

The best British performance was that of Abecassis who finished 11th overall, but with insufficient speed to

make an impression in the over 2,000cc sports class. Moss's winning average was to remain unbeaten during the remaining two years in which the race was held. Among other finishers was Barsotti who took 20hr 44min 44sec to complete the course with his Rover 75 saloon and was classified 271st, tenth from last. Inevitably, there had been an accident and fatalities included a child. A major problem with spectators is that it was impossible to ensure through the whole length of the race that spectators watched from relatively safe positions.

There was more than one reason why the 1955 Mille Miglia became the most famous, best-remembered of all the races in the series. It was one of only two won by a foreign car, in both cases Mercedes-Benz, a company that had come very close, on the basis of its performance in 1952, to making it three wins. Daimler-Benz had spent

Wolfgang Seidel, partnered by Helmut Glöckler, finished eighth overall in 1955, driving this Porsche 550, and won the 1,500cc Sports class from an OSCA and another Porsche. (Porsche-Werkfoto)

This is the OSCA that Descollanges/Nicol drove to second place in the 1,500cc class of the 1955 race. They were a little over 21 minutes behind the class-winning Porsche. The car has what might be described as the 'standard' OSCA body of the period. (Spitzley-Zagari Collection)

vast sums on winning the race and then did much the same publicising the victory.

Denis Jenkinson, who rode with Moss, was Continental Correspondent of *Motor Sport* (then Britain's highest circulation motoring journal). Jenkinson's account in the June 1955 *Motor Sport* was one of the greatest pieces of motor racing writing. As a result Jenkinson was transformed from being an erudite journalist, little-known outside motor racing circles, to a public personality.

In 1955 the Donald Healey Motor Company entered a team of Austin-Healey 100S competition cars. Ron Flockhart drove this car and is seen at Ferrara, not long after the start. When he crashed through the parapet of a bridge near Rimini, the car plunged into the water. The young Scot was lucky to escape with a bad shaking. (Spitzley-Zagari Collection)

Results:

General classification:

1st Moss/Jenkinson (Mercedes-Benz), 10hr 7min 48sec (97.98mph/157.65kph)
2nd Fangio (Mercedes-Benz), 10hr 39min 33sec
3rd Maglioli/Monterferraio (Ferrari), 10hr 52min 47sec
4th Giardini (Maserati), 11hr 15min 32sec
5th Fitch/Gesell (Mercedes-Benz), 11hr 29min 21sec
6th Sighinolfi (Ferrari), 11hr 33min 27sec
7th Gendebien/Wascher (Mercedes-Benz), 11hr 36min 0sec
8th Seidel/Glöckler (Porsche), 12hr 8min 17sec
9th Bellucci (Maserati), 12hr 9min 10sec
10th Casella (Mercedes-Benz), 12hr 11min 15sec

Class results:

Diesel: Larcher/Retter (Mercedes-Benz), 17hr 12min 14sec (58.82mph/94.65kph)

Class results, Special Touring (Modified Production):

750cc: Galtier/Michy (Renault), 14hr 44min 58sec (67.29mph/108.28kph)
1,300cc: Mandrini/Bertassi (Fiat), 13hr 48min 12sec (71.91mph/115.70kph)
Over 1,300cc: Cestelli Guidi/G. Musso (Alfa Romeo), 13hr 14min 5sec
     (75.00mph/120.67kph)

Class results, Sub-classes:

Up to 350cc: Cippola (Isetta), 20hr 8min 9sec (49.29mph/79.31kph)
500cc: Seibert (Citroën), 18hr 24min 33sec (53.92mph/86.75kph)
1,000cc: K. Spiliotakis/E. Spiliotakis (DKW), 15hr 3min 50sec
     (65.89mph/106.02kph)
1,600cc: Cagli/Banti (Borgward), 15hr 47min 19sec (62.86mph/101.15kph)
Over 2,000cc: Zeidlitz/Diemer (Mercedes-Benz), 15hr 33min 13sec
     (63.81mph/102.68kph)

Class results, Special Grand Touring:

750cc: Viola (Fiat), 14hr 32min 50sec (68.23mph/109.78kph)
1,300cc: von Frankenberg/Oberndorff (Porsche), 12hr 58min 39sec
     (75.86mph/122.06kph)
Over 1,300cc: Fitch/Gesell (Mercedes-Benz), 11hr 29min 21sec
     (86.39mph/139.00kph)

Class results, Grand Touring:

1,600cc: Günzler (Porsche), 12hr 52min 46sec (76.47mph/123.04kph)
2,000cc: D. Leto di Priolo/M. Leto di Priola (Fiat), 13hr 21min 36sec
     (74.29mph/119.54kph)

Class results, Sports Group:

750cc: Storez (DB), 13hr 21min 3sec (74.34mph/119.62kph)
1,100cc: Bourillot (OSCA), 13hr 1min 21sec (76.22mph/122.63kph)
1,500cc: Seidel/Glöckler (Porsche), 12hr 8min 17sec (81.77mph/131.57kph)
2,000cc: Giardini (Maserati), 11hr 15min 32sec (88.16mph/141.84kph)
Over 2,000cc: Moss/Jenkinson (Mercedes-Benz), 10hr 7min 48sec
     (97.98mph/157.65kph)

1956

28–29 April
Starters: 365; Finishers: 182; Distance: 998 miles (1,606km).
Circuit: see page 247.
Weather: initially dry, but then heavy rain and slippery roads throughout the
remainder of the race.

Main contenders for victory:

505 Olivier Gendebien/Jacques Wascher (Ferrari 250GT, Scaglietti berlinetta, 2,953cc)
547 Cesare Perdisa (Maserati 300S, 2,993cc)
548 Eugenio Castellotti (Ferrari 290MM, Scaglietti spider, 3,490cc)
551 Peter Collins/Louis Klemantaski (Ferrari 860 Monza, Scaglietti spider, 3,431cc)
553 Piero Taruffi (Maserati 300S, 2,993cc)
554 Stirling Moss/Denis Jenkinson (Maserati 350S, 3,483cc)
556 Luigi Musso (Ferrari 860 Monza, Scaglietti spider, 3,431cc)
600 Juan Manuel Fangio (Ferrari 290MM, Scaglietti spider, 3,490cc)

*Weather conditions in the 1956 race were wet, stormy and
thoroughly unpleasant. Eugenio Castellotti's drive represented a
brilliant combination of speed, car-control, restraint and
maturity. It revealed that the young Italian was becoming a
truly great driver. Here he is seen throwing up spray as he
hustles his 3.4-litre Tipo 290MM V12 Ferrari through Modena.
At the finish he led team-mate Collins by over 12 minutes.*
(Spitzley-Zagari Collection)

Mercedes-Benz 300 SL Entries:

443 Fritz Riess/Hermann Eger
446 Wolfgang von Trips/Horst Straub
448 E. Ruttgens
450 Jacques Pollet/Flandrak
452 Alberico Cacciari/Franco Bordoni
454 Wolfgang Seidel/Helmut Glöckler
455 Arnaldo Bongiasca/Mario Bogiasca
457 Armando Zampiero/Lucilleo Sacchiero
500 Guido Cestelli/Guidi
501 Fernando de Mascarenhas/Manuel J. Palma
502 Helmut Busch/Wolfgang Piwco
504 Prince Paul Metternich/Wittigo von Einsiedel
509 Erwin Bauer/Eugen Grupp

British entries (only listed where car and drivers were British):

227 Nancy Mitchell/Pat Faichney (MGA, 1,489cc)
229 Peter Scott Russell/Tom Haig (MGA, 1,489cc)
234 Bruno Ferrari/F. Dari (AC Ace, 1,991cc)
242 Leslie Brooke/Stan Astbury (Austin-Healey 100S, 2,660cc)
247 Tom Wisdom/Walter Monaco (Monaco was American, Austin-Healey 100S, 2,660cc)
254 Sheila van Damm/Peter Harper (Sunbeam Rapier, 1,390cc)
301 Gregor Grant (MG Magnette ZA, 1,489cc)
545 John Heath (HWM-Jaguar, 3,442cc)

There were no changes to the circuit, but there were great
concerns about safety following the disaster at Le Mans
the previous year. Accordingly, it was decided to restrict
the entry to 400 cars with drivers who had previous

racing experience. After non-starters, this meant that there were 365 runners.

In towns there was now a rather more serious attempt to properly marshal spectators, but this was not always the case. In theory, at least, marshalling of the course was much more comprehensive and effective than in the past. There were, however, still young lads, unsupervised, who played 'chicken' with the cars – which meant that they tried to touch the sides of competing cars as they sped by. Flag marshals indicated to drivers every corner and curve, bridge, bump and level crossing. The roads were now officially closed until the last car had passed.

Clearly, Ferrari was the favourite for victory, with a strong team of four sports-racing cars, two V12s and two four-cylinder. The strongest opposition came from Maserati and Mercedes-Benz. Originally, there were two of the new Tipo 350S Maseratis with 3,485cc engines and reworked suspension to be driven by Stirling Moss and Piero Taruffi. Taruffi, however, made the decision that he would drive a standard 300S and Perdisa, likewise, was entered with one of these cars. It was to be a near-disastrous entry and Moss wrote in *My Cars, My Career*:

"Our Mille Miglia car was completed so late that I only managed the briefest tests just before the great race. Jenks and I had been out on a recce in an old 1954 car rigged with right-hand drive and a detuned Formula 1 engine in which we covered 2,000 miles [3,220km] in 2½ days. The new car wasn't ready. But the Maserati people were crestfallen when we suggested that we should race a 300S instead …

"Two days before the race the new car had still only progressed as far as the bodyshop with 22 mechanics swarming all over it. We kicked our heels around the works all that Friday, poised to try the car, until finally night fell and it still wasn't finished. Eventually we were told to get some sleep, and return at 5.30 next morning.

"When we arrived, the 350S was finished at last, and Bertocchi had already tested it at Modena Aerautodromo two hours earlier! A protruding spoiler had been added under the radiator intake and there were mutterings about the nose lifting above 130mph [209kph], but this would cure it …

"I wanted to try the car back-to-back against our spare 300S, so with Bertocchi driving the spare car we went up to the Raticosa Pass where we chose a 10km [6.214-mile] stretch for timed runs both up and downhill. After three runs each way, the new 350S was clearly quicker, but I can tell you that it was a whole lot harder to drive.

"On the way from Modena I had wound it up to about 5,200rpm in fifth, which was about 145mph [233kph], but at that speed the nose really did wander most disturbingly. I

In the very wet 1956 race, Juan-Manuel Fangio drove this Ferrari V12 Tipo 290MM car. Fangio never was as comfortable in a sports car as he was in a single-seater, and here his car was letting in water badly. Overshadowed by the performances of his team-mates, he finished fourth. It was very much a Ferrari race: Maranello entries took the first five places. (Author's Collection)

Paul Frère's drive with a Renault Dauphine

I crashed heavily with a Ferrari in the sports car Swedish Grand Prix in 1955 and I did not race again until the 1956 Mille Miglia. Neubauer had offered me a 300 SL Gullwing coupé for the race, but I decided, instead, to drive one of the five works Renault Dauphines. These were very stylish little 845cc saloons with a four-cylinder water-cooled engine mounted at the rear. Although these cars looked like the production model and retained standard suspension, they were quite substantially modified under the skin.

There was a supplementary fuel tank in what would otherwise have been the 'boot' and the steering was higher-geared than on the standard cars. Engine modifications included a special camshaft, a cylinder head with enlarged ports and valves, a very large twin-choke, 35mm Solex carburettor and the compression ratio raised to 8.5:1. The result was an increase in power from a modest 30bhp at 4,500rpm to 52bhp at 5,800rpm with an engine speed limit of 6,500rpm. Renault also fitted a five-speed gearbox and although the cars were on the heavy side, they had an excellent performance.

In this race I opted to drive solo, but I made my reconnaissance of the course with that very able lady driver Gilberte Thirion. Near Pescara we had gearbox trouble, but with that tremendous enthusiasm for the Mille Miglia that was pretty well universal in Italy, the head mechanic in a small workshop stripped and rebuilt the gearbox, without making a single error – and charged a very modest price.

In the race the main opposition in our class came from Robert Manzon who was driving a French DB with a glass-fibre body, possessing excellent aerodynamics and weighing quite a bit less than the Dauphines. However, both Gilberte and I knew the course better than Manzon and we thought that we could give him a good run for his money. Initially Manzon gained on us, but when heavy rain began to fall, he dropped back and by the Pescara control I led him by six seconds.

I could not go any faster in the terrible weather and there was thick fog at the summit of the Radicofani Pass. I

think that my Dauphine was suffering from carburettor icing. I had already slid into the straw bales just before Pescara and as I descended the Radicofani, I went into a corner quite fast. It was not the corner that I had expected, the car slid off the edge of the road, somersaulted and came to rest a few yards from a raging torrent. Luckily, I was completely unhurt, but I thought that my race was over.

Spectators, however, loomed out of the mist and rain and with their help I got the Dauphine back on its wheels and then on to the road. With its crushed-in roof, it looked a sorry sight and the steering was bent. It was still drivable at reduced speed and I carried on to the finish. Manzon won the class, although Gilberte drove an excellent race to finish second. Despite all my problems, I was fifth in the class.

Paul Frère was – and still is – a great technical journalist and he was also a works driver for Ferrari, Aston Martin and Jaguar. In the 1956 Mille Miglia he drove a works Renault Dauphine but overturned it. (Author's Collection)

also found on the Raticosa that should I enter a corner too fast and induce understeer to help slow and steady the car, there was then no way that I could convert that initial understeer into oversteer to bring the tail round and point the nose back into the corner.

"This was most disconcerting – quite unlike 300S behaviour – and although the car was much quicker than the 300S it left terribly little margin for error. It was most unforgiving, and if there was one thing necessary for the Mille Miglia, it could be forgiveness."

The behaviour of the car in the race met Moss's worst apprehensions and in reality there was no serious Maserati challenger for a win.

There was only one other car among the large-capacity sports-racers that needs mentioning. John Heath had followed in the footsteps of his partner George Abecassis by entering an HWM and it was the latest car with Jaguar D-type engine, improved suspension and a more streamlined body. Heath very much wanted to drive

One of the best performances was that of Belgian driver Olivier Gendebien who, accompanied by his brother-in-law Jacques Wascher, drove this works 250GT into a superb fifth place overall and thrashed the Mercedes-Benz 300 SL Gullwing opposition. These early Ferrari GT cars, with Pinin Farina bodies, were elegantly styled but shoddily built. (Spitzley-Zagari Collection)

in the Mille Miglia, but he had not driven competitively for a year or so. Friends and family urged him to be sensible and give up the idea, but without success.

A fifth works Ferrari was the very light and very highly tuned pioneer of a long and famous line, the first of the 3-litre 250GTs with what was probably an engine to full race tune. It ran in the Special Touring/GT class in which it faced 14 Mercedes-Benz 300 SL coupés driven with various degrees of competence. Certain of these, notably the cars driven by von Trips, Riess and Seidel were works entries with full works back-up including the presence of racing manager Alfred Neubauer, assisted by former works Mercedes-Benz driver Karl Kling. Neubauer believed that if the weather was bad, the 300 SLs would have a chance of scoring an outright victory.

In the 750cc sports class there was a new OSCA model and the make was also strongly represented in the 1,100cc and 1,500cc sports classes. Notable OSCA drivers in the 1,500cc class were Giulio Cabianca, Umberto Maglioli and veteran Luigi Villoresi. In 1955 Maserati had introduced the Tipo 150S four-cylinder car and works driver Jean Behra had driven one of these to a win in that year's Nürburgring 500km race. It was a one-off, for, overall, neither these cars nor the 200S 2-litre version were successful, but Behra drove a 150S in the 1956 1,000-mile race. The 2-litre class was fought out between the older A6GCS six-cylinder Maseratis, without the Ferraris making their presence known.

My first Mille Miglia
by Sheila van Damm

(Adapted from The Autocar *for 11 May 1956)*

If you have ever driven a family sports saloon at 96mph [154kph] in darkness and a blinding rainstorm along roads lined with excited Italians – then you will know what the Mille Miglia 1,000-mile road race is like.

I drove in a new Sunbeam Rapier with Peter Harper, a team-mate of mine in many international rallies. This time, as before, we were members of the Rootes Group official works team. It was our first Mille Miglia – indeed it was the first motor race for both of us – and it demanded a completely new driving technique.

After the race we were told that we had been driving under the worst conditions experienced in the Mille Miglia. Hearing that, I did not feel quite so badly about those hectic moments I had experienced when sitting in the passenger seat beside Peter during my non-driving period. It is always worse, of course, in a race to have to sit and do nothing, but if I must do so, I would rather Peter Harper at the steering wheel than almost anyone I know.

At the finish, after 1,000 miles and 15 hours' motoring, we found that we had come second in our class, beating a strong contingent of Continental cars, including a number of specially prepared Porsches.

Our average speed on the first 600-mile [965km] section was 72mph [116kph] and our final overall average for the race was 66.3mph [106.7kph] – an average in weather so bad that the winning 12-cylinder Ferrari averaged only 85mph [137kph] – considerably less than last year's record figure.

Our car, although it had been fully tested, had never before taken part in an international competition event of any sort; it was a 1,390cc four-cylinder family sports saloon, not a racing car, and we were in a class that catered for 1,600cc models. The Sunbeam Rapier, however, did us proud – we exceeded 96mph [154kph] on many stretches and she clung to those shiny, wet mountain bends like a limpet.

The race, itself, for me is now rapidly merging into a rather hazy hotchpotch of blurred faces slipping past the window, and near-torrential rain beating down on the bonnet and hard top. Certain highlights, however, stand out like milestones on a moorland road.

The whole atmosphere before the race, for instance, was unlike anything I have ever known before. Brescia – indeed the whole of Italy – seemed to en fête for the event, and there was a carnival atmosphere about the place that was infectious.

Recalling those few days of preparation, I must thank my old friend, Stirling Moss, who gave me many tips on the circuit and its snags. [Moss drove for the Sunbeam-Talbot rally team in 1952–53.] We were sitting in a café in Brescia before the start when Stirling joined us for a cup of coffee. In no time at all the place was inundated by small boys waving autograph books. We slipped away, but I later learned that Stirling had sat there signing steadily for nearly two hours.

The start itself I shall always remember. Each competitor was sent off at minute intervals out into the night and the rain. Eventually our turn came and I drove the car on to the yellow ramp, four feet high, into a blaze of light. Thousands of people were watching and shouting from stands specially erected, and voluble Italian was issuing from the loudspeakers of the public address system. It was a relief to get away and to take that first bend, where many a competitor has smashed his car before now.

Peter Harper took the wheel for the middle section of 538 miles [865km], and I drove at the beginning and the end. Everywhere we found enthusiasm – an excited, happy atmosphere, which not even the rain could wash away.

A significantly large number of Maseratis started the race, 27, compared to 16 Ferraris. Alfa Romeo Giuliettas competed in vast numbers but there were only seven Lancias, all Aurelias. It was also significant of trends and growing popularity that there were 19 Porsche entries. The fastest of these were two new and much-improved Porsche 550A Spyders, with space-frame chassis and more powerful engines. Although it seemed of little importance at the time, a Fiat running in the 1,100 Special Touring/GT class was driven by Ludovico Scarfiotti, later a Ferrari works driver, whose father had driven an Alfa Romeo in the race in the early days.

The French Renault company had entered a strong team of modified Dauphine saloons with rear-mounted 845cc engines. These cars had only just entered production and over an eight-year period Renault was to sell two million of this model. The handling of these cars has been much criticised, mainly by those who have never driven one, and they went very well in the 1,000-mile race. Other French contenders were the 750cc DB-Panhards and one of these was driven by Robert Manzon, who had vast racing experience and was a leading French driver of the post-war years, mainly at the wheel of Gordini single-seaters.

Of considerable interest was the new Alfa Romeo Sportiva, based on 1900 components, with a power

Sheila Van Damm was the daughter of the owner of London's Windmill Theatre which, during the Second World War blitz, boasted 'we never close'. The Windmill was famous for its risqué shows but – unlike the scantily-clad chorus girls who, on the instructions of the Lord Chamberlain, were not allowed to move on stage, or look at the audience, lest this imperil public morals – Sheila Van Damm was very fast, at the wheel of Sunbeam and Sunbeam-Talbot cars. At this lively-looking interview, the man with his back to the camera is Raymond Baxter, former RAF fighter pilot and BBC commentator. (LAT)

Even in the mountains crowds were waving us on with soaked handkerchiefs.

Along the course we saw about 12 crashes in all, although, strangely enough considering the conditions, we ourselves had very few near misses. Once in the mountains, when Peter was at the wheel, we were roaring down a hill coming into a rather wicked bend, when the car started to slide. It was tricky for a few seconds but Peter held it, and

we straightened out and accelerated across a bridge and up the hill. Only after we were over and through did I look back. I saw a 50ft drop and some rather unpleasant wreckage at the bottom – just at the spot where we would have gone if the car, and the driver, had not been first-class.

We stopped four times for petrol, taking no more than 30 seconds at each stop. We were filling up at Florence rather breathlessly when my window was tapped by a grinning, wet figure who shouted "Hi." It was film star Anthony Steel, another old friend. Like the rest of the roadside crowd, he was soaked to the skin.

I had heard so much of the danger of crowds blocking the course that I was pleasantly surprised to find that, although the spectators' enthusiasm seemed to know no bounds, their common sense kept them on the kerbs. Once I caught a fleeting glimpse of a man stepping out dangerously close to us as we approached, but then I saw a policeman grab him by his coat and pull him back in a most unceremonious – and Italian – kind of way. In some of the more crowded villages we often had to drive towards what seemed like a solid mass of people, but they always parted and we drove on, rather like a high-speed ice breaker.

For one thing I was grateful – we were warm and dry. Many of the people in the sports cars had to be almost lifted out of the open cockpits at the end of the race. Peter and I were not particularly tired at the finish, thanks to our rally training, and I think that we could have carried on quite happily.

The difference between sports car racing and rallying? Not as great as one would suppose at first although, of course, in a race the average speeds are much higher, and the effort and thrills are concentrated into a much shorter time. The feature which I found so strange was the intense enthusiasm of the spectators, which meant that one drove through an avenue of people for most of the race.

Whatever my personal reactions at the end of the weekend, I am certain of one thing – my first Mille Miglia was a wonderful thrill.

output of 138bhp at 6,000rpm, Bertone spider body and a maximum speed of close to 140mph (225kph). The driver was works head tester Consalvo Sanesi, but like so many other cars in this race, it crashed. It was a project that Alfa Romeo quietly forgot, although it seemed to have tremendous potential as a limited numbers production car. Among the British cars were four Triumph TR3s, one with the Northern Ireland pairing of Ronald Adams and Ernie McMillen, the rest with Belgian and French drivers; another British car was a Jaguar XK 140 driven by Guyot.

The two MGAs were works cars, the first race entry by the company since the appearance of the Ex182 MGA

prototypes at Le Mans and in the Tourist Trophy in 1955. These cars were built to long-distance racing specification which included 20-gallon fuel tanks with central filler, twin fuel pumps, stiffer suspension, oil coolers, raised rear axle ratio and close-ratio gearboxes. They were painted red (in the interests of greater sympathy from Italian level-crossing keepers and the Italian public generally) and they were driven by Peter Scott Russell/Tom Haig (the latter, MG's chief test driver) and Nancy Mitchell/Pat Faichney.

The first car away was Santinello's Fiat 600 at 23hr 0min 30sec (the first 'starter' failed to appear) and, as was often the case, there was no real consistency in

Cesare Perdisa, another of Italy's very promising drivers, was entered in the 1956 race with this Maserati 300S. The 300S was a beautifully balanced, superb-handling car, although somewhat deficient in engine power. As usual, Maserati preparation was poor and, although Perdisa won the 3,000cc class, he finished well down the field because of delays caused by mechanical problems. (Spitzley-Zagari Collection)

starting times. The earliest starters were numbered 1 to 77 and then at 23.37pm, car number 2337 left the ramp and thereafter the departures were at minute intervals. Fangio was the last away, number 600, at 6am. There were to be many crashes in this race and the first was Giacobi who went off the road near Desenzano, killing two spectators and injuring a number of others.

Castellotti set the pace and averaged 121.4mph (195.3kph) to Padua, where heavy rain had begun to fall; already he was comfortably ahead of Taruffi and Moss in second and third places. For the remainder of the race the drivers would battle with gusting winds, torrential run and mud, stones and other debris that had slid down the hillsides on to the road. At Ravenna, Castellotti still led by 19seconds from Taruffi and next up was von Trips with his 300 SL. Cabianca held an incredible fifth place with his 1,500cc OSCA. Taruffi had brake problems caused by water entering the drums and he went off the road and out of the race just after Ravenna.

Near Ravenna John Heath lost control of his HWM-Jaguar which gyrated into a ditch, flipped and crushed him. Initial reports were that his injuries were not life-threatening, but they were mistaken and he died in hospital. His partner in HWM, Abecassis, always blamed the accident on the fact that Heath had fitted very low-geared steering to reduce the effort needed on the mountainous sections of the course. When the rear end of the HWM lost adhesion, the low gearing prevented

Heath from steering into the slide quickly enough. Heath had done so much for post-war British motor racing and it was he who brought Stirling Moss, Lance Macklin and Peter Collins into Formula 2 racing with his HWMs.

By Pesaro von Trips had taken the lead and headed Castellotti and Riess. It seemed that the 300 SLs had a distinct advantage because of their properly built closed bodywork. As refined production cars, they had cockpits that were well insulated from the elements, proper ventilation and demisting equipment and excellent windscreen wipers. In contrast Gendebien's GT Ferrari had a rather ropey specimen of Scaglietti bodywork that leaked just about everywhere and had an incredibly loud resonance in the cockpit, but it was lighter and more powerful than the 300 SLs.

After the very fast run down the Adriatic coast to Pescara, Castellotti was back in front, 1min 49sec ahead of von Trips and with Riess still third, 6min 33sec behind the leader. Behind this trio the order was Collins, Fangio, Moss, Musso, Gendebien, Perdisa and then Cabianca who had dropped back on the fast roads. Two of the leaders were soon out of the race.

Moss had been fighting against the odds with the 350S Maserati, but as he left Pescara the rain increased in intensity and when the brakes locked, the Maserati crashed through a stone wall, careered up the hillside and over the crest of the hill, and then over a three-foot retaining wall, through a concrete retaining wall, carrying on until it hit a tree. Shortly afterwards, von Trips under pressure, misjudged an overtaking manoeuvre, hit a series of marker stones and crashed heavily.

Gordon Wilkins wrote of Moss and Jenkinson, "First to stop was Fangio's Ferrari and although still well placed in the race, he offered to remove the metal cover from his passenger seat and give the two Englishmen a lift to the next control. Astonished and delighted at this terrific sporting gesture, they nevertheless waved him frantically on, and got a more leisurely lift in a competing Alfa Romeo saloon, the driver of which was nevertheless going fast enough to terrify Moss.

"Eventually they got to Rome, borrowed a couple of ill-fitting suits and raincoats, and with their soaked overalls and crash helmets in paper parcels under their arms, presented themselves at the railway station, looking like a couple of refugees, to buy a train ticket back to Bologna." Fangio's offer may have been very kind, but it also reflected the Argentinean World Champion's disenchantment with Ferrari in general and the Mille Miglia in particular.

By Rome, Castellotti had extended his lead to nine minutes, with Peter Collins in second place, Riess now third and driving magnificently, followed by Fangio and Musso; Gendebien was sixth with the Ferrari 250GT and then Cabianca came with his OSCA. Perdisa was 11th with his surviving 300S Maserati, but he gradually fell back because of mechanical problems. The section from Rome onwards was the most difficult part of the course and the mountain passes were even more challenging than usual because of thick fog and debris all over the roads.

Brooke/Astbury crashed their Austin-Healey at the Siena Bridge when Brooke lost control, hit the parapet and rolled on down the embankment to stop just short of the river. The car was badly damaged, but the drivers suffered only a shaking and some bruises. By Florence, Castellotti still led Collins by nine minutes, with Musso, Fangio and Gendebien in the next three places. Gendebien was more than a match for Riess over the mountainous passes and, also, the leading 300 SL had gone off tune.

Gregor Grant, Editor of *Autosport*, drove his road-going MG Magnette saloon into 150th place overall and fifth in his class. He wrote, "The Futa Pass was frightfully dangerous, with thick cloud and slippery roads. All crews must have gaped to see a Giulietta on the roadside, with a waterfall coming through a smashed rear window, and cascading through the remains of a front door!

"Just before the Futa, Fangio went by me on the approach to a very dangerous section with new-laid gravel not yet rolled. The Ferrari did some remarkable gyrations, but the World Champion kept it on the road. It was truly dicey around here. Juan Manuel treated every corner cautiously, and to my delight it was some while before he went out of sight."

Enzo Ferrari was at Bologna to urge on his drivers and the Ferraris went on to take the first five places, a level of domination not seen since Alfa Romeo's successive wins in pre-war days. All the works Ferrari drivers handled their cars superbly and Castellotti had proved that he was the Italian's number one driver. It was a great tragedy that he was killed in a testing accident with the latest Tipo 801 Formula 1 Ferrari at Modena Aerautodromo in March 1957.

The Mercedes-Benz 300 SL Gullwing of Fernando de Mascarenhas and Manuel Palma shows signs of damage to the front, inflicted in an off-road excursion, and it is obvious that this prevented the passenger door from closing properly. Apart from very wet roads, there was fog, which can be seen hanging round the edge of the road. This 300 SL finished 31st overall and tenth in the over 2,000cc GT class. (Spitzley-Zagari Collection)

Juan Fangio had a particularly miserable drive and his manager Marcello Giambertone wrote in *My Twenty Years of Racing*: "News reaching racing headquarters indicated that [Fangio's] performance had been less brilliant than usual. When he stopped I ran towards him, scarcely recognising him. He was extremely pale and shivering as though in the grip of a high fever.

"Painfully he got out of his seat. I looked down. The cockpit was almost awash, soaked with water right up to the driver's seat. After swallowing a hot grog, at my insistence and in spite of his dislike of alcoholic drinks, Fangio told me what had happened.

"At a certain spot on the body of his Ferrari, a hole had been specially made by a factory mechanic, so that air could enter to help cool the brakes. An excellent idea, if the result had not been so unexpectedly disastrous. That year the Mille Miglia took place in a downpour from beginning to end. Water thrown up by the wheels flooded into the car and Fangio had to drive under appalling conditions for 11 hours.

"'Every time I braked,' he said, 'a sheet of water came over me, soaking me up to my waist.'"

Just like Alfa Romeo in pre-war days, the Ferrari team had faced no opposition that combined speed with reliability. Although poor Riess fell back to finish tenth overall, there were four 300 SLs in the top ten and if von Trips had not crashed, he could well have beaten Gendebien in the GT category. Maserati had proved a

Veteran Monégasque driver Louis Chiron with his 750cc OSCA at the start of the 1956 race. Chiron retired because of mechanical problems and another OSCA, driven by Capelli, won the 750cc Sports class. This was one of Chiron's last race appearances, but the very final one was his drive with André Testut in the 1957 Mille Miglia. They finished second at the wheel of a Citroën DS19 in the 2-litre Special Touring class. (Author's Collection)

great disappointment and just about the only consolation for Modena was that Perdisa won the 3,000cc Sports Class, despite dropping back to 28th place overall.

The OSCAs put up a particularly strong showing, humiliating Stanguellini, Maserati and Porsche. Capelli's win in the 750cc class with the new OSCA model ahead of two Stanguellinis was particularly impressive. OSCAs were first and third in the 1,100cc class. In the 1,500cc class the new 1,500cc Porsche 550As driven by Herrmann and Bracco retired, as did the OSCAs of Maglioli and Villoresi. Giulio Cabianca with his car won the class from Behra who had been badly delayed with his Maserati.

A tyre chafed through a brake pipe on the Maserati and the brakes failed as he came down the mountains near Rome. He slowed the car on the gearbox and then pussy-footed until he came to a garage. There he purchased a brake pipe, fitted it and rejoined the race. Fiat 8Vs took the first three places in the 2,000cc GT class. An outstanding performance was that of the new Alfa Romeo Giulietta Sprint coupés which defeated the Porsche 356s and took the first five places in the 1,300cc Touring and Gran Turismo class. Particularly impressive

was the drive of the class-winners Sogbati/Zanelli, who finished 11th overall and a mere ten seconds behind the ailing 300 SL of Riess/Eger.

British finishers included the class-winning Sunbeam of Sheila Van Damm/Peter Harper in 72nd place overall, 70th and 74th places by the MGAs (Scott Russell/Haig beating Mitchell/Faichney) and 77th overall by Tom Wisdom, which was good enough for second place in the 3,000cc Sports class. When a race is run in such appalling weather conditions, it cannot be regarded as great whatever the outcome. That comment cannot be applied to Castellotti. In 1955 he had driven as though demented. In 1956 he drove like a maestro and it was a terrible tragedy when he was killed in 1957.

Results:
General Classification:

1st	Castellotti (Ferrari),	11hr 37mim 10sec (85.42mph/137.44km)
2nd	Collins/Klemantaski (Ferrari),	11hr 49min 28sec
3rd	Musso (Ferrari),	12hr 11min 29sec
4th	Fangio (Ferrari)	12hr 25min 50sec
5th	Gendebien/Wascher (Ferrari),	12hr 29min 58sec
6th	Metternich/Einsiedel (Mercedes-Benz),	12hr 36min 38sec
7th	Seidel/Glöckler (Mercedes-Benz),	12hr 38min 24sec
8th	Pollet/Flandrak (Mercedes-Benz),	12hr 49min 56sec
9th	Cabianca (OSCA),	12hr 57min 11sec
10th	Riess/Eger (Mercedes-Benz),	13hr 6min 31sec

Class Results, Special Touring (Modified Production):
750cc: Ogna (Abarth), 16hr 48min 6sec (59.06mph/95.03kph)
1,100cc: Thirion (Renault), 15hr 14min 10sec (65.01mph/104.60kph)
1,300cc: Stern/Barbey (Alfa Romeo) 13hr 47min 59sec (71.91mph/115.70kph)
1,600cc: Van Damm/Harper (Sunbeam), 15hr 4min 37sec (66.30mph/106.68kph)

Class Results, Touring and Gran Turismo:
750cc: Michey (Renault), 14hr 34min 55sec (68.07mph/109.52kph)
1,000cc: Manzon (DB), 14hr 36min 13sec (67.97mph/109.36kph)
1,100cc: Scarfiotti (Fiat), 14hr 39min 15sec (67.73mph/108.98kph)
1,300cc: Sgorbati/Zanelli (Alfa Romeo), 13hr 6min 42sec (75.70mph/121.80kph)
1,600cc: Persson/Blomquist (Porsche), 13hr 32min 54sec (73.26mph/117.87kph)
2,000cc: Toselli/Caneparo (Fiat), 13hr 19min 20sec (74.48mph/119.84kph)
Over 2,000cc: Gendebien/Wascher (Ferrari), 12hr 29min 58sec (79.41mph/127.77kph)

Class Results, Sports Group:
750cc: Capelli (OSCA), 15hr 41min 15sec (63.27mph/101.80kph)
1,100cc: Brandi (OSCA), 14hr 48min 42sec (67.01mph/107.82kph)
1,500cc: Cabianca (OSCA), 12hr 57min 11sec (76.84mph/123.64kph)
2,000cc: Scarlatti (Maserati), 13hr 19min 2sec (74.53mph/119.92kph)
3,000cc: Perdisa (Maserati), 13hr 47min 17sec (71.99mph/115.82kph)
Over 2,000cc: Castellotti (Ferrari), 11hr 37min 10sec (85.42mph/137.44kph)

Class Results, Price Category (2 million lire, £1,200 equivalent):
2,000cc: Saucken (Porsche), 14hr 50min 14sec (66.89mph/107.63kph)
Over 2,000cc: Guyot (Jaguar), 14hr 7min 15sec (68.28mph/109.86kph)

Eugenio Castellotti

Born in Lodi, Milan on 10 October 1930, Eugenio Castellotti was the most talented of that batch of Latin drivers, de Portago, Musso, Perdisa, who shot to the fore in the mid-1950s. He started racing with a Ferrari Tipo 166MM 2-litre sports-racing car when he was only 20. His first appearance was in the Mille Miglia in 1951 when he finished 24th overall, but early successes included a win in the 1952 Portuguese Grand Prix for sports cars, second place in the 1952 Monaco Grand Prix held that year as a sports car race and a third place at Bari.

During 1953 he became Italian mountain champion (for the first of three times); partnered by Musitelli he won the Messina Ten Hours Night Race and at the end of the year he was brought into the Lancia team for the Carrera Panamericana Road Race. He drove an older D23 model and finished third overall behind other Lancia drivers Fangio and Taruffi. What was most conspicuous about Castellotti's driving was that he was so very fast, even when it was not necessary or tactics dictated otherwise. It was as if he suffered from a great excess of testosterone and nothing (except, maybe, a bad woman) could control his constant thrusting and pushing.

Castellotti became a regular member of the Lancia team in 1954, and his main hopes were pinned on driving the new D50 Grand Prix car when it became available. For the whole season he drove only Lancia sports-racing cars and achieved very little success. He was holding third place in the Mille Miglia when his engine failed, mainly because young Castellotti was giving it too much right foot. A number of successes in those long, mountainous Italian hill climbs followed, but that was the sum of his successes.

The D50 Grand Prix car was first raced in the 1954 Spanish race in October. In 1955 Castellotti drove these cars regularly. At Monaco he finished second with his D50 and following Ascari's death Lancia entered the Belgian Grand Prix, their final event before withdrawing from racing. They sent only a single car for Castellotti and he in fact ran as a private entry. In a rather wild, forceful effort he was second fastest to Fangio (Mercedes-Benz) by a half-second and held third place until his gearbox broke a little short of half-distance.

Eugenio had been driving for Ferrari in sports car races since the beginning of the 1955 season. Castellotti's wild driving and the high speed and poor reliability of the latest six-cylinder sports cars were well-matched. In reality, he knew that his Ferrari sports cars would not last and so he simply drove them flat-out until they broke. After Ferrari had

Two Lancia-Ferraris in the 1956 British Grand Prix at Silverstone: Eugenio Castellotti leads Alfonso de Portago. It was very much a Ferrari race. Peter Collins took over de Portago's car, to finish second behind Fangio with a Lancia-Ferrari. Castellotti's car was mechanically sick and handed over to de Portago as the most junior member of the team. De Portago finished 11th and last, nine laps behind the winner. (T. C. March/FotoVantage)

Arrogant, immature, but one of the fastest and most courageous of all Italian drivers – Eugenio Castellotti is seen in conversation with Peter Collins at Monza in 1956. (LAT)

taken over the Lancia Formula 1 cars, Castellotti became a member of the Maranello F1 team and took an excellent third place in the Italian Grand Prix behind the W196 Mercedes car.

Castellotti's win in the 1956 Mille Miglia was that of a driver who was both inspired and was putting into practice all the experience that he had gained over the previous years of racing. It was a brilliant performance in the most dreadful conditions and overall not matched by his performance in Formula 1 that year. Throughout the Grand Prix season Castellotti and Musso vied to the point of madness, each desperate to prove that he was the greatest Italian driver. His most successful performance was in the French race in which he finished second to Peter Collins.

His most dramatic race was the European Grand Prix at Monza. Englebert were still incapable of making tyres that could cope with the high speeds and performance demands of the Lancia D50s. In some ways it was a replay of what had happened at Monza in 1955, save that the Ferrari-entered Lancias started the race. Before the race Fangio talked to both Castellotti and Musso, pointing out that he needed only third place to win the Championship.

He proposed that he should lead until ten laps from the finish and they could battle for the lead in those remaining laps. It was a suggestion made with a view to them driving in a much more restrained manner and conserving their cars.

But Castellotti and Musso wanted to fight out the race in a hot-headed Latin way. Their battle for the lead, with constant locking of the wheels under braking and spinning their wheels all round the circuit meant that excessive tyre wear and tyre failures were inevitable. Castellotti spun violently into a barrier and out of the race, but he seemed completely unfazed by his accident and, in the words of Alan Henry, he was "dauntlessly enthusiastic and somewhat unimaginative." The Castellotti in Formula 1 in 1956 was a very different man from the one who had displayed such cool, calm, calculating skill in the Mille Miglia.

After driving in the Argentine Grand Prix and the other two 'Temporada' races in early 1957 Castellotti and his fiancée, film actress Gila Scala, went on holiday. Ferrari called him back to test the latest Lancia-Ferrari Formula 1 car at Modena Aerautodromo on 14 March 1957. He crashed into a small stand at the exit of the chicane and was killed. He had been under great pressure from his fiancée to retire from racing. De Portago was killed in the 1957 Mille Miglia; following the death of Castellotti young Cesare Perdisa retired from racing and Luigi Musso was killed at the wheel of his Ferrari in the 1958 French Grand Prix.

1957

11–12 May

Starters: 298; Finishers: 163; Distance: 998 miles (1,606km).

Circuit: see page 247.

Weather: fine initially, but rain in the closing stages.

Main contenders for victory:

417 Olivier Gendebien/Jacques Wascher (Ferrari 250GT, 2,953cc, Scaglietti berlinetta)
530 Giorgio Scarlatti (Maserati 300S, 2,993cc)
531 Alfonso de Portago/Ed Nelson (Ferrari Tipo 335S, 4,023cc, Scaglietti spider)
532 Wolfgang von Trips (Ferrari Tipo 315S, 3,783cc, Scaglietti spider)
533 Hans Herrmann (Maserati Tipo 350S V12, 3,495cc)
534 Peter Collins/Louis Klemantaski (Ferrari Tipo 335S, 4,023cc, Scaglietti spider)
535 Piero Taruffi (Ferrari Tipo 315S, 3,783cc, Scaglietti spider)
537 Stirling Moss/Denis Jenkinson (Maserati Tipo 450S, 4,477cc)

British entries (car and drivers):

212 Peter Harper/Peter Reece (Sunbeam Rapier, 1,494cc)
213 Sheila Van Damm/Humphrey (Sunbeam Rapier, 1,494cc)
300 Nancy Mitchell/Pat Faichney (Triumph TR3, 1,991cc)
306 Tom Clarke (AC Aceca-Bristol, 1,971cc)
337 Gregor Grant (Lotus Eleven-Climax 1,098cc)
338 Bruno Ferrari (Lotus Eleven-Climax 1,098cc)
347 Peter Simpson/John Blaksley (MGA, 1,489cc)
353 J. M. Sparrowe/Reid (MGA, 1,489cc)
357 Rob Carnegie (MGA, 1,489cc)
358 R. W. Fitzwilliam (MGA, 1,489cc)
404 Tony Hogg/Jones (MGA, 1,489cc)
412 Peter Riley/Bill Meredith Owens (Ford Zephyr, 2,553cc)
414 Tom Wisdom/Cecil Winby (Austin-Healey 100-Six, 2,639cc)
518 Ron Flockhart (Jaguar D-type, 3,442cc)
520 Dickie Steed/John Hall (Cooper-Jaguar, 3,442cc)

Some modern writers have said that the race was doomed, that sooner or later (probably sooner) there would be a really bad accident and that the organisers, if they had two hap'orth of common sense, should have been fully aware of the situation. This is hindsight with a vengeance. In Italy at this time road racing was still commonplace and the Targa Florio in Sicily, perhaps equally hazardous, was to survive until 1974. Of course, we all knew that there was the risk of fatal accidents, but, rightly or wrongly, we were not expecting a tragedy on any great scale.

It should, however, be remembered that although the roads had steadily improved in post-war days, they were not keeping abreast of the increasing speeds of the fastest cars. The cars were getting a tremendous pounding on the bumps and potholes and the fastest cars were taking off over the really severe bumps. To state the obvious, the faster the cars became, the greater the skill needed to control them and it was not always there in the last years of the race.

For what was to prove the last race, the circuit remained unchanged. There were concerns about safety and so the entry was restricted to 350 competitors, but the actual number of starters was only 298. Sports car racing was passing through a difficult period. Both Jaguar and Mercedes-Benz had withdrawn from racing – and Maserati was to follow at the end of the year. Jaguar had never seriously tackled the race and Flockhart's Écurie Ecosse entry in the 1957 race was as serious as anything that had emanated from the Coventry works. Aston Martin had received too many bloody noses in the Mille Miglia and was concentrating on racing their new DBR1 on more conventional circuits.

Porsche still raced only 1,500cc cars, brilliantly successful in their class, but Zuffenhausen's really great days were yet to come. So Ferrari was to dominate the last Mille Miglia, just as it had done in most post-war years. It seemed that Maserati would present a serious threat with the two monstrous V8s cars to be driven by Moss/Jenkinson and Jean Behra, but it was not to be. On the eve of the race Behra was carrying out late practice when he collided with a lorry. The Maserati was wrecked and the French driver was badly injured.

In 1957 Maserati had their best-ever chance of winning the race but Moss, partnered by Jenkinson and seen here on the starting ramp at Brescia, retired within a few kilometres of the start because of a broken brake pedal. (Author's Collection)

Olivier Gendebien and Jacques Wascher had another brilliant drive in 1957, finishing third overall in this Ferrari 250GT. (LAT/The Autocar)

Umberto Maglioli drove his 550A Porsche solo in the 1957 race. He finished fifth overall and won the 1,500cc Sports class. (Porsche-Werkfoto)

Moss did make the start with his 450S, but he was out of the race in less than four minutes. Of his retirement he wrote in *My Cars, My Career*:

"The [Maserati] was clearly the most powerful and fastest car in the entire entry. I drove it gently down the starting ramp, and we were hardly out of Brescia itself before we were up into high-ratio fifth and the rev counter was hovering on 6,700rpm, which as near as dammit was 180mph [290kph] and we couldn't help grinning at each other. It was a fantastic experience …

"I notched it down into normal fifth as we entered a series of fast swerves, and then about 3½ minutes into the race, as we approached a tighter left-hander at something like 145mph [233kph], I hit the brakes to take off more speed.

"Everything seemed fine; early in the race, not trying anything really heroic. The car began to slow.

"Then my foot suddenly banged down to the floorboards and the car seemed to leap forward as the brakes were released.

"The brake pedal had just snapped off.

"My brain momentarily just couldn't take it in.

"Had my foot slipped off the pedal?

"I search frantically for the pedal with my foot.

"It just wasn't there.

"Jenks sensed this was no longer normal cornering and curled up in his seat. I was trying simultaneously to see where the car was going and look down at the pedals and I changed down through the box as quick as I could – all this far quicker than it takes to read these words.

"I managed to scratch round at about 120mph [193kph] and then Jenks was wagging his finger at me, indicating it was a bit early to start dicing. I just pointed numbly down at the floor; he glanced down, and his jaw dropped …

"We coasted almost to a halt, then jumped out and brought the car finally to rest by hand. There was no way that we could repair it. The pedal had sheared off just above the pivot and there wasn't even a usable stump left. So our Mille Miglia was over before it had really begun."

This meant that there was no serious challenger to Ferrari. Hans Herrmann's 3.5-litre V12 Maserati was purely experimental and it was not expected to make it to the finish. There was also a 3-litre 300S Maserati with larger 450S brakes driven by Giorgio Scarlatti, but neither car nor driver was fast enough to be a serious contender for victory. Flockhart's D-type Jaguar was a brave effort, but its roadholding, designed for the smooth expanses of Le Mans and Reims, was not suitable for road races. At one stage the D-type was in fifth place, but it retired when the rear of the bodywork collapsed.

Akton Miller's Chrysler Special, which he called *El Caballo de Hierro II* ('The Iron Horse, the Second'), was another brave effort. This car was based on a Kurtis-Kraft tubular chassis with solid axles front and rear, a modified Chrysler 5,427cc engine (some sources say 6.5 litres) developing around 400bhp and, by European standards, a rather bizarrely styled body featuring twin streamlined headrests. It was a true enthusiast's effort and Miller and co-driver Doug Harrison had to overcome a lot of

niggling problems before the race. Just 30 minutes before the start, the engine refused to fire up and panic ensued.

It was another car unsuitable for this event, mainly because of inadequate roadholding and braking and it suffered badly from the pounding from the roads. A brake drum cracked and the exhaust manifold started to come adrift, so the Americans pulled into a small garage and carried out some welding. They then drove slowly back to Brescia, gladdened by the fact that they had started the race, but deeply disappointed by their failure.

There were 11 Mercedes-Benz 300 SL coupés entered in the race, all private entries and no match for the latest Ferrari 250GTs. Nine of these cars started the race, but none finished. In the main this dismal effort was the result of failure of a bolt attaching the dynamo and resulted in the loss of water from an engine water jacket. Although the general quality of the entry was lower than in recent Mille Miglias, the British entry was steadily growing and there were 15 British car and driver entries.

Ron Flockhart with the Écurie Ecosse Jaguar D-type that won at Le Mans in 1956. It was not suitable for the Mille Miglia, but Flockhart was determined to have a go. Note the advertisements: at the back, Gaggia coffee-making machines, so very popular in the 1950s coffee-bar era, and at the front, OM, then still an independent maker of commercial vehicles. (Author's Collection)

Paul Frère – my 1957 Mille Miglia

I again drove a works Renault Dauphine, actually the same car as the year before, but with a big difference: the entire rear end was now properly located by two longitudinal arms linking the swing-axle half-shafts to the chassis platform, and the rear springs were shortened to give the wheels some negative camber. This really transformed the handling and I had a much better race than in 1956. There were again four works cars, driven by Jean Lucas, Maurice Michy and the Italian crew Giancarlo Sala/M. Vigliani in addition to mine. In the 750–1,000cc class our 'Special Touring Cars' were mixed with the GT cars, most of which were DB-Panhards and Renault-Alpines.

As things turned out, I was unlucky to be the first starter in the class at 23hr 30, so I could not get any information of the other cars' progress. When I reached Ferrara, 140 miles [225km] from the start, the clutch began to slip. I suspected a lack of free motion of the pedal, but in the darkness I could do nothing about it. The problem became progressively worse and along the Adriatic coast, I was crawling at a mere 75mph [120kph] before reaching the Pescara check point.

Of our team, Jean Lucas was first to pass me, followed by Garnache, a private entrant who drove a very fast Dauphine prepared by Ferry in Paris [Ferry was a Renault tuning and development specialist]. Immediately after Pescara I stopped, crawled under the car and adjusted the clutch release lever, but when I restarted many other cars in our class had sailed past, and it took about 30 minutes before the clutch cooled down and gripped again.

This was the 11th time that I had driven the complete course, which was a help. I caught and passed Lucas and reached the Rome control just as Garnache left it. Michy's car was stationary at the Rome check-point because it was damaged and was being worked on. When I left Rome, I was out to catch Garnache and his very fast Ferry-Dauphine. Two or three DBs and other GTs had passed me on the long straights of the Adriatic coast because of their superior top speed. In the Abruzzi Mountains I was able to repass them, thanks to the Dauphine's five-speed gearbox.

As we reached Florence, 186 miles [300km] after Rome, the flying Garnache was still not in sight. At the check-point the Renault crew gave me a note informing me that my average speed was 71mph [114kph], but telling me nothing about my position. The next check-point was Bologna, 67 miles [107km] away over the famous Futa and Raticosa Passes on bumpy, winding roads, perhaps the

Peter Collins, partnered by photographer Louis Klemantaski, drove this 4.1-litre Ferrari in the 1957 race. He is seen at the Ravenna control. Collins drove magnificently and was leading at Rome, but retired because of final drive problems. (LAT/The Autocar)

All these except the D-type were contenders for success only in the lesser classes, but manufacturers were convinced that there was good publicity to be derived even from a mediocre performance.

The two Sunbeam Rapiers had the engines bored out to 1,494cc, within the limits permitted by the Special Touring Class rules, and a little more power. There were larger, 10in (254mm) finned brake drums with wider

Opposite: *After so many disappointments over many years of competing in the Mille Miglia, everything came right for veteran driver Piero Taruffi in the 1957 race. Driving steadily, but swiftly, and conserving the weak transmission of his V12 Ferrari as far as possible, he scored a fine win, three minutes ahead of Wolfgang von Trips in another Ferrari. Here Taruffi speeds through Bologna. Some Italians rate Taruffi as the fastest of all Mille Miglia drivers. (Spitzley-Zagari Collection)*

most famous of all Mille Miglia sections. Here I really squeezed out all that the Dauphine could give, to such effect that covering this distance took me only 3min 13sec more than it took Maglioli in his Porsche 550 Spyder and 15 seconds less than Strahle's Porsche Carrera that won its class.

But Garnache's yellow Dauphine was still not in sight. I had now lost all hope of catching it when, to my amazement, the Renault crew at the Bologna check-point assured me that mine was the first Dauphine that they had seen. Brescia was now 300km away, mostly over long straights on which our maximum speed was 93mph [150km]. At Mantova we saw the first road signs, "Brescia 65km" [40 miles] – next to nothing when you have driven over 930 miles [1,500km] non-stop, I thought.

Probably poor Alfonso de Portago must have thought the same, but Guidizzolo [where he crashed] was still a few kilometres away ... Mine was the first Renault at the finish in Brescia, but for the class victory, I was beaten by Jean-Pierre Vidilles' DB by three seconds, the closest finish ever in the history of the Mille Miglia. And where was Garnache? Just after the Rome check-point he had missed the turn into the Via Cassia heading north and disappeared out of sight behind the straw bales with no damage done. He finished third in the class, 12min 35sec behind me.

Although the 1957 Renault Dauphines still looked very standard, they had modified engines and rear suspension. Paul Frère, seen here driving over cobbles at Loiano, finished second in his class behind another French car, a DB. (Spitzley-Zagari Collection)

First time – impressions of the 1957 race by Peter Simpson of the Fitzwilliam MGA team

(Reproduced from Autosport *of 12 July 1957)*

My first Mille Miglia was certainly exciting, both for John Blakesly and me. John drove as far as Rome, where I took over. The sole moment was when he hit a straw bale, causing the mudguard to be impaled on a tyre. This took us, maybe, a couple of minutes to sort out and then we carried on. We had a little rain in the mountains, not an awful lot, but enough to make the roads extremely slippery – particularly on the Raticosa Pass, which I thought was the most arduous section of the route.

We called, without any trouble, at our final refuelling stop some 100 miles [160km] from Brescia. At one corner, a simple second gear affair, I must have hit the disc brakes a little too hard, and the front wheels locked. Although the road was perfectly dry, I shot straight on through a couple of straw bales, causing the crowds to scatter. Fortunately there was no damage, either to the car or the spectators.

The crowds of people were, to say the least of it very disconcerting. I had experienced nothing like the Mille Miglia before and I was not too happy finding people literally all over the road, and apparently wandering around without much in the way of control. However, in the towns, the police kept them back successfully. As for flag-marshalling, all I can say is that it was superb – no criticisms anywhere on that score.

As the car lacked full insulation, it was rather hot in the cockpit. The engine did not seem to run hot, the water temperature never going above 175° Centigrade or Fahrenheit, I don't know which, but I do know that it was well within the safety mark. Oil pressure was a constant 75psi, and dropped to 70 when we were climbing in the mountains. The car hardly used a scrap of oil, and we had absolutely no trouble at all with the engine.

I considered that the disc brakes were a real advantage, once we had got used to the different feeling of them compared with drum brakes. There was absolutely no sign of fade, grab or pulling. In fact, without discs, we should have had to work that much harder.

We aimed at an approximate fuel consumption figure of 20 miles per gallon, knowing full well that the theoretical [he meant actual] consumption would be much lower than that. We refuelled three times, putting in 60 litres [13.2 Imperial gallons] on each occasion, and never once did we need more, as this filled the tank completely. Maximum revs in our MG were 5,600. This we could hold effortlessly, without any sign of strain on the car at all.

Seating was extremely comfortable, mainly because of the ideal driving position. The only real trouble was an annoying one; the steering column top bracket came adrift, and we had to stop and fix it with wire because the column was shaking about.

One does have dices with other cars in the Mille Miglia, and we had a couple of interesting ones with a pair of Alfa Romeo Sprint Veloces, passing and repassing, but eventually the MG managed to get away from them. The Porsches we met [356s], we passed quite easily, and I was most interested to find that in the Passes we could hold the bigger Ferraris. They were making absolutely nothing on us at all and, if anything, we closed up on them, which surprised me a lot. On the straights, of course, they just sailed away from us. It was gratifying and good for morale.

Our most amusing incident was at a level crossing. Our team manager, John Keeling, had told us that if we did come to a crossing with the barrier down, we should at least have a shot at getting under it. We only met one with the barrier down, and discovered that the 'A' would just go underneath if John and I ducked our heads. We saw the train approaching rapidly and scooted through very smartly indeed. That did create quite a laugh among the onlookers. We didn't care who won, as long as it wasn't a dead heat!

It has been suggested that if the car had been painted red, the barrier would not have been down. Personally, I

linings, remote-control floor-mounted gear-lever, 20-gallon fuel tank, Laycock-de-Normanville overdrive and, as on the Alpine Trial cars, channels that fed cool air to the rear shock absorbers. Tommy Wisdom's Austin-Healey 100-Six was originally listed as a sports car, but was transferred to the Gran Turismo class. His co-driver was Cecil Winby of the Bricovmo company that manufactured Brico and Covmo pistons.

The works-entered Triumph TR3 of Nancy Mitchell/Pat Faichney was to standard specification, including optional wire-spoked wheels and hardtop, but with a 28-gallon fuel tank. Tom Clarke (the man who had accompanied Falkner in Aston Martins in pre-war days) rolled his AC Aceca-Bristol after two girls on scooters pulled across in front of him in practice. The AC was repaired in time for the race, but the fuel tank split and although he made it to the finish, he was averaging 10mpg and consumed 198 gallons (900 litres) of fuel. He was classified 147th.

Two Lotus Eleven sports-racing cars were entered, but these were far too flimsy to be practical

There was a very successful entry of British 1,489cc MG production sports cars in 1957. This car, seen passing the Ferrari slogans at Loiano, was entered by the Fitzwilliam Racing Team for Simpson and Blakesly. (Spitzley-Zagari Collection)

don't think that this made any difference at all. There was plenty of enthusiasm for our green-painted machine. Anyway, the name MG certainly appears to be making an impact in Italy. Back in Brescia before the start, the MG agents were wonderfully kind and helpful. Nothing was too much for them and they are the sort of enthusiasts that one finds back home.

In all, it was a wonderful experience, and I believe our team, on the whole, did very well – especially Robin Carnegie who took fourth place in the 1,500cc (sports) class and would have probably have been third if he'd known that the Porsche that took that place was only a minute or so ahead. I believe that he had a certain amount of trouble passing a BMW, the driver of which wanted the Raticosa to himself; this may have lost him some time.

Note: the cars driven by Peter Simpson/John Blakesly and Carnegie were rebuilt 1955 works Ex182 cars with

aluminium-alloy bodies and this, together with the disc brakes, meant that they had to run in the 1,500cc sports class alongside sports-racing Porsche 550s and OSCAs. Carnegie, driving solo, finished 31st overall. The team also ran a near-enough standard MGA (the car with which Fitzwilliam/Carnegie had won the 1956 Autosport Series Production Sports Car Championship). Fitzgerald drove this solo, carried on after crashing into a tree, but retired because he needed treatment for a broken nose.

propositions in a road race. At Le Mans, where the works Lotus team was so successful, specially built, strengthened cars were used. Gregor Grant, editor of *Autosport* magazine, had borrowed his car from the works and something of his trials and tribulations are described on page 233. Bruno Ferrari, the driver of the other Lotus, was in fact British and a relatively unknown driver in Club events (he had competed with an AC Ace in the 1956 Mille Miglia). He retired because of mechanical problems.

The first of the 298 cars left from 11pm onwards on the Saturday, in cool weather and under a sky that was overcast but the race was to remain dry throughout. With Moss out so early, the race became a battle between the fastest Ferraris. At Padua German Ferrari driver Wolfgang von Trips led by about 30 seconds from Collins and had averaged 121.3mph (195.2kph); behind them the order was Taruffi, de Portago and then Gendebien with the Ferrari 250GT. Sheila van Damm departed from the race near Verona where she hit a

Eddie Nelson, the skiing instructor of the Marquis Alfonso de Portago, has a rather concerned look on his face in the 1957 Mille Miglia. Nelson was not unaccustomed to partnering de Portago and rode in his winning GT Ferrari in the 1956 Tour de France high-speed rally. This photograph was taken shortly before the accident in which both men were killed, and it may be that a damaged tyre was already affecting the handling of the Ferrari. (Author's Collection)

This 750cc OSCA was driven in the 1957 race by Masperi/Foglietti and had beautifully smooth lines. It is interesting to compare this photograph with that of the Lotus on page 233. The Italian car was quite high, sturdy and generally ideal for endurance racing. The Lotus was very low, very light and aerodynamically advanced. The OSCA finished in this race, but it was down the field in 143rd place because of unexpected mechanical problems. Note the advertising that was unofficially permitted on cars in 1957. (Spitzley-Zagari Collection)

house with her Sunbeam Rapier and damaged it too badly to continue.

Flockhart held sixth place until the D-type began to fall apart and the Cooper-Jaguar was an early retirement because of brake trouble. Herrmann's V12 Maserati had hardly been tested at all, the suspension and roadholding had not been sorted and this car was soon out because of a broken stub axle. In the smaller-capacity classes Maglioli with his Porsche 550RS and Cabianca with an OSCA were particularly impressive. On the eve of the race Cabianca's 1,500cc engine had broken, so he switched to a 750cc OSCA fitted with a 950cc engine, all that was available, and he completely dominated the 1,100cc class.

Peter Collins, partnered by the bearded Louis Klemantaski, had taken the lead near Forli and he still led at Pescara, but Taruffi was up in second place. The order behind the two leaders was von Trips, de Portago and Gendebien, followed by Scarlatti enjoying a smooth race with the underpowered Maserati 300S and Flockhart struggling with the D-type. Nancy Mitchell retired her Triumph TR3 near Pescara after the car became airborne over a level crossing; she lost control and hit a straw bale, damaging the radiator. Ron Flockhart was forced to retire near L'Aquila.

Collins, with a lead of over five minutes, seemed uncatchable when he arrived at Rome and the victories of Moss and Castellotti had dispelled any legends about 'he who leads at Rome' not winning the race – or so it seemed. Behind Collins the order was unchanged, save that Gendebien had passed de Portago and Maglioli was now seventh with the Porsche. Collins realised that all

was not well with his transmission, but he made it to Parma where the Ferrari's final drive failed.

Taruffi took the lead and, on his 13th attempt, won the race by a margin of three minutes. He, too, had been worried by transmission problems and had been nursing his car in the later stages of the race. He did not know that he had won until he reached Brescia and was told his times, those of von Trips and what had happened to Collins. On hearing of his victory, he immediately retired from racing. Von Trips took second place, a mere three minutes in arrear. Gendebien and brother-in-law Wascher in the 3-litre GT Ferrari finished third.

The Marquis Alfonso de Portago, partnered by his friend and skiing instructor Ed Nelson, should have finished third. Instead this great sportsman and driver of immense potential had crashed at Guidizzolo, a mere 25 miles from the finish, killing himself, Nelson and ten spectators. The accident and the repercussions are discussed in greater detail on page 250 onwards.

Scarlatti brought his 300S 3-litre Maserati across the line in fourth place and Maglioli, winner of the 1,500cc class with his Porsche, was fifth overall. The next five cars were all Ferraris: Camillo Luglio/Umberto Carli sixth with a Zagato berlinetta-bodied 250GT, 'Ippocrate' (Paolo Ferrario) seventh with a Scaglietti berlinetta-bodied 250GT, Gino Munaron eighth and winner of the 2,000cc Sports class with a Scaglietti spider-bodied 500 Testa Rossa, Albino Buticchi ninth with a Scaglietti berlinetta-bodied 250GT and Gottfried Köchert was tenth with a Scaglietti spider-bodied 500 Testa Rossa.

Cabianca, winner of the 1,100cc class, was 26th overall. Other finishers of interest were Peter Harper second in class and 93rd with his Sunbeam Rapier (after co-driver Jackie Reece had bodged a throttle repair with a screwdriver and wire). Veteran Louis Chiron, at the wheel of a Citroën DS19 with André Testut as co-driver, finished 103rd overall and second in class. Of the MGs, the story of Peter Simpson/Blakesly is recounted on pages 228–229, as is Fitzwilliam's fate. Carnegie finished 31st with his car.

Paul Frère with his Renault Dauphine won the 1,000cc Special Touring class and tells his story on pages 226–227. The Ford Zephyr of Riley/Meredith Owens finished 115th overall and fourth in the over 2,000cc GT class. Robin Carnegie (MGA) won the limited price class from Wisdom/Winby (Austin-Healey), Simpson/Blakesly (MG) and John Hogg (MGA).

Results:
General classification:

1st	Taruffi (Ferrari), 10hr 27min 47sec (94.86mph/152.63kph)	
2nd	von Trips (Ferrari), 10hr 30min 48sec	
3rd	Gendebien/Wascher (Ferrari), 10hr 35min 53 sec	
4th	Scarlatti (Maserati), 11hr 0min 58sec	
5th	Maglioli (Porsche), 11hr 14min 7sec	

An unexpected contender was the Ford Zephyr of Riley/Meredith Owens, which turned in a surprisingly competent performance to finish 115th overall and fifth in class. (Spitzley-Zagari Collection)

6th	Luglio/Carli (Ferrari), 11hr 26min 58sec	
7th	'Ippocrate' (Ferrari), 11hr 30min 55sec	
8th	Munaron (Ferrari), 11hr 32min 4sec	
9th	Buticchi (Ferrari), 11hr 44min 27sec	
10th	Köchert (Ferrari), 11min 49min 2sec	

Class results, Modified Touring Cars:

750cc:	Lohmander/Kronegard (Saab), 16hr 40min 22sec (59.53mph/95.78kph)
1,000–1,300cc:	Faggi (Fiat), 14hr 31min 23sec (68.3mph/109.9kph)
1,600cc:	Guiraud/Chevron, 14hr 12min 28sec (69.8mph/112.3kph)
2,000cc:	Fona/Della Torre (Alfa Romeo), 13hr 56min 30sec (71.19mph/114.55kph)

Class results, Special Touring Class:

750cc:	Chardin (Renault), 15hr 59min 47sec (62.03mph/99.8kph)
1,000cc:	Frère (Renault), 13hr 47min 55sec (71.9mph/115.7kph)
1,100cc:	Mandrini/Bertazzi (Fiat), 14hr 8min 3sec (70.7mph/113.7kph)
1,300cc:	de Lageneste (Peugeot), 13hr 34min 17sec (73.13mph/117.67kph)
1,600cc:	Springer (Peugeot), 13hr 46min 54sec (72.0mph/115.8kph)
2,000cc:	Aumas (Alfa Romeo), 13hr 56min 24sec (71.20mph/114.56kph)
Over 2,000cc:	Heuberger (BMW), 12hr 54min 33sec (76.6mph/123.2kph)

Class results, Grand Touring Class:

750cc:	Thiele (Abarth), 13hr 32min 33sec (73.3mph/117.93kph)
1,000cc:	Vidilles (DB), 13hr 47min 42sec (71.95mph/115.77kph)
1,100cc:	L. Mantovani (Lancia), 13hr 20min 22sec (74.41mph/119.72kph)
1,300cc:	Martin/Convert (Alfa Romeo), 12hr 39min 44sec (78.39mph/126.12kph)
1,600cc:	Strahle/Linge (Porsche), 12hr 10min 8sec (81.56mph/131.24kph)
2,000cc:	Nobili/Cagnana (Fiat), 13hr 0min 49sec (76.27mph/122.72kph)
Over 2,000cc:	Gendebien/Wascher (Ferrari), 10hr 35min 53sec (93.65mph/150.69kph)

Class results, Sports Class:

750cc:	Rigamonti (OSCA), 13hr 29min 41sec (73.55mph/118.34kph)
1,100cc:	Cabianca (OSCA), 12hr 51min 46sec (77.16mph/124.16kph)
1,500cc:	Maglioli (Porsche), 11hr 14min 7sec (88.34mph/142.14kph)
2,000cc:	Munaron (Ferrari), 11hr 32min 4sec (86.05mph/138.45kph)
Over 2,000cc:	Taruffi (Ferrari), 10hr 27min 47sec (94.86mph/152.63kph)

Ron Flockhart and the Écurie Ecosse Jaguar D-Type

(Based on discussions with Écurie Ecosse mechanic Pat Meahan, the late 'Wilkie' Wilkinson's son-in-law)

In 1956–57 David Murray's Écurie Ecosse team, running D-type Jaguars, was at the peak of its power. It had won Le Mans in 1956 with one of its original 1955 'production' D-types and following the withdrawal of Jaguar from racing at the end of 1956 the team was racing long-nose ex-works cars. It was to win again at Le Mans that year. Ron Flockhart was number one Écurie Ecosse driver, so far as the team had a number one driver.

Flockhart, born in Edinburgh on 16 June 1923, raced motorcycles originally, but then took up four-wheel racing with MG and Cooper-Vincent cars in 1948. He bought Raymond Mays's famous black ERA D type R4D in 1952 and enjoyed a prolifically successful season with it the following year before becoming a works BRM driver. He drove a works Austin-Healey 100S in the 1955 Mille Miglia and started to drive for Écurie Ecosse in 1956.

He yearned to race in the Mille Miglia again and he persuaded Murray to run him in the 1957 race with one of the team's D-types. The team still retained the 1956 Le

The D-type was taken by transporter to the Nürburgring immediately after the race. The rear bodywork and fuel tank had collapsed onto the rear axle, making the car undrivable. (Pat Meahan)

Mans winner, a so-called 'production' car, but the team's chief engineer 'Wilkie' Wilkinson had carried out extensive development work and it was generally agreed to be a more practical proposition than one of the long-nose ex-works cars. Everyone knew that Flockhart would not win, but a good effort would bring excellent publicity.

Écurie Ecosse took the D-type to Italy in one of their transporters, a pre-war Leyland Tiger coach, with a big door inserted in the rear end and ramps that enabled one car to be driven in and then raised by the ramps and a second car to be driven in below it. Apart from Murray and Wilkinson, there were three mechanics at the race, Sandy Arthur, Ron Gaudion and Pat Meahan. The team stayed at Count Maggi's villa. Ron reconnoitred as much of the circuit as he could in a Jaguar Mark VII saloon, accompanied by Wilkinson, but he drove single-handed in the race.

On the day of the race Pat Meahan drove Flockhart to Brescia, retrieved the D-type from its lock-up garage, carried out a final pre-race check, saw Flockhart on to the starting ramp and watched him go off. Flockhart was car number 518, leaving at 5.18am. As had been discussed between them, he accelerated away gently, for they had both seen an earlier starter gun his car down the ramp only to break a half-shaft yards from the start.

Pat Meahan then caught a train to Bologna where with the help of the local Esso representative they set up the pit for Flockhart's final refuelling stop. All he had to do then was to wait for car number 518 to arrive. Later Ron Gaudion travelled from his pit in Rome to report that Flockhart had retired. He had gone well during the first half of the race, rising as high as fifth place, but on the twisting mountain roads near L'Aquila the fuel tank and rear bodywork broke away from the main structure of the car and collapsed on to the back axle. The D-type was undrivable and retirement was inevitable.

Ron Flockhart with the Écurie Ecosse D-type Jaguar at Ravenna; at this early stage in the race the car was still looking very pristine and Flockhart was well up with the leaders. (Author's Collection)

Meahan and Gaudion stayed at Bologna watching the rest of the runners scream into the pits area. Pat remembers the Marquis de Portago standing up in the cockpit of his works Ferrari and shouting at the mechanics as they refuelled the car and changed the wheels. "The drama in the pits was electric," he recalls, "with hundreds of Italian enthusiasts shouting and clapping. The noise of the open exhausts as the cars accelerated away and the smell of petrol, oil and overheated rubber was intoxicating." This eyewitness account sinks the story that de Portago refused a tyre change at Bologna to save time which, by implication, led to his accident.

It was some time later, after the faster cars had gone through, that they saw a lone Lotus creep slowly down the hill towards the pits and then stop in front of them. "The driver flopped out of the car and fell full-length on the ground, obviously ill. We took off his helmet and got him into a seating position. After some minutes he began to recover. The problem was petrol fumes.

"The Lotus had an extra fuel tank mounted on the scuttle and this had split. Both car and driver [Gregor Grant, editor of the magazine Autosport] were saturated with petrol. We made a temporary repair by stuffing rubber from the seat into the split, it seemed to hold, and off he went, brave man, with flames shooting dangerously from the side exhaust."

Although the Jaguar D-type was built for the smooth surfaces of Le Mans and Reims, several D-type drivers, including Duncan Hamilton and Bob Berry, regularly drove their cars on the road (after the transporter for the latter's Broadhead-owned car broke down at Tours in France, Bob drove the D-type on the road to Porto). As late as 1956 the works team drove the complete entry on the road to the Nürburgring. What had happened to Flockhart's D-type seemed uncharacteristically severe.

The mechanics loaded it on to the transporter and drove with it to the Nürburgring where Pat Meahan photographed it. The team repaired it in time to run in the 1,000Km race at the German circuit, another circuit for which the D-type was totally unsuitable, and Ninian Sanderson/Dickie Steed drove it into 16th place overall. Ron Flockhart died on 12 April 1962 at the controls of his P51D Mustang aircraft when it broke up in severe turbulence over the Dandenong Mountains near Melbourne while he was testing it prior to a Sydney–London record attempt.

As for Gregor Grant in the Mille Miglia, he later wrote in Autosport, "When my fuel tank finally burst, I was drenched with about 80 litres of high octane fuel, and had to bale out rapidly with only 70 miles left to go. By a miracle the Lotus did not catch fire, nor did it hit anything when it came gently to rest by the roadside. Main danger was when cigarette-smoking Italians came running to help me to my feet. When I saw them coming, I took to my heels yelling 'Benzina – benzina – pericolo'! It had the desired effect".

Gregor Grant, editor of Autosport *magazine, borrowed this Lotus Eleven with 1,098cc Coventry Climax FWA engine from the works and ran it in the 1957 race. He turned in a determined and gutsy performance, but was forced to retire because of a split fuel tank. Lotus Elevens were extraordinarily flimsy cars, but this was a 1956 Le Mans entry of rather sturdier construction. (Spitzley-Zagari Collection)*

Count Giannino Marzotto

Giannino Marzotto is one of four brothers, all of whom competed in motor racing: Vittorio born 13 June 1922 (died 4 February 1999), Umberto born 12 April 1926, Giannino born 13 April 1928, and Paolo born 9 September 1930. The Marzotto family's main business has always been textiles, but some 200 years ago they became involved in transportation and also entered the restaurant and hotel business. The company is a major international concern and Count Giannino remains President. Count Marzotto retired from racing in 1954 to concentrate on the family business.

This chapter is based on an interview conducted at the Count's family home at Trissino, near Vicenza at the foot of the Berici Mountains, on 23 June 2006. Throughout the meeting the Count chain-smoked Gitanes Blondes and drank the finest malt Scotch whisky as though it were mineral water. Count Marzotto has approved the contents of this section.

I first started competing in 1947 with a Lancia Aprilia and I continued to compete with these cars until the end of 1949. My brothers were saying that I was driving very badly, so I found a small event here in the mountains, the Tortima-Tresché-Conco-Asiago hill climb. Marco Crosara, a friend from schooldays accompanied me. He had some confidence in my driving, but not that much! I won the event outright with my Aprilia.

After that my brothers said that I was not driving so badly and I began to compete more frequently. In 1948 I competed in the Tour of Sicily (which was also the Targa Florio), the Mille Miglia (in which I was partnered by my brother Umberto), together with three other shorter events. In the Mille Miglia I finished 28th overall and ninth in my class. In the 1949 Mille Miglia I hit the kerb on a very difficult corner and broke a wheel. It has been written that in the Mille Miglia we used advertisement hoardings for the hotels to indicate corners and other hazards. This is a load of cock and we did no such thing.

In October 1949 Ferrari gave me a 2-litre Tipo 166MM car to drive in the Vermicino-Rocca di Papa hill climb near Rome. I do not really know why he did this. Among my opponents was Giovanni Bracco, 'king of the mountains', with a Maserati, a very manoeuvrable car. I do not know how I won, but I did. The President of the Royal Italian Auto Club said that the timekeepers had been making errors. I have to admit that he was probably right.

Ferrari then made a Tipo 195S with Touring berlinetta body available to me for the Mille Miglia. As a family we had no special relationship with Ferrari, but I did personally. To him I was like a son and to me he was like a father. At this time he needed some help and I tried to give him what help I could. He was a very proud man and he had constant financial difficulties. When Ascari and Villoresi were racing the Formula 1 Grand Prix cars, the team was so short of money that it took chewing gum to races to seal the radiators, should they start to leak.

I won the 1950 Mille Miglia race after the retirement of Ascari and Villoresi with the new 3.3-litre cars and I had a race-long battle with Serafini who was driving a similar car. He started after me, so at the finish I looked

Opposite: Count Giannino Marzotto, partnered by brother Umberto, drove this Lancia Aprilia in the 1949 Mille Miglia and finished ninth in the Touring category. (Author's Collection)

This Ferrari, based on a modified Tipo 212 Export chassis with a berlinetta body designed by Giannino Marzotto, ran in the 1951 race. Because of the rather odd styling the car was known as the 'Egg'. It was not a great success. Marzotto retired because of a chunked rear tyre that he incorrectly identified as a possible problem with the prop-shaft. (Author's Collection)

at my watch to see whether he had made up enough ground to beat me. He had not and I won by a margin of over seven minutes. I was very lucky in that race and I never in fact broke a car. I was always very sympathetic to the mechanics of my cars. I am tired and bored with

Count Marzotto, seen in Brescia for the 1951 race, with (left) Count Lurani, an anglophile who ran Scuderia Ambrosiana and (right) race-founder Count Aymo Maggi. The car in the foreground is of course the 2,562cc Tipo 212 Ferrari-based 'Egg'. (Spitzley-Zagari Collection)

questions about me wearing a suit and silk tie in this race. It all started with questions that a Brescia newspaper asked me. The suit was the one that I used to go to work in every day. I was the youngest winner ever of the Mille Miglia at the age of 22.

In 1951 I built my own cars, which were very, very fast. They were the fastest cars in the field at most races, but they were not reliable. I had concluded that Ferrari was not obtaining the best performance from his cars, which is why I went my own way, and I proved it. I designed the very streamlined coupé body that was called the 'egg' and I had it built for me by Fontana who was a coachbuilder, not a designer or stylist. My car was technologically better and technically much worse.

By that I mean that the technical concept was vastly superior, but the realisation was much worse. I retired in both the Tour of Sicily and the Mille Miglia. The Mille Miglia was run in heavy rain and I was a good driver in the wet. I had an advantage in wet races, because I drove very smoothly and smooth driving is so important in wet races. I had a tyre bulge, but all I could hear was the thumping of the tyre against the bodywork. On a previous occasion I had prop-shaft failure and I thought that it had happened again, so I stopped.

Later that year I had two successes with my streamlined car, a win in the 423-mile (680km) Tuscany Cup and third place in the 128-mile (206km) Rome Grand Prix. It is credible that I said about these very fast sports-racing cars that it was easy to go from zero to 120mph (193kph) – but the difficulty was to go from 120mph to zero.

I did a favour to Ferrari in 1951 by taking over the Formula 2 cars, for Ferrari needed to concentrate his resources on the Formula 1 team. I said to him that I would help, but he said that he did not want help. He said if I gave him the money, he would give me something in return. That is how I acquired the Formula 2 cars. I did not like single-seaters and although I drove these cars at Rome and Rouen (where I won), they were not for me.

In 1952 I drove very little because I was the owner of the Marzotto team and I did not think that the owner of the team was supposed to drive. I had been promised an Alfa Romeo for the 1953 Mille Miglia, but I was away on business in the Lebanon and when I came back I found that Alfa Romeo had no car for me. So I asked Lancia, but they could not let me have a car either. So I decided to run the 'egg' in the Mille Miglia. Crosara was a very good friend of Enzo Ferrari and when he heard about this he went to Ferrari to ask him for a car for me. Ferrari found an old 4.1-litre car and I raced this with Crosara.

I had a battle with Fangio at the wheel of an Alfa Romeo. Ferrari claimed that I was racing at 300kph (186mph), which was absolutely not true. The maximum speed that I could make was 230kph (143mph). During the race my tachometer failed. Fangio told me that with his Alfa Romeo he was attaining a speed of 250kph (155mph).

Although there was talk of the 4.1 Ferrari producing up to 300 horsepower, the true figure was 220 to 230 horsepower. The lies that were told were incredible. The Ferrari was not as fast as the Alfa Romeos, but it was a very reliable car. When Fangio saw that I was ahead at Bologna, he believed that I would win because he thought my car was faster than his. Enzo Ferrari was there in Bologna and he urged me on.

They said that Fangio's Alfa Romeo had steering trouble, but Fangio told me that the race was won at the very end. He raced at very high speed from Florence to Bologna and the worst that could have been wrong with his car was wheel shimmy. You would not be able to cover 130 miles or so (209km) with only one wheel responding to the steering. The problem was greatly exaggerated. If you see film of Fangio's Alfa near the end of the race, it is clear that there is no obvious problem with the front wheels.

I drove again for Ferrari at Le Mans in 1953. I had one of the beautiful Tipo 340MM cars with Pinin Farina berlinetta body. I co-drove with my brother Paolo. Ascari and Villoresi had one of these cars, but with a 4.5-litre engine, while another 4.1-litre was driven by Giuseppe Farina and Mike Hawthorn. It was not a successful race for Ferrari, as the race was dominated by the disc-braked Jaguar C-types which finished first, second and fourth.

Farina/Hawthorn were disqualified because the brake fluid was topped up before the necessary number of laps had been covered. Ascari set a new lap record with the car that he was sharing with Villoresi, but the 4.5-litre car was retired because of clutch failure. Paolo and I kept going steadily with our 4.1 and finished fifth, which was quite good in all the circumstances.

I raced only once more when I drove the 5-litre 375 Plus Ferrari in the 1954 Mille Miglia. My sister-in-law Gioia (Joy) Tortima was my passenger. I said to Ferrari that I did not take responsibility for whether I finished the race with the 5-litre car. So I said that I would not race with my friend Crosara who was an expert. I would race with my sister-in-law, the youngest fast girl in the world. She is the sister of my wife.

I told Gioia that if anyone asked me why I retired, I would say it was my fault and not your fault, but I did not think that anyone would believe this. The Ferrari retired; there was a vibration and this vibration broke away part of the bodywork and the mounting for the oil tank. I was not prepared to drive at 140–150mph (225–240kph) with the car in this condition.

You ask me whether I ever used pace notes in the Mille Miglia. I deny that there was a benefit from

Giannino Marzotto is raised shoulder-high by supporters after his unexpected win in 1953.

practising over the course. If I practised over the course, I would find a truck coming or a horse or a carriage. I would not derive the benefit of taking corners at the maximum speed I would during a race.

As a matter of fact, if I practised, I would remember things wrongly. As far as I was concerned, I was reckoned to have a trigonometric eye, that is to say, each time I saw a curve or a hill, my trigonometric eye would determine the maximum speed at which I should take curve or hill. I had no experience, but the maximum flexibility. There were no notes at all, if Crosara had notes, he would have lost them! He had no sense.

When you drove in a road race, you had to concentrate on what you are doing and rely on your eye. Moss and Jenkinson were professionals who started to practise on the course three months before the race. This was a very different approach to the race from that taken by Ferrari. Ferrari could not have afforded prolonged training. Moss was not the fastest driver in road racing at the time and I believe that Taruffi was faster. Taruffi, of course, broke his car in 1955. And, of course, you always needed luck.

Hans Herrmann

Hans Herrmann was born in Stuttgart on 23 February 1928. Although his mother was German, his father was a stateless person. His father was virulently anti-Hitler and it was through him that Hans formed an acute dislike of the Nazi government. Herrmann's father formed friendships with forced labourers from France, Belgium and Poland, something which was hardly politically acceptable during the war years. As a result he was arrested and subsequently executed. Hans Herrmann's early racing career with Porsche and Mercedes-Benz ended in a bad crash with a W196 car in practice for the 1955 Monaco Grand Prix.

Although his injuries were bad, he made a full recovery and thereafter drove once more for Porsche. Notable exceptions were the 3.5-litre V12 Maserati that he drove in the 1957 Mille Miglia and the British Racing Partnership BRM; he crashed spectacularly with the BRM at Avus in 1959 and was thrown from the car. Hans Herrmann's long racing career ended when he and Richard Attwood drove the winning Porsche 917 at Le Mans in 1970. It was a good note on which to retire. This section is based on an interview with Herr Herrmann at Stuttgart-Untertürkheim in April 2005.

When I was young, I and my friends played at being racing drivers and I always chose to be Caracciola, while others took on the roles of von Stuck, Rosemeyer or von Brauchitsch. At this time boys had ambitions to be a naval captain, a pilot or a train driver, but I always wanted to be a racing driver. My first car was a BMW Dixie, based on the Austin Seven. Later I raced a BMW-based Veritas and then I was able to buy a series production Porsche 356.

In the main I drove the Porsche in minor events such as reliability trials and rallies. I had to do this to qualify for my competition licence. In 1953 I won my class of the German Championship with a Porsche 356. I also drove my Veritas in the German Grand Prix that year, but it was not competitive and I finished 14th.

Neubauer was getting together his team to race Mercedes-Benz W196 Grand Prix cars in 1954. He took on Fangio, who was the best driver in the world at that time and the second driver was Karl Kling, who had raced Mercedes-Benz 300 SLs in 1952 and was also vastly experienced with Veritas cars.

To choose the third driver Neubauer held tests at the Nürburgring and it was obvious that the fastest would get the place in the team. Apart from me, there was Karl-Günther Bechem who raced Borgward sports cars, Hans Klenk who was another Veritas driver and had ridden with Kling in 300 SLs in 1952 and Paul Frère. I was fastest and won the place in the team.

My first drive in the Mille Miglia was earlier than that when I shared a Porsche 356 1500S with Erwin Bauer in the 1953 race. Before the war Bauer had been a factory driver, but he no longer had factory support. We received some sponsorship from Bons, a mineral firm. Our planning for the race was very simple, we lapped the complete circuit once and we had a road book supplied by Hans Klenk, which he had used when he partnered Karl Kling in a Mercedes-Benz 300 SL. We finished 30th overall and won our class.

In 1954 I drove the new Porsche 550 Spyder in the Mille Miglia and my co-driver was Herbert Linge. I remember that the cars were taken to the race by transporter and not driven there on the road as sometimes happened. That year we practised more thoroughly and completed two or three laps of the complete circuit. I had wanted Herbert Linge as co-driver, because he had good technical knowledge and would be very helpful if anything went wrong with the car. The race was a sensational success, as we were sixth in general classification and won the 1,500cc class.

We could cover about 300km on a tankful of petrol and so we had to refuel four or five times during the race. Everything about the course was demanding. There was the long run alongside the Adriatic Sea in the direction of Pescara and the mountains, which were especially demanding. The roads over the Futa and the Radicofani and other passes were particularly difficult because they had not been repaired since the winter. When it rained, our clothing became soaked and our goggles misted up. It was the same, of course, for all drivers of open cars.

One of the greatest difficulties that we faced was railway level crossings. These were dangerous because at some the rails of the track were lower than the wooden sections between the rails and at some the wood sections projected above the rails, which could be very dangerous at speed. Also, the keepers at level crossings closed the gates far sooner than they needed to. They did this as soon as the train came into sight, maybe 150 or 160 metres away.

There was an occasion we came round a curve in the Spyder and some 50 or 80 metres ahead of us the cross-keeper had already closed the crossing. He waved his flag at us and wanted us to stop. On my left was a hillside that blocked my view, but when I looked right there was no sign of a train. I decided not to stop at the crossing, so at that moment I tapped Linge on the head so that he understood what I intended.

I thought that we could just scrape under the pole. We crouched down in the cockpit and just passed under the barrier. When we crossed the track, the train was only five metres away. For the next five minutes or so we were quite pale after our narrow escape, we had been much closer than we intended! Anyway, that was our 1954 race.

In 1955 I drove a Mercedes-Benz 300 SLR, although we used 300 SL Gullwing coupés for training. It would not have been possible to have had a more experienced Racing Manager than Alfred Neubauer, who had held this position since before the War. He combined firm discipline with a friendly approach. We trained for some 2½ weeks. We used to set out from Brescia in the morning at around 6.30am or seven and we drove in the direction of Rome. By the evening we reached Montefascione, some 50 kilometres beyond Rome on the route back to Brescia.

There we would stay overnight. We would continue on to Brescia the following morning, taking about half a day to complete the lap. Neubauer was with us and I had to be back in the hotel by 11pm or midnight and this caused some ill-feeling. We covered the complete course at least ten times in the 2½ weeks. Many sections we covered over and over again until Neubauer was satisfied.

I did not use any kind of route notes or book, but obviously the more times I covered the course, the better I got to know it. In comparison with the 2½-litre W196 Grand Prix car, the 300 SLR was altogether heavier. It was a very comfortable car to drive and it was immensely powerful. It was not an easy car to control. The road surface varied throughout the circuit and as the surface varied, so did the amount of grip. There was a stretch of road near Padua that was exceptionally difficult and very slippery in the wet.

In this race I was partnered by Hermann Eger, who was the head mechanic in charge of Fangio's Formula 1 car. We had carefully worked out our tactics. Fangio disliked road races over such long distances, as in the Mille Miglia, he'd had more than enough of them in the Argentine and he much preferred to race on a circuit. Naturally, he was in the team for the Mille Miglia and so was Karl Kling.

Both Fangio and Kling drove in the race without a co-driver. This had advantages and disadvantages. Reduction in weight was one advantage in not having a co-driver. But both Moss and I had the advantage that having a mechanic helped prevent us from driving at, say, 240kph (150mph) when the road was fit for only 200kph (125mph). It was for this reason that we chose to have co-drivers.

Moss was off like an arrow at the start and Eger, relying on his technical knowledge, said, "Hans, that Moss will run out of brakes in 300 or 400km (186 or 248 miles)." That, of course, is not how it worked out.

An artist's impression of Herrmann and Linge with their Porsche 550, squeezing under the poles of a level crossing during the 1954 race. Herrmann reckons that they crossed a mere five metres ahead of the train. In the 1950s, motoring artwork issued by German manufacturers was usually lurid and tasteless. (Porsche-Werkfoto)

Our car was very heavy and we decided to concentrate our efforts on the last third of the race. We had to stay not far behind Moss and track his times.

Over the section of the course from Brescia to Ravenna the fastest driver was Castellotti with a Ferrari in 1hr 34min; Moss was second fastest in 1hr 36min, then it was Taruffi (1hr 37min), Herrmann (1hr 39min), Kling (1hr 41min) and Fangio (1min 43sec). Then came the Ravenna to Pescara section over which Taruffi was fastest, then Herrmann, Moss, Kling and Fangio. Always Moss, Herrmann, Taruffi and Fangio were in close contact. Later in the race Fangio dropped back 25 minutes behind Moss and finished the race at much-reduced speed because of fuel-injector problems.

At Rome our car was refuelled to the brim with 280 litres (61.6 gallons). There was a bayonet fixing for the fuel filler cap which was under a flap in the streamlined driver's headrest immediately behind me. When this cap was replaced by the mechanic during the refuelling stop, rather stupidly it became twisted and the filler was not fastened properly. With a full tank we were not aware of any problem, but as the tank started to empty, so the fuel sloshed around and leaked from the filler pipe.

Hans Herrmann (right) and mechanic Hermann Eger are seen with their 300 SLR Mercedes-Benz before the 1955 Mille Miglia. Herrmann drove a superb race, constantly challenging for the lead until he ran into problems because of a fuel leak. (Hans Herrmann Collection)

As the fuel leaked over me, my first reaction was how wonderfully cool it felt. Hermann Eger was much more sensible and realised immediately what was happening. He furiously indicated to me "stop, stop, stop!" I wanted to try to reach our next depot at Bologna. There the problem could be solved and there was not much after Bologna to worry about except Cremona and Mantua. It would not have been so bad if we were using ordinary pump fuel, but the 300 SLR was running on a special fuel mixture made in Hamburg. Soon the fuel began to burn our skin and itch.

The cockpit also became much hotter, intolerably hot. Fuel was running down my goggles and it became increasingly difficult for me to see where I was going. I remember panicking and wondering whether the car was already on fire. As we came round a curve on the Bologna side of the Futa Pass, I hit a rock at the side of the road, I lost control and the Mercedes spun several times. I realised that Eger was no longer sitting next to me, but was standing on his seat ready to abandon the car. There was a flash of fire, he jumped out of the car and I followed him as quickly as possible. That was the end of our Mille Miglia in 1955.

Shortly afterwards I crashed in practice for the Monaco Grand Prix with a W196 Formula 1 car. I was having difficulty with a locking brake, but I was trying very hard to turn in a good lap time. Positions on the starting grid at Monaco were critically important because of the rush of cars into the Gasometer hairpin just after the start and the great difficulty in overtaking at any

point on this circuit. I came past the Hôtel de Paris close to the limit, passed the Casino and over the rise, when I lost control of the car and hit a stone balustrade.

I was badly injured and did not race again until 1956. By this time there had been the terrible Le Mans accident which cost the lives of so many spectators and Mercedes-Benz had withdrawn from both sports and Formula 1 racing. In 1956 I again drove a Porsche 550 Spyder in the Mille Miglia. The team manager was Huschke von Hanstein and our preparation work was excellent. My co-driver was Werner Enz, an engine specialist who worked for Hans Metzger. In later years Metzger became best known as a Formula 1 engine racing specialist. We relied on the pace notes prepared by Hans Klenk that we had used in 1953 and 1955.

The car ran well until we reached L'Aquila or near there where it became clear that there was a problem with the engine. The engine went on to three cylinders and Enz spent half-an-hour working on it. He could not cure the problem and although we could have completed the course to Brescia, it would have been at much reduced speed and we would not have been in the running for a place in our class and so we retired. That was my 1956 Mille Miglia!

I was asked to drive a works Maserati in the 1957 Mille Miglia and this came about because Fangio, who was the team leader at Maserati, did not like the race. In this race I drove the car without a co-driver. I was given a

Hans Herrmann's 300 SLR is seen after his accident on the Futa Pass in 1955. Not long after this he crashed a Mercedes-Benz W196 Formula 1 car in practice for the Monaco Grand Prix and put himself out of racing until 1956. (Hans Herrmann Collection)

new and experimental 3.5-litre V12 model and it had not been fully developed or adequately tested. Before the race I completed a number of laps over the circuit. This was because parts were difficult and other parts could have changed since 1956. The amount of practice that we did, however, was totally inadequate.

My troubles soon started and after 300 or so kilometres, on the start of the run down to Pescara alongside the Adriatic the car developed a steering problem and was pulling to the left, towards the sea. Later I retired from the race because a front stub axle broke. The race was a complete catastrophe for me and I had never driven such a bad car. Retiring was probably the best thing that could have happened.

After the Mille Miglia this car was repaired and taken to the Nürburgring 1,000Km race in which I also drove for Maserati. With the V12, every corner at the Nürburgring was a struggle. It was not, however, short of power, just about the only good thing about this car. Fangio took it out and when he came into the pits, he said that the roadholding was so bad that it was undrivable.

The Circuits

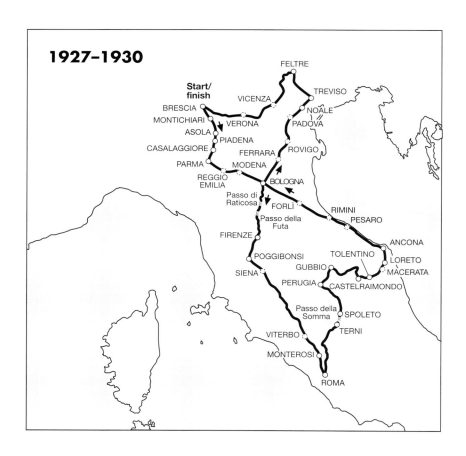

1927–1930

The original circuit had a length of 1,018 miles (1,638km) and was chosen to reflect all the different road conditions that a motorist would meet in Italy at this time. About one-third of the course was unmetalled, but this proportion steadily reduced as more road works were undertaken by Mussolini's fascist government.

Note when reading the circuit maps:
Roma = Rome, Firenze = Florence, Venezia = Venice,
Mantova = Mantua, Padova = Padua, Torino = Turin,
Milano = Milan, Livorno = Leghorn

1931–1933

The popularity of the Mille Miglia was such that many other Italian towns were clamouring to be included in the route. From 1933 the circuit was extended to 1,022 miles (1,644km) to take in Cremona, an important city.

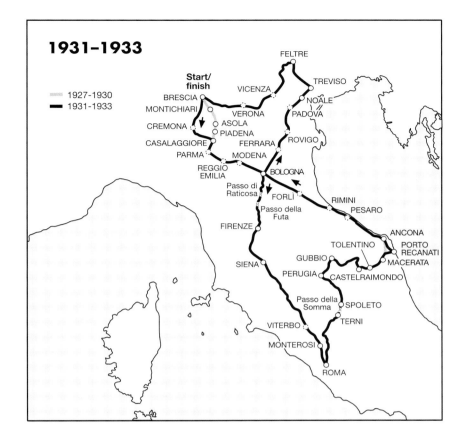

1934–1935–1937

Already extensive works had been carried out to the roads incorporated in the Mille Miglia and the much-improved surfaces were reflected in rising speeds. The worst-surfaced parts of the course were still the passes in the Apennine Mountains. Feltre was dropped from the circuit in 1934 and, significantly, Venice was included, reached by a bridge over the Lagoon, which the competitors crossed in both directions. The length of the course was now reduced to 1,009 miles (1,624km).

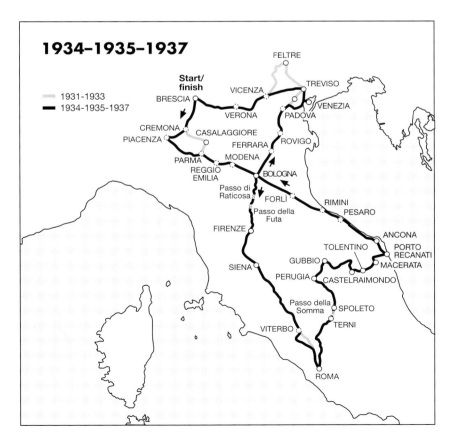

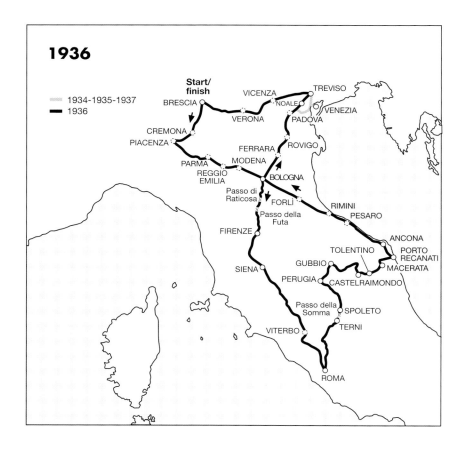

1936

1934-1935-1937
1936

Start/finish

BRESCIA
VICENZA
TREVISO
NOALE
VERONA
VENEZIA
PADOVA
CREMONA
PIACENZA
ROVIGO
FERRARA
PARMA
MODENA
REGGIO EMILIA
BOLOGNA
Passo di Raticosa
FORLÌ
RIMINI
PESARO
Passo della Futa
FIRENZE
ANCONA
TOLENTINO
PORTO RECANATI
GUBBIO
MACERATA
SIENA
PERUGIA
CASTELRAIMONDO
Passo della Somma
SPOLETO
VITERBO
TERNI
ROMA

1936

The only change made to the circuit for 1936 was the exclusion of Venice. Why this happened is far from clear, but it may have been because Venice was unwilling to increase its contribution to the costs of running the race. The length of the course was reduced to 998 miles (1,606km), making it the shortest used before the Second World War.

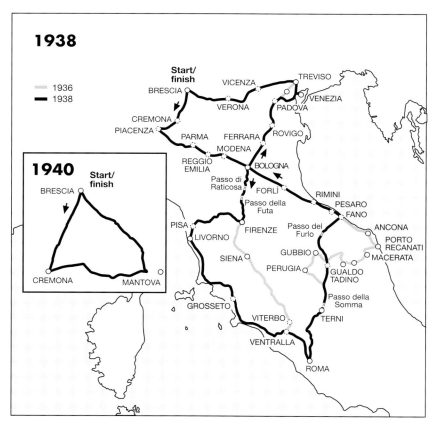

1938

1936
1938

Start/finish

BRESCIA
VICENZA
TREVISO
VERONA
VENEZIA
PADOVA
CREMONA
PIACENZA
PARMA
FERRARA
ROVIGO
MODENA
REGGIO EMILIA
BOLOGNA
Passo di Raticosa
FORLÌ
RIMINI
PESARO
FANO
Passo della Futa
PISA
Passo del Furlo
FIRENZE
ANCONA
LIVORNO
PORTO RECANATI
SIENA
GUBBIO
MACERATA
PERUGIA
GUALDO TADINO
Passo della Somma
GROSSETO
VITERBO
TERNI
VENTRALLA
ROMA

1940

Start/finish

BRESCIA
CREMONA
MANTOVA

1938

There were very substantial changes made to the southern part of the course. Instead of following the inland route to Rome through Siena and Viterbo, the route followed the Mediterranean coastline and, after Rome, took a more more direct, northerly route to the Adriatic coastline. The length was 1,013 miles (1,630km).

1940

Following the very bad accident in 1938 that caused the abandonment of the race for two years, it was revived in 1940 under the title 'Gran Premio di Brescia della Mille Miglia' – previously the title was 'Coppa della Mille Miglia'. The race – held over a flat, fast, closed circuit of triangular shape – followed the route Brescia-Cremona-Mantua-Brescia, the city centres of both Cremona and Mantua were bypassed to avoid heavily built-up areas. The length of the circuit was 103 miles (166km) and the race distance was 927 miles (1,492km).

1947–1948

When the race was resumed after the war, the direction was reversed and the cars now ran in a clockwise direction and – to avoid complete congestion in Bologna – they passed through this city only once, on the routine leg up the west of Italy. Another important change was the inclusion of Turin and Milan, which enabled competitors to finish the race on the fast Autostrada that ran directly to Brescia. The race was at its longest ever, with a distance of 1,139 miles (1,833km).

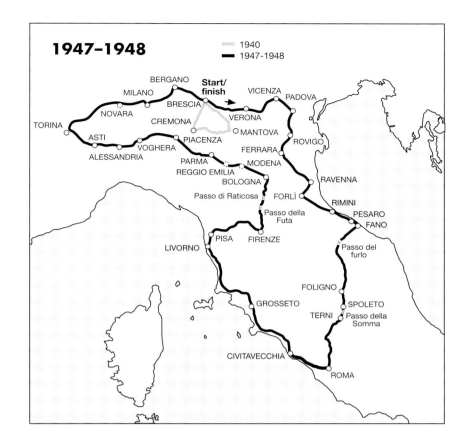

1949

Substantial changes were again made to the course, which reverted to an anti-clockwise direction. Both Turin and Milan were now excluded, as was Bologna and the Futa Pass. The cars now took the Cisa Pass, which was between Parma and La Spezia. Instead of continuing north at Terni, the course veered east to Pescara, and then followed the Adriatic coastline northwards, rejoining the 1947–48 course at Fano. The distance was 996 miles (1,602km).

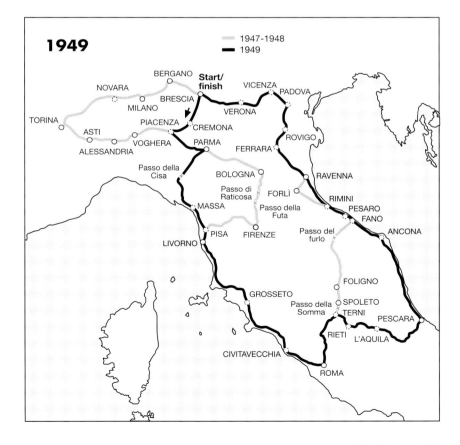

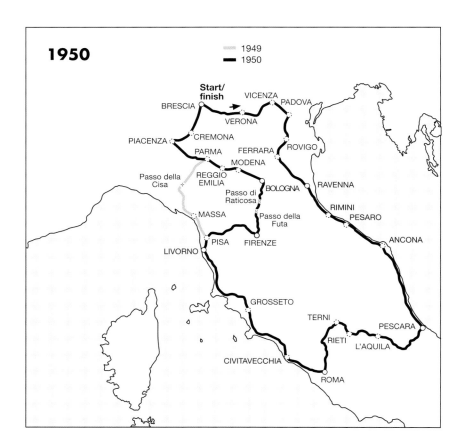

1950

A major change was the adoption once again of the Autostrada between Pisa and Florence. From Florence the course went north to Bologna and then cut across the Po Valley to Piacenza. Because of these changes the course was now longer, at 1,022 miles (1,644km).

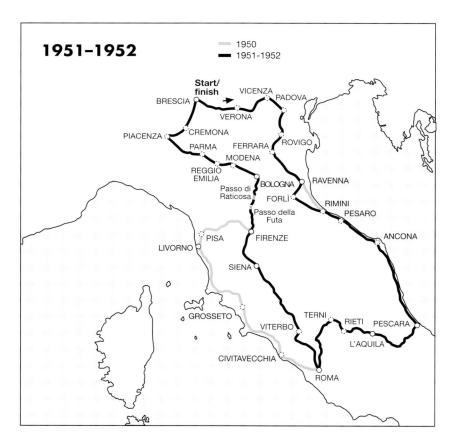

1951–1952

Forli was again incorporated in the course and remained until the final race. From Rome the course stayed well inland, routed via Viterbo and the Radicofani Pass to Siena. At Florence the route joined that of the 1950 event back to Brescia and included the very fast section from Bologna onwards. The route was now essentially settled, and only minor changes were to be made over the following years. The course distance in 1951–52 was 978 miles (1,574km).

1953

The only change for 1953 was that Terni was excluded and the course ran directly from Rieti to Rome. This reduced the distance to 945 miles (1,521km).

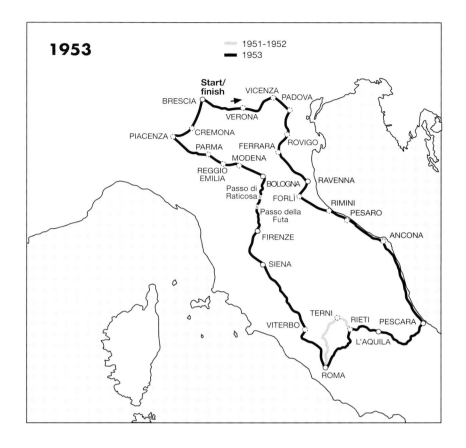

1954–1957

Following the death of Tazio Nuvolari in August 1953, for 1954 onwards the organisers included Mantua, Nuvolari's home town, as a tribute to the great driver.

The competitor setting the highest average speed over the stretch of the course running Cremona-Mantua-Brescia was awarded the Gran Premio Tazio Nuvolari. The race distance was now 998 miles (1,606km) and the course remained unchanged until the final Mille Miglia in 1957.

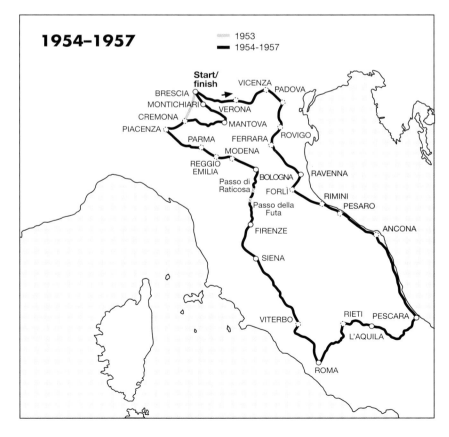

Aftermath

The Mille Miglia was marred and brought to an end by de Portago's terrible accident near Guidizzolo and so very close to the finish. It cost the lives of de Portago, then holding third place in the race, Eddie Nelson, his close friend and skiing instructor and ten spectators. This is how the accident was described in the American magazine *Road & Track*:

"Alas the joy [of Taruffi's win] was too great to last, and soon was to be dispersed by the terrible news that only 25 miles away from the finish, drama had struck brutally. In one of the long stretches before Brescia, the Marquis de Portago, driving contentedly in third place at a speed of some 165mph [265kph], suddenly left the road and crashed first into a series of stone markers and then plunged into the crowd after cutting a telephone pole in two.

"The car literally flew into the air for 150 yards before plunging into a small canal. Both de Portago and his inseparable companion Nelson were instantly killed by the impact, which also took the lives of ten other people. Two wonderful persons had just disappeared from the scene of our lives. It was not de Portago's fault: by the irony of destiny, for once he had been driving a smooth, well-planned race, taking no chances."

Some reports suggest that 11 spectators were killed and it is believed that five of them were children.

The Marquis Alfonso de Portago was a great sportsman; he was French amateur jockey three times (although the family was Spanish and Alfonso was born in London on 11 October 1928, the family home was in the very fashionable Avenue Foch in Paris) and he rode in the Grand National steeplechase at Aintree twice. He was a brilliant swimmer and created the Spanish bobsleigh team that competed in the 1956 Winter Olympics. De Portago was a godson of King Alfonso XIII of Spain,

who abdicated in April 1931, and it seems likely that the family left Spain for France at much the same time as the monarch.

De Portago did not behave like a member of the nobility. He was long-haired, often unshaven; he was scruffy and looked as though he needed a good wash (which he probably did need). When Roy Salvadori met him on an Aerolineas Argentinas flight to Buenos Aires in early 1954, he thought that de Portago was a mechanic.

He took up motor racing in 1954 and co-drove Harry Schell's 3-litre V12 Tipo 250MM Ferrari to second place in that year's Buenos Aires 1,000Km race; a quite remarkable performance for a first race. Early that year he took delivery in Paris of a 2-litre Maserati A6GCS sports-racing car and competed with it throughout 1954. He drove a Ferrari sports car in the races at Nassau in the Bahamas at the end of 1954, winning the 70-mile (113km) Governor's Trophy and finishing second to Masten Gregory with another Ferrari in the 210-mile (338km) Nassau Trophy.

By 1955 de Portago was appearing as a member of Scuderia Ferrari, but he was paying for his drives. He drove at non-Championship Formula 1 events with an old Tipo 625 car, but with sports cars he was second to Fangio in the Venezuelan Grand Prix and in the races at Nassau in the Bahamas he won the Governor's Trophy ahead of Phil Hill and finished second to Phil Hill with another Ferrari in the 210-mile Nassau Trophy. The Nassau results were exactly the same as he had achieved in 1954.

Ferrari included de Portago in the Scuderia's 1956 team on merit, although he was the most junior member. He appeared regularly as a member of the Formula 1 squad at the wheel of the Scuderia's ex-Lancia D50 cars. Successes were few and far between, but in the British Grand Prix at Silverstone he was in third place when

Peter Collins took over his car and brought it across the line to finish second. With sports cars his greatest success was a win in the Tour de France accompanied by Ed Nelson. In this high-speed rally (which could almost be described as a French version of the Mille Miglia) the Marquis was at the wheel of a Ferrari 250GT.

His racing style and performance had improved and early in 1957 he took over Gonzalez's Ferrari to finish fifth in the Argentine Grand Prix and he was one of four drivers to share the third-place Ferrari in the Buenos Aires 1,000Km race. By this time he was highly rated and highly regarded within the small International motor racing world. De Portago believed that the Mille Miglia was an exceptionally and unnecessarily dangerous race, but as a works Ferrari driver he could not avoid taking part.

All of the motoring magazines had an opinion as to the fate of the race and those of two apologists are set out below:

Edward Eves in the British magazine Autocourse:

"The sensational press in Italy and at home have made a great song-and-dance about the de Portago accident. The body of opinion in Italy that wants to take the Mille Miglia away from Brescia will most certainly use the English daily press reports as a powerful argument in favour of discontinuing the race. Of course the race *is* dangerous for the spectators; one cannot control a crowd of five million, and the sight of cars travelling at 180mph [290kph] between [walls] of humanity chills the blood of even the most unimaginative.

"Yet the argument can be made that just as many people are killed on a normal Sunday over that stretch of road. It is certain that something will have to be done to preserve the good name of motor racing. Some kind of regulations to limit the maximum speed of the cars and to preserve their mechanical condition throughout the race is called for. There are those in Italy who say we have seen the last Mille Miglia in its present form – we shall see."

The car that Peter Collins and Louis Klemantaski drove in the 1957 race was this 4,023cc Tipo 335 Sport, chassis number 0700, with Scaglietti spider body. In later years it was acquired by Peter Sachs, owner of the Klemantaski library of photographs. In 1996 he and Louis Klemantaski took the car on the Mille Miglia Storica event, where this photograph was taken. (The Klemantaski Collection)

Eves' reference to the number of people killed 'on a normal Sunday over that stretch of road' is ludicrous. If Eves meant Bologna to Brescia then the suggestion that 11 people were killed over it every Sunday was nonsensical. Even on a bad day those numbers of people were not killed on the whole circuit.

This portrait of de Portago was taken at Brescia before the 1957 race and captures well his character and attitude. Whatever the extent of his wealth, he was above all a very great motor racing enthusiast. (LAT)

"The Mille Miglia probably won't be held again next year. Every person who has driven or witnessed this race will very much regret this state of things. The Mille Miglia is really part of the automobile sport, and nothing can replace it. It is because it is unique in its form that we hope that it will not really pass away completely but will come back again in future years. There is no doubt that its dynamic organisers, M. Castagneto and Count Maggi, will find a new way to run it again.

"It is a fact that cars travelling at 200mph [322kph] are a great danger for a most undisciplined public which crowds the roads but this unfortunate accident, which took again too many dear lives, shouldn't stop the Mille Miglia from being run again. Let's always remember how much the Mille Miglia did for the progress of the automobile sport and let's also not forget that more people are killed on the Mille Miglia road on any other ordinary weekend of the year than on this day. A new Mille Miglia with a new safer base, yes, but no Mille Miglia at all? No!"

There are two questions that must be tackled, even if they cannot be adequately answered. Firstly, what was the cause of de Portago's accident? Secondly, was it right for the Italian government to ban the race? After the race two Mille Miglia Ferraris were impounded for inspection as part of the official inquiry into the accident, but there was never any conclusion reached as to what caused it. It was a move that deeply upset Enzo Ferrari and his pride. In Italy, he had come to be regarded as part of the establishment and his *amour propre* was badly damaged.

The first and most likely cause of the accident was tyre failure. Fifty years ago racing tyres were very different from the slicks of today. They were normal treaded tyres with quite deep sidewalls (much stronger than today's racing tyres) and apart from the choice of tread pattern they were generally similar to that used on touring cars. What was of paramount importance was the compound. A hard compound was suitable for endurance racing provided that the weather was dry and it was possible for cars to run through a full 1,000km or so race without wheel-changes. A softer tyre gave, generally better grip, especially in the wet, but the rate of wear was high.

Traditionally, Ferrari used Englebert tyres made in Belgium. Although the brand name still appears on some tyres manufactured for classic cars, it is generally long forgotten. There was some history of the failure of Englebert tyres on Ferraris. In September 1955, when Ferrari ran the Lancia D50s for the first time at the Italian Grand Prix at Monza, these cars were plagued by thrown treads on their Englebert tyres. Lancia had used Pirelli tyres, but Englebert (and there was a Monsieur

A Zagari shot of the Ferrari of de Portago and Nelson on the cobbles at Loiano. The cause of the Ferrari's accident still remains a matter of speculation. (Spitzley-Zagari Collection)

Englebert who was seen at races) refused to let Ferrari switch to Pirellis for this race because it would have been a breach of his company's contract as sole supplier. So the D50s non-started.

More problems followed in 1956 when the Ferrari drivers found that their cars were 'under-tyred' for the high speeds which they were now attaining and were greatly worried about driving on Englebert tyres in the Mille Miglia. Paolo Marzotto pressured Enzo Ferraris on behalf of all the drivers and the result was that the team made a late change to Pirellis for this race. What Monsieur Englebert had to say remains unknown. The problems were still there at the Italian Grand Prix and there seemed no excuse for continuing tyre failures.

One theory as to the cause of the accident was that de Portago had struck a kerb near Bologna, the last control before the finish. At the control the mechanics wanted to change the damaged wheel, but de Portago refused to let them. This seems not to have been the case and the reader's attention is directed to what Pat Meahan says on page 233. Whether the accident was caused by a tyre deflating remains speculative, but in a road-race of this kind, the Ferraris were fitted with very durable tyres and they should, within reason, have survived any impact with kerbs.

According to Fitzgerald & Merritt, "Ferrari's own investigation revealed that as de Portago drifted through the Volta Matovana bend, his front tyre clipped one of the 'cats-eye' reflectors set in the road, causing the blow-out which sent him careering into a crowd of spectators at the edge of the road." This version does not specify which tyre failed, but it seems that it would have been that on the left side. For this to have happened, the tyres must have been flimsy indeed. In any event Ferrari switched to British Dunlops for 1958.

There is only one other theory about the cause of the accident that is remotely feasible. The transmission of 1957 Ferraris incorporated a four-speed gearbox in unit with the final drive and this was a weak feature of these cars. It caused the retirement of Collins's car on which there was a "pitiful whine from the differential" (according to Klemantaski) until about 130 miles from the finish when the car lost the drive to the rear wheels. We know that the race winner, Piero Taruffi, also had transmission problems and was concerned that the transmission might fail.

It was reported by Edward Eves that Sparrowe, a British driver of an MGA, saw a wheel and part of the rear axle of de Portago's car become detached immediately before the car went out of control. De Portago's Ferrari was so badly damaged in the crash that it was impossible to ascertain what components if any broke before the crash and may have caused it.

There remains the question of whether or not the race should have been banned following this accident. There are a number of 'precedents' and of course the most important was Le Mans following the 1955 disaster involving Levegh's Mercedes-Benz that cost over 80 lives. There is little doubt that if Le Mans had been banned, it would have been the end of motor racing in much of the world. Following the accident, racing was temporarily banned in France, Spain and Switzerland. The ban became permanent in Switzerland and so the use of the brilliant, beautiful Bremgarten circuit at Bern was lost.

The biggest difference was that Le Mans was run on a circuit of only 8.34 miles (13.42km), admittedly on public roads, but closed and controlled when racing was taking place. All the spectators, theoretically, were in safe enclosures or grandstands and if anyone was killed while in an unauthorised area, that was their problem. What had happened at Le Mans was a freak accident, made possible by old and inadequate pit facilities and narrow roads near the pits. Over the next 12 or so months substantial works were carried out and thereafter the circuit remained substantially safe.

In the British Isles there were two precedents, both involving road circuits used for the Tourist Trophy sports car race. Between 1928 and 1936 the race was run on the 13.6-mile (22km) Ards road circuit near Belfast. As the circuit was used only once a year, safety precautions including making available proper enclosures and clearly marked prohibited areas was impractical and not thought necessary – until Chambers's Riley skidded broadside on to the pavement at Newtownards in the 1936 race killing eight spectators and injuring another 15.

The spectators were standing unprotected on the pavement. The use of this course was abandoned and although it happened prior to the banning of the Mille Miglia for the first time, the reasons were the same: the impossibility of providing protection for spectators. Between 1950 and 1955 the Tourist Trophy was run at Dundrod, another road circuit near Belfast with a length of about 9½ miles. It was a difficult, winding, narrow circuit that required great skill and on which overtaking was very difficult. It was abandoned after the 1955 race in which three drivers were killed. It is perhaps worth mentioning in passing that racing on public roads was never permitted on the British mainland.

The background of the Mille Miglia, the fact that it had been banned once already and the major consideration that it was impossible to properly marshal all tipped the scales against its survival. There were also the lurid condemnations in the popular press that did not assist the future of the race. Within limits, competitors may kill themselves and racing continue unaffected (and that remains the position with the Tourist Trophy motorcycle races still held on closed public roads in the Isle of Man), but you can't kill spectators, especially children. There was also the feeling that the Mille Miglia had been rather sneakily restored after the war and that went against any proposals to let the race continue.

In addition there was nothing further that the organisers could do to ensure the safety of spectators that would not destroy the complete character of the race, for example by running it as a short circuit event. In fact it was not quite the end of the Mille Miglia which has continued in far from totally emasculated form, something that would only be possible in Italy. From 1958 until 1961 the Mille Miglia was run as a rally, but Count Maggi would not have anything to do with it in that form.

The Mille Miglia Retrospective was first held in 1987 and is now the premier classic motor racing event of the year. Owners of Mille Miglia-type cars drive at top speed over roads approximating to those used for the road race and with a police escort. It may not have the death toll of the original race, but it remains a dangerous event and at least one competitor (sorry, entrant, the drivers are not supposed to be competing with each other) has been killed. Even the long-term future of the Retrospective must be uncertain.

Bibliography

Balestra, Nino and De Agostini, Cesare, *Cisitalia Catalogue Raisonné*, Automobilia, Milan, 1991

Berthon, Darell, *A Racing History of the Bentley, 1921–31*, The Bodley Head, 1956

Borgeson, Griffith, *The Alfa Romeo Tradition*, Foulis/Haynes, 1990

Buckley, J. R., *Cars of the Connoisseur*, B. T. Batsford, 1960

Cancellieri, Gianni, and Marchianò, Michele, *La Fiat va alla Mille Miglia*, Giorgio Nada Editore, 1998

Canestrini, Giovanni, *Mille Miglia*, Automobile Club d'Italia/L'Editrice dell'Automobile, 1967, Revised edition 1990

Caracciola, Rudolf, *A Racing Driver's World*, Cassell & Company, 1963

Curami, Andrea, *Mercedes-Benz & Mille Miglia*, Giorgio Nada Editore, 2005

De Agostini, Cesare, *La Saga dei Marzotto*, Giorgio Nada Editore, Not dated

Fangio, Juan Manuel, in collaboration with Giambertone, Marcello, *My Twenty Years of Racing*, Temple Press, 1961

Farrell, Nicolas, *Mussolini, A New Life*, Weidenfeld & Nicolson, 2003

Fitzgerald, Warren W. and Merritt, Richard F., *Ferrari: The Sports and Gran Turismo Cars*, Bond Publishing Company, 1968

Frère, Paul, translated by Louis Klemantaski, *On the Starting Grid*, B. T. Batsford, 1957

Fusi, Luigi, *Alfa Romeo, Tutte Le Vetture Dal 1910*, Third edition, Emmetigrafica, 1978

Garnier, Peter and Healey, Brian, *Donald Healey: My World of Cars*, Patrick Stephens, 1989

Georgano, G. N., edited, *The Complete Encyclopaedia of Motorcars*, Second Edition, Ebury Press, 1973/76

Healey, Geoffrey, *More Healeys*, Gentry Books

Henry, Alan, *Ferrari, The Grand Prix Cars*, Second edition, Hazleton Publishing, 1989

Hilton, Chris, *Nuvolari*, Bredon Books, 2004

Hull, Peter and Slater, Roy, *Alfa Romeo, A History*, Cassell & Company, 1964

Kling, Karl, with Günther Molter, translated by Peter Myers, *Pursuit of Victory*, The Bodley Head, 1956

Ludwigsen, Karl, *The Mercedes-Benz Racing Cars*, Bond/Parkhurst Books, 1971

Lurani, Count Giovanni ('Johnny'), *Nuvolari*, Cassell & Company, 1959

Lurani, Count Giovanni ('Johnny'), *Mille Miglia, 1927–57*, Edita, 1981

Marzotto, Giannino, *Red Arrows, Ferraris in the Mille Miglia*, Giorgio Nada Editore, 2001

McKenzie, W. A., *Motormania*, Cassell & Company, 1972

Montagu of Beaulieu, Lord, with Sedgwick, Michael, *Lost Causes of Motoring, Europe, Volume 1*, Cassell & Company, 1969

Moore, Simon, *The Alfa Romeo 412*, Thoroughbred & Classic Cars, November 1981

Moss, Stirling, with Nye, Doug, *My Cars, My Career*, Patrick Stephens, 1987

Nixon, Chris, *Racing the Silver Arrows: Mercedes-Benz Versus Auto Union, 1934–39*, Osprey Publishing, 1986

Orsini, Luigi and Zagari, Franco, *The Scuderia Ferrari*, Editorale Olimpia SpA, 1979

Orsini, Luigi and Zagari, Franco, *Stanguellini, Big Little Racing Cars*, Giorgio Nada Editore, 2003

Posthumus, Cyril, *The Farmer's Son*, chapter in *The Motorist's Weekend Book*, edited by Michael Frostick and Anthony Harding, B. T. Batsford, 1960

Posthumus, Cyril, *The Man Who Crashed Twice*, chapter in *The Motorist's Miscellany*, edited by Anthony Harding, B. T. Batsford, 1964

Pritchard, Anthony, *Maserati: A Racing History*, Haynes Publishing, 2003

Pritchard, Anthony, *Aston Martin: A Racing History*, Haynes Publishing, 2006

Scott-Moncrieff, David, with Nixon, St John and Paget, Clarence, *Three-Pointed Star*, Cassell & Co., 1955

Trow, Nigel, *Lancia Racing*, Osprey Publishing, 1987

Venables, David, *Bugatti: A Racing History*, Haynes Publishing, 2002

Whyte, Andrew, *Jaguar Sports Racing & Works Competition Cars to 1953*, Haynes, 1982

Magazines and newspapers: *Autosport, Autocourse, Classic & Sports Car, Classic & Thoroughbred Cars, Daily Telegraph, Il Messagero, Motor Racing, Motor Sport, Old Motor, Road & Track, The Autocar, The Motor, The Times*

Index

Marques, models and teams